A very learned work, amazing in its mastery of primary sources.

Daniel J. Harrington, S.J., Ph.D., D.S.S.
Professor of New Testament
Weston School of Theology
Cambridge, Massachusetts

I render homage to the prodigious erudition and the profound faith that inspires this immense work.

Francois Dreyfus, O.P., Ph.D.
Professor of Biblical Studies
Ecole Biblique et Archéologique
de Jérusalem, Israël

This work is both a theological presentation and a Christian meditation. It is highly informed by biblical, Jewish and patristic texts and gives not only the fruit of the author's study, but also an annotated collection of texts that will enrich one's knowledge both of Scriptural passages and of important themes in salvation history from the creation of Adam to the revelation of the Son of Man. It reflects something of the author's own pilgrimage in Christ and, thus, is able to offer to all who read it, spiritual edification for their own lives.

E. Earle Ellis, Ph.D.
Research Professor of Theology
Southwestern Baptist Theological Seminary
Fort Worth, Texas

Levi Khamor's meditation and study have produced something unique in *The Revelation of the Son of Man*. This great labor displayed with perfect clarity provides an authoritative commentary on Jesus as the Son of Man: the personification of understanding, of labor, suffering, service and humility. Levi Khamor shows that through Jesus' fidelity, they who accept him are led from darkness to the light of Truth. He fully vindicates the historical Jesus as the Messiah of the Jews.

Professor J.D.M. Darrett, Ph.D., LL.D., D.C.L. (Oxford)
Professor Emeritus of Oriental Law,
University of London, England
Author of Law in the New Testament,
Midrash in Action as a Literary Device,
Midrash, the Composition of the Gospels
and Discipline, *etc.*

This book on Jesus Christ, the Son of Man, is a work of understanding and of love. It is neither a theological treatise (Christology) nor a work of biblical exegesis (in the technical sense of the terms). It is an instrument for reflection, a quarry from which stones are cut in order to enrich our meditation of the Word of God. It is full of riches, coming from the Bible (Old Testament and New Testament), as read in a community of living faith. A special trait of this work can be seen in the various and rich quotations borrowed from the Jewish heritage, bringing thus new perspectives to our Christian reading of the Word of God....

The rich variety of quotations found here is based on an accurate selection of Hebrew and Greek terms used in the biblical texts: they center on the person of Our Lord, Jesus Christ; they lead us to Him, our Savior, the Anointed One, who is the Messiah, the only Son of God who has revealed to us the Father (see John 1:18).

Professor Léo Laberge, O.M.I., Ph.D., D.S.S.
Professor of Old Testament
University of St. Paul
Ottawa, Canada

This remarkable book is a sustained study and meditation on the basic questions of human existence and on Jesus (or Yeshua) as the Son of Man. It draws on a vast range of literature: not only the whole of Christian Scripture, including the deuterocanonical books, but also the inter-Testamental literature, including the Dead Sea Scrolls, and the early Christian fathers. A special feature is the extensive use of Jewish sources to shed light on Scripture. Few Christian scholars are really competent to handle the mass of Rabbinic writings or to chart a course through "the ocean of the Talmud," but this book offers a unique compilation of rabbinic parallels.

... The writer, throughout, seeks to uncover the hidden, spiritual significance of Scripture and he illuminates the meaning of key terms and concepts by extensive cross-references and comparisons. New light is shed on numerous texts and passages of the Bible.

... One has the feeling that this work is the product not just of lengthy study but also of lengthy meditation and of a life deeply committed to the service of God. Those who want to explore the hidden depths of Scripture will find this book an almost inexhaustible treasure house.

Professor Charles H. Scobie, Ph.D.
Head of the Dept. of Religious Studies
Mount Allison University
Sackville, New Brunswick
Canada

THE
REVELATION
OF
THE SON OF MAN

The Revelation of the Son of Man

Levi Khamor

ST. BEDE'S PUBLICATIONS
Petersham, Massachusetts

NIHIL OBSTAT AND IMPRIMATUR:
+ Donat Chiasson
Archbishop of Moncton, N.B., Canada

Cover painting by Deb Hoeffner, Kinnelon, NJ

LIBRARY OF CONGRESS CATALOGING-IN-PUBLICATION DATA

Khamor, Levi, 1923-
   The revelation of the Son of Man / Levi Khamor.
      p.   cm.
   Bibliography: p.
   ISBN 0-932506-51-8
   1. Son of Man.   I. Title.
BT232.K48   1989   88-22794
232'.1—dc19   CIP

Published by St. Bede's Publications
      P.O. Box 545
      Petersham, MA 01366-0545 U.S.A.

1948 — 1988

At the age of forty, a man is ready for understanding.
—Mishnah, *Pirke Aboth* V.24

Dedicated to

His people the Jews
who suffered and died
in all the persecutions
of the world
and in the great Shoah

Contents

Before the beginning was known
And the end was understood

Before the heavens were stretched out
And the earth was formed

Before the mountains were begotten
And the hills were brought forth

God knew Man
The Lord understood the Son of Man

Introduction

Many years ago I was hospitalized, and because I was in critical condition the Chaplain was called to anoint me and give me the Last Sacraments of the Church. I remember looking at a cross and promising the Lord that I would do something for Him if I lived. I recovered and began to find out about Him, what He said, what He did, how He lived and who He was. For if I really wanted to do something for Him I thought I had better get to know Him first. Only then would I be able to discover what was dearest to His heart, and what He desired the most so that I could try my best to do it for Him.

I see now that it all begins with wanting to, for if we really want to do something for Him with all our heart and with all our soul, God does the rest. So He then prompted me to give up my medical practice in beautiful western Montana, sell my house and land, pull up my roots and leave to do volunteer work at isolated Mission hospitals overseas. Thus, He led me to the poor and needy, and by working among them I began to get to know Him. We may read about Him in Bibles and books but there is no surer way of knowing Him than to reach out towards another human being in need of our compassionate aid, because whatever we do for someone in need we have done for the Lord.[1] And is not this to know Him?[2]

To know the Lord is to love Him, and to want others to know and love Him too. For we become aware how insignificant is our love for Him compared to His love for us. And so we seek to expand it as a little taper does when it lights up one by one a myriad glowing candles. But there would be no lighting up of the hearts of others unless the flame first burns in our own. Only words that come from the heart can penetrate the heart of another.

I now understand why it was, while working in the Missions, that I first heard the call to become a monk or a hermit. I thought to myself that it was just a normal reaction to the very active schedule I had, seeing patients from morning to night, operating, doing hospital rounds, and traveling by ambulance to the outlying district medical stations. For what busy physician has not sometimes had the desire to get away from it all? But it was on an occasion when I was able to get camping gear and provisions into a Land Rover and drive far away to a lonely beach that the call to a life of silence and solitude became a cry that could no longer remain unheeded.

I knew that having found Him in the poor, He now wanted me to find Him within myself, but to be able to do that I had to follow the call to leave all and be alone with Him. I had to confront myself before His eyes and become aware of what He saw in my heart and soul. It is the goodness of God which leads us to repentance.[3] He was drawing me to the wilderness for it was there that He wanted to speak to my heart.[4] He did not have to say a word, I suddenly saw that I had all these years kept from Him what He desired the most: the 'me' in me hiding in the innermost chamber of my heart. For we may give all, and do all, but we shall have done nothing for Him unless we have first given Him our very self.

And so it was that after having found someone to replace me at the Mission hospital, I left Africa and became a hermit. I have been one for the past twenty-four years and live in a hermitage in the woods of a Cistercian Abbey in Canada.

Silence is a great teacher and teaches best those who listen attentively to the voice of His words. Behind every word of God is His wisdom, understanding and knowledge, and within it is His Truth.

Long ago, when I went to live deep in the forest, I learned that if we wish to be truly able to understand His words, we must do what they say. For it is written that: 'a good understanding have all those who do His command'.[5] Thus, the Lord said to Joshua: 'Do according to all the Law which Moses My servant commanded you . . . that you may understand . . . do all that is written in it for then you shall make your way prosperous and you shall understand'.[6] Had not Moses told His people Israel to: 'Keep them [the Commandments] and do them; for that will be your wisdom and your understanding in the sight of the nations,'[7] and to 'be careful to do the words of this covenant that you may have understanding in all that you do'?[8] For 'he who keeps the Law of the Lord gets the understanding thereof'.[9] Thus, it is referred to as 'the Law of life and good understanding'.[10] Truly, 'whoever keeps the Law is an understanding son',[11] and he knows why the wise man said: 'My son, do not forget my Law but let your heart keep my commandments . . . so shall you find favor and good understanding in the sight of God and man'.[12] 'Keep the charge of the Lord your God, to walk in His ways, keep His statutes and His commandments and His judgments, and His testimonies as it is written in the Law of Moses, so that you may understand'[13]. Hezekiah 'held fast to the Lord; he did not depart from following Him, but kept the commandments which the Lord commanded Moses',[14] therefore 'the Lord was with him and he understood'.[15] And so did the Psalmist who said: 'Through Your commandments You have made me wiser than my enemies for they [the Commandments] are ever with me'.[16] He also said 'I understand more than the ancients because I keep Your precepts'[17] for he knew that 'through Your precepts I get understanding'.[18]

'Who is wise and will observe these things . . . they will understand the lovingkindness of the Lord'.[19] 'If you desire Wisdom, keep the commandments and Lord shall give her to you'.[20] And 'if you keep silence in purity of heart you shall understand'[21] and be wise for 'with the chaste is wisdom'[22] because 'the wisdom from above is first of all chaste'.[23] 'An understanding which is chaste and untainted by any evil,'[24] is able to grasp His wisdom, and His knowledge as well, because 'His knowledge is pure'.[25] The early Fathers of the Church knew that 'pure as regards corporeal lusts and pure in respect of holy thoughts are those who attain to the knowledge of God'.[26] Because 'from chastity arises understanding'[27] and 'the reward of chastity is knowledge'.[28] The rabbis also knew that 'the adornment of the commandments is chastity'[29] because 'God loves nothing better than chastity'[30] and 'if you follow after chastity and purity with patience and prayer and with fasting in humility of heart the Lord will dwell in you because He loves chastity'[31] and He 'reveals what is hidden to the pure'.[32] Thus, the patriarch Jacob on his deathbed is said to have told his children: 'Purify yourselves of uncleanness and I will tell you the hidden secrets, the concealed date of the End, the reward of the righteous and the punishment of the wicked and what the pleasures of Paradise will be'.[33] Did not the pious Jew, Ben Sirach say: 'I found Wisdom in purity and through her guidance I obtained understanding'?[34]

We shall not be able to see Him nor find Him within ourselves unless we have been cleansed by Him and by the Truth of His word. 'How shall a young man cleanse his way? by observing Your word'.[35] 'Your word have I hid in my heart that I may not sin against You'.[36] Thus, the Lord said to His disciples: 'Now, you are clean through the word I have spoken to you'.[37] And He prayed to the Father: 'Sanctify them through Your Truth. Your word is Truth'.[38] For we are 'sanctified through the Truth'.[39] O Lord, 'cleanse us as only Your Truth can cleanse'.[40]

When we have been cleansed by the Truth of His word, we shall realize that 'the perfection of the word is Truth',[41] and 'the end of considering spiritual things is Truth'.[42] We shall understand that it is the will of the Lord to 'have all humanity to be saved and to come to the full knowledge of the Truth'.[43] But we should not forget that 'the full knowledge of the

Truth is according to godliness'[44] because Truth is the reward of goodness. 'Thou wilt reward the righteous with lovingkindness and Truth'.[45] It is those who are true who shall bring forth the Truth.

He is 'the Way, the Truth, and the Life'.[46] And I learned that if we desire to bear witness to the Truth in Him, we need the help of another because it takes two to bear witness to the Truth.[47] The day came when the two met and agreed before the Lord to pray and to work towards the same goal until the task was accomplished. For the Son of Man shall be revealed before His own when a Man and a son of Man have borne witness to Him, through His knowledge and understanding.

[1] St. Matthew 25:35–40

[2] Jeremiah 22:16

[3] Romans 2:4

[4] Hosea 2:14

[5] Psalm 111:10

[6] Joshua 1:7,8, Literal Translation

[7] Deuteronomy 4:6, Literal Translation

[8] Deuteronomy 29:9, Literal Translation

[9] Sirach 21:11, Literal Translation

[10] Sirach 45:5, Hebrew Text

[11] Proverbs 28:7

[12] Proverbs 3:1,4

[13] 1 Kings 2:3, Literal Translation

[14] 2 Kings 18:6

[15] 2 Kings 18:7, Literal Translation

[16] Psalm 119:98

[17] Psalm 119:100

[18] Psalm 119:104

[19] Psalm 107:43

[20] Sirach 1:26

[21] Testament of Naphtali 3:1

[22] Proverbs 11:2, rabbinic rendering of the Hebrew word TSANA (see Hebrew Dictionary)

[23] St. James 3:17

[24] Letter of Aristeas v. 292

[25] Maaseroth II.49d, Jerusalem Talmud

[26] Clement of Alexandria, *Stromata* IV c.6

[27] Shepherd of Hermas Book I, *Vision* III.8.7

[28] Clement of Alexandria, *Stromata* VII.xii.72

[29] Derek Eretz Zutta V.4

[30] Pesikta Rabbati 185b

[31] Testament of Joseph 10:2

[32] 2 Baruch 54:5

[33] Targum Ps. Jonathan on Genesis 49:1

[34] Sirach 51:20

[35] Psalm 119:9

[36] Psalm 119:11

[37] St. John 15:3

[38] St. John 17:17

[39] St. John 17:19

[40] Clement, *First Epistle to the Corinthians* 60:2

[41] Philo, *L.A.* III.4

[42] Philo, *Praem.* V.28

[43] 1 Timothy 2:4

[44] Titus 1:1

[45] Targum of the Amidah, see also Isaiah 61:8; Proverbs 11:18

[46] St. John 14:6

[47] Deuteronomy 17:6; 19:15; St. Matthew 18:16; St. John 8:17

Abbreviations

CBQ	Catholic Biblical Quarterly
NASB	New American Standard Bible
RSV	Revised Standard Version Bible
Abr.	De Abrahamo
Agr.	De Agricultura
Cher.	De Cherubim
Conf.	De Confusione Linguarum
Congr.	De Congressu Eruditionis Gratia
De Ios.	De Josepho
De Prov.	De Providentia
De Virt.	De Virtutibus
Decal.	De Decalogo
Det.	Quod Deterius Potiori insidiari soleat
Deus	Quod Deus sit Immutabilis
Ebr.	De Ebrietate
Fug.	De Fuga et Inventione
Her.	Quis rerum divinarum heres sit
L.A.	Legum Allegoriarum
Mig.	De Migratione Abrahami
Mos.	De Vita Mosis
Mut.	De Mutatione Nominum
Op.	De Opificio Mundi
Plant.	De Plantatione
Post.	De Posteritate Caini
Praem.	De Praemiis et Poenis
Q. Exod.	Quaestiones et Solutiones in Exodum
Q. Gen.	Quaestiones et Solutiones in Genesin
Sacr.	De Sacrificiis Abelis et Caini
Som.	De Somniis
Spec.	De Specialibus Legibus

MAN
AND
SON OF MAN

[For those who believe]

Chapter 1

'Who Is This Son Of Man?'
—St. John 12:34

'There exists Man and the son of Man' —Apocryphon of John 14:15

We shall not be able to know who the Son of Man is unless we understand from the very beginning who Man was. But to be able to do that we must have faith so that we may enter the wonderful garden found in the narrative of Genesis, a garden that is only opened to those who believe.

When we are told in the book of Genesis (1:26; 2:6–7) that the Lord God created Man in His own image and likeness, and formed him from the moistened dust of the ground, we are given the basis of understanding the nature of Man, his origin and his end. Man is truly an Earthman, and he shall return to the earth at the end of his days: 'the Lord created Man out of earth and turned him back to it again' (Sirach 17:1; Genesis 3:19). Since 'Adam was created out of earth' (Sirach 33:10) all his progeny are 'offspring of him who was first formed from the earth' (Wisdom 7:1), and so back to the earth they shall also return (Job 10:9, Ecclesiastes 3:20; 12:7). 'What then is Man but he who is only earth and potter's clay and will return to dust?' (1QH 10:3–4; 1QS 11:22, Dead Sea Scrolls; Isaiah 45:9; 64:8).

In forming Man from the dust of the ground, the Lord God made him from topsoil: that 'highest part of the dust of the world' (Proverbs 8:26) which is potentially the most fertile portion of the earth pending a good water supply. Man (Adam) was formed of earth *and* water: 'a mist went up from the earth and watered the whole face of the ground, then the Lord God formed Man of the dust from the ground' (Genesis 2:6–7). Previous to that, the rest of the ground was not yet productive, 'for the Lord God had not caused it to rain upon the earth' (Genesis 2:5). 'The dust of the earth can be blessed only through water' (Midrash Genesis Rabbah 41.9).

Having formed Man from the moistened dust of a field where 'he was taken from' (Genesis 3:23), the Lord God brought him to a fruitful Garden, a superlative place for growth and production, where the soil was best and the supply of water plentiful (Genesis 2:8–15). There was no better spot to bring a living plot of potentially fertile ground into, should one have desired to sow upon it, and obtain from it fruit in abundance. It was after He had brought Man into the Garden that 'the Lord God commanded [VAYTZAV] upon [AL] the Man [HA-ADAM]' not to eat the fruit of the tree of the knowledge of good and evil (Genesis 2:16–17). It is literally written in Hebrew that 'the Lord God commanded *upon* [AL] Adam', as one would place a 'seed . . . upon [AL] the earth' (Genesis 1:11), and wait to have it accepted, kept and brought into fruit by the ground. It is the nature of good ground to bear fruit from seed, and to nurture what has sprung forth from it.

Upon the great truth that Man is literally an earth-man formed from the dust of the ground, rests all our understanding as to his nature and potential. Thus, Man's relationship with his Maker is basically that between earth and Sower; ground and Seed; garden and Gardener; matter and Life. That is why the Word of God is often described as a seed implanted in Man: 'As . . . seed to the sower . . . so shall My word be that goes forth out of My mouth' (Isaiah 55:10,11). 'The Seed is the Word of God' (St. Luke 8:11). 'The Sower sows the Word' (St. Mark 4:14). 'Receive with meekness the implanted Word which is able to save your souls' (St. James 1:21). 'Born again, not of perishable seed but of imperishable: through the Word of God which lives and abides forever' (1 Peter 1:23). Philo, a Jewish philosopher (20 B.C.–A.D. 42), described the Word of God as being 'the invisible seminal artificer: the Divine Word' (Philo, *Her.* 67), and as such it is the vitalizer through which God effects His will in Man, and also gives life to him, because the original starting point of a new life is in the seed.

A plot of earth in a garden is most productive when it bears a fruit tree. When 'the Lord God took the Man, and put him into the Garden of Eden to work it and to keep it' (Genesis 2:15), He brought him to a place full of fruit trees which the Lord had made to grow out of the ground (Genesis 2:8–9). Man was brought there to take care of the Lord's own garden, but as an Earthman he had, figuratively speaking, the capability to bring forth a fruit tree himself from seed sown upon him. Earthman could have been not only the ground in the garden of the Lord, but also the fruit bearing tree sprung forth from it, had he kept the seed of God's command. Thus, more than two thousand years ago it was said that 'the Paradise of the Lord, the Trees of life, these are His holy ones, their planting is rooted forever' (Psalms of Solomon 14:3–4; 1QH 8:5–6, Dead Sea Scrolls). Again, 'What blessings God bestows on those who love Him as they should since they become a paradise of delights, they rear *in* themselves a fruitful tree in fullest bloom and are adorned with a variety of fruit' (Epistle to Diognetus 12:1–2).

The Lord God commanded Adam not to eat fruit from the tree of the knowledge of good and evil, giving this commandment to Earthman as a seed to be kept by him. What the Lord forbade Adam was extrinsic knowledge acquired by consuming fruit and casting seed aside: the seed of God's command. Within that particular seed was the promise of fruit, if it had been kept: the fruit of the knowledge of God which is only for those who obey Him.

It is by keeping the seed of His commandments that we shall receive the fruit of knowledge. Jesus said: 'If any man does His will, he shall know . . . ' (St. John 7:17); 'they have kept Thy word, now they know . . . ' (St. John 17:6,7). For in doing His will we gain His friendship and thereby His knowledge because friends confide in one another (St. John 15:10,14–15). Long ago, the wise scribes knew that the prohibition given by the Lord God to Adam was indeed a commandment whose keeping would result in 'knowing':

> 'Thou [Adam] hast forsaken My commandment which I delivered unto thee to keep it' –Book of Adam and Eve 23:3.

> You commanded *upon* him [Adam] just one commandment that he may know . . . –2 Esdras 3:7, Armenian Text.

> Is not the keeper . . . he who knows? –Proverbs 24:12.

> If they do not obey . . . they shall die without knowledge –Job 36:12.

Thus, 'the fruit of whose knowledge is upon his body' (Sirach 37:22, Hebrew Text), is he who has kept the commandment entrusted to him as a seed, towards the 'bearing *fruit* . . . and increasing in the *knowledge* of God' (Colossians 1:10) expected of him.

Moreover, in discarding the seed of God's command and devouring the forbidden fruit, Adam (Man) cast away life, and consumed in the ripe fruit the dissolution that follows maturity: death. 'Growth is effected by seed' (Philo, *L.A.* II. 37) and not by fruit substance. There is life within a seed, life that engenders itself in the ground that holds the seed fast and nurtures it. Let us not forget that when good ground keeps the seed, it awakens life in it which results in growth and the bringing forth of fruit full of children seeds.

The Lord does all things well. 'What can be known about God is plain' (Romans 1:19) because 'ever since the creation of the world His invisible nature, namely, His eternal power and deity, has been clearly perceived in the things that have been made' (Romans 1:20). And just as clear shall His ways be, if we understand His works.

Though lowly and small in size, there is great potential stored within a seed. The garden ground that accepts a seed, accepts in reality the fruitful tree that shall spring forth from it—if that seed is held fast by the heart of the ground. A wonderful thing happens to the earth that keeps the seed, after a time, its lifeless elements are taken up to form part of a living tree, and thereby matter enters into life.

In keeping the seed of God's command, Earthman would not only have received the fruit of knowledge from it but he would have entered into the life of the tree sprung forth from it, as well. Obedience would have gained for Man the knowledge of God and life everlasting.

A rich young man once asked the Lord, 'What good deed must I do to have eternal life?' And Jesus said to him, 'If you would enter life (eternal), keep the commandments' (St. Matthew 19:16, 17). For the seed of 'His commandment is life everlasting' (St. John 12:50) for those who keep it. 'If anyone keeps My word, he will never see death' (St. John 8:51) said the Lord, for His 'words . . . are spirit and life' (St. John 6:63), they are 'Words of eternal life' (St. John 6:68) for those who keep them. Is it not written 'You shall therefore keep My statutes and My ordinances by doing which a man shall live'? (Leviticus 18:5). 'Blessed are they who do His commandments that they may have right to the tree of life' everlasting (Revelation 22:14; Genesis 3:22).

'God created Man to be immortal and made him to be an image of His own eternal Self' (Wisdom 2:23; Ibid., 3:4; 6:18–19; 8:13,17; 15:3; Enoch 69:11; see also Philo *Op.* 37; 1 Corinthians 15:42,50,53 etc.). But the Lord God formed Man from the moistened dust of the ground to be truly an Earthman. If by the keeping of a living seed it is possible for earth to enter into life, would not the Lord have made it possible for man to enter eternal life by the keeping of the Lord's seed-command? 'For the word of God is alive and powerful' (Hebrews 4:12), and it works in the heart of man to 'bring forth fruit unto life everlasting' (St. John 4:36). Indeed, 'His commandment is life everlasting' (St. John 12:50) for those who hold that seed fast.

Man was created to give glory to God, and because he was formed from the dust of the ground, Man gives glory to God the same way the ground may be said to give glory to a sower: by bringing forth fruits in abundance for him from the seeds that he sowed. Thus, the Lord said, 'in this is My

Father glorified, in that you bear much fruit' (St. John 15:8), for Man is meant to bear fruit for God: 'fruit of praise' (1QS 10:9, Dead Sea Scrolls). 'Praise to God . . . is the fruit' (Hebrews 13:15) brought forth by the 'trees of righteousness, the planting of the Lord that He might be glorified' (Isaiah 61:3), by their fruits of praise (Psalm 50:23).

Before Earthman could have participated in the eternal life of God, he had to keep the seed of the Lord's command, and thereby enter into the everlasting life of that seed-word of God. And before Man would have been able to give glory to God he needed to have the knowledge of God brought forth as fruit from that seed. We know that Adam had been commanded not to eat *fruit* of knowledge that was not his, but hidden in that command was *seed* of knowledge to be kept, so that he would be able to bring forth fruit of knowledge from that seed. The first commandment God gave Adam and Eve was to 'be fruitful and multiply' (Genesis 1:28), but Man had to learn that there is no fruition and increase without first keeping the seed. If we 'keep knowledge' (Proverbs 5:2; Malachi 2:3) as seed, 'knowledge shall be increased' (Daniel 12:4) in 'the fruit of knowledge' (Sirach 37:22, Hebrew Text) we shall bring forth from that seed to His praise and glory. For 'when the earth shall be full of the knowledge of the Lord' (Isaiah 11:9) then 'all the earth shall be filled with the glory of the Lord' (Numbers 14:21).

The truth is that through obedience Earthman was meant to become a Treeman bearing the fruit of knowledge and eternal life. For the Lord gave Earthman a Seed to keep so that He would receive fruit from him as a Treeman in the end.

But because he did not keep the seed of God's command, Man became 'unfruitful in the knowledge of our Lord' (2 Peter 1:8). Even 'Wisdom is a tree of life (in the end) to those who take hold of her' as a seed in the beginning (Proverbs 3:18).

From what happened in the Garden of Eden we can see that the term 'Man' in Holy Scripture has the connotation of immanent perfection, knowledge, immortality and an exalted state along with the intimation of pride, impenitence, instability and disgrace through disobedience.

'I see men that I behold as trees walking' (St. Mark 8:24 Literal Translation) said the blind man who was given insight as well as natural vision by the Lord, because 'the Lord gives wisdom to the blind' (Psalm 146:8, Greek Text) before He gives them sight. May 'the eyes of your understanding be enlightened' (Ephesians 1:18).

Chapter 2

Breadman

From the Garden we can learn about Man, and from the Field we can begin to understand about the Son of Man. When Earthman was taken to a well watered garden but failed to produce in that optimal place of fruition, 'the Lord God sent him (away) to till the ground from which he was taken' (Genesis 3:23). Man was sent back to the *field* where he was formed. There, he was to learn that bearing fruit is easy in a garden but not in a field. For in a field the ground must be plowed, harrowed and tilled before it can bear fruit from seed. And just as Man was expected in Eden to be as a garden plot bearing of himself a fruitful tree, so in the field is he expected to bring forth of himself a crop of grain and be made bread for God.

It may be easy for the ground of a garden that has kept the seed to bring forth a fruit tree, but the ground of a field must be worked upon before it can 'make [ASAH] fruit' (Leviticus 25:19,21; 2 Kings 19:30; Isaiah 37:31 etc.) from seed. In the Garden of Eden, Man did not have to produce his own food, the Lord provided for him out of the herbs, seeds and fruits of His creation (Genesis 1:11,29; 2:8–9.16). But when Man was exiled to the field, he had to labor in sorrow (Genesis 3:17–19) for his nourishment and make his own food: bread. For the soil of a field is 'the earth whose fruits are raised by labor' (Testament of Issachar 5:5). Man and the sons of Man in the field have to plow, harrow, sow, till, reap, thresh, winnow, grind, knead, mould and bake before they can eat the bread they have made. And because Man and the sons of Man have to suffer before they can eat 'the bread of men' (Ezekiel 24:17,22), our bread is referred to as 'the bread of affliction' (Deuteronomy 16:3; 1 Kings 22:27; 2 Chronicles 18:26), 'bread of sorrows' (Psalm 127:2), and 'bread of adversity' (Isaiah 30:20) for it is 'bread gotten by sweat' (Sirach 34:26, Latin Vulgate; Genesis 3:19).

Thus, in the field 'Man is land suffering' (Epistle of Barnabas 6:9), because 'his fruitful field both soul and body' (Isaiah 10:18), can only be fruitful through labor and suffering. A son of Man in the field can consider his own 'back as the ground' (Isaiah 51:23), and say as King David did: 'Upon my back have the plowers plowed and made their furrows long' (Psalm 129:3).

But God is good, for when Man has worked in the field 'to the exhaustion of his strength' (Sirach 31:4, Hebrew Text), the Lord makes the ground 'yield . . . her strength' (Genesis 4:12) to him. So that from the 'bread [LEHEM] out of the ground' (Psalm 104:14), Man receives his strength back, being nourished by that 'bread which strengthens man's heart' (Psalm 104:15; 1 Samuel 28:20,22), and 'comforts' him (Judges 19:5,8).

A garden is for fruit trees and a field for grain and vineyards. Life in a garden would have been the destiny of Man, but because he disobeyed, life in the field of exile is the lot of all the sons of Man. We know that if he had kept the seed of God's command in the Garden of Eden, Man would have become, in a certain way, a Treeman bearing the fruit of the knowledge of God. By the same token, if they keep the seed of His Word, the sons of Man shall become, as it were, a Fruitful Field providing 'bread of understanding' (Sirach 15:3, Hebrew and Greek Texts) for God from the words that He sowed in them.

The prophet is like a shepherd according to the Lord's own heart (Jeremiah 3:15) in that he is able to feed his people with the fruit of knowledge and the bread of understanding. Jeremiah's enemies may have had the two divisions of mankind in mind when they plotted against him saying, 'Let us destroy the tree and its bread [LEHEM]' (Jeremiah 11:19, Literal Translation of the Hebrew Text). Did not the Psalmist and St. John the Baptist in analogous verses (Psalm 1:3–4; St. Matthew 3:10,12) describe mankind in terms of trees and grain? If a good man is 'like a tree planted by streams of water that yields his fruit in his season,' and in the same Psalm, 'the wicked . . . are like chaff which the wind drives away' (Psalm 1:3,4), are not the righteous like grains of wheat? 'The righteous, all of them are as wheat fit for storage,' said the rabbis (Midrash Song of Songs Rabbah 7.3; see also Targum to Jeremiah 23:28). They also said that 'the fruit of the tree of knowledge was wheat' (Midrash Genesis Rabbah 15.7; Berakoth 40a, Babylonian Talmud). But of course, in this instance, they were mistaken, for it takes labor and suffering to bring forth wheat, and there was no sorrow in the Garden of Eden. However, they may have been speaking, in a hidden sense, of the ideal Man full of knowledge from the fruit of knowledge, and of understanding from the 'bread of understanding' (Sirach 15:3). Long ago, Eliphaz had said concerning the obedient who accept suffering: 'You shall come to your grave in ripe old age as a sheaf of grain is gathered in its season' (Job 5:26).

In the field, the sons of Man are not only likened to a fruitful field, grains, and sheaves of wheat (Genesis 37:5–8; Job 5:26), but also to dough: 'Purge out the old leaven that you may be a new dough' (1 Corinthians 5:7;

see Philo, *Sacr.* 107; Midrash Genesis Rabbah 14.1; 17.8; 34.10; Tanchumah on Genesis 1.28; 3.53; Tanchumah Noah 1; Mezora 9; Berakoth 17a; Shabbath 31b–32a, Babylonian Talmud; Tosephta Kiddushin 5.2; Yalkut to Proverbs 962; Sifre to Deuteronomy 45). 'We many are one bread' (1 Corinthians 10:17; see Numbers 14:9) and not one 'tree' because we are not sons of Man in the Garden of Eden but in the field of exile. Being 'bread' we can see why there were twelve loaves (Numbers 24:5–8) always set before the Lord in the Tabernacle of the sojournings, and in the Temple at Jerusalem; each loaf of bread representing one of the twelve tribes. Moreover, according to Jewish tradition, the two loaves offered to the Lord at the time of the wheat harvest were large enough to be human-sized (Mishnah, *Menachoth* 6:6; 7:1; Maimonides', *Book of the Temple Service,* section Daily Offerings, par. 10). 'May he be as a flourishing field of grain', said the rabbis of the Messiah (Midrash Genesis Rabbah 48.10; 86.1; Midrash Ecclesiastes Rabbah 1.9), for He was to live among the sons of Man in the field. And 'kiss the wheat' (BAR means either 'son' or 'wheat' in Psalm 2:12), was interpreted by them to mean, 'kiss the Messiah' (Rabbi David Kimchi's Commentary on Psalm 2:12). Thus, when the Son of Man came, He referred to Himself as 'a grain of wheat' (St. John 12:24), and the living and true 'Bread of life' (St. John 6:51,32,48). And 'if anyone eats of this Bread, he will live forever' (St. John 6:51 and v. 58).

We know that a field is for growing grain, but it is also the place for planting a vineyard. Both require hard labor and the discipline of cultivation to bring forth fruit in abundance. The vine must be pruned and staked to make it give the full cluster. Shall there be wine without treading the grape? In the field of the sons of Man we 'are God's cultivated land' [GEORGION] – 1 Corinthians 3:9. And there we are also His vineyard and His vine. In the Psalms and in the books of the prophets Isaiah, Jeremiah and Hosea, we find the Lord referring to the people of Israel as His vineyard, and the tribe of Judah as His 'planting' (Isaiah 5:7) from which the Davidic line of Kings issued. It was from the stump of that vine that the Messiah was later on to sprout as a glorious 'Branch' (Isaiah 11:1–5). The Lord remonstrated through His prophets that although He had cultivated His vineyard with loving care, it produced no fruits of understanding for Him. Therefore because 'its branches are withered they will be broken off; the women come and set them on fire, because it is a people of no understanding' (Isaiah 27:11; see vv. 2–3): a people without 'the fruits of understanding' (Sirach 37:22) on their branches. The Lord looks for 'profitable fruitage . . . yielded by the understanding' (Philo, *Som.* II. 22). 'O Lord . . . cultivate our understanding whereby fruit may come' (2 Esdras

8:6), otherwise, our 'understanding is unfruitful' (1 Corinthians 14:14).

'Bread of understanding' (Sirach 15:3), and vine-'fruits of understanding' (Sirach 37:22 and v. 23) are what the Lord expects from the sons of Man in the field. The Garden of Eden was meant to be the world of Man, but 'the field is the world' (St. Matthew 13:38) of the sons of Man. And just as Man in the garden was meant to bring forth of himself a tree bearing fruit of knowledge, so are the sons of Man in the field envisioned as bringing forth of themselves bread and wine of understanding (for 'the fruit of the vine' is wine; see St. Matthew 26:27–*29*). We can now see why it is written in the book of Proverbs: As for him who lacks *understanding,* Wisdom says to him, 'Come eat of my *bread* and drink of the *wine* I have mingled' (Proverbs 9:4– 5). And we can understand the sadness of the sage who 'went by the *vineyard* of the man devoid of *understanding,* and behold, it was all grown over with thorns, and nettles covered its surface, and its stone wall was broken down' (Proverbs 24:30–31), because that man neglected to cultivate his vine of understanding. Let us not forget that 'he who tills his own ground [ADAMAH] will be satisfied with *bread,* but he who follows after worthless pursuits is devoid of [bread of] *understanding'* (Proverbs 12:11), and his field is without fruit. Thus, if Man in the garden was meant to be a tree of knowledge, a son of Man in the field is meant to be bread and wine of understanding. This is why in the end the Son of Man gave Himself to us in the form of Bread and Wine, for He is not only 'the true Bread' (St. John 6:32) but also 'the true Vine' (St. John 15:1).

In the term 'son of Man' there is the connotation of labor and suffering, servitude and understanding, humility and righteousness with final exaltation through fidelity.

Man was concerned with the Fruit itself, the Son of Man concentrates on the Seed. 'In the original creation of all things . . . God caused all the trees and plants to spring out of the earth perfect, having fruits not unripe but at their prime . . . also a provision for the perpetual reproduction of their kind containing within them the seed' (Philo, *Op.* 42,43). 'All issued forthright complete and perfect out of the earth . . . the fruit was created first' (Midrash Haggadol, *Bereshith* I. 581; Torah Behukothai I. 561; Torah Shelemah I. 384,389). 'Like all creatures formed in the six days of creation, Man came forth from the hand of the Creator fully and completely developed' (Ḥullin 60a; Ḥagigah 12a, Babylonian Talmud), but not the sons of Man, for they were born from seed. And they understand that there is no perfect fruit for them in the end, unless a seed has been kept from the very beginning by the heart of the ground.

Wisdom said:

> 'I was exalted like a cedar in Lebanon, and like a cypress tree
> upon the mountains of Hermon.
> I was exalted like a palm tree in En-gedi, and as a rose plant
> in Jericho, as a beautiful olive tree in the field, and like a plane
> tree by the water, I was exalted' —Sirach 24:13–14.

Wisdom was exalted by the good ground in the hearts of the sons of Man
who held her words fast as a seed.

> 'O Lord . . . shall the dust praise You? shall it declare Your truth?'
> —Psalm 30:8,9.

Yes Lord, if You sow and rain upon it, it shall bring forth praise as fruit
to Your glory, and declare that the truth is in the seed of Your word.

Chapter 3

Man And The Son Of Man

'Happy the Man who finds wisdom
and the son of Man who knows understanding'
—Proverbs 3:13, Syriac Text

If the term 'Man' represents 'Knowledge', then the designation 'Son of Man' symbolizes 'Understanding'. Man was created to have immortality and knowledge of God as a reward, but he forfeited that reward when he discarded the seed of God's command. The knowledge he acquired through disobedience was the knowledge of good and evil, but not the knowledge of God. For 'by this do we know that we know Him, if we keep His commandments. He who says, 'I know Him,' and does not keep His commandments, is a liar, and the truth is not in him' (1 John 2:3–4). Nevertheless, because of the episode in the Garden of Eden, the motifs of 'Knowledge' and 'Man' became closely associated in the Holy Scriptures. The sons of Man did not eat of the tree of the knowledge of good and evil so they could not be said to have Man's knowledge, however, they possess understanding because when God created Man, He formed him to be an understanding being (Philo, *Q.Gen.* I. 53; Torah Shelemah 2.126). It is through obedience, labor, and suffering in the field of exile that the understanding of the sons of Man shall advance to the knowledge of God.

In the Holy Scriptures, when the terms Man and Son of Man are used in conjunction, the same sequence of *Man* and *knowledge,* and *son of Man* and *understanding* is observed even when the phrasing is oblique. Let us take Psalm 144:3 as an example:

> 'What is *man* that You *know* [YADA] him? or the *son of man* that You *take account* [CHASHAB] of him?'

Knowing the hidden sequence we can render it:

> 'What is man that You know him? or the son of man that You understand him?'

because it takes understanding to be able to 'take into account':

'How shall I understand [SAKAL] unless You take account [CHASHAB] for me?' —1QH 10:6,7, Dead Sea Scrolls.

Do take account and understand —Apocalypse of Abraham 29:3.

Let him who has understanding take into account —Revelation 13:18.

There is also close association between *remembering* and *knowing*: 'Remember [ZAKAR] now . . . that you may know' (Micah 6:5). We find that remembering and knowing are used interchangeably in variant texts of Sirach 16:17:

'I shall not be *remembered* among so many people' —Vaticanus and Ephraemi Greek Texts.

'I shall not be *known* among so many people' —Sinaiticus, Alexandrinus and MS 248 Greek Texts; Hebrew, Syriac, Vetus Latina and Latin Vulgate Texts.

Furthermore, there is also a relationship between being *visited* by the Lord and *understanding*: 'The Most High will *visit* the world . . . then you will *understand*' (2 Esdras 9:2,4). Thus, Psalm 8:4:

'What is man that You remember [ZAKAR] him? and the son of man that You visit him?'

may be rendered:

'What is man that You know him? and the son of man that You make him understand?'

Humanity stems forth from two great engenderings: the generation of Man, and the generation of the son of Man. From Adam sprang the generation of Man, and from Noah, that of the sons of Man. The first generation perished in the Flood, the second endures to the present. We are descended from the generation of a son of Man: Noah. In the stylistic parallelism of the Creation narrative and the Flood account we can see that Noah—son of Man—is considered a second Adam. There is close similarity in both accounts:

Genesis

Creation	Flood
1:27	9:6
1:28	9:1–2
1:29–30	9:3
2:19	9:2
2:17	8:21

Adam is par excellence Man, and Noah pre-eminently Son of Man. Adam's generation and 'the world that then existed perished, being flooded with water' (2 Peter 3:6). 'The world which now exists' (2 Peter 3:7), and our present generation from the time of Noah, is the generation of the sons of Man. 'Good and upright is the Lord' (Psalm 25:8), therefore 'God made Man [ADAM] upright' (Ecclesiastes 7:29) and good (Genesis 1:27,31). And Man remained good and upright until he disobeyed and lost not only his uprightness, but his right to be called righteous, because righteousness comes from keeping the commandments of God. When God created Man in His own image and likeness He made Man a pure and perfect being: 'Man [ADAM] came forth from the hand of the Creator fully and perfectly developed' (Midrash Genesis Rabbah 14.7; 8.1; Midrash Numbers Rabbah 12.8; Midrash Song of Songs Rabbah 3.11; Sifra 26.4; Zohar I. 123b). Nevertheless, Man (Adam) is never called 'righteous' in the Holy Scriptures because he disobeyed. The first one to be called righteous is Noah, a son of Man:

> Noah was a righteous man, perfect in his generations, Noah walked with God —Genesis 6:9.

> The Lord said to Noah . . . 'I have seen that you are righteous before Me in this generation' —Genesis 7:1.

> Noah . . . the righteous one —Paraleipomena Jeremiou 7:8.

> Noah . . . from whom came all righteous men —2 Esdras 3:11.

'Noah [son of Man] was found righteous' (Sirach 44:17, Hebrew Text), because 'Noah did according to all God commanded him' (Genesis 6:22; 7:5), but Adam (Man) was not found 'righteous' because he disobeyed. It is the pure who are able to see God (St. Matthew 5:8), and it is the perfect who can attain to His knowledge (Ephesians 4:13) because 'the full knowledge of the truth is according to godliness' (Titus 1:1). In turn, it is the righteous sons of Man who have understanding: 'the understanding [PHRONĒSEI] of the righteous' (St. Luke 1:17). 'A righteous man understands' (Proverbs 21:12): that it is the prerogative of Man, who was created perfect, to have the knowledge of God (if he had obeyed), and it is the priviledge of the righteous sons of Man to understand Him: 'O, God of righteousness and understanding' (1QH Fragment 7:8, Dead Sea Scrolls) by 'Your righteousness You make them understand' (11Q Ps^a xix.3, Dead Sea Scrolls).

We have seen the relationship between *Man* and *Knowledge* and *Son of Man* and *Understanding;* and between *Man* and *perfection* and *Son of Man* and *righteousness:* 'the Son of Man who has righteousness' (Enoch 46:3; 71:14,16). We can now understand why it is written:

'Your wickedness affects a man [as it did Adam] and your righteousness a son of man' —Job 35:8.

'I know that righteousness is not of man [it is of the sons of Man] nor of the sons of man perfection of way' [it is of Man who was created perfect] —1QH 4:30,31, Dead Sea Scrolls.

'What is man that he should be pure [ZAKAH]? and he who is born of woman [i.e. a son of Man; see Sirach 50:22–24, Syriac; Enoch 15:12] that he should be righteous?' —Job 15:14.

'How can man be righteous with God? [by keeping His commandments] or how can he be pure who is born of woman?' [by 'going on towards perfection' and becoming one with 'righteous men made perfect' and pure through obedience and suffering —Hebrews 6:1; 12:23; 2:10] —Job 25:4.

'Shall mortal man [i.e. a son of Man; see Sirach 17:30] be more righteous than God? Shall a strong man [as Adam was strong] be more pure than his Maker?' —Job 4:17.

Furthermore, knowing that righteousness concerns the *sons* of Man we can discover the same sequence in other verses:

'Give the King Your judgments, O God, and Your righteousness to the King's son' —Psalm 72:1.

The mercy of the Lord is from everlasting to everlasting on those who fear Him. And His righteousness to children's children —Psalm 103:17.

The mountains will bring peace to the people, and the little hills [sons of mountains], by righteousness —Psalm 72:3.

Noah . . . his heart was righteous in all his ways. And Noah son of Man said: 'My children, hear, work judgment and righteousness that you may be planted in righteousness over the face of all the earth' —Book of Jubilees 5:19; 7:34.

They petitioned and interceded for the sons of Man and righteousness flowed before them as water —Enoch 39:5.

'In Your righteousness You do visit the sons of Man' —Psalms of Solomon 9:8.

He [God] visits the righteous —Psalms of Solomon 3:14.

The righteous . . . in the time of their visitation they shall shine forth —Wisdom 3:1,7; Ibid., 4:15.

'What is . . . the son of man that You visit him?' —Psalm 8:4.

The Son of Man who has righteousness, and understanding —Enoch 46:3.

Chapter 4

Knowledge And Understanding

'Who will tell me what I do not know?
Great and wonderful things which I do not understand?'
—Job 42:3, Greek Text

Man came before the Son of Man, and he ate 'the fruit of . . . knowledge' (Sirach 37:22, Hebrew Text) before he learnt to make 'the bread of understanding' (Sirach 15:3). Therefore, most Scriptural texts place knowledge before understanding:

Out of His mouth comes knowledge and understanding
—Proverbs 2:6.

'I will give you shepherds after My own heart, who will feed you with knowledge and understanding' —Jeremiah 3:15.

Everyone having knowledge and having understanding
—Nehemiah 10:28.

All the inhabitants of the earth shall know, and all who are left in the world shall understand —Sirach 23:27, Syriac Text.

He who knows all things knows her, He has found her out with His understanding —Baruch 3:32.

Know therefore and understand —Daniel 9:25.

'That you may know and understand' —St. John 10:38.

'What do you know that we do not know? What do you understand that is not in us?' —Job 15:9.

'I neither know nor understand what you are saying' —St. Mark 14:68.

Have you not known? . . . have you not understood? —Isaiah 40:21.

Thus His eyelids understand and try the sons of Man since understanding and righteousness concern the sons of Man:

> This is the Son of Man who has righteousness, and with whom dwells righteousness —Enoch 46:3.

> This is the Son of Man who is born to righteousness and righteousness abides over him —Enoch 71:14.

If the Lord tries and refines the righteous sons of Man, it is to make them pure and perfect as Man was meant to be:

> The Lord tries the righteous —Psalm 11:5.

> 'O Lord of Hosts who triest the righteous' —Jeremiah 20:12.

> The righteous . . . God proved and found them worthy of Himself; like gold in the furnace He has tried them, and like a sacrificial burnt offering He accepted them. In the time of their visitation they shall shine forth —Wisdom 3:1,5–7.

> 'When He has tried me I shall come forth as [shining] gold' —Job 23:10.

> He will purify for Himself some of the sons [MIBBENE] of Man ['ISH] to expel every spirit of perversity [from them] —1QH 4:20, Dead Sea Scrolls.

> The Lord tried them and their spirits were found pure —Enoch 108:9.

Holding on to the same pattern of thought that relegates Knowledge to Man and Understanding to the sons of Man, and not forgetting about 'seeing' and 'knowing', and 'hearing' and 'understanding', we shall have insight regarding other texts:

> Who is the man who can know the command of God? And who is there among the sons of man who can hear [and understand] the words of the Holy One? —4Q Enoch IV. [Pl. XXIV.10–14], Dead Sea Scrolls [Cave 4 Aramaic Fragments of the book of Enoch].

> The first man did not know her [Wisdom] perfectly, nor shall the

last [son of] man find her out [i.e., 'understand her'] —Sirach
24:28
But He who knows all things knows her, and has *found her out
with His understanding* [SUNESEI] —Baruch 3:32.

In the verses above, we can see again that Man precedes sons of Man, and
knowledge precedes understanding. We shall also find the key words
'knowing', 'command' and 'perfectly' associated with the word 'Man', and
the words about 'searching' and 'finding', 'hearing' and 'understanding' associated with the words 'sons of Man'. For it is expected of the sons of Man
that they understand: 'Understand, O son of man' (Daniel 8:17), and that
they search for Wisdom, and even for understanding if they do not have
it: 'the *sons* [UIOI] of Hagar, who seek for understanding [SUNESEŌS] on
the earth' (Baruch 3:23) because they know that they are really 'sons of
man according to His understanding [SAKAL]' —1QH Fragment 11:4,
Dead Sea Scrolls. Notice that it refers to 'His' and not 'their' understanding [SAKAL] because all 'wisdom, understanding [SAKAL], and insight of
things are from the Lord' (Sirach 11:15, Hebrew Text).

The tradition of knowledge preceding understanding is very old, and we
can discover the same thought pattern in the writings of other ancient
peoples:

> That men may *know* the tale, and that the multitudes of the
> earth may *understand* it —Baal Text VI.iii, ll.15–16.

> Tell it so that the sons of El may *know,* and the assembly of the
> stars may *understand* it —Baal Text IV.i, ll.3–4.

> A word which men do not *know* and the multitudes of the earth
> do not *understand* —Anat Text III. ll.23–25; Ibid., IV. ll.59–60.

> Who *knows* the will of the gods in heaven? who *understands* the
> plans of the underworld gods? —Ludlul bel Nemeqi ll.36–37
> [Ashurbanipal Tablet K3972].

> One cannot *know* the spot where he [the god of the river Nile]
> is, nor can his cavern be *understood* from the writings —
> Egyptian Hymn to the Inundation ll.45–46 [*Journal of Near
> Eastern Studies* vol. 34, no.I p. 18].

Precedence of knowledge before understanding is found in all these
texts not because mankind was meant to go from knowledge to under-

standing, but because there is the collective memory that from the earliest beginnings primeval Man stole 'eternal knowledge' (1QS 2:3; 8:9; 1QM 17:8, Dead Sea Scrolls), he usurped it. For in creating Man, God endowed him with wisdom and understanding but He did not give him knowledge:

> The Lord created Man of the earth . . . He endowed them with strength proper to themselves, and made them according to His image . . . counsel, and a tongue, and eyes and ears, and a heart He gave them to understand. He filled them with the insight [EPISTĒMĒN] of understanding [SUNESEŌS] and *showed* them [*not* gave them knowledge of] good and evil . . . besides this He *gave* them insight [EPISTĒMĒN] and the law of life for a heritage —Sirach 17:1,3,6–7,11.

> 'I [God] commanded Wisdom to create man' —2 Enoch 30:8.

> Wisdom preserved the first formed father of the world, who was created alone . . . and gave him power to rule all things —Wisdom 10:1–2.

Man was meant to acquire Knowledge through obedience: through the keeping of the seed of God's command, which would have eventually brought forth in him the fruit of knowledge—if he had kept that seed. Knowledge belongs to the realm of good judgment and in the eyes of God no one is fit to judge who has not been tried and found true. 'Good *judgment* and *knowledge*' (Psalm 119:66) go together. 'Shall anyone teach God *knowledge*, since He *judges* those who are on high?' (Job 21:22). 'By the knowledge of the Lord they were distinguished' (Sirach 33:8), because it is through knowledge that we are able to distinguish things and distinguish between good and evil and between right and wrong so that we can make a good judgment. When the Lord said in Jeremiah 3:15: 'I will give you shepherds after My own heart, who will feed you with knowledge [DEAH] and understanding,' He meant that He will give us pastors who will teach us good judgment to enable us to uphold righteousness and condemn wickedness. For when He Himself shall come as a Shepherd to feed His flock (Ezekiel 34:15), He will with the same knowledge and understanding give the wicked their due: 'I will feed them with judgment' (Ezekiel 34:16). 'The Lord is a God of judgment' (Isaiah 30:18) because 'the Lord is a God of knowledge [DEAH]' —1 Samuel 2:3.

To be able to judge with true knowledge is in a certain way to be able to judge as God does. When the Satanic serpent tempted Eve to eat the fruit of the tree of the knowledge of good and evil, it induced her to do so saying that if they ate the fruit of that tree they would become 'like gods [ELOHIM] knowing good and evil' (Genesis 3:5). ELOHIM, the Hebrew word for 'God' used in over two-thousand and seven-hundred instances in Holy Scripture, is the same word used for 'judges' [ELOHIM, as in Exodus 21:6; 22:8,9,28], because all judgment belongs to God and no one is able to make a true and righteous judgment unless he possesses the knowledge of God. But God does not give His knowledge to us unless He has proved us worthy of His true knowledge.

We have seen how in many texts of the Bible knowledge precedes understanding. We shall now become aware that when the Lord gives us His gifts of wisdom, understanding, and knowledge, He gives them to us in that order of precedence, for we are to be truly wise and understanding before we shall be given the knowledge of God:

> When the wise is made to understand [SAKAL], he receives knowledge −Proverbs 21:11b.

> 'I have filled him with the spirit of God in wisdom, and in understanding, and in knowledge' −Exodus 31:3.

> He was filled with the spirit of God in wisdom, and understanding, and knowledge −Exodus 35:31.

> He was filled with wisdom and understanding and knowledge [DAATH] −1 Kings 7:14.

> Wisdom rains down understanding [EPISTĒMĒN] and knowledge [GNŌSIN] −Sirach 1:19.

> He [God] makes *wisdom* abound as Pishon and as Tigris in the days of the new fruits. And He makes *understanding* abound like Euphrates and as the Jordan in the days of the harvest, and makes the instruction of *knowledge* appear as light, as Gihon in the time of vintage −Sirach 24:25–27, Sinaiticus and MSS. 248,55,155,253,254 etc.

> He [God] gives wisdom to the wise and [He gives] knowledge to those who know [all about] understanding −Daniel 2:21.

> 'My son, pay attention to my *wisdom,* and incline your ear to my *understanding* so that you may observe discretion and your lips may keep *knowledge'* −Proverbs 5:1–2.

We must first understand before we shall be given knowledge by God. And the first thing we should understand is that 'to depart from evil is understanding' (Job 28:28), for we must be good before we can really understand and have 'the understanding [PHRONESEI] of the righteous' —St. Luke 1:17. 'A righteous man understands' (Proverbs 21:12, Literal Translation) but 'none of the wicked shall understand' (Daniel 12:10). And 'the righteous one knows . . . but the wicked do not understand knowledge' (Proverbs 29:7, Literal Translation), 'but knowledge is easy to him who understands' (Proverbs 14:6), because he who understands is good and the righteousness of the Lord in him has earned him the friendship of God. They who are friends of God truly know Him. All these things 'are plain to him who understands, and right to them who find knowledge' (Proverbs 8:9). Adam and Eve usurped knowledge, but for us there is no knowledge unless we first understand for 'if there be no understanding, there is no knowledge' (Pirke Aboth 3:21). 'Wisdom brings forth understanding for a man' (Proverbs 10:23, Greek Text), and 'understanding throws open the way to knowledge' (Corpus Hermeticum, *Libellus* IV. 6a). Thus, the Lord says through the prophet Hosea (14:9): 'Who is wise and he shall understand these things? (Who is) understanding [BIN] and he shall know them?' 'The heart of the understanding [BIN] gets knowledge' (Proverbs 18:15a). If we hope for knowledge, let us ask for understanding so that we may 'know':

> 'Give me understanding that I may learn' —Psalm 119:73.

> 'Understanding loves to learn and advance to knowledge' —Philo, *Decal.* I. 9.

> 'Give me understanding that I may know' —Psalm 119:125.

> 'By Your understanding I have knowledge' —1QH 14:12, Dead Sea Scrolls; Ibid., 15:12.

> 'These things I have known because of Your understanding' —1QH 1:21, Dead Sea Scrolls.

> 'We know these things because of Your understanding' 1QM 10:16, Dead Sea Scrolls.

> 'Within whose heart You have set understanding so that he may open the fountain of knowledge to all who understand' —1QH 2:18, Dead Sea Scrolls.

'That they might know You according to the measure of their understanding' —1QH 1:31, Dead Sea Scrolls.

'I give You thanks O Adonai! For you have given me understanding of Your truth and have made me know Your marvelous mysteries' —1QH 7:26,27, Dead Sea Scrolls.

'And I gifted with understanding, I have knowledge of You' —1QH 12:11,12, Dead Sea Scrolls.

'Let him who glories glory in this, that he understands and knows Me' —Jeremiah 9:24.

'You will know for you have understanding' —*Didache* 2:21.

'The heart of him who has understanding seeks knowledge' (Proverbs 15:14), because he knows that although he may be wise and understanding he still has to acquire knowledge. They who understand know that 'the fear of the Lord is the beginning of knowledge' (Proverbs 1:7) because 'they who fear the Lord keep His commandments' (Sirach 2:21, Latin Vulgate; Deuteronomy 5:29). Let us not forget that it is within the seed of His commandment that the potential fruit of knowledge is found. 'The Lord takes pleasure in those who fear Him' (Psalm 147:11), and keep His commandments. Therefore, 'whoever fears the Lord will receive His instruction' (Sirach 32:14), and the Lord will confide in him as a friend because he pleases the Lord. Thus, 'the secret of the Lord is for those who fear Him; He makes known to them His covenant' (Psalm 25:14).

Remembering that we 'see and know' and that we should understand before we can have knowledge, we shall have insight into Psalm 73:16:

'When I sought to *know* this, it was hard labor [AMAL] to my eyes, until I went into the sanctuary of God; then I understood [BIN] their end . . . for indeed, [I know now that] those who are far from You shall perish' —Psalm 73:16,27, Literal Translation.

And we shall also see the insight that Joshua, son of Nun had when the elders said to him:

'Moses is dead. Take the garments of his wisdom and put them on you, and gird your loins with the girdle of his *knowledge*'. . . . And Joshua took the garments of wisdom and put them on and girded his loins with the girdle of *understanding,* and when he put it on, his understanding was kindled and his spirit was stirred up —Ps. Philo's, *Biblical Antiquities* XX. 2,3.

Let us rejoice! for 'the Son of God has come, and has given us *understanding,* to *know* Him who is true' —1 John 5:20.

Chapter 5

The Most High And The Almighty

'What is His name, and what is
His Son's name? Surely you know!' —Proverbs 30:4

Just as the association of Man with knowledge precedes that of Son of Man with understanding, the divine designation God 'Most High' precedes that of God 'Almighty' (Genesis 14:18–20,22; 17:1). In turn, the attributes of knowledge and understanding are also respectively linked to each of these titles of God. The Most High is God of knowledge, and it is He who gives knowledge to man:

> The Most High possesses knowledge —Sirach 42:18c, Masada Scroll.

> The knowledge of the Most High —Numbers 24:16; 2 Esdras 14:50; 1QS 4:22, Dead Sea Scrolls.

> The Most High knows all knowledge —Sirach 42:18, Sinaiticus and Ephraemi Greek Texts.

> The Most High who knows all —Sibylline Oracles, Fragment i.4.

> The Most High has given knowledge to men that He may be honored in His wonders —Sirach 38:6, Latin Vulgate.

> 'Blessed be the Most High who gave you wit and knowledge' —Story of Ahikar 7:19, Arabic Text.

> 'I will say . . . to the Most High: Support of my goodness! Source of knowledge!' —1QS 10:11,12, Dead Sea Scrolls.

> 'He has caused His knowledge to abound in me . . . the Most High has given it' —Odes of Solomon 12:3,4; 6:6,10–12.

Knowing that the 'Most High' is the title of God who 'knows', we can understand the particular phrasings in the book of Job and in the Psalms:

> Is not God [Most High] in the *heights* of the heavens? . . . and you
> say, 'What does God *know?*' [being the Most High in the heavens
> He should know] —Job 22:12,13.

> 'How does God know? Is there knowledge in the Most High?'
> —Psalm 73:11.

Yes, indeed! although 'such *knowledge* is too wonderful for me, it is *high*
I cannot attain to it' (Psalm 139:6). But, if we 'walk in the knowledge of
the Most High' (Odes of Solomon 23:4, H Text) we shall 'receive the
knowledge of the Most High' (Odes of Solomon 8:9). 'O Most High . . . by
Thy grace alone we received this light of knowledge' (Corpus Hermeticum,
Asclepius III).

Having seen the relationship between *God Most High* and *knowledge* we
can go on to that between *God Almighty* and *understanding*. 'God is
mighty . . . He is mighty in power and understanding' (Job 36:5), inasmuch as 'understanding has mighty power' (Corpus Hermeticum, *Libellus*
IX. 10); 'whoever has understanding is wholly lordly, and independent
and masterful' (Philo, *Q. Gen.* III. 22, Greek Fragment). Thus, we hear
about 'a mighty man [GIBBOR] of understanding' (Jeremiah 50:9), and being able to 'understand mightily [MEOD]' —Jeremiah 2:10. If we want to
become 'powerful in understanding' (4 QSl 39, I. 21, [Angelic Liturgy],
Dead Sea Scrolls), and have 'the understanding of the powerful' (Sirach
10:3, Literal Translation), let us ask the Almighty, for we know that 'the
understanding possessed by Bezaleel was from the *Almighty'* (Midrash Exodus Rabbah 48.4). 'The *understanding* of the *Almighty'* (Judith 8:13,
Greek Codex 58, Syriac and Vetus Latina Texts) is 'infinite' (Psalm 147:5).
'The Lord, the Creator of the ends of the earth does not faint, nor does He
get weary [because he is *Almighty,* All Strong] there is no searching of His
understanding' (Isaiah 40:28). 'The *Almighty* Lord . . . He has *understanding'* (Sirach 42:17,18, Codex Sinaiticus and Alexandrinus Texts). When it
is time for the sons of Man to understand, it is 'the breath of the *Almighty*
which gives them *understanding'* (Job 32:8), 'to them alone the *Almighty*
God has given discreet counsel and faith and an excellent *understanding*
in their hearts' (Sibylline Oracles III. 584–585). 'The *Almighty* . . . will He
not *understand?'* (Job 11:7,11). Of course, He will, for He is 'mighty in understanding' (Judith 11:8). 'God . . . is *mighty* in *power* and *understanding'*
(Job 36:5).

Furthermore, just as Man is 'father' to Son of Man, it may be said that
the title of God: 'Most High' is 'Father' to that of 'God Almighty'. It is the

Most High who is called 'Father' and who has 'sons' but not the Almighty, although the Almighty is called the Most High's Son:

> The Most High Father —Odes of Solomon 23:18.

> 'All of you sons of the Most High' —Psalm 72:6; Book of Jubilees 21:11.

> 'Be like a father to orphans and instead of a husband to their mother; so shall you be like the son of the Most High' —Sirach 4:10.

> 'Love your enemies, do good and lend hoping for nothing in return; and your reward will be great, and you will be sons of the Most High' —St. Luke 6:35.

> Jesus, He will be great, and will be called the Son of the Most High —St. Luke 1:31,32.

We must not forget that Jesus the Son of Man is 'Jesus, Son of the Most High God' (St. Mark 5:7; St. Luke 8:28; see also Odes of Solomon 23:16) but He is also 'the Almighty' (Revelation 1:8; see also Ladder of Jacob 7:20 and Ignatius', *Ep. to Philippians* VII.1), who is therefore the Most High's Son.

As 'Father' the Most High 'knows' and makes things known to His children:

> The Most High Father —Odes of Solomon 23:18, Syriac Text.

> The Most High who knows —Sibylline Oracles Fragment i.4; see also Testament of Joseph 9:3.

> 'The Father taught Me' —St. John 8:28; 5:19–20.

> 'The Father knows Me' —St. John 10:15.

> 'He [the Father] who knew Me and brought Me up is the Most High in all His perfection' —Odes of Solomon 17:7; 41:13–14.

> 'Let the father tell it to his son and make him know it' — Babylonian Epic of Creation VII. ll.126–128.

In turn, as 'Son' of the Most High Father, the Almighty 'understands' and is the Giver of understanding because it is the prerogative of *sons* to understand:

> God has decreed and created the sons of man to understand words of knowledge —4Q Enoch XII.3, Dead Sea Scrolls [Cave 4 Aramaic Fragments of the Book of Enoch].

> 'Behold, My son will understand' —Ascension of Isaiah 4:21.

> 'Understand, O son of man' —Daniel 8:17.

> A son, a man of understanding —Sirach 47:12, Greek and Hebrew Texts.

> An understanding son —Proverbs 10:5; 28:7; Ibid., 17:21, Greek Text.

> 'He is your understanding [PHRONIMOS] son' —Hosea 13:13, Greek Text.

> 'They brought us a man of understanding [SAKAL], of the sons of Mahli' —Ezra 8:18.

> 'There is no one else who knows you [the god Aton] except your son whom you make to understand your plans and your power' —Egyptian Hymn to Aton, l.12.

> 'O [Ninib] *mighty son,* firstborn of Bel, perfect *son* of Isara . . . warlike you are, perfect in *understanding*' —Babylonian Ninib Texts I and IV.

We know that Abraham is par excellence the 'father' not only of the Jews but of many nations (Genesis 17:4; Isaiah 51:2; Sirach 44:19; St. Matthew 3:9; St. Luke 16:24,30; 19:9; St. John 8:53,56; Acts 7:2; Romans 4:12 etc.) and that Jacob is Abraham's grand-'son'. Therefore, it was only fitting that the God of Abraham should be the Most High, and the God of Jacob, the Almighty:

The Most High and Abraham

> 'Blessed be Abram [Abraham] of the Most High God, possessor of heaven and earth' —Genesis 14:19.

He [Abraham] prayed that night and said: 'My God, God Most High, You alone are my God' —Book of Jubilees 12:19.

'You, the Most High, are my [Abraham's] God forever' —Book of Jubilees 13:16.

Abraham . . . who kept the Law of the Most High and was in covenant with Him —Sirach 44:19,20.

The Almighty and Jacob

The Mighty One of Jacob —Genesis 49:24; Psalm 132:2,5.

'I the Lord am your Saviour and your Redeemer, the Mighty One of Jacob' —Isaiah 49:26; 60:16.

The remnant of Jacob [will return] to the Mighty God —Isaiah 10:21.

'Sing aloud to God our *strength,* and make a joyful shout to the [Mighty—All Strong] God of *Jacob'* —Psalm 81:1.

They [the wicked] say, 'The Lord shall not see [and know], neither shall the God of Jacob [the Almighty] understand [BIN] it' [the Almighty is the One who is All-Understanding] —Psalm 94:7.

Thus Isaac said to Jacob: 'God Almighty bless you and increase and multiply you' —Book of Jubilees 27:11.

And Jacob said to Joseph: 'God Almighty appeared to me at Luz in the land of Canaan and blessed me' —Genesis 48:3.

Following the usual Scriptural sequence that places the word *'Man'* before *'son of Man'* (see Numbers 23:19; 2 Samuel 7:14; Job 15:14; 16:21; 25:4; Psalms 8:4; 80:17; 90:3; 144:3; Isaiah 51:12; 52:14; 56:2; Jeremiah 49:18,33,50; 50:40; 51:43; Judith 8:16; Sirach 10:18; 1QS 11:6,15; 1QH 4:30, Dead Sea Scrolls, etc.), and *'knowledge'* before *'understanding',* the divine title *'God Most High'* precedes that of *'God Almighty'* or *'Mighty One'* whenever they are used in conjunction:

The utterance of him [Balaam] who . . . knows the knowledge of the *Most High,* and sees the vision of the *Almighty* —Numbers 24:16.

He who dwells in the secret place of the *Most High* shall abide under the shadow of the *Almighty* —Psalm 91:1.

The *Most High* shall visit to judge righteously and execute judgment . . . neither will the *Almighty* be patient towards them — Sirach 35:17,18, Alexandrinus and MS 248 Greek Texts.

He called upon the *Most High* God . . . and he followed the *Mighty One* —Sirach 46:5,6.

For a remembrance before the *Most High* . . . to worship their Lord *Almighty* —Sirach 50:16,17.

And Esdras blessed the Lord God *Most High* . . . the *Almighty* —1 Esdras 9:46.

'Your voice has been heard before the *Most High,* and the *Almighty* has seen your righteous dealing' —2 Esdras 6:32.

'I besought the *Most High* night and day . . . and we gave great glory to the *Mighty One*' —2 Esdras 9:44,45.

'Your arrogance has reached the *Most High,* and your pride to the *Almighty*' —2 Esdras 11:43.

'You are remembered before the *Most High,* and the *Almighty* has not forgotten you' —2 Esdras 12:47.

'O *Most High, Almighty God*' —3 Maccabees 6:2.

The *Most High* has commanded . . . hear the word of the *Mighty God* —2 Baruch 6:6,8.

The *Most High* . . . the *Mighty One* —2 Baruch 25:1,4; 2 Esdras 13:23, Syriac and Ethiopic Texts.

'I have besought the *Most High* . . . the *Mighty One* has explained to you' —2 Baruch 56:1,2; Ibid., 77:21,26; 81:1,4; 82:2,5.

In righteousness possessing the Law of the *Most High* . . . to them alone the *Almighty* has given . . . understanding —Sibylline Oracles III. 580, 584.

In the first chapter of the book of Genesis, God 'created' [BARA] and 'made' [ASAH] all things including Man. And in the second chapter we are told that 'the Lord God formed [YATSAR] Man of the dust of the ground, and breathed into his nostrils the breath of life; and Man became a living being' (Genesis 2:7). Thus, the divine activity of creating and making came before the act of forming (please note that in the second chapter v. 19, there is also mention of the 'forming' of every beast and every bird). It takes knowledge to be able to think a design and bring it into being. God creates and makes things through His knowledge:

'In Your thought is all knowledge' —1QH 11:7,8, Dead Sea Scrolls.

'Knowledge in every design' —1QS 4:4, Dead Sea Scrolls.

By His knowledge all things are brought into being —1QS 11:10, Dead Sea Scrolls.

From the God of knowledge [i.e., the Most High] comes all that is and shall be, before all things came into being [through His creative knowledge] He established all their design —1QS 3:15, Dead Sea Scrolls.

'Before creating them You had knowledge of all their works' —1QH 1:7, Dead Sea Scrolls.

'Yours, O God of knowledge, are all the works' —1QH 1:26, Dead Sea Scrolls.

'You have created . . . the fountain of knowledge' —1QH 12:28,29, Dead Sea Scrolls.

'You have created all the hosts [i.e., angelic spirits] of knowledge' —1QH 18:23, Dead Sea Scrolls.

We need knowledge to be able to create and 'to know how to work all manner of work' (Exodus 36:1), but before we are able to 'form' anything we need understanding, the Lord even forms understanding for us:

He [God] sought to form [in us] an understanding —Epistle to Diognetus 9:6.

'By what means can I obtain understanding unless You form it for me?' —1QH 10:6, Dead Sea Scrolls.

'I [the Lord] . . . formed the understanding' —Odes of Solomon 8:18.

They form his understanding −Philo, *Q. Exodus* II. 13.

He formed in His understanding −Epistle to Diognetus 8:17.

The Lord is also pleased to take away from the travail of his soul, to show him light, and to form him with understanding −Isaiah 53:11, Greek Text and Isaiah [1QIs[a]] Dead Sea Scroll.

Set in motion and formed and given life by the understanding −Philo, *Op.* 9.

'All the people have known of your understanding because the formation of your heart is good' −Judith 8:29, Literal Translation.

'The Lord . . . forms the spirit of man within him': 'the spirit which gives understanding' −Zechariah 12:1; 1QH 4:31, Dead Sea Scrolls; Enoch 49:3.

'Homage to thee O Ra! Supreme Power . . . who forms the earth by his understanding' −The Litany of Ra 1.66 [Egyptian hieroglyph at Thebes (Biban El-Marduk)].

Knowing that it takes knowledge to 'create' and to 'make'; and that understanding is needed in order to be able to 'form', we shall see that because of His knowledge, the *Most High* has the role of *Creator* and *Maker,* and because of His understanding, the *Almighty* has the role of *Former:*

'My God, God *Most High,* You alone are my God, and You and Your dominion I have chosen. You have *created* all things, and all things are the work of Your hands' −Book of Jubilees 12:19.

'The *Most High* who *created* heaven and earth' −Book of Jubilees 22:6.

'Who *formed* man and put a heart in the midst of his body and gave him breath, life, and understanding. Yes, the Spirit of *God Almighty*' −2 Esdras 16:66.

'The *Most Mighty formed* us' −Ps. Philo's, *Biblical Antiquities* XVI. 5.

We know that unbelievers scoffed at the knowledge of the Most High

(Psalm 73:11). We shall discover them also deriding the understanding of the Almighty if we recall the pattern which places the Most High before the Almighty; the Creator and Maker before the Former; and knowledge before understanding:

> Shall the thing made [ASAH] say of its Maker [the Most High], 'He did not make me'? Or shall the thing formed [YATSAR] say of its Former [the Almighty], 'He has no understanding'? —Isaiah 29:16.

> The Almighty . . . will He not understand [BIN]? —Job 11:7,11.

> He [the Almighty] who formed [YATSAR] the hearts of all, He understands [BIN] —Psalm 33:15.

Let us 'worship the *Most High,* the *Holy One of Israel'* (Sirach 50:17b, Hebrew Text), and we shall also know that 'the *Holy One of Israel* (who) has *created* it' (Isaiah 41:20) is the Most High (see also Sirach 47:8; Enoch 10:1).

Chapter 6

The Creator And The Former

Before an artist gives form and shape to a work of art, he visualizes it in his imagination, he has an image of it in his mind before he brings it into actual form. Thus, in the book of Genesis, 'creation' takes place before the act of 'formation'. Moreover, the term 'image', as a rule, precedes the word 'form' when they are both used in conjunction in Holy Scripture:

> 'I could not discern the image [MAREH = appearance, 'visage'] thereof, [but soon after] a form [TEMUNAH] was before my eyes' —Job 4:16.

> His visage [MAREH] was marred more than any man, and his form [TOAR] more than the sons of man —Isaiah 52:14.

We see a good example of this sequence in the narrative of King Saul's visit to the witch of Endor:

> Saul said to her, 'bring me up Samuel'. And the woman saw [RAAH] Samuel . . . and the king said to her . . . 'What have you seen?' And the woman said to Saul, 'gods [ELOHIM] have I seen coming out of the earth.' And he said to her, 'What is his form [TOAR]?' And she said, 'That of an old man comes up, and he is covered with a mantle.' And Saul knew that it was Samuel —1 Samuel 28:11,12,13,14.

She first saw Samuel in the concept of his office as 'judge' [ELOHIM], and then she more specifically described his form.

The first chapter of the book of Genesis tells us that in creating Man, God made him in His own image and likeness. We thereby receive the abstract concept of Man as a creature made in the image and likeness of God. In the second chapter we can visualize the form of Man taking shape as the Lord God fashions him from the moistened dust of the ground and we can behold him as a human being. The initial Divine acts of 'creating' and 'making' Man, are demarcated from the subsequent 'forming' of Man by the Lord God. God is not only called 'Creator' [BARA, as in Ecclesiastes

12:1; Isaiah 40:28; 45:15], and 'Maker' [ASAH, as in Job 4:17; 35:10; Psalm 95:6; Proverbs 14:31; Isaiah 51:13 etc.], but He is also called 'Former' [YATSAR, as in Isaiah 22:11; 29:16; 44:2; 45:9 etc.]. Furthermore, we have seen how it is as the *Most High* that God 'creates' and 'makes' with His *knowledge,* and it is as the *Almighty* that the Lord God 'forms' with His *understanding.* Jeremiah knew that the Almighty God of Jacob is the Former of all things:

> The portion [i.e., *God;* see Psalms 16:5; 73:26; 119:57; 142:5; Lamentations 3:24] *of Jacob* is not like them [the false idols], for He [the Almighty] is the *Former* [YATSAR] of all things — Jeremiah 10:16.

Throughout the Holy Scriptures the acts of 'creating' and 'making' precede that of 'forming', just as the Creator and Maker precedes the Former:

> 'Did not He . . . make [POIEŌ] and form [PLASSŌ] you?' — Deuteronomy 32:6 Greek Text.

> 'Have you not heard from afar how I have made [ASAH] it? And from ancient times how I have formed [YATSAR] it?' — 2 Kings 19:25; Isaiah 37:26.

> Did not He who made me in the womb make him? And did not One fashion us in the womb? — Job 31:15.

> The sea is His, He made it and His hands formed the dry land — Psalm 95:5.

> 'Thy hands have made [POIEŌ] me, and formed [PLASSŌ] me' — Psalm 119:73, Greek Text.

> 'I will praise Thee for I am fearfully and wonderfully made . . . I was made [ASAH] in secret . . . my members were formed [YATSAR]' — Psalm 139:14,15,16.

> 'You have not looked on its Maker [ASAH], neither have you seen its Former [YATSAR] of long ago' — Isaiah 22:11.

> 'It is a people of no understanding. Therefore He who made [ASAH] them will have no mercy on them, and He who formed [YATSAR] them will show them no favor' — Isaiah 27:11.

> Shall the thing made [ASAH] say to its Maker, 'He did not make

me'? Or shall the thing formed [YATSAR] say to its Former, 'He has no understanding'? —Isaiah 29:16.

Thus says the Lord who created [BARA] you, O Jacob, and He who formed [YATSAR] you, O Israel —Isaiah 43:1.

'For My glory I have created [BARA] him, yes, I have formed [YAT-SAR] him' —Isaiah 43:7.

Thus says the Lord your Maker [ASAH] and your Former [YAT-SAR] from the womb —Isaiah 44:2.

Thus says the Lord Creator of the heavens, Who is God, Former [YATSAR] of the earth —Isaiah 45:18.

Thus says the Lord the Maker of the earth, the Lord who formed [YATSAR] it to establish it —Jeremiah 33:2.

Even in the making of idols the pagans were said to have 'made [POIEŌ] them and . . . formed [PLASSŌ] them' —Wisdom 15:16. The same sequence is found in the Egyptian and Babylonian creation narratives:

Egyptian Texts

'O Ra . . . thou art the god who didst come into being in the beginning of time. Thou didst create the earth, thou didst form man' —Papyrus of Hunefer, Sheet I (British Museum Papyrus no. 9901).

'I am the creator of what has come into being, and I myself came into being in the images of Khephera . . . I formed myself from the primeval matter which I had created. I formed myself from primeval matter, my name is Osiris' —British Museum Papyrus no. 10,188, col. XXVIII.

'Ptah . . . who created his own image, who formed his own body, who has established Truth [MAAT] in all the two lands' —Hieroglyphic Inscription found in R.V. Lanzones', *Dizionario di Mitologia Egizia* p. 240, Turin, 1886.

'O Ptah-Tenen creator of the gods . . . builder of his own limbs, and former of his own body' — Hymn to Ptah-Tenen, pl. 118 found in C.R. Lepsius, *Denkmaler aus Aegypten und Aethiopien* vol. 6, Berlin, 1859, Leipzig 1913.

'Ptah who made the earth according to the plans of his heart . . . Ptah who formed the gods and men and all animals, and who created (beforehand) all lands, coastlines, and the great ocean in his name Creator of the earth' — Ptah Hymn pl. III. 1 and pl. VII. ll. 6–8 (Berlin Papyrus no. 3048).

'Re . . . lord of the heavens, lord of the earth who made the things which are above and the things which are below . . . who made the countries and created man, who made the sea and created the Nile . . . who formed man and beast' — Papyrus of Ani 15A found in E.A.W. Budge's, *The Book of the Dead. Facsimiles of the Papyrus of Ani in the British Museum,* London 1890.

Babylonian Texts

'Narru, King of the gods who created mankind . . . and Mami who formed them' — pl. XXXVI. ll. 276, 278 (British Museum Babylonian Tablet no. 34773).

'The creator of destiny finished them . . . the figures of peoples, Mami formed' — col. IV, ll. 11–14 Babylonian Tablet of the J. Pierpont Morgan Library (*Keilinschriftliche Bibliothek* vol. VI.1, p. 288).

'Ummu-Khubur, who created all things . . . in all eleven monsters of this kind she formed' — col. II, ll. 19,32 Babylonian Tablets 40559 and 93015 (British Museum).

Even the ancient Mayas of Southern Mexico and Central America knew the proper sequences in their creation narratives:

'Four creations . . . by the Maker [TZAKOL] and the Former [BITOL]' — *The Popol Vuh* (The Book of Counsel) *of the Quiche Maya of Guatemala,* Edited by M. Edmonson. (Publication of the Middle American Research Institute, Tulane University, Lousiana).

'Their Maker, their Former, the Creator of them' — Ibid.

'They gave thanks to Maker and Former' —Ibid.

'Thanks to you that we are created, that we are made, that we are formed' —Ibid.

Philo Judaeus differentiated between created man and formed man:

'There is a vast difference between the man thus formed [Genesis 2:7], and the man who came into existence earlier [Genesis 1:26–27] after the image of God' —Philo, *Op.* 134.

'The formed man is the sense-perceptible man . . . but the man made [anteriorly] in accordance with God's image is incorporeal and a likeness of the archetype' —Philo, *Q. Gen.* I. 4.

When Moses (who wrote the book of Genesis) had called the genus 'Man', he added that it had been created 'male and female', and this though its individual members had not yet taken shape (i.e., been formed) —Philo, *Op.* 76.

The Jewish scribes and the early Christian fathers were also aware of these two distinct workings of God:

'Every thing that is called by My name it is for My glory, I have created it, I have formed it' —Pirke Aboth 6:11.

'You shall love Him who made you, and fear Him who formed you' —Epistle of Barnabas 19:2.

'The artisan . . . has never made an image [as God has] that breathes, or formed flesh out of the earth' —Clement of Alexandria, *Exh.* lxviii, 18, 98; *Paed.* i,98; *Stromata* ii,131; v,87 ff.; vi,80 ff.

Knowing that 'creating' and 'making' came first and the act of 'forming' came after, we can understand why Behemoth (Job 40:15–24) who 'is the first of the ways of God' (Job 40:19) was said to have been 'made' by Him, and Leviathan (Job 41:1–34) who came after is said to have been 'formed' by the Lord:

'Behold now Behemoth which I made [ASAH]' —Job 40:15.

'Leviathan, whom You have formed [YATSAR]' —Psalm 104:26.

Similarly, because the name 'Jacob' antedates 'Israel' (Genesis 32:28; 35:10), Jacob is said to have been 'created' and Israel 'formed':

> Thus says the Lord who created you, O Jacob, and He who formed you, O Israel —Isaiah 43:1.

If it is said that Wisdom existed before all things (Proverbs 8:22–31) then, of course, our understanding of Wisdom would come after, and we shall surely find that she was 'created' and understanding was 'formed':

> Wisdom has been created before all things, and understanding of prudence [was formed; see pp. 35–36 for the 'forming' of understanding] from the time of the ages [AIŌNOS] —Sirach 1:4.

Remembering the association of Man with knowledge and the son of Man with understanding, we may expect the term 'image' to be linked with 'Man', 'knowledge', and 'creating':

> 'Put on the new *Man* who is renewed in full *knowledge* [EPIGNŌSIN] after the *image* of Him who *created* him' —Colossians 3:10.

Furthermore, we shall understand why that which concerns the image [i.e., 'visage', 'appearance', 'likeness'] is linked to Man, and that which concerns the form, to the sons of Man:

> His *visage* [i.e., image] was marred more than any *man*.

> And his *form* more than the *sons of man* —Isaiah 52:14.

If Man is known by his appearance (or image) and knowledge, we may be sure that a son of Man is known by his form and understanding:

> 'A man is known by his appearance, and one who has understanding [i.e., a son of man] is known by [the form of] his face when you meet him' —Sirach 19:29.

When 'God *created Man* in His own *image* . . . male and female He created them' (i.e., Man) —Genesis 1:27. 'He *made* them according to His own *image*' (Sirach 17:3), but 'He *formed* the *Son of Man* with His hands' (Aphraates, *Demonstration* XVII. 7).

As the Son of God the Lord Jesus 'Christ . . . is the image of God' (2 Corinthians 4:4), He 'is the image of the invisible God' (Colossians 1:15); but as the Son of Man He took flesh and form in the virginal womb of Mary so that the image and form of God may be seen in Him. For thus says the Lord concerning Him:

'I am He, before Me there was no God [EL] formed [YATSAR], nor shall there be after Me' —Isaiah 43:10.

Chapter 7

The Father And The Son

Apart from love, what the fathers among men desire the most from their children is their understanding. In the book of Proverbs the father says to his son: 'My son, give me your heart' (Proverbs 23:26). By that he means to say, 'My son, give me your understanding,' because it is in the heart that we understand:

> 'God . . . made the heart for understanding' —Testament of Naphtali 2:8.

> 'The heart is the seat of understanding' —Midrash on Psalm 103.3.

> 'He gave them a heart to understand' —Sirach 17:6.

> 'I give You thanks, O Adonai, who have put understanding in the heart of Your servant' —1QH 14:8, Dead Sea Scrolls.

> 'The Great One has given to the sons of Man . . . to understand in their heart' —4Q Enoch XIII. 2, Dead Sea Scrolls.

In Holy Scripture the word 'heart' is synonymous with the word 'understanding'. Thus, when the Alexandrian Jewish scribes translated the Hebrew Bible into Greek they sometimes rendered the Hebrew word for 'heart': LEB, into the Greek words for 'understanding' [SUNESIS, PHRONĒSIS, DIANOIA, NOUS]:

> 'Wisdom will enter your *heart*' —Proverbs 2:10, Hebrew Text.

> 'Wisdom will enter your *understanding* [DIANOIAN]' —Ibid., Greek Text.

> 'Set Your *heart* upon him' —Job 7:17, Hebrew Text.

> 'Set Your *understanding* [NOUN] upon him' —Ibid., Greek Text.

'Wise in *heart*' —Exodus 28:3; Job 9:4, Hebrew Text.

'Wise in *understanding* [DIANOIA]' —Ibid., Greek Text.

For 'the wise in heart is a man of understanding' —Proverbs 16:21, Syriac Text. Thus, when the father says to his son: 'My son, if your heart is wise, my heart will be glad' (Proverbs 23:15), he means to say that if his son is understanding, his heart will rejoice. For the joy that a wise father receives comes from having his wisdom and knowledge understood by an appreciative son. Moreover, the wise father desires that his son shall become as wise and knowledgeable as him. 'My son, be wise and make my heart glad' (Proverbs 10:1; 15:20). But that which makes a father rejoice exceedingly is to know that he has a righteous son: 'the father of the righteous [son] will *greatly* rejoice' (Proverbs 23:24) because that wise father knows that it is the righteous who really understand wisdom and knowledge:

'A righteous man understands [SAKAL]' —Proverbs 21:12.

'The righteous one knows' —Proverbs 29:7.

'To the righteous who do His command, He has made known the words of His good pleasure' —Targum to Isaiah 40:13.

Thus, to say that 'Wisdom rests in the heart of him who has *understanding*' (Proverbs 14:33, Hebrew Text) is to say that 'Wisdom rests in the heart of the *righteous*' (Proverbs 14:33, Syriac Text). 'Who is the man of understanding [SAKAL] who may rightly boast of understanding? It is he who, recognizing the sinful thing, keeps himself aloof from it' (R. Joseph Kimchi's, *Shekel Hakodesh* 129) for 'to depart from evil is understanding' (Job 28:28). They knew that 'the heart of him who has *understanding*' (Proverbs 15:14, Hebrew Text) is 'the heart of the *righteous*' (Proverbs 15:14, Syriac Text). Man rejoices in having a righteous and understanding son [of Man]. Therefore, the attributes of righteousness and understanding are closely associated with the Son of Man (see pp. 13–14, 15–17, 21–23). What does the Lord look for in the sons of Man?

'The Lord looked down from heaven upon the sons of Man to see
if there are any who *understand,* who seek God' —Psalm 14:2.

If no one with understanding was found among the sons of Man then, it was because none among them was righteous:

> As it is written (Psalm 14:2–3; 54:1–3), 'There is none righteous, no, not one; there is no one who understands; there is no one who seeks after God. They have all gone out of the way, they have together become unprofitable; there is no one who does good, no, not one' —Romans 3:10–11.

It is the righteous sons of Man who understand and seek God because they know that 'they who seek the Lord understand *all* things' (Proverbs 28:5) and have become ready for the knowledge of God because the Lord 'gives wisdom to the wise and knowledge to those who know understanding' (Daniel 2:21). He shall 'open the fountain of knowledge [DAATH] to all who understand' (1QH 2:18, Dead Sea Scrolls) because they are righteous; only 'the upright will understand the knowledge of the Most High' (1QS 4:22, Dead Sea Scrolls). If we want to 'improve understanding by knowledge' (Proverbs 9:6, Greek Text), we must strive to be good and to depart from evil (Job 28:28) so that we may have the understanding we need to be able to know God. 'None of the wicked will understand' (Daniel 12:10), and none of the wicked will 'know' because 'they have no understanding to know' (Isaiah 44:18, Greek Text); 'the wicked do not understand knowledge' (Proverbs 29:7, Literal Translation). 'Have all the workers of iniquity no knowledge?' (Psalm 14:4; 53:4). Yes, for 'their wickedness blinded them, they do not know the Mysteries of God' (Wisdom 2:12,22), they are 'ever learning and never able to come to the knowledge of the truth' (2 Timothy 3:7), because 'the full knowledge [EPIGNŌSIN] of the the truth is according to godliness' (Titus 1:1). Thus, 'the way of the wicked is darkness, they do not know' (Proverbs 4:19), and 'the works of the ungodly are far from knowledge' (Proverbs 13:19, Greek Text) for 'to do good they have no knowledge' (Jeremiah 4:22) because they are 'disabled from knowing [GNŌNAI] the things that are good' (Wisdom 10:8). 'Miserable indeed, are all men by nature in whom there is no knowledge [AGNŌSIA] of God' (Wisdom 13:1). But happy indeed, are all those who strive for perfection, because they have as their reward the greatest happiness: the joy of knowing God. Truly, O Lord, 'to know You is perfect righteousness' (Wisdom 15:3), and so it is that the righteous 'know You according to the measure of their understanding [SAKAL]' —1QH 1:31, Dead Sea Scrolls. 'All His sons of Truth shall rejoice in eternal knowledge' (1QM 17:8, Dead Sea Scrolls): the knowledge possessed by the children of God.

We know that what is expected of true sons of Man is righteousness and understanding. But what is it that is required of true children of God?

First of all, obedience, the perfect obedience taught by Jesus the Son of God:

> 'I came down from heaven not to do My own will but the will of Him who sent Me' —St. John 6:38.

> 'I do not seek My own will but the will of the Father who sent Me' —St. John 5:30.

> 'As the Father gave Me commandment so I do' —St. John 14:31.

> 'I have kept My Father's commandments and abide in His love' —St. John 15:10.

> 'My food is to do the will of Him who sent Me and to finish His work' —St. John 4:34.

> 'I have glorified You on the earth. I have finished the work which You have given Me to do' —St. John 17:4; 19:30.

> 'Not My will but Yours be done' —St. Luke 22:42.

> 'The Son can do nothing of Himself, but what He sees the Father do; for whatever He does, the Son also does in like manner' —St. John 5:19.

> 'The Father has not left Me alone for I do always those things that please Him' —St. John 8:29.

> 'Christ did not please Himself' —Romans 15:3.

The rabbis knew that 'when we obey God, He is called our Father; otherwise He is our Master' (Kiddushin 36, Babylonian Talmud). Even the ancient Egyptians knew what 'a splendid thing is the obedience of an obedient son, that which is desired by the god is obedience; disobedience is abhorred by the god' (Instruction of Ptah-Hotep 1.38, Prisse Papyrus). 'The Holy Spirit whom God has given to those who *obey* Him' (Acts 5:32) is the same Holy Spirit who shall make us children of God 'for as many as are led by the Spirit of God, these are the sons of God' (Romans 8:14) and 'the Spirit Himself bears witness with our spirit that we are children of God' (Romans 8:16, Galatians 4:6)—through obedience.

Following 'obedience and love' (Sirach 3:1, Latin Vulgate), God the Father expects to be honored by His children just as Jesus honored and glorified His Father:

'I honor My Father' —St. John 8:49.

'I have glorified You [the Father] on the earth' —St. John 14:13.

Because good children honor their fathers and give glory to them:

'Honor your father with your whole heart' —Sirach 7:27; Exodus 20:12; Deuteronomy 5:16.

'A son honors his father' —Malachi 1:6.

'Whoever fears the Lord will honor his father . . . honor your father by word and deed' —Sirach 3:7,8, Greek MS. 248, Syriac and Latin Vulgate Texts.

'A man's glory comes from honoring his father' —Sirach 3:11.

'Whoever honors his father will be gladdened by his own children' —Sirach 3:5.

'He who gives glory to his father shall have length of days' — Sirach 3:6.

'As he who honors his father is a lover of his father, so he who [as a son] honors God is a lover of God' —Clement of Alexandria, *Stromata* VII. 4.1–2.

From time immemorial 'God has made the father honorable to the children' (Sirach 3:3, Latin Vulgate), and we are exhorted to honor our fathers on this earth, but the fathers of the sons of Man know that all honor and glory really belong to God and they do not ask glory and honor for themselves from their children because all honor and glory are His:

'Give to the Lord glory and strength, give to the Lord the glory due to His name' —Psalms 29:1,2; 96:7,8.

'Declare His glory among the nations, His wonders among all peoples' —1 Chronicles 16:24.

'I am the Lord, that is My name; and My glory I will not give to another' —Isaiah 42:8; 48:11.

Having understanding, the sons of Man are able to praise God:

'Sing praises with understanding [SAKAL-SUNETŌS]' —Psalm 47:7, Hebrew and Greek Texts.

'I will sing with the understanding' —1 Corinthians 14:15.

'I give You thanks, O Lord, who have put understanding in the heart of Your servant . . . that he may praise Your name' —1QH 14:8,9,10.

'I will give them a heart and they shall understand, and ears and they shall hear, and they shall praise Me' —Baruch 2:3, Latin Vulgate.

'He granted as their portion a heart to understand, and He set His eye upon their hearts to show them the greatness of His works so that they might praise His holy name' —Sirach 17:6–7, Latin Vulgate.

'Praise God, you who fear the Lord, with understanding [EPISTĒMĒ]' —Psalms of Solomon 2:37.

'They shall praise the Lord who seek Him' —Psalm 22:26.

Because 'they who seek the Lord understand all things' —Proverbs 28:5.

And in a certain way the sons of Man may even be said to be able to glorify God, because whoever offers praise to God glorifies Him (Psalm 50:23; 2 Corinthians 4:15). But who can give glory to God? Who can honor Him with 'the glory that comes from God alone'? (St. John 5:44). No one but the children of God, for they alone are able to reflect it back to Him. Having been created originally in the image and likeness of God, 'Man . . . is the image and glory of God' (1 Corinthians 11:8), but since the Fall of Adam and Eve 'all have sinned and fallen short of the glory of God' (Romans 3:23). Only in the Lord Jesus 'who is the radiance of His glory and the exact image of His person' (Hebrews 1:3), shall we see 'the light of the knowledge of the glory of God in the face of Jesus Christ' (2 Corinthians 4:6). Our hope of glory is in Jesus the Son of God (Colossians 1:27; St. John 14:13; Romans 5:1–2; 15:5–7; 16:27; 2 Corinthians 1:19–20; 3:18; Ephesians 1:5–6,10–12; 3:21; Philippians 1:11; 2:11; Colossians 3:4; 2 Thessalonians 2:14; 2 Timothy 2:10; Hebrews 2:9–10; 1 Peter 5:10; 2 Peter 1:2–3), because it is through Him that we can become children of God (St. John

1:12; Galatians 4:4–5; Ephesians 1:5; 1 John 5:1,11–12), and be able to reflect His glory when the time comes that the Son of God shall be revealed (1 John 3:2; 1 Peter 1:7; 5:10; Romans 8:14–19) in all His power and glory (St. Matthew 24:30; St. Mark 13:36; St. Luke 21:27; 1 Peter 1:13; 4:13; 5:1; 2 Thessalonians 1:7,10).

Perfection and knowledge pertain to the sons of God just as righteousness and understanding are relevant to the sons of Man. It is not enough for the former to have the righteousness of the truly righteous (St. Matthew 5:20), because perfection is required from the children of God:

> 'Be ye perfect as your heavenly Father is perfect' –St. Matthew 5:48.

Only the perfect shall be 'perfect in knowledge' (Job 36:4) and possess the 'eternal knowledge' (1QS 2:3; 8:9, Dead Sea Scrolls) of the children of God. It was when 'Enoch was found *perfect* [TAMIM]' that he 'was taken as a sign of *knowledge* [DAATH] to all generations' (Sirach 44:16, Hebrew Text).

We know that we can become righteous through keeping His commandments. But how do we become perfect children of God? 'Righteous men made perfect' (Hebrews 12:23), are made 'perfect through sufferings' (Hebrews 2:10). Just as Jesus set an example for us 'through what He suffered . . . being made perfect' (Hebrews 5:8,9), and sanctifying Himself for our sakes, that we 'might also be sanctified' (St. John 17:19). Because all suffering is 'for the perfecting of the holy ones . . . until we all attain to the unity of the faith, and of the full *knowledge of the Son of God,* to a *perfect* [TELEION] man, to the measure of the stature of the fullness of Christ' (Ephesians 4:12,13); having through Him 'put on the new nature which is renewed in full knowledge according to the image of its Creator' (Colossians 3:10). For Adam and Eve were created to have the knowledge of God and to become His children *through* obedience. And for us, the price of that renewal and knowledge is still perfect obedience to His will, and in addition, acceptance of our lot of suffering. Thus St. Paul said: 'for the excellency of the knowledge of Christ Jesus my Lord . . . I have suffered the loss of all things . . . that I may know Him' (Philippians 3:8,10). For 'what does he know, who has not been tried?' (Sirach 34:9, Latin Vulgate), 'he who has not been tried knows little' (Sirach 34:10, Greek Sinaiticus Text). 'Now brethren, we make known to you . . . that in a great trial of affliction . . . you abound in everything, in faith, in utterance, and in knowledge' (2 Corinthians 8:1,2,7). Through the trials and afflictions that are sent to us, we are purified to receive His 'holy knowledge' (2 Maccabees 6:30). When the pious Essenes prayed for constancy and knowledge, they first asked to be forgiven and purified: 'forgive my sin, O Lord, and purify me from my iniquity, and graciously grant me a spirit of constancy and knowledge' —11Q Ps^a col. XIX, ll. 13–15 (Plea for Deliverance, Dead Sea Scrolls).

As fire purges the dross and makes the refined silver shine, so does suffering purify and enable us to reflect His glory and 'the light of knowledge' (Hosea 10:12, Greek and Syriac Texts; Testament of Levi 18:13). Long ago, it dawned on man that 'suffering leads to knowledge' (Herodotus I. 207; Aeschylus, *Ag.* 176f., 249f.; Sophocles, *Oed. Col.* ll. 1–7; Corpus Hermeticum, *Libellus* IX. 4b). The learned Jewish scribes who translated the Hebrew Holy Scriptures into Greek had the same insight because they rendered 'the *misery* of man is great to him' (Ecclesiastes 8:6, Hebrew Text) into 'the *knowledge* [GNŌSIS] of man is great to him' (Ecclesiastes 8:6, Greek Text). If we search through the Holy Bible we shall find a close relationship between discipline and knowledge: 'reprove one who has understanding [BIN], and he will understand knowledge [DAATH]' (Proverbs 19:25), and become prudent. For 'he who takes a reproof to heart is prudent' (Proverbs 15:5), and 'every prudent man acts with knowledge' (Proverbs 13:16). 'A threat breaks down the heart of one who understands, but a fool though scourged knows not' (Proverbs 17:10, Greek Text) that the rebuke which breaks down the heart of one who understands releases knowledge from it. Truly 'he who pricks the heart makes it to show her knowledge' (Sirach 22:19). Therefore, 'whoever loves discipline, loves knowledge, but he who hates reproofs is brutish' (Proverbs 12:1); he is 'brutish in his knowledge' (Jeremiah 10:14; 51:17); 'altogether brutish and foolish' (Jeremiah 10:8). But 'he who has knowledge will not complain when he is disciplined' (Sirach 10:25, Greek Text, Cursives 248,70,106,307), for he knows all about 'the disciplines [YASAR] of knowledge' (1QS 3:1, Dead Sea Scrolls; see also Philo, *Q. Gen.* IV. 4). 'There is no limit to trials; but the man of understanding increases his knowledge by their means' (Ibn Gabirol, *Mibchar ha-Peninim*). Indeed, 'the godly man . . . makes his sufferings contribute to the increase of his knowledge' (Corpus Hermeticum, *Libellus* IX. 4b; Ibid., I. 4f., 482).

The reward of the suffering Servant in the book of Isaiah, is the gift of the fruit of knowledge acquired through his obedience and acceptance of the trials and sufferings sent him by God, in expiation for the sins of the people:

'He was despised and rejected by men, a man of sorrows, and knowing [YADA] suffering . . . he was despised and we did not esteem him. Surely he has borne our griefs and carried our sorrows; yet we esteemed him stricken, smitten by God and afflicted. But he was pierced through for our transgressions, he was bruised for our iniquities; the chastisement for our peace was upon him, and by his stripes we are healed . . . the Lord has laid on him the iniquity of us all. He was oppressed and he was afflicted, yet he did not open his mouth; like a lamb that is led to the slaughter, and like a sheep that is silent before its shearers, so he did not open his mouth . . . yet it was the will of the Lord to bruise him, and put him to grief, and though he makes himself a guilt offering, he shall see his offspring, he shall prolong his days; and the good pleasure of the Lord shall prosper in his hand. He shall see [as a woman sees the fruit of her womb after labor] the travail of his soul and be satisfied. By [the fruit of] his knowledge [gained through suffering] shall My righteous Servant make the many to be accounted righteous' —Isaiah 53:3,4,5,6,7,10–11.

We can also see in other passages of the Holy Bible how the Lord makes the people have knowledge of Him through successive trials and punishments:

'When they were tried . . . though they were disciplined in mercy, they thoroughly knew [EGNŌSAN] . . . for You did admonish them' —Wisdom 11:9,10

'An agonizing conflict she [Wisdom] decided for him [Jacob] that he might know [GNŌ] that godliness is stronger than all things' —Wisdom 10:12; Proverbs 28:1.

'My people have gone into captivity [to suffer] because they do not have knowledge' —Isaiah 5:13.

'Misery will suddenly come upon you, I have caused you to be tried among nations and you shall know Me' —Jeremiah 6:27, Greek Text.

'I will pour out My wrath on you, and spread My anger against you . . . I will punish you according to your ways . . . then you will know' —Ezekiel 7:8,9.

'I will execute great vengeance upon them, with furious rebukes; then they shall know' —Ezekiel 25:17.

'When I have broken (through punishments) their wanton heart which has departed from Me . . . then they shall know' —Targum to Ezekiel 6:9,10, and Latin and Syriac Texts.

'The days of visitation have come, the days of retribution have come, Israel shall know' —Hosea 9:7.

'He afflicted you and let you be hungry . . . that He might make you know' —Deuteronomy 8:3, Literal Translation.

'Through the sufferings . . . knowing Him whom before they refused to know, they then fully knew [EPEGNŌSAN] Him to be the true God' —Wisdom 12:27.

'Brought to know . . . by torment' —2 Esdras 9:12.

'His limbs were much pained by a grievous bruising of the body . . . he lived in sorrow and in pain . . . by this means being brought down from his great pride [the proud do not know God; see 1 Timothy 6:4; Psalms of Solomon 2:35; 2 Baruch 48:40 etc.], he began to come to full knowledge [EPIGNŌSIN] by the scourge of God' —2 Maccabees 9:7,9,11.

'Let Him repay [with punishment] the man himself, and he will know [YADA]' —Job 21:19, Literal Translation.

'You shall also *know* in your heart [after being chastised] that as a man chastises his son, so the Lord your God chastises you [to make you know]' —Deuteronomy 8:5.

Obedience and humble acceptance of the trials and afflictions sent by God, play a great role in the purification of the sons of Man so that they may become perfect children of God, and be able to glorify Him with the light of His knowledge. When 'the earth shall be full of the knowledge [DEAH] of the Lord' (Isaiah 11:9) then 'all the earth shall be filled with the glory of the Lord' (Numbers 14:21) because the children of God shall 'give knowledge [DEAH] of the glory of the Lord' (11Q Ps^a xviii.5, Dead Sea Scrolls) to all flesh.

God the Father requires our obedience, for He desires to make us His perfect children full of the joy of being able to glorify Him with the fruit of knowledge that obedience shall gain for us. We must not forget that the fruit of knowledge is full of 'the light of knowledge' (Hosea 10:12, Greek Text; Testament of Levi 4:3; 18:3), which is why it is also known as 'the fruit of light'. And 'the fruit of light [PHŌTOS] is found in all goodness and righteousness and truth' (Ephesians 5:9). If we hope to have 'the light of the knowledge of the glory of God' (2 Corinthians 4:6) shine in our faces as it did in His, we should strive for the goodness and perfection of the only begotten Son of God: Jesus Christ.

Chapter 8

The Children Of Light
And The Children Of Darkness

We have to know a person very well and have knowledge of all the good qualities of that person before we can eloquently honor him or her. The more intimate our relationship, the greater our knowledge. No one knows God the Father better than His only begotten Son:

> 'No one knows the Father except the Son, and he to whom the Son wills to reveal Him' —St. Matthew 11:27.

> 'I know Him, for I am from Him' —St. John 7:29.

> 'O righteous Father, the world has not known You, but I have known You' —St. John 17:25.

Even the ancient Egyptians knew that 'there is no one who knows you [the god Aton] except your son whom you made to understand your plans and your power' (Hymn to Aton, 1.12). 'For every secret did I reveal to him as a Father' —3 Enoch 48C:7.

Being His Son, it is Jesus who glorified the Father and made Him known to us:

> 'Father . . . I have glorified You on the earth . . . I have manifested Your name . . . I have declared to them Your name' —St. John 17:1,4,6,26.

Jesus was able to glorify the Father because He is the Truth (St. John 14:6) and in Him is all wisdom and knowledge (Colossians 2:2,3). There is light in truth, wisdom, and knowledge; the light that gives glory to God. When the time comes for 'the light of His glory' (Baruch 5:9) to be revealed, it is the children of 'the Father of lights' (St. James 1:17) who shall reflect it to His glory. These children of God are also 'children of light' (St. John 12:36), because 'God is light' (1 John 1:5).

It is from the dust of the ground from which Adam was formed that we are called to become children of light. We who 'were once darkness but are now light in the Lord' (Ephesians 5:8), become children of light by bringing forth from our hearts: 'the fruit of light which is found in all goodness, righteousness and truth' (Ephesians 5:9). God the Father is glorified by our fruits: 'by this is My Father glorified, in that you bear much fruit' (St. John 15:8). From the very beginning the Word of God is given to us as a seed to be kept in the ground of our hearts (see pp. 3–7). Within the seed of His Word, God has concealed His light, wisdom, understanding, knowledge, and truth. And He waits for us to bring them forth to light in the fruit—to His glory.

They who 'bear fruit to God' (Romans 7:4) bring forth 'fruit towards holiness and . . . eternal life' (Romans 6:22), the everlasting life possessed by the children of God. There is no bearing of fruit unless the seed is kept. 'The seed is the word of God' (St. Luke 8:11). If the seed of His word is kept by the good ground of our hearts, a wonderful thing shall happen: it will open up to reveal the light hidden within, for 'the unfolding of Thy words gives light' (Psalm 119:130). Truly, 'light [OR] is sown [ZARA] for the righteous' (Psalm 97:11) for they are the ones expected to bring forth 'the fruit of light' (Ephesians 5:9). Thus, if we keep 'the seeds of wisdom' (Philo *Q. Gen.* III. 32) we shall bring forth 'the fruits of wisdom' (Philo, *Ebr.* 212; Sirach 6:19) to His praise, for 'without wisdom it is not possible to praise the Creator of all things' (Philo, *Q. Gen.* I. 6) on that great day when 'praise shall be uttered in wisdom and the Lord will prosper it' (Sirach 15:10). Remember that 'wisdom is given to make known the glory of the Lord' (11Q Ps^a xviii.3, Dead Sea Scrolls; Testament of Levi 13:8). Again, if we keep and cultivate 'the seeds and plants of understanding' (Philo, *Cong.* 123) we shall bring forth 'the fruits of understanding' (Sirach 37:22) to His glory, for 'He has given men understanding that He may be glorified in His marvelous works' (Sirach 38:6). Let us 'keep knowledge' (Proverbs 5:2; Malachi 2:7) as a seed so that 'knowledge will be increased' (Daniel 12:4) and continue 'increasing in the full knowledge of God' (Colossians 1:10) until we bring forth 'the fruit of knowledge' (Sirach 37:22, Hebrew Text) and be able to 'sing with knowledge . . . to the glory of God' (1QS 10:9, Dead Sea Scrolls). And let us keep 'the seeds of truth' (Justin Martyr, *Apol.* I. 44.29) so that we may become true and bring forth 'the fruit of truth' (Shepherd of Hermas, *Sim.* IX. 19.96:2); then 'all the nations shall know Your truth, and all the peoples Your glory' (1QH 6:12, Dead Sea Scrolls).

If we hope to understand the deep things of God, we should ever keep in mind that we are truly earthpeople, and that God relates to us as Farmer to field and Seed to ground. Thus, before He explained the parable of the Sower to His disciples, Jesus said to them, 'Do you not know (as Earthmen should) this parable? How then will you know *all* the parables?' (St. Mark 4:13). If we do not know and understand that we are the ground upon which God sows His Word as seed, how shall we understand that we are to bring forth fruit from it to His glory? For 'praise to God . . . is the fruit' (Hebrews 13:15); 'praise: the firstfruits of the lips from a *holy* and *righteous heart*' (Psalms of Solomon 15:5). The fruit of praise comes from those who have kept the seed of His Word. And in that glorious fruit brought forth for Him are the many children seeds from the One seed that was sown. The good ground not only brings the seed to fruit but also multiplies it into many children seeds so that the seed of His Word may abound to His glory.

We know that those who obey Him become children of God. They also become *'children of light'* (St. John 12:36; St. Luke 16:8; 1 Thessalonians 5:5; 1QS 1:9; 2:16; 3:13,24,25; 1QM 9:11,13, Dead Sea Scrolls), and *'children of truth'* (1QS 4:5,6; 1QM 17:8; 1QH 6:29; 7:29,30; 9:35; 10:27; 11:1, Dead Sea Scrolls) because *'God is light'* (1 John 1:5), and *'God is truth'* (Horeb, *Mitzvoth* V. 482; Odes of Solomon 38:4; Epistle to Diognetus 7:4–5; St. John 14:6).

The work of sanctification that perfects one into a child of light is done by the Holy Spirit (Romans 15:16), who labors within so that we may bear fruit for Him and become in our conduct manifest children of God (Philippians 2:15). For 'the fruit of the Spirit is love, joy, peace, patient endurance, kindness, generosity, faithfulness, modesty and chastity' (Galatians 5:22) before the eyes of the world, that people may give glory to God the Father when they see His goodness shine in His children.

God the Father shares His glory with His children: 'those who glorify Me I will glorify' (1 Samuel 2:30). The 'inheritance of light' (1QS 3:19, Dead Sea Scrolls; Colossians 1:12) and 'the lot of truth' (Sirach 17:20, Latin Vulgate) are given to the children of Light and the children of Truth who have brought them forth for Him. Thus, 'the wise (children of God) shall inherit glory' (Proverbs 3:35) and His 'sons of truth . . . shall be glorified according to their knowledge' (1QH 10:27, Dead Sea Scrolls), the fruit of knowledge they have brought forth to His glory.

Just as there are children of God there are also 'children of the evil one': 'children of the devil' (St, Matthew 13:38; 1 John 3:10; St.. John 8:44; Acts 13:10), and just as there are 'children of light' there are also 'children of darkness' (1QS 1:10; 1QM 1:1,10,14; 13:16; 1QH 6:18, Dead Sea Scrolls) recipients of 'the inheritance of darkness' (1QM 1:11, Dead Sea Scrolls) and 'the lot of deceit' (1QS 4:24, Dead Sea Scrolls). For they are led by 'the spirit of wickedness' (1QS 5:20; 10:18,19, Dead Sea Scrolls) and 'the spirit of error' (1QS 4:9; 1QH 11:12, Dead Sea Scrolls) so that they become 'children of deceit' instead of 'children of truth'. 'All dominion over the children of deceit is in the hands of the angel of darkness' (1QS 3:20,21, Dead Sea Scrolls) and 'all their works are in darkness' (1QS 4:9,11, Dead Sea Scrolls; see Romans 13:21) for they are 'works of deceit' (1QH Fragment 3:10). 'The fruit of the wicked' (Proverbs 10:16) is 'the fruit of lies' (Hosea 10:13), for they 'travail with iniquity and conceive mischief, and bring forth lies' (Psalm 7:14), 'conceiving and uttering from the heart words of falsehood' (Isaiah 59:13). The end of the children of deceit is inglorious because their 'understanding is unfruitful' (1 Corinthians 14:14) and they are 'unfruitful in the knowledge of our Lord Jesus Christ' (2 Peter 1:8). They who 'do not obey, shall perish by the sword, and they shall die without knowledge' (Job 36:12) and remain in the darkness because they do not have 'the light of Truth' (Odes of Solomon 38:1).

Chapter 9

Sons Know And Servants Understand

'A son honors [KABED] his father' (Malachi 1:6) and is able to 'glorify' [KABED = to glorify and thereby 'honor'] him because an obedient son knows his father, for he has knowledge of his father's will, thoughts, desires, ways and deeds. Moses cried out to the Lord, 'Make me to know [YADA] Your way, that I may know You' (Exodus 33:13), because from the understanding and knowledge of the ways of God we arrive at His knowledge. It is for His children and friends to have personal knowledge of Him, and it is for His servants to understand Him and His ways.

The Holy Scriptures teach us that we go from slavery to freedom, from bondage 'to the glorious liberty of the children of God' (Romans 8:21), and from understanding to the knowledge of God. Adam was created to have dominion over all things, but when he was put 'in Eden, the garden *of* God' (Ezekiel 28:13; Genesis 13:10) he was told 'to tend and keep' (Genesis 2:15) the garden of the Lord as a servant. He was also expected to tend and guard the seed of God's command (see pp. 3–7) in the ground of his own heart so that he would have been able to go from life to immortality, and from being a creature to becoming a child of God through obedience. Man failed to keep the command of the Lord God. Consequently, he was exiled from the garden of God to the field where he was once taken from, a field now thorny and brambled which Adam had perforce to work and till before the life-giving seeds within it would be able to bear fruit to nourish him.

Out of love for his father, a son willingly obeys him, but a slave has no choice but to obey his master if he hopes to keep on living and not be flogged. The main concern of a good servant is to be able to really understand what his master says and wants done, for he seeks to give good service to his lord and master:

'I am Your servant, give me understanding' —Psalm 119:125.

'Give me understanding that I may learn Your commands' — Psalm 119:73.

The slave fears and serves his master, and the son loves and honors his father. Thus, the Lord says through the prophet Malachi:

> 'If I then am a Father, where is My honor? And if I be a Master, where is My fear?' —Malachi 1:6.

The son is privy to his father's confidences while the slave remains unknowing outside the chamber, even though he understands his master's commands.

Although sons lived in close intimacy with their father and shared their confidences, they were disciplined and treated like servants to train them to be good and worthy sons. For it was well known that 'foolishness is bound up in the heart of a child, but the rod of correction will drive it far from him' (Proverbs 22:15), because 'the rod and reproof give wisdom, but a child left to himself brings shame' (Proverbs 29:15). The fathers knew that just as 'an unbroken horse becomes stubborn . . . a son unrestrained becomes reckless' (Sirach 30:8). That is why the wise man asked: 'Do you have sons? Chastise them' (Sirach 7:23, Hebrew Text), 'chastise your son while there is hope' (Proverbs 19:18). 'He who loves his son causes him to feel the rod often, so that he may have joy from him in the end. He who chastises his son shall have praise from him and shall take pride in him among his acquaintances' (Sirach 30:1–3, Greek Sinaiticus Text). Sons were not only disciplined but they were also treated as servants: 'Give him no authority in his youth, do not wink at his follies. Bow down his neck in his youth, and beat him in the sides while he is a youngster, lest he become stubborn and disobey you and you have sorrow of soul from him. Chastise your son and make his yoke heavy lest his shameless behaviour be an offense to you' (Sirach 30:11–13, Greek MS. 248, Syriac and Old Latin Texts). The discipline exerted by the father was founded on love for his son, for 'he who spares his rod hates his son, but he who loves his son disciplines him diligently' (Proverbs 13:24). Thus, the fatherly corrections were called 'chastisements of love' (Berakoth 5a, Babylonian Talmud; Sifre 73b on Deuteronomy 8:5). When the son grows older and understands the love behind the discipline, he loves and honors his father for it in return: 'Discipline your son and he will love you, and give honor to your soul' (Proverbs 28:17, Greek Text).

When God chastised His people to turn them away from their iniquities, He was likened to a loving Father disciplining his children:

> 'Whom the Lord loves He disciplines, just as a father the son in whom he delights' —Proverbs 3:12.

'My son do not disdain the discipline of the Lord, nor be discouraged when you are rebuked by Him. For whom the Lord loves He disciplines and scourges every son whom He receives. If you endure chastening, God deals with you as with sons; for what son is there whom a father does not discipline?' —Hebrews 12:5–7.

'As a man disciplines his son, so does the Lord your God discipline you' —Deuteronomy 8:5.

God disciplines His people for their good so that they 'might be partakers of His holiness' (Hebrews 12:10), the 'holiness without which no man shall see the Lord' (Hebrews 12:14) for only the holy and pure in heart shall see God (St. Matthew 5:8), and know Him. It is the children of God who know Him, and not His servants. We become children of God through obedience after we have proven ourselves to be faithful servants through many tribulations.

In the book of Genesis (Chapters 27–32), the devious 'supplanter': Jacob, following many years of afflicting service and an arduous contest with the angel of the Lord, is given a new name: Israel. Jacob, the servant, having thereby been proven, becomes Israel, the child of God. Henceforth, in the Holy Scriptures, the people of God are sometimes collectively called either 'Jacob' or 'Israel' depending on their status as servants or children of God. Thus, we see His people referred to as '*Jacob,* My servant' (see Isaiah 44:1–2; 45:4; 48:20; Jeremiah 30:10; 46:28; Ezekiel 28:25; 37:25; Baruch 3:36) and '*Israel,* My son', 'child', 'firstborn' (see Exodus 4:22–23; Hosea 11:1–2; Sirach 36:12; Pirke Aboth 3:18). In the dimension of being a 'son', His people 'Israel' know Him and are expected to know Him:

'Is there any other people who know You besides Israel?' —2 Esdras 3:22.

'Israel shall know' —Hosea 9:7.

'All Israel knew [YADA]' —2 Samuel 3:37.

'Israel will cry to Me, "My God, we know You" ' —Hosea 8:2.

'O Israel, happy are we, for the things that are pleasing to God are made known to us' —Baruch 4:4.

'Hear now, I beg you, O heads of Jacob, and you princes of Israel: is it not for you to know judgment?' —Micah 3:1.

'The ox knows its owner ... but Israel [sadly] does not know' —Isaiah 1:3.

'Are you such fools, you sons of Israel that without judgment [ANAKRINANTES] or clear [SAPHES] knowledge [EPIGNONTES] you have condemned a daughter of Israel?' —Daniel, History of Susanna, v. 48.

Rightly so, it is from Israel His 'son' that the Lord expects to receive 'glory':

'O Israel, in whom I will be glorified' —Isaiah 49:3.

'Praise Him all ye seed of Jacob, glorify and fear Him all ye seed of Israel' —Psalm 22:23.

'The Lord has redeemed Jacob, and glorified Himself in Israel' —Isaiah 44:23.

And if Israel His 'son' is also sometimes called His 'servant' (see Isaiah 41:8– 9; 44:21; 49:3), it is because God relies on service from His sons:

'Thus says the Lord: "Israel is My *son*, My firstborn ... let My son go that he may *serve* Me" ' —Exodus 4:22,23.

But 'is Israel a servant? is he a homeborn slave?' (Jeremiah 2:14). No, he is really a son: 'Israel His beloved' (Baruch 3:36). Being a 'son', Israel is referred to as a 'prince' (Micah 3:1,9; Numbers 1:44; 7:2,84; 10:4; 16:2; 17:6; 36:1; Joshua 22:14,30; 1 Chronicles 22:17; 23:2; 27:22; 28:1; 2 Chronicles 12:6; 21:4; Ezekiel 19:1; 22:6) and the 'inheritance' belongs to Israel (Deuteronomy 1:38; Jeremiah 12:14; Numbers 32:18; Joshua 14:1).

A true 'Israelite' is one who is upright and without guile (St. John 1:47). Jacob did not receive the name Israel until he had been tried. In ancient times 'Israel' was interpreted to mean the 'man [ISH] who saw [RAAH] God [EL]':

'Jacob is the supplanter, and Israel is he who sees God' —Philo, *Mut.* 81; *Abr.* 57; *Praem.* 44; *Conf.* 56; see also Tanna debe Eliyyahu, ER, p. 138–139.

'The seer of God that is Israel' —Philo, *Her.* 78; *L.A.* 186.

'Israel [he] who has the clear vision of God' —Philo, *Sac.* 134.

'Accordingly He calls Israel His 'firstborn' (Exodus 4:22), making it evident that he who sees God is the recipient of this honor' — Philo, *Post.* 63.

'Israel . . . the race that has eyes to see Him' —Philo, *Mig.* 54; *Deus.* 144; *Cong.* 51; *Som.* II. 173.

They knew, in those days, that 'they who live in the knowledge of the Holy One are rightly called "sons of God" ' (Philo, *Conf.* 145), and what son is there who does not see the face of his father? 'Blessed are the pure in heart for they shall see God' (St. Matthew 5:8) and they shall be called His children. 'Truly God is good to Israel: to those who are pure [BAR] of heart' (Psalm 73:1, Literal Translation) and have thereby as sons seen Him.

The sons of God who see and know Him are free for they possess the glorious liberty of the children of God. But the sons of Man are still His servants, and when the Lord (Psalm 14:2) looks down from heaven upon them, He ascertains if they understand and seek God to serve Him, for the Lord expects His servants to understand and to attend to Him. Good servants are noted for their understanding:

'Behold, My Servant shall understand [SAKAL-SUNĒSEI], He shall be exalted and extolled and be very high' —Isaiah 52:13, Hebrew and Greek Texts.

'The King's favor is towards an understanding [SAKAL] servant' —Proverbs 14:35.

'Free men shall serve the servant who is understanding' —Sirach 10:25, Greek Sinaiticus Text and Cursives 248,23,106,307.

'An understanding servant calms a man's anger' —Proverbs 18:14, Greek Text.

'Who then is a faithful and understanding [PHRONIMOS] slave, whom his master made ruler over his household?' —St. Matthew 24:45.

'An understanding [SAKAL] servant shall have rule over a son who causes shame' —Proverbs 17:2.

'Let your soul love an understanding [SAKAL-SUNETON] servant' —Sirach 7:21, Hebrew Text, and Sinaiticus, Alexandrinus and Cursive 248, Greek Texts.

'I am Your servant, give me understanding' —Psalm 119:125.

'Blessed are You O God of knowledge, who has given understanding of knowledge to Your servant' —1QH 11:27,28, Dead Sea Scrolls.

'A servant who has understanding [SAKAL] shall be exalted' —Sirach 10:24, Hebrew Text; see Isaiah 52:13.

We read in the Holy Scriptures that 'labor [INYAN] is grief' (Ecclesiastes 2:23) and that Qoheleth had 'seen the labor [INYAN] which God has given to the sons of Man to be exercised in it' (Ecclesiastes 3:10), for a 'heavy yoke is upon the sons of Man' (Sirach 40:1) because they are His servants. The Lord relies on the fidelity of His servants (Numbers 12:7; 1 Samuel 22:14; Nehemiah 13:13; St. Matthew 24:45; St. Luke 12:42; 1 Corinthians 4:1–2), and if He finds them faithful He no longer considers them servants but friends and beloved ones. Abraham the 'servant' of God (see Genesis 26:24; Deuteronomy 9:27; Psalm 105:6,42; 2 Maccabees 1:2) 'when he was tried, was found faithful' (Sirach 44:20), and became henceforth known as Abraham, 'the friend of God' (St. James 2:23; 2 Chronicles 20:7; Isaiah 41:8) and His 'beloved' (Daniel, Song of the Three Holy Children, v. 12; 2 Esdras 3:14). We know that good servants desire to have understanding so that they may really be able to learn His commandments and do them (Psalm 119:125,73). In the wisdom of God, the Lord grants them their hearts' desire by rewarding their obedience and fidelity with the gift of understanding:

'Keep therefore, the words of this covenant and do them so that you may understand [SAKAL]' —Deuteronomy 29:9.

'Be careful to do according to all the Law which Moses My servant commanded you, turn not from it to the right hand or to the left, so that you may understand [SAKAL]' —Joshua 1:7.

'A good understanding [SAKAL] have all those who do His commandments' —Psalm 111:10.

'Keep the charge of the Lord your God, to walk in all His ways, to keep His statutes, His commandments, His ordinances, and His testimonies, as it is written in the law of Moses, that you may understand [SAKAL] in all that you do and wherever you turn' —1 Kings 2:3.

'Hezekiah . . . trusted in the Lord God of Israel . . . he held fast to the Lord; he did not depart from following Him, but kept the commandments which the Lord commanded Moses. And the Lord was with him and he understood [SAKAL]' —2 Kings 18:1,5,6,7.

'Behold, I have taught you statutes and judgements . . . keep therefore and do them for this is your wisdom and understanding in the sight of the nations' —Deuteronomy 4:5,6.

'Everyone who hears these words of Mine, and does them, shall be likened to a man of understanding [PHRONIMŌ]' —St. Matthew 7:24.

'It is only by doing God's will that man can attain to the understanding of those things which he desires to know' —St. Augustine, *Homilies on Psalms,* re Psalm 119:104.

'I understand more than the aged, because I have kept Your precepts' —Psalm 119:100.
For 'through Your precepts I get understanding' —Psalm 119:104.

'He who keeps the Law ['of the Lord'] gets the understanding thereof' —Sirach 21:11, Greek Text and Cursives 106,248.

Thus to be a good servant is to be an understanding servant:

'Let your soul love a *good* [AGATHON] servant' —Sirach 7:21, Greek Vaticanus and Ephraemi Texts and Cursives 68,157.

'Let your soul love an *understanding* [SAKAL-SUNETŌN] servant' —Sirach 7:21, Hebrew Text, and Greek Sinaiticus and Alexandrinus Texts and Syriac Text.

We know that as 'sons', the 'sons of Man' are concerned with understanding (see pp. 13–14, 21–23, 46–47). They may also expect to understand as obedient servant-sons of Man. Thus, the term 'son of Man' has connotations of service and understanding:

'The Son of Man did not come to be served, but to serve' —St. Matthew 20:28; St. Mark 10:45.

'I am among you as the One who serves' —St. Luke 22:27.

'I do not seek My own glory' —St. John 8:50.

'Christ did not glorify Himself' —Hebrews 5:8.

'Jesus Christ [the Son of Man], though He was rich, yet for your sakes He became poor, that you through His poverty might become rich' —2 Corinthians 8:9.

'Christ Jesus, who, being in the form of God, did not consider equality with God a thing to be grasped, but emptied Himself, taking the form of a servant' —Philippians 2:5–7.

'Jesus . . . rose from supper and laid aside His garment, took a towel and girded Himself. After that, He poured water into a basin and began to wash the disciples' feet and to wipe them with the towel with which He was girded' —St. John 13:3,4–5.

'All who heard Him [Jesus, Son of Man] were astonished at His understanding' —St. Luke 2:47.

'We have the understanding [NOUN] of Christ' —1 Corinthians 2:16.

'He [Jesus] opened their understanding [NOUN] so that they might understand the Scriptures' —St. Luke 24:45.

'The Lord [Jesus] will give you understanding in all things' —2 Timothy 2:7.

And as suffering played an important part in the life of a servant (Genesis 39:1–2,20; Psalm 105:17–18; Exodus 1:11–14; Isaiah 50:6; 52:14; 53:1–11) so did the Servant-Son of Man have to suffer:

'The Son of Man will suffer at their hands' —St. Matthew 17:12.

'The Son of Man shall be betrayed to the chief priests and scribes, and they will condemn Him to death' —St. Matthew 20:18.

'The Son of Man must be delivered into the hands of sinful men, and be crucified, and on the third day rise' —St. Luke 24:7.

'It is written of the Son of Man that He will suffer many things and be treated with contempt' —St. Mark 8:31; St. Luke 24:25–26,46.

We know the role of suffering in making us understand and purifying us to receive His holy knowledge (see pp. 51–55). Did not He who understands all things as the Son of Man, and who knows all as the Son of God, have to suffer? For He who was innocent and sinless (St. John 8:46; 14:30; 15:10; Romans 10:4; 2 Corinthians 5:21; Hebrews 4:15; 7:26; 1 Peter 1:19; 2:22; 1 John 2:1; 3:3,5,7), and 'became obedient to the point of death' (Philippians 2:8), chose, nevertheless, to wholly share our lot of suffering, fulfilling all righteousness (St. Matthew 3:15) so that we may ever confidently lean on Him who so fully understands and knows us.

The Servant-Son of Man said: 'Learn from Me, for I am meek and humble of heart' (St. Matthew 11:29). There is wisdom and understanding in the humility and meekness of good servants:

'With the humble is wisdom' —Proverbs 11:2.

'A man of understanding is humble in spirit' —Targum to Proverbs 17:27.

'Let a man first grasp the way of humility and then ask God for understanding' —Tanna debe Eliyyahu Zutta p. 31 (Friedman).

'To the way of humility I incline, and thus will my heart gain understanding' —R. Joseph Kimchi, *Shekel Hakodesh* 79.

'Humility discloses to us the light of understanding' —St. Gregory, *Morals on Job,* XXV. 30.

Much understanding and humility —R. Joseph Kimchi, *Shekel Hakodesh* 67.

Humility of understanding —Colossians 3:12.

He who has a humble understanding —Sotah 5b; Sanhedrin 43b (Babylonian Talmud).

Meekness and wisdom —R. Joseph Kimchi, *Shekel Hakodesh* 120.

A wise [SOPHIAS] meekness [PRAUTĒTI] —St. James 3:13.

'Be meek to hear the Word of God so that you may understand' —Sirach 5:13, Latin Vulgate.

Meek understanding —Philo, *Q. Gen.* III. 26.

'Many are exalted and esteemed but the Mysteries of God are revealed to the meek' —Sirach 3:19, Greek Sinaiticus Text and Cursives 248, 106, 253.

Good servants are not only humble and meek, they are also patient, and patience, too, gives them understanding:

'He who is slow to anger has great understanding, but he who is quick-tempered exalts folly' —Proverbs 14:29.

'And a man of violence does not receive understanding' —Sirach 32:18, Hebrew Text, MS. E.

'A quick tempered man acts ill-advisedly, but a man of understanding holds his peace' —Proverbs 14:17, Greek Text.

'He who restrains his lips is understanding [SAKAL]' —Proverbs 10:19; 11:12.

'He who restrains his tongue shall be filled with understanding' —Proverbs 15:4, Greek Text.

'Even a fool, when he keeps his peace, is considered wise, and he who restrains his lips is esteemed a man of understanding' —Proverbs 17:28.

'A patient man is understanding' —Proverbs 17:27, Greek Text.

'The understanding [SAKAL] of a man makes him slow to anger' —Proverbs 19:11.

Because 'anger leads the mind to frenzy and does not allow understanding to work in men' —Testament of Simeon 4:8.

'The spirit of anger blinds his eyes and . . . darkens his understanding' —Testament of Dan 2:4.

'A man of impatient spirit is very much without understanding [A-PHRŌN]' —Proverbs 14:29, Greek Text.

'Be patient and of good understanding' —Shepherd of Hermas, *Mand.* V. 1. 33:1.

Have 'a spirit of humility and slowness to anger, and great compassion and eternal goodness, and understanding, and insight, and mighty wisdom' —1QS 4:3,4, Dead Sea Scrolls.

'Beware, that you be not greatly enraged and be like those who are wanting in understanding' —Sirach 13:8, Hebrew Text.

'Bad temper is first of all foolish, impetuous and without understanding [A-PHRŌN]' —Shepherd of Hermas, *Mand.* V. 2. 34:4.

'My son, if fierce anger seizes you, do not say a word lest you be called one without understanding' —Story of Ahikar v. 26, Slavonic Text; Ibid. v. 28, Greek Text.

The angry man 'vacillates in everything he does, being pulled here and there by the evil spirits, and totally blinded from a good understanding' —Shepherd of Hermas, *Mand.* V. 2. 34:7.

'The temperate understanding repels all these malignant passions ['violence, love of power, empty boasting, arrogance, loudness and slander' v. 15] as it also repels anger: for it masters even this' —4 Maccabees 2:16.

'The temperate understanding is able to be superior to the passions' —4 Maccabees 2:18.

'A patient man will bear for a time and afterwards joy shall spring up to him . . . the lips of many will declare his understanding' —Sirach 1:22,23.

Those who are patient accept reproof, and 'he who listens to a reproof gets understanding' (Proverbs 15:32). Servants are proverbially poor and despised although it is 'the poor man who knows' (Ecclesiastes 6:8) and it is 'the poor man who has understanding' (Proverbs 28:11); yet 'the poor man's wisdom is despised, and his words are not heard' (Ecclesiastes 9:16), 'if a poor man speaks with understanding he is not listened to, and he is called a fool' (Story of Ahikar v. 112 Slavonic Text). But 'the rich man speaks and his helpers are many, and though his words are ugly they are veneered over. The poor man . . . speaks with understanding [SAKAL] and there is no place for him' (Sirach 13:21, Hebrew Text), because he is poor. Poor 'men of understanding . . . are counted as refuse' (Sirach 26:28). But 'do not despise the poor man who has understanding' (Sirach 10:22, Hebrew Text) because the day will come when 'the poor man is honored for his understanding' (Sirach 10:29, Hebrew Text). Then 'the wisdom of the poor man shall lift up his head and make him sit in the midst of nobles' (Sirach 11:1, Hebrew and Greek Texts). For thus says the Lord: 'My Servant will understand [SAKAL], he shall be exalted and extolled and be very high' (Isaiah 52:13) and although 'he was despised and rejected by men . . . and we did not esteem him' (Isaiah 53:3), on that day His 'Servant who has understanding [SAKAL] shall be exalted' (Sirach 10:24, Hebrew Text). For when the day shall come that 'a man shall be praised according to his understanding [SAKAL]' (Proverbs 12:8), then shall we know that the Son of Man is Understanding.

Chapter 10

Fidelity And Lovingkindness

The righteousness of the sons of Man becomes manifest in their understanding and fidelity; and the perfection of the children of God in their knowledge and lovingkindness. All righteousness conduces towards peace, and all perfection leads to loving as God does. No one is called truly righteous until he has been proven faithful, and no one is presumed to be perfect who has not been found to be kind. Perfection and lovingkindness go hand in hand:

> 'Be *perfect* just as your heavenly Father is perfect' —St. Matthew 5:48.

> 'Be *compassionate* just as your Father is also compassionate' —St. Luke 6:36.

> 'If you want to be *perfect,* go sell what you have and *give* to the *poor*' —St. Matthew 19:21.

> 'Be a *support* to the *poor* all you *perfect* of way' —1QH 1:36, Dead Sea Scrolls.

For 'love is the bond of perfection' (Colossians 3:14), and love longs to give to those in need. 'Lovingkindness towards the poor and love of enemies are the marks of perfection' (St. Ambrose, *De Officiis* I. II. 37). We walk towards the perfection of the children of God when we act with compassion: 'Be like a father to orphans, and instead of a husband to their mother; you will then be like a son of the Most High, and He will love you more than does your mother' (Sirach 4:10). The children of God love, for 'God is love' (1 John 4:16) and 'love is of God, and he who loves is born of God and knows God' (1 John 4:7) as a son knows his father.

When the Lord said through the prophet Hosea: 'Sow for yourselves righteousness, and reap the fruit of lovingkindness' (Hosea 10:12), He hid good counsel in that exhortation. He taught thereby that righteousness bears fruit in lovingkindness. We know that ultimately the seed is perfected in the fruit, but before that happens the fragrant flower is the first manifestation of the fruit that is to come. Thus, the prophet Isaiah also cried out:

> 'All flesh is grass and all its lovingkindness is as the flower of the field' —Isaiah 40:6, Literal Translation.

Those who become children of God are made manifest by their unreserved lovingkindness (St. Matthew 5:44–48), and as such they are the pride of the human race just as the flowers are the glory of the grassy meadows.

They who in their lovingkindness give graciously to the poor, give to the Lord Himself (St. Matthew 25:35–40,45; Proverbs 19:17; 14:31), and the Lord makes Himself known to them through their acts of lovingkindness towards Him:

> 'He [the righteous one] judged the cause of the poor and needy . . . was not this to know Me? says the Lord' —Jeremiah 22:16.

Surely, they shall know the Lord who exercise His lovingkindness, judgement and righteousness in the land, for the Lord shall delight in them (Jeremiah 9:24). Because 'the Lord loves judgment' (Psalm 37:28; 33:5; Isaiah 61:8) and He 'delights in lovingkindness' (Micah 7:18). But where there is no lovingkindness there is no knowledge of God:

> 'There is no truth, nor lovingkindness, nor knowledge of God in the land' —Hosea 4:1.

> 'I desired lovingkindness, and not sacrifice; and the knowledge of God more than burnt offerings' —Hosea 6:6.

If the seed of righteousness is kept it shall bear 'the fruit of righteousness' (St. James 3:18; Hebrews 12:11; Philippians 1:11), which is lovingkindness (Hosea 10:12). Within that glorious fruit we shall find the children seeds of Truth because the seed-'word of righteousness' (Hebrews 5:13) that was sown in the heart is multiplied and made manifest in the well arrayed children seeds of Truth within the fruit. And just as the sower is rewarded in the end with a share of the crop so 'to him who sows righteousness (there will be) a reward of Truth [EMETH]' —Proverbs 11:18. Therefore the Lord said through Isaiah: 'I will give them their wages [PEULLAH] in Truth [EMETH]' —Isaiah 61:8. 'Thou wilt reward the righteous with lovingkindness and Truth [EMETH]' —Targum of the Amidah (the Eighteen Benedictions). In the end, the righteous who have kept 'the (hidden) seeds of truth' (Justin Martyr, *Apol.* I. 44.29) shall receive a portion of 'the fruit of truth' (Shepherd of Hermas, *Sim.* IX. 19.96:2) which they have brought forth by their righteousness.

King David knew that the words of the Lord are Truth: 'O Lord God You are God and Your words are Truth [EMETH]' —2 Samuel 7:28. Truth is the very kernel of the seed of His word. With patience and perseverance, fruit shall be brought forth from that seed, and the Truth shall become manifest: 'the word that is sown is hidden in the soul of the learner as in the earth . . . through time and labor, truth will shine forth' (Clement of Alexandria, *Strom.* I. chap. 1) 'and the truth which has been so long without fruit shall be made manifest' (2 Esdras 6:28). Because 'Truth [EMETH] shall spring up from the earth' (Psalm 85:11) 'and the plant of righteousness and truth shall appear' (Enoch 10:16) to be seen and heard by all. Truly, 'he who speaks the truth shows forth righteousness' (Proverbs 12:17), for it takes a life of righteousness to bring forth the truth from our hearts. 'He who walks uprightly and works righteousness . . . speaks the truth from his heart' (Psalm 15:2). Long ago, they knew that 'the offspring of a perfected soul are perfect words and deeds' (Philo, *Q. Gen.* III. 32) for truth and lovingkindness are the children of perfection.

However, we should always remember that all perfection commences with being righteous: with keeping His commandments. When 'Jerusalem . . . shall be called a city of righteousness' (Isaiah 1:1,26) then 'Jerusalem shall be called a city of Truth [EMETH]' (Zechariah 8:3); 'Jerusalem, the holy city' (Isaiah 52:1). On the other hand, where 'there is neither truth nor righteousness' (1 Maccabees 7:18), there is wickedness. There is a close association between righteousness and truth, and 'to speak righteousness' is to speak truth:

> 'You love evil more than good and lying rather than to speak righteousness' [i.e., to tell the truth] —Psalm 52:3.

> 'I the Lord speak righteousness [i.e., the truth], I declare things that are right' —Isaiah 45:19.

'The judgments of the Lord are truth and righteousness' (Psalm 19:9), and He is our 'God in truth and in righteousness' (Zechariah 8:8). When we shall see that 'corruption has come to an end, and intemperance has been abolished, and infidelity has been cut off' then we shall know that 'righteousness has grown up, and Truth has arisen' (2 Esdras 7:43,44 [113,114]).

We shall recognize the perfection of the children of God in those who are true and who speak the truth at all times and who are always kind to all, even towards their enemies:

> 'If any one makes no mistakes in what he says, he is a perfect man' —St. James 3:2, RSV.

> 'Love your enemies, bless those who curse you, do good to those who hate you, and pray for those who spitefully use you and persecute you, so that you may be sons of your Father in heaven; for He makes His sun to rise on the evil and on the good, and sends His rain on the righteous and on the unrighteous' —St. Matthew 5:44– 45.

Thus, God's perfect lovingkindness and Truth are found side by side in the Holy Scriptures:

> 'You, O Lord, are a God full of compassion, and gracious, long-suffering, and abundant in lovingkindness and truth' —Psalm 86:15; Exodus 34:6.

> 'Righteousness and justice are the foundation of Your throne; lovingkindness and truth shall go before Your face' —Psalm 89:14.

> 'God shall send forth His lovingkindness and His truth' —Psalm 57:3.

> 'Your lovingkindness is great to the heavens, and Your truth to the clouds' —Psalm 57:10.

> 'All the paths of the Lord are lovingkindness and truth' —Psalm 25:10.

> 'Your lovingkindness is before my eyes, and I have walked in Your truth' —Psalm 26:3.

> 'Praise the Lord, all nations! Extol Him, all peoples! For great is His lovingkindness towards us; and the truth of the Lord endures forever' —Psalm 117:1–2.

> 'Not to us, O Lord, not to us, but to Your name give glory, for the sake of Your lovingkindness and Your truth' —Psalm 115:1.

'I will praise Your name for Your lovingkindness and Your truth' —Psalm 138:2.

'I have not concealed Your lovingkindnes and Your truth' —Psalm 40:10.

'Bid lovingkindness and truth watch over him [the king]' —Psalm 61:7.

'Lovingkindness and truth watch over the king' —Proverbs 20:28.

'Let not lovingkindness and truth forsake you' —Proverbs 3:3.

'Let Your lovingkindness and Your truth continually watch over me' —Psalm 40:11.

'By lovingkindness and truth iniquity is redeemed' —Proverbs 16:6; see 1 Peter 4:8; St. James 5:19–20.

'Do they not err who devise evil? But lovingkindness and truth are for those who devise good' —Proverbs 16:6.

'Deal with lovingkindness and truth towards me' —Genesis 47:29; 24:49; Joshua 2:14.

'Execute judgment of truth, show lovingkindness and tender compassion every man to his brother' —Zechariah 7:9.

'Lovingkindness and truth have come together; righteousness and peace have kissed' —Psalm 85:10.

For when lovingkindness and truth shall become one, then justice and peace shall reign over the whole world. And when we 'shall deal with *lovingkindness* and truth' (Joshua 2:14) towards one another, we shall 'then have dealt truly and *perfectly*' (Judges 9:19).

Chapter 11

Wisdom And The Coming Of The Son Of Man

Long ago, Wisdom was described as a beautiful and desirable maiden created by God and living in His heavens:

'The Lord Himself created Wisdom' –Sirach 1:19.

'Wisdom came forth from God' –Sirach 15:10, Latin Vulgate.

'The Lord created me [Wisdom] at the beginning of His way, before His works of old' –Proverbs 8:22.

'Follow after and pursue the genuine and unmated virgin, the Wisdom of God' –Philo, *Q. Gen.* II. 3.

'Pursue Wisdom as a hunter and lie in wait in her ways' –Sirach 14:22.

'If you desire Wisdom, keep the commandments and the Lord shall give her to you' –Sirach 1:26.

'With You is Wisdom who knows Your works and was present when You made the world, and who understands what is pleasing in Your sight' –Wisdom 9:9.

'Wisdom does not depart from the place of Your throne nor turns away from Your presence' –Enoch 84:3.

'I [Wisdom] was beside Him as one brought up and I was daily His delight, rejoicing always before Him' –Proverbs 8:30.

'O God . . . send Wisdom forth out of the holy heavens, and from the throne of Your glory send her, that she may be with me and work and that I may know what is pleasing to You' –Wisdom 9:1,10.

God made Wisdom radiant (Wisdom 6:12; 7:10,26,29–30; 8:1), and beautiful so that she would be desired by us:

> 'Come to me [Wisdom] all you who desire me, and be filled with my fruits' —Sirach 24:19.

> 'Wisdom hastens to make herself known to those who desire her' —Wisdom 6:13, RSV.

> 'Wisdom is easily seen by those who love her, and found by those who seek her' —Wisdom 6:12.

> 'Wisdom is near to those who seek her, and he who gives his desire to her shall find her' —Sirach 51:26, Hebrew Text.

Those who love Wisdom seek to have knowledge of her, just as a man desires to know the woman he loves:

> 'I loved Wisdom and sought her from my youth, and I desired to make Wisdom my spouse, and I became enamoured of her beauty' —Wisdom 8:2.

> 'My soul longed with desire for Wisdom' —Sirach 51:19, Hebrew Text.

> 'My inmost being burned with desire for Wisdom to look upon her' —Sirach 51:21, Hebrew Text.

> 'I went about seeking how to take Wisdom for myself' —Wisdom 8:18.

> 'I determined to take Wisdom to live with me' —Wisdom 8:9.

> 'But I knew that I could not take her [Wisdom] unless God gave her to me, and it was a mark of understanding to know whose gift she was' —Wisdom 8:21; Sirach 1:26; Ecclesiastes 2:26.

We shall not be able to 'know' Wisdom unless we first understand. Because it is through our understanding that we are able to encompass and apprehend Wisdom:

> 'I encompassed [SABAB] with my understanding to know and to search out Wisdom' —Ecclesiastes 7:25.

> It is the attribute of understanding to apprehend —Philo, *Mig.* 78; *Deus.* 78.

Apprehend by means of the understanding —Philo, *Abr.* 58; *Spec.* I. 46.

The immaterial, the invisible, the apprehended by the understanding alone —Philo, *Spec.* I. 20.

Spoken words contain symbols of things apprehended only by the understanding —Philo, *Abr.* 119; *Q. Gen.* IV. 163.

The understanding stretches out to seize —Philo, *Q. Gen.* II. 34.

Things unseen by sense but seized by the understanding — Philo, *Spec.* IV. 192; *Agr.* 53.

Seize [KATALĒPSONTAI] Wisdom —Sirach 15:7.

And 'take firm hold [EGKRATĒS] of Wisdom and do not let her go' (Sirach 6:27). 'Cleave to Wisdom that you may prove yourself wise' (Sirach 2:3, Syriac Text) but 'understand first' (Sirach 11:7) that 'men without understanding will not be able to seize Wisdom' (Sirach 15:7, Literal Translation), but 'every man of understanding knows Wisdom' (Sirach 18:28). If 'a man of understanding has Wisdom' (Proverbs 10:23) it is because 'a man of understanding is faithful to the Law of God' (Sirach 33:3, Latin Vulgate). Therefore, 'if you desire Wisdom, keep the commandments and the Lord shall give her to you' (Sirach 1:26), for 'whoever keeps the Law is an understanding [BIN] son' (Proverbs 28:7). 'A wise heart that has understanding will abstain from sins' (Sirach 3:32, Latin Vulgate) because 'Wisdom will not enter a deceitful soul, nor dwell in a body enslaved to sin' (Wisdom 1:4), but 'Wisdom rests in the heart of him who has understanding' (Proverbs 14:33). 'Generation by generation entering into holy souls, Wisdom makes them beloved by God' (Wisdom 7:27) because 'those who get Wisdom obtain friendship with God' (Wisdom 7:14) for 'the Lord loves those who love Wisdom' (Sirach 4:14). Indeed, 'God loves nothing so much as the man who lives with Wisdom' (Wisdom 7:28). Wisdom lives with *a man of understanding* for he alone is full of desire for her and is able to know her.

Just as Wisdom is portrayed as a beautiful and desirable *woman,* so is Understanding described as a strong and virile *man:*

'The understanding in each of us is in the true and full sense: the Man' —Philo, *Her.* 231.

> The understanding may be truly called the Man within the man
> —Philo, *Cong.* 97; *Q. Gen.* I. 33.

> The understanding in us, call it: 'Man'   —Philo. *Cher.* 57; *Q. Gen.* I.25,53,94; *L.A.* I. 92.

> That which is, one might say, naturally male in us is the understanding —Philo, *Q. Gen.* III. 46.

> The understanding . . . holding to its own nature of true manhood has the strength to be victor —Philo, *Her.* 274.

Thus, to say: 'if you have *understanding,* answer your neighbor' (Sirach 5:12, Greek Text), is to say that 'if you have *manhood* [ISH] with you, answer your neighbor' (Sirach 5:12, Hebrew Text). And where 'there is no wisdom, nor *understanding,* nor counsel against the Lord' (Proverbs 21:30, Hebrew Text), 'there is no wisdom, nor *manliness* [ANDREIA] nor counsel' (Proverbs 21:30, Greek Text) against Him. 'Hear me, you *men* of heart' (Job 34:10, Hebrew Text, Literal Translation) and 'hear me, you who are *understanding* [SUNETOI] of heart' (Job 34:10, Greek Text). 'Gird up the loins of your understanding' (1 Peter 1:13), 'be strong and act manfully that you may be understanding [SUNĒS] in all that you do' (Joshua 1:7, Greek Text), and you shall be like Joshua who 'girded up his loins with the girdle of understanding' (Ps. Philo, *Biblical Antiquities* XX. 3) like a true man. Conversely, the effeminate 'men of Sodom' were 'blind in understanding' (Philo, *Fug.* 144), yes, 'the sodomites . . . were barren of wisdom and blind in the understanding' (Philo, *Conf.* 27), for they were not like 'real men [ANDRES] with no blindness of the understanding' (Philo, *Agr.* 81), men who know that 'we contribute to lack of understanding [APHROSUNĒ] by slackness, indolence, luxury, effeminacy, and by complete irregularity of life' (Philo, *Ebr.* 20,21). 'O my understanding, never show weakness or slacken' (Philo, *Mig.* 222), 'be firm [ESTĒRIGMENOS] in your understanding' (Sirach 5:10), 'possess a piercing [OXUN] understanding' (Letter of Aristeas v.276) 'and penetrating understanding' (Zohar, *Midrash Haneelam,* Bereshith 17). Then, 'come to Wisdom with all your understanding' (Sirach 6:26, Syriac Text), and 'draw near to Wisdom . . . and when you draw close to her do it as a hero and a mighty one' (Sirach 1:22, Greek Sinaiticus Text) with your understanding, for 'every man of understanding knows Wisdom' (Sirach 18:28). It is because understanding is given a masculine imagery just as wisdom is given a feminine one that we can understand the rationale behind these Scriptural quotations:

'I made a covenant with my eyes; why then should I understand [BIN] upon a virgin?' —Job 31:1.

Be ashamed . . . to thoroughly understand [KATANOĒSEŌS] upon another man's wife —Sirach 41:21.

Do not understand [BIN] upon a virgin —Sirach 9:5, Hebrew Text.

Our innate 'understanding' [BIN = 'basic understanding'] is the one which has masculine connotations. But besides Wisdom, the gifts of Insight [BINAH] and great Understanding [TEBUNAH] come from God, and because He wants us to yearn for them, they are also presented to us as desirable women:

Say to Wisdom, 'You are my sister', and call Insight [BINAH] your kinswoman —Proverbs 7:4.

Does not Wisdom cry out, and great Understanding [TEBUNAH] lift up her voice? —Proverbs 8:1.

Let us also desire and ask the Lord for these His gifts so that we may really understand His holy things and be able to glorify Him.

When it is said that Wisdom 'delights' in being with the *'sons of Man'* (Proverbs 8:31), and that the 'voice' of great Understanding [TEBUNAH] is directed to the *'sons of Man'* (Proverbs 8:1,4), it is because both rejoice in being comprehended by those who are supposed to understand: the sons of Man (see pp. 13–14, 21–23, 46–47, 66–67). We have previously seen that whenever the terms 'Man' and 'Son of man' are used in conjunction in the Holy Scriptures, *'Man'* implies *knowledge,* and the term *'Son of Man', understanding.* To understand is the particular prerogative of the 'sons of Man', and that is why Wisdom and great Understanding have a predilection for them instead of 'Man' for Wisdom's great desire is to be understood. Thus, 'Wisdom went forth to make her dwelling among the *sons of Man'* (Enoch 42:2), hoping to find them understanding her.

Having her dwelling place in heaven (Enoch 84:3; Wisdom 7:25–26; Sirach 24:4; Baruch 3:29), Wisdom came down to earth seeking to be understood, but she was also disappointed in the sons of Man as the Lord was (see Psalms 14:2–3; 54:1–3), when He found no understanding among them either. We are told that Wisdom then 'returned to her place (in heaven) and took her seat among the angels' (Enoch 42:2c,d) until the time comes when she will be fully understood by a true son of Man.

Just as Wisdom is hypostatized as a beautiful woman; Understanding can be personified as a son of Man. That is why when 'the Word was made flesh' (St. John 1:14), 'the Understanding which has come down from heaven' (Philo, *Her.* 274) was also made flesh and dwelt in our midst in Jesus, for the Lord Jesus Christ is that Son of Man who understands all things:

> Christ, in whom are hidden all the treasures of wisdom and knowledge —Colossians 2:2,3.

> The Son [Jesus Christ] is the Understanding, Word and Wisdom of the Father —Athenagoras, *Emb.* XXV; 1 Corinthians 1:24.

> Christ . . . the door which we who desire to understand God must discover —Clement of Alexandria, *Exh.* I. 10.2.

> Where the Lord [Jesus Christ] dwells there is much understanding. Cleave to the Lord and you will understand and perceive all things —Shepherd of Hermas, *Mand.* X. 1. 40:6.

> Why do you not ask the Lord [Jesus] for understanding and receive it from Him? —Shepherd of Hermas, *Sim.* V. 4. 57:4.

> Ask the Lord [Jesus] to receive the insight to understand —Shepherd of Hermas, *Sim.* IX. 2. 79:6.

> The Lord [Jesus] give you understanding in all things —2 Timothy 2:7.

> We know that the Son of God has come and has given us understanding in order that we might know Him who is true —1 John 5:20.

> We have the understanding of Christ —1 Corinthians 2:16.

> Jesus . . . opened their understanding so that they might understand the Scriptures —St. Luke 24:36,45.

> Through Jesus Christ, our foolish and darkened understanding springs up to the light —Clement of Alexandria, *Strom.* IV. c.17.

> Jesus . . . through Him the eyes of our heart have been opened —First Clement 36:2.

> The eyes of the understanding being opened by [Jesus] the

Teacher who rose on the third day —Clement of Alexandria, *Strom.* V. c.11.

We thank You for the life and knowledge which You have made known to us through Jesus —*Didache* 9:3.

Blessed is our Lord [Jesus] who has placed in us wisdom and understanding of His secrets —Epistle of Barnabas 6:10; 10:12; 9:1,4.

He [Stephen], full of the Holy Spirit, gazed into heaven and saw the glory of God, and *Jesus* standing at the right hand of God, and he said, 'Behold, I see the heavens opened, and *the Son of Man* standing at the right hand of God' —Acts 7:55–56.

No one has ascended into heaven but He who descended from heaven, the Son of Man —St. John 3:13; Ephesians 4:9–10; St. Mark 16:19; St. Luke 24:51–52; Acts 1:9–11.

And because He *is* Understanding, He came down from heaven as the Son of Man, not in glory but in 'the form of a servant', 'to serve and to give His life as a ransom for many' (Philippians 2:7; St. Matthew 20:28), and save us from our sins. He also came down from heaven to teach us that it is the meek and humble servant-sons of Man who really understand.

THE
REVELATION
OF
THE SON OF MAN

[For those invited to believe]

Chapter 12

The Revelation Of The Son Of Man

'It is the nature of understanding to be very deep, not superficial, it does not display itself openly but loves to hide itself in secrecy.'[1] Thus Job asked: 'Where is the place of understanding? For it is hidden from the eyes of all living and concealed from the birds of the heavens.'[2] 'There is no searching of His understanding,'[3] and no finding it out until He determines that the time has come for it to be known and understood.

Long ago it was said of a patient man that 'he will hide his words until his time (to be exalted), and the lips of many shall (then) declare his understanding.'[4] The Word of God incarnate came and sowed 'His seed'.[5] For almost two thousand years He has patiently waited for us to bring forth from His implanted words: 'the fruits of understanding'.[6] Behold, the fruits are ripe, and the gatherers are here, for the time has come for the Son of Man to be exalted by His understanding. Let us drink this cup of astonishment to His glory, and our trembling.

Yeshua the Messiah came to us as the Son of Man who descended from heaven to dwell in our midst and to teach us, for in Him are hidden all the treasures of wisdom and knowledge. We shall see that Yeshua fulfilled all things relevant to understanding because as the Son of Man He is Understanding personified.

Understanding is associated with the 'dawn', the 'East', and the 'morning star':

> Understanding [PHRONĒSIS] is truly a thing of the dawn, all radiancy and brightness —Philo, *Plant.* 40.

> 'Understanding' is 'like one enlightened by the flash of the sun's beam after night' —Philo, *Cher.* 62.

> If the sun shall have risen, that is, the Understanding that shines so brilliantly in us —Philo, *L.A.* III. 35.

> The understanding [NOUS] is the sight of the soul illuminated by rays peculiar to itself, whereby the vast and profound darkness of ignorance is dispelled —Philo, *Deus.* 46.

'If you do not adapt yourself to the vision of holiness, you will end your life in blindness, unable to see the [rising] sun of understanding' –Philo, *Q. Exod.* II. 51.

'We have erred from the way of Truth, and the light of justice has not shined on us, and the sun of understanding has not risen upon us' –Wisdom 5:6, Latin Vulgate.

By His understanding He established the dawn –11Q Ps[a] xxvi.4 (Hymn to the Creator, Dead Sea Scrolls).

I understood [BIN] it in the early morning –1 Kings 3:21.

Words of the man of understanding [SAKAL] addressed by him to all the sons of the dawn [i.e., to those who understand] –Cave 4 Fragment, Dead Sea Scrolls.

Since the sun rises in the East we can expect understanding to be found in the East and knowledge in the West.

'Pass over to the coasts of Cyprus [to the West] and see [and know; see pp. 19–21] and send to Kedar [to the East] and understand [BIN] mightily' –Jeremiah 2:10.

Therefore, the term 'morning star' which rises in the East, denotes Understanding; and the Son of Man, who is the giver of understanding, is Himself named the 'Morning Star':

We have the prophetic word made more sure, to which you do well to pay attention as to a lamp shining in a dark place, until the day dawns and the morning star [i.e., understanding] rises in your hearts –2 Peter 1:19.

'I [Yeshua] . . . am the Root and the Offspring of David, the bright and Morning Star' –Revelation 22:16.

'He who overcomes, and keeps My works until the end, to him will I give power over the nations . . . I [Yeshua, the Son of Man] will give him the morning star' –Revelation 2:26,28; 2 Timothy 2:7; 1 John 5:20.

The prophet Jeremiah prophesied concerning the Messiah:

'Behold, the days are coming, says the Lord, when I will raise for

David a Branch of righteousness, and He shall reign as King and understand [SAKAL-SUNĒSEI], and shall execute judgment and righteousness in the earth' —Jeremiah 23:5, Hebrew and Greek Texts.

His people knew that the One the prophets called 'the Branch' (Isaiah 4:2; 11:1; Jeremiah 23:5; 33:15; Zechariah 3:8; 6:12) who was to rule and understand, was the promised Messiah who was going to be exalted in His day:

In that day the *Branch* of the Lord shall be beautiful and glorious —Isaiah 4:2.

At that time the *Messiah* of the Lord shall be for joy and for glory —Targum to Isaiah 4:2.

A shoot will come forth from the stump of Jesse, and a *Branch* shall grow out of his roots —Isaiah 11:1.

A king shall come forth from the sons of Jesse, and the *Messiah* shall grow up from his sons' sons —Targum to Isaiah 11:1.

Thus says the Lord of Hosts, saying: 'Behold, the Man whose name is the *Branch.* From His place He shall branch out, and He shall build the temple of the Lord; Yes, He shall build the temple of the Lord. He shall bear the glory, and shall sit and rule on His throne' —Zechariah 6:12,13.

Thus says the Lord of Hosts, saying: 'Behold the Man whose name is the *Messiah* who shall be revealed etc.' —Targum to Zechariah 6:12.

'Behold the days are coming, says the Lord, when I will raise for David a *Branch* of righteousness, and He shall reign as King and understand [SAKAL]' —Jeremiah 23:5.

'Behold the days come says the Lord that I will raise up unto David a righteous *Messiah* and he shall reign as King and understand' —Targum to Jeremiah 23:5; Ibid., 33:15.

The Messiah King who was named the Branch was before His exaltation a Servant of the Lord, a simple man:

'Behold, I am bringing forth My Servant the Branch' —Zechariah 3:8.

'Behold, the man whose name is the Branch' —Zechariah 6:12.

Let us ask ourselves, 'How did this Servant-Branch-man become exalted and reign gloriously as a King?' We should not forget that servants are exalted by their *understanding*, and it is by their *understanding* that they may someday be given to rule:

'A servant who has understanding [SAKAL] is exalted' —Sirach 10:24, Hebrew Text; Ibid., 10:29.

'Behold, My Servant shall understand [SAKAL], he shall be exalted and extolled and be very high . . . Kings shall shut their mouths because of him, for that which has not been recounted to them they shall see [and know], and that which they have not heard they shall understand [BIN]' —Isaiah 52:13,15.

'An understanding [SAKAL] servant shall have rule over his masters' —Sirach 20:27, Syriac Text.

'An understanding [SAKAL] servant shall have rule over a son who causes shame' —Proverbs 17:2.

'Nobles shall serve a servant who has understanding' —Sirach 10:25, Greek Sinaiticus Text and Cursives 248,23,106,307.

We can see from the Targums to the Prophets that His people knew that the *'Branch'* of the Lord was the *'Messiah'* (Targum renderings of Isaiah 4:2; 11:1; Jeremiah 23:5; 33:15; Zechariah 6:12). They also knew that the *'Servant'* of the Lord who shall understand was none other than 'My Servant, the *Messiah'* (Targum to Isaiah 52:13) who shall be exalted and extolled the day we recognize His great understanding.

'When God created man, He implanted within him his passions and moral nature. And at that time he enthroned above all the holy ruler Understanding [NOUN]' —4 Maccabees 2:21,22. For there is hidden mastery, power and kingship in understanding. 'Whoever has understanding [PHRONĒSEI] is wholly lordly and independent and masterful' (Philo, *Q. Gen.* III. 22, Greek Fragment and Armenian Text). Nevertheless, because he understands, he keeps 'the power of understanding' (Job 36:5; 2 Esdras 4:22) hidden within himself, for those who understand are by nature patient and 'humble in understanding' (Sirach 32:3, Hebrew Text; Colossians 3:12; Sotah 5b; Sanhedrin 43b, Babylonian Talmud). Truly, 'a man of understanding is humble in spirit' (Targum to Proverbs 17:27). The understanding of a son of Man makes him wait until 'the lips of many shall declare his understanding' (Sirach 1:24). In the end the poor and meek and humble servants of the Lord shall be exalted by their understanding.

Without understanding there is no exaltation from the Lord:

> 'You have hidden their heart from understanding [SAKAL], therefore You will not exalt them' —Job 17:4, Literal Translation.

Therefore, if you want to be exalted you must 'with all your getting get Understanding [BINAH], extol her and she will exalt [RUM] you, she will bring you to honor . . . she will place on your head a garland of grace; she will deliver to you a splendid crown' (Proverbs 4:7–9).

The Lord Himself shall be exalted when He makes us understand:

> 'Now I will arise' says the Lord, 'Now I will be glorified, now will I be exalted [because] now you shall see, and now you shall understand' —Isaiah 33:11, Greek Text.

> 'They shall lay it to heart and know that I am the Lord their God, for I will give them a heart and ears to hear [and understand] and they shall praise Me' —Baruch 2:30–32.

For 'He has given men understanding so that He may be glorified' (Sirach 38:6). 'I will exalt You, O my Rock . . . I will praise You . . . for You have made me to know the secret of Truth, and have revealed Your wonders to me' (1QH 11:15,16,17, Dead Sea Scrolls). 'Sing praises to God, sing praises, sing praises to our King, sing praises. For God is King of all the earth, sing praises with understanding' (Psalm 47:6–7, Hebrew and Greek Texts). 'Praise God with understanding' (Psalms of Solomon 2:37; 1 Corinthians 14:15). If it is said that 'a man shall be praised according to his understanding [SAKAL]' (Proverbs 12:8) it is because 'good understanding [SAKAL] wins favor' (Proverbs 13:15); 'he who has understanding will please great men' (Sirach 20:27) because there is wonderful counsel in good understanding: 'the counsel of understanding' (Sirach 6:24, Latin Vulgate; Ibid., 22:16; 44:3; Proverbs 1:5; 1 Chronicles 27:32; 26:14; 2 Enoch 66:3). 'Seek counsel always from the understanding' (Tobit 4:18, Vaticanus B Greek Text).

Understanding is exalted, praised and rewarded because of its life-giving and enlightening counsel. Thus the wise scribes who translated the Hebrew Bible into Greek rendered:

> 'In that day the *Branch* of the Lord shall be beautiful and glorious' —Isaiah 4:2, Hebrew Bible,

into

> 'In that day God shall shine gloriously in *counsel* on the earth' —Isaiah 4:2, Greek Septuagint Text.

They knew that the Branch of the Lord would be beautiful and shine gloriously the day the understanding and counsel of God would be revealed in him. He would no longer be the despised and abject Servant of the Lord (Isaiah 52:14; 53:1–10), but glorious in the sight of all because of his revealed knowledge and understanding (Isaiah 53:11; 52:13). The same wise scribes rendered the Hebrew word used for the Messiah: TSEMACH ['branch'] into ANATOLĒ, the Greek word for 'East' and 'Sunrise':

> 'Behold, I will bring forth My Servant the East [ANATOLĒN]' —Zechariah 3:8(9), Greek Text.

> 'Behold, the Man whose name is the East [ANATOLĒ]' —Zechariah 6:12, Greek Text; see also Philo, *Conf.* 62–63.

It was an appropriate paraphrase because the Branch of the Lord: the Messiah, was to spring forth from the stump of Jesse of the tribe of Judah whose alloted place was on the eastern side:

> 'On the east side, towards the sunrise, the divisions of the camp of Judah are to encamp under their standard; and Nahshon the son of Amminadab shall be the leader of the children of Judah' —Numbers 2:3.

In ancient times the East had not only special significance as regards Understanding but it was also the place of origin of the gods, god-kings of Egypt, and the promised One:

> 'I go on this eastern side of the sky where the gods were born' —Ancient Egyptian Pyramid Texts, Utterance 473, Section 928.

> 'The King is bound for the eastern side of the sky for the god-king

was conceived there, and the god-king was born there' —Ancient
Egyptian Pyramid Texts, Utterance 668, Section 1960; see also
Revelation 16:12.

'And from the East, God shall send a King who shall give every
land rest from the bane of war' —Sibylline Oracles III. 652; see
also Tacitus, *Histories* V.13 and Suetonius, *Vespasian,* 4.

Through holy inspiration, the prophets knew that things have their
beginning in the East and their completion in the West. The seed of righteousness sown in the East brings forth the perfect fruit of lovingkindness
from the West. If a righteous one shall come to sow from the East shall
he not return to gather from the West?

'Who raised up from the East the righteous one?' —Isaiah 41:2,
Literal Translation.

'I will bring your seed from the East, and gather you from the
West' —Isaiah 43:5.

Along with Judah, the tribes of Levi, Issachar, and Zebulon were also
stationed on the eastern side (Numbers 3:38–39; 2:5–9). Thus, the east
side was the place delegated to the priests and Levites, the kingly tribe
of Judah, and the tribes of Issachar and Zebulon which settled in the
region of Galilee wherein it was prophesied that:

'In Galilee of the Gentiles, the people who walked in darkness
have seen a great light; those who dwelt in the land of the
shadow of death: Light has shined on them' —Isaiah 9:2 [Inter-
preted Messianically in Zohar III, *Shemoth* 7b, 9e].

The Messiah came to fulfill all that the prophets had said and written
about Him (St. Luke 24:27), and about the dawn of His coming:

'Through the tender mercy of our God . . . the East [ANATOLĒ]
from on high will visit us' —St. Luke 1:78.

He did come and visit us 'to give light to those who sit in the darkness
and in the shadow of death and to guide our feet into the way of peace'
(St. Luke 1:79). He is 'the East' [ANATOLĒ] and 'the Sunrise' [ANATOLĒ]
because 'from the East is the direction where light comes forth' (Pesikta
Rabbati, Piska 46.3) and Yeshua the Messiah is 'the Light of the world'
(St. John 8:12; 9:5; 12:46). 'His [the Messiah's] name is "Light-giver" '

(Midrash Lamentations Rabbah I.16). 'The Messiah . . . will give light to the eyes of Israel' (Pesikta Rabbati Piska 36.1; see also Midrash Genesis Rabbah I.6).

When He was born in the little Judean town of Bethlehem, were not the wise men from the East the first Gentiles aware of His coming?:

> When Jesus was born in Bethlehem of Judea in the days of King Herod, behold, there came magi from the East to Jerusalem, saying, 'Where is He who is born King of the Jews? For we have seen His star in the East, and have come to worship Him' —St. Matthew 2:1–2.

Furthermore, seeing that Yeshua the Messiah of the tribe of Judah is Understanding incarnate, we may also be sure that the archangel who was sent to announce His Incarnation (St. Luke 1:26–38) is not only the angel who makes us understand but also the angel whose place is in the East as protector of the kings of Judah:

> 'Gabriel, make this man to understand the vision' –Daniel 8:16.

> 'And Gabriel said to me [Daniel], "Understand, O son of Man" ' –Daniel 8:17.

> 'Gabriel's place is in the East, it corresponds to that of Moses and Aaron and of the kingdom of the house of David [i.e., Judah]' –Pesikta Rabbati, Piska 46.3.

> 'Gabriel in front [of the eastern encampment] represents the kingship of Judah' –Midrash Numbers Rabbah 2.10.

> 'Gabriel the herald of the light' –Pirke R. Eliezer 11.3; see Ginzberg's *The Legends of the Jews,* vol. 5, p. 70, n. 13.

When Yeshua: 'the East from on high' (St. Luke 1:78) came to visit us, a member of the tribe of Levi whose place was also 'on the side of the camp that faces East' (Pesikta Rabbati, Piska 46.3) was sent as a forerunner 'to bear witness to the Light' (St. John 1:7). St. John the Baptist came 'in the spirit and power of Elijah, to turn the hearts of the fathers to the children, and the disobedient to the understanding of the righteous, to make ready a people prepared for the Lord' (St. Luke 1:17). It is of him that the Messiah said that 'he was a burning and a shining lamp' (St. John 5:35) as all the sons of the East should be.

And 'adjacent to the tribe of Judah shall be Issachar (the tribe) who is master of the *light* of the Torah' (Pesikta Rabbati, Piska 46.3), and the tribe of Zebulon (Numbers 2:5–7) out of whom were 'they who could handle the pen of the scribe [SAPHAR]' – Judges 5:14; see also Midrash Numbers Rabbah 3.12. We know that from the tribe of Levi – also adjacent to Judah – came the first verbal witness to Yeshua the Davidic Messiah. We may expect that the companion tribes of Issachar and Zebulon are prophetically symbolic of the future two witnesses who shall establish the truth of His coming. It is by these two witnesses that the Messiah shall be revealed and His Truth established. In an ancient Jewish apocryphal work of the second century B.C. called the Testament of the Twelve Patriarchs it was written that Issachar was noted for his righteousness and singleness of heart (Testament of Issachar 3:1–8; 4:1; 7:1–6), and Zebulon for his compassion and lovingkindness (Testament of Zebulon 1:4–7; 2:4–6; 5:1–2; 6:4–6; 7:1–4). Indeed, what better witnesses to the Truth can there be than Fidelity and Mercy?

[1] Philo, *Som.* I. 6.
[2] Job 28:20,21.
[3] Isaiah 40:28.
[4] Sirach 1:24.
[5] St. Luke 8:5.
[6] Sirach 37:22.

Chapter 13

Bethlehem

When the times were fulfilled for the Messiah to be born, He chose to come to us from the tribe of Judah. Judah was the fourth child of Leah and Jacob. The Messiah could have come forth from any of the three tribes preceding Judah, or even from the tribe of Benjamin who was the youngest and only child of *Israel* (Jacob was named 'Israel' at the time he fathered Benjamin; see Genesis *32*:28; *35*:18,21). After all, Benjamin was the only one among his brothers born in the Holy Land, the rest were born in Aram. Nevertheless, it was from the stump of Jesse of the tribe of Judah that the Messiah branched forth.

Perhaps, the reason for the choice of Judah was that Judah alone was named to the praise of the Lord (Genesis 29:35), and according to the rabbis (Sifre Torah I.89b), God's name is included in the name Judah ('I will praise the Lord' – Genesis 29:35), while all the rest of the children were named for ulterior motives (Genesis 29:32–34; 30:1–24; 35:18). Moreover, was not Judah the first man to offer himself as a ransom for the sake of his brothers? (Genesis 44:9–34; Mekilta, *Beshallah* VI. 28–44, 66–70; Sotah 37a, Babylonian Talmud). We shall come closer to the wisdom of the Lord's choice when we see that from the very beginning Judah's matrimonial connections contained more non-Israelite elements than any other tribe. Judah's first wife was Bath-Shua, a Canaanitess (Genesis 38:1–5,12), then Tamar, an Aramean (Philo, *De Virt.* 221–222; Midrash Numbers Rabbah 20.25). In the Messianic line of the tribe of Judah (St. Matthew 1:1–16) are found Rahab, the harlot of Jericho (Ps. Philo, *Biblical Antiquities* XX. 21), the Moabitess Ruth, and Bathsheba, the wife of Uriah the Hittite. Who has not heard about the seven hundred wives and three hundred concubines of King Solomon taken from the Egyptians and other 'women of the Moabites, Ammonites, Edomites, Zidonians and Hittites'? (1 Kings 11:4; 14:21).

Ancient rabbinic tradition traces the genealogy of King David from the marriage of Miriam, the sister of Moses, to the Kenezite Caleb (Midrash Exodus Rabbah 1.17; 40.1; 48.4; Pirke de Rabbi Eliezer 45; Sifre to Numbers 78; Midrash Tanchumah I. 52; II. 121–123; Sotah 11b–12a, Babylonian Talmud; Targum to 1 Chronicles 2:19; 4:4; Tanchumah wa-Yakhel 4–5; see also Ginzberg's, *The Legends of the Jews* vol. II, p. 253; vol. IV, pp. 81–82). 'Caleb, the son of Jephunneh the Kenezite' (Numbers 32:12; Joshua 14:6,14), was a descendant of Kenaz, a son of Eliphaz who was the son of 'Esau the father of the Edomites' (Genesis 36:9–11). The foreign Kenezite clan to which Caleb belonged became incorporated with the tribe of Judah by the time Caleb was born. It is in the Calebites that the progeny of Esau (Kenezites) and Jacob (Judahites) were *united*.

We first hear about Caleb in the narrative of the scouting done in the land of Canaan by the spies chosen from each of the twelve tribes (Numbers 13:1–14:30). It was during the time that the tribes were still sojourning in the wilderness with Moses and Aaron and were encamped in Kadesh-Barnea, an oasis in the desert of Paran close to the Promised Land. Moses had assembled the tribes and selected from each tribe a delegate to spy out the land of Canaan and determine the strength of its cities and inhabitants. What wonderful names the scouts had (see Yalkut I. 743; Midrash Genesis Rabbah 16.5): from the tribe of Reuben, Shamua ('Renowned'); from Simeon, Shaphat ('Judge'); from Dan, Ammiel ('My people are strong'); from Naphtali, Nahbi ('Consolation'); from Gad, Geuel ('God of salvation'); from Asher, Sethur ('Protected one'); from Issachar, Igal ('Deliverer'); from Zebulon, Gaddiel ('Fortune of God'); from Manasseh, Gaddi ('Lucky one'); from Ephraim, Hoshea ('Salvation'); from Benjamin, Palti ('The Lord delivers') [see Young's *Analytical Concordance to the Bible*]; but from Judah: Caleb ('Dog'). That Caleb [KLB] means 'dog' is attested not only by the Hebrew meaning of the word (see *Jewish Encyclopedia* Vol. III, p. 498), but also by the same meaning for the word KLB found in the Ugaritic Texts: *Keret* I. 3.19; 5.10; 11.1.15; *Baal* V. 3.60, and in the *Lachish* (Tell el-Amarna) *Letters* II. 4, and ancient Canaanite inscriptions (*Corpus Inscriptionum Semiticarum,* pt. I. 86; pt. II. 56; pt. III. 22–25, Paris, 1881). Even in the Babylonian Tablets VAT 9933; 13836; 10349 (Berlin Museum), KLB means 'dog'.

When the spies returned from their expedition, almost all of them gave the people a discouraging report, frightening them with their accounts that told of great walled cities, high mountains, deep rivers, and gigantic inhabitants next to which they appeared to be mere grasshoppers in size. Only Caleb spoke up bravely saying, 'Let us go up at once and possess it, for we are well able to overcome it' (Numbers 13:30). Along with Joshua, Caleb continued exhorting the frightened people: 'The land which we passed through to search is an exceedingly good land. If the Lord delights in us, then He will bring us into this land and give it to us, a land flowing with milk and honey. Only do not rebel against the Lord, nor fear the inhabitants of the land for they are bread for us. Their defense is departed from them, and the Lord is with us, do not fear them' (Numbers 14:7–9).

They spoke to no avail, and as the still badly demoralized people proceeded to stone them to silence, the Lord intervened, rebuked and condemned the people and the rest of the spies—except Caleb and Joshua—to wander in the wilderness for forty years until all of them who came out of Egypt had died. The Lord then spoke to Moses in praise of Caleb, saying, 'But My servant Caleb, because he had another spirit with him and has followed Me fully, him will I bring into the land where he went, and his children shall possess it' (Numbers 14:24). Seven times do the Holy Scriptures tell us that Caleb 'wholly followed the Lord' (Numbers 14:24; 32:12; Deuteronomy 1:36; Joshua 14:8,9,14; Sirach 46:10), as a loyal dog follows its master (Tobit 11:4; Story of Ahikar 2:8, Armenian Text). Caleb, the faithful Kenezite from the tribe of Judah believed in the Lord's promises (Exodus 3:8; 13:5; Leviticus 20:23–24). The partly Edomite man named 'dog' (Caleb) showed faith in the Lord when none of the rest of the children of Jacob did. Because of his fidelity, the Lord gave him first choice on any parcel of land he desired when the Holy Land was to be divided later on among the twelve tribes. And Caleb chose Hebron as his very own city and gave it as a heritage to his descendants. There was wisdom in Caleb's choice of the city of Hebron and its environs for himself and his children (Joshua 14:12–15; Judges 1:20), because, excepting Rachel and Joseph, all the tribal patriarchs and matriarchs: Abraham, Sarah, Isaac, Rebecca, Jacob, Leah and all the rest of the children of Jacob were buried in Hebron. Caleb chose and obtained Hebron as his possession so that 'all the children of Israel might see that it is good to follow the Lord' (Sirach 46:10), and that they may know that it was only fitting that a man named 'dog' should ask and get to keep the place where the holy bones of his ancestors were buried. There is a tongue in cheek mention of Judah's 'dog' in 'Hebron' in the Testament of the Twelve Patriarchs (Testament of Judah 2:6).

Bethlehem, a city fifteen miles north of Hebron, was founded by Salma, the grandson of another Calebite called Caleb (1 Chronicles 2:51,54,9,18–19,42,50). The Calebite cities: Hebron and Bethlehem figure prominently in the history of King David.

Shortly after the death of King Saul and Prince Jonathan, David asked the Lord where to reside, and the Lord answered: 'Hebron' (2 Samuel 2:1). It was in Hebron, the chief city of the Calebites, that David was anointed

King over Israel (2 Samuel 5:1–3), and there 'he reigned for seven and a half years over Judah' (2 Samuel 5:5). At that time six sons were born to King David from six of his wives among whom were the Calebite Abigail (1 Samuel 25:3; 2 Samuel 2:2), and Maachah, the daughter of the foreign King of Geshur (2 Samuel 3:3; 1 Chronicles 2:42,43).

King David himself may have acknowledged his Caleb family connections by addressing himself as 'son' to a Calebite (1 Samuel 25:2–3,8). That same Calebite was not only said to be a 'fool' (1 Samuel 25:25) but literally a 'dog-man' [ANTHRŌPOS KUNIKOS, in the ancient Greek Text of 1 Samuel 25:3]. Did not King David use such self-deprecatory expressions as: 'After whom do you pursue? After a dead dog? After a flea?' (1 Samuel 24:14; 26:20). In praising King David the Lord extolled him with the same terms he had used for His servant Caleb: 'My servant David, who kept My commandments and who followed Me with all his heart' (1 Kings 14:8), just as Caleb the faithful 'dog'-man did.

We know that King David was born in Bethlehem, 'the city of David' (St. Luke 2:4,11,15) which was founded by the Calebite Salma (1 Chronicles 2:51), and that he was anointed King in Hebron and from there reigned seven and a half years over Judah. Notwithstanding that Hebron belonged to Caleb and his descendants, it also fell by lot to the Levites (Joshua 21:11,13; 1 Chronicles 6:54–57), because they were allied to the Calebites through the tradition of the marriage of Caleb to Miriam the sister of Moses and Aaron. By the same token, Levites were also found in Bethlehem (Judges 17:7–13; 18:30; 19:1). Was it not written that 'David's sons were priests [KOHEN pl.]'? – 2 Samuel 8:18, Literal Translation. And did not King David's son Solomon bless the people, consecrate the Temple, and offer sacrifices to the Lord just as a priest? (1 Kings 8:14,55,62–64; see also 2 Samuel 15:12 re Absalom's 'offering of the sacrifices'). The tribe of Judah from which the Davidic line and the Messiah sprung forth, was united to the tribe of Levi not only by the marriage of Caleb and Miriam but also by that of Aaron and Elisheba the daughter of Amminadab and great-great-great-granddaughter of Pharez the son of Judah and Tamar (Exodus 6:23; Ruth 4:18–22; Genesis 46:12).

In the tribe of Judah were also found the bloodlines of the Canaanites (Bath-Shua), Arameans (Tamar), Kenezites (Caleb), Moabites (Ruth), and Ishmaelites (according to rabbinic tradition, the wife of Jesse was the daughter of the Ishmaelite Ithra; see Yebamoth 8:3,9b, Jerusalem Talmud). It is also mentioned that while they were in Egypt, the tribe of Judah intermarried with the Egyptian women (Midrash Numbers Rabbah 13.8). Such was the history of foreign intermarriages in the tribe of Judah, that the very name 'Judah' became synonymous with those who cohabit with foreign women (Sanhedrin 82a,b, Babylonian Talmud).

In common with his brother Judah, Simeon also married a Canaanite woman (Genesis 46:10; Book of Jubilees 34:20; 44:13; Sepher ha Yashar 54a; Midrash Haggadol I.682), and his descendants commingled with the Midianites and Cushites (Sanhedrin 82a,b, Babylonian Talmud; Midrash ha Shiloah IX. 360). The children of Simeon were held in low esteem because their tribe was the poorest, and all impecunious schoolteachers, and itinerant beggars were deemed to have come from them (Midrash Genesis Rabbah 88.7; Midrash Numbers Rabbah 21.8; Yalkut to Genesis 158; Rashi re Genesis 49:7 and Joshua 19:8–9). Although the tribe of Simeon did not share in the blessing of Moses (Deuteronomy 33), there was an ancient tradition that 'Moses attached Simeon to the tribe of Judah' (Midrash to Psalms 90.3; Zohar II. *Vayehi* 236a; Judges 1:3,17), because just as the Calebites received 'a portion among the children of Judah' (Joshua 15:13), so did the tribe of Simeon receive a share 'in the midst of the inheritance of the tribe of Judah' (Joshua 19:1,9). And so close were the ties between the tribe of Simeon and the tribe of Judah, that the cities which were said to belong to the tribe of Judah, were also cities that belonged to the tribe of Simeon. Thus, Maladah, Beersheba, Hazar, Shual, Baalah, Ezem, Ziklag, Ain and Rimmon were cities of Judah (in Joshua 15:26,28,29,31,32) but also cities of the tribe of Simeon (in Joshua 19:2,3,5,7). And the Negev region of Judah (1 Samuel 27:10) and of Caleb (1 Samuel 30:14), was the same Negev region of the tribe of Simeon (Joshua 19:1–9; Tamid 31b–32a, Babylonian Talmud). Residing in the southernmost section of the Holy Land where the wise are said to abide (Obadiah 8; Baba Bathra 158b, Babylonian Talmud; Midrash Genesis Rabbah 16.4), the Simeonites were noted for their wisdom (Tamid 31b–32a, Babylonian Talmud), and careful attention to the Law. The very name 'Simeon' was interpreted to mean, 'he who listens to the words of God' (Midrash Genesis Rabbah 71.4). Thus, many of the scribes were traditionally from the tribe of Simeon (Midrash Genesis Rabbah 98.5; 99.7; Tanchumah I. 218–219; Aggadat Bereshith 82, 159–160; Targumim Genesis 49:5–7; Shitah Hadashah 2; Tanchumah Vayehi 9–10; see also Tertullian, *Adversus Marcion* 3.18; *Adversus Judaios* 10, and Hippolytus re Genesis 49:5).

Consequently, through intermarriage and proximity, the tribes of Levi and Simeon partially merged with the tribe of Judah, and so did many non-Israelites. Thus, in the House of Judah, the royal, priestly and scribal lineages blended, and the Jew and Gentile became consanguineous in that 'universal' tribe chosen by God to bring forth His Messiah: Yeshua.

Long ago, His people knew that the Messiah would come forth from the tribe of Judah and the House and lineage of King David (Targums on Genesis 49:8–12; Ruth 3:15; Jeremiah 23:5; 30:9; 33:15; Hosea 3:5; Micah 5:1; Berakoth 5a; Sukkah 55a; Taanith 64a, 68b, Jerusalem Talmud; Erubin 43a,b; Yoma 10a; Sukkah 52a,b; Megillah 17b; Yebamoth 62a; Nazir 23a; Sotah 48b; Baba Kamma 38a,b; Sanhedrin 38b; 93; 94a; 96b; 97a; 98a,b; Abodah Zarah 5a; Niddah 13b; Kallah Rabbathi 52a; Derek Eretz Zuta 59a, Babylonian Talmud; Midrash Genesis Rabbah 50.10; 51.8; 85.19; Midrash Exodus Rabbah 25.12; 30.3; Midrash Numbers Rabbah 13.11; Midrash Ruth Rabbah 3.14; 7.15; 8.1; Midrash Song of Songs Rabbah 2.13; Midrash Lamentations Rabbah, *Proems* 21, 23; 1.16 sect. 51; Midrash on Psalms 18.36; 21.11; 43.5; 60.3; 87.6; 92.10; Midrash Mishlei (on Proverbs) re Prov. 19:21; Midrash Haggadah [Buber] on Genesis 15:12; 19:15; 38:15; Midrash Haggadol I. 735–739; Pesikta R. Kahana, Piska 5.9; Pesikta Rabbati, Piska 15.14–15; 36.2; Pirke R. Eliezer, Perek 30,31; Yalkut Shimoni f. 160; Yelammedenu 35; *Beth haMidrash* [Jellinek] vol. V, pp. 167–168, 187–188; vol. VI. Introd. 22, 25– 26, 84; Zohar I. 25b, 82b, 188b, 238a; II. 203b, 278b; Sekel Tob [Buber] re Genesis 32:5; 49:8; Rashi on Genesis 49:8–12; *Otzar Midrashim* [Eisenstein] 466; Maimonides', *Thirteen Principles of the Faith* 12–13; *Yad haHazaqa, Shoftim, Hilkhot Melachim* 11–12, etc.).

They also knew from the prophet Micah that the Messiah from the tribe of Judah would be born in Bethlehem:

'And you, Bethlehem-Ephrathah, though you are little among the thousands of Judah, from you shall come forth for Me *the One* who is to be ruler in Israel, whose goings forth have been from old, from the days of eternity' —Micah 5:2.

'And you Bethlehem-Ephrathah who are too little to be counted among the thousands of the house of Judah, from you in My name shall come forth *the Messiah* who is to be ruler in Israel and whose name has been called from eternity, from the days of old' —Targum Jonathan on Micah 5:2.

'The *King Messiah* . . . from where does he come forth?' 'from the royal city of *Bethlehem* in Judah' —Berakoth 5a, Jerusalem Talmud; see also Midrash Lamentations Rabbah, *Proem.* I. 1.16; Bereshith Rabbati, pp. 130–131; St. Matthew 2:1–6; St. John 7:42.

Before we shall understand why He chose to be born in Bethlehem-Ephrathah, let us recall that He came as the Son of Man to live among the children of men. For He desired to share our life in the great field which is the world (St. Matthew 13:38), and where He was to become our Bread of life and understanding.

Previous to the occupation of the promised land by the twelve tribes, Bethlehem was known by its old name: Ephrathah (Genesis 35:16,19; 48:7). It was known as the *'fruitful'* (Ephrathah) before it was named Bethlehem ('House of *Bread*'). The change in name evokes not only the normal precedence of fruit before bread but it also reminds us of the two stages of mankind: Man in the fruitful garden of Eden, and Man in the field where he was taken from, and where he labored to make bread for the sons of Man. Thus King David was said to be not only 'a son of Jesse the Bethlehemite' (1 Samuel 16:18), but also 'the son of that Ephrathite of Bethlehem whose name is Jesse' (1 Samuel 17:12). If the Messiah was to come forth from 'Bethlehem-Ephrathah' (Micah 5:2) it is because He is not only the 'Living Bread' (St. John 6:51) of Man but also 'Messiah the first-fruits' (1 Corinthians 15:23) from whom we have received 'the bread of understanding' (Sirach 15:3) and 'the fruit of . . . knowledge' (Sirach 37:22, Hebrew Text). And because the Lord expects both fruit and bread from us, the first offering to the Lord was 'a *sheaf* [OMER] of the *firstfruits*' of the barley harvest. Later on, at the time of the wheat harvest the second offering presented to the Lord was that of the two freshly made loaves of leavened wheat *bread* (Leviticus 23:10–17). In Ephrathah-Bethlehem we have the two motifs of 'fruit' and 'bread'.

Bethlehem is truly a city of kings. The village of Bethlehem and its surroundings played an important part in the history of Israel because in the road by the fields a mile north of 'Ephrathah which is Bethlehem', Benjamin was born (Genesis 35:16–19), from whom descended Saul the first King of Israel and founder of the royal house of Benjamin (1 Samuel 9:1–2; 10:1,24). And in Bethlehem itself were born King David, the founder of the royal house of Judah, and his descendant Yeshua the Messiah. Important as it may have become later on, there was no mention of the royal city of David among the one hundred and twenty five cities listed as belonging to the tribe of Judah (Joshua 15:20–63). The omission is remarkable because many of the cities in that complete list were smaller than Bethlehem-Ephrathah. Perhaps Bethlehem was not listed because it was a city of Calebites, having been founded by Salma of the house of Caleb, and that particular clan of the tribe of Judah seemed to be held in low esteem even long after King David's time when the Hebrew Scriptures were translated in Greek:

'The man [i.e., Nabal] was harsh and evil in his doings, and he was of the house of Caleb' – 1 Samuel 25:3, Hebrew Text.

'The man was harsh and evil in his doings and he was a dog [KUNIKOS] man [ANTHROPOS]' – 1 Samuel 25:3, Greek Text (3rd Century B.C.)

According to old tradition, King David's mixed ancestry was also derogatorily referred to by his enemies (Midrash on Psalms 1.2; 4.8,9; 116.9; Midrash Numbers Rabbah 18.17; see 1 Samuel 20:30–31; 22:7–9). There was also a tradition that David himself was despised by his brothers and banished by them and relegated to tending sheep because they falsely presumed that he was the offspring of Jesse's dalliance with a slave girl (Pesachim 119a, Babylonian Talmud; Midrash Shemuel 19,104; see also Ps. Philo, *Biblical Antiquities*, LIX.4). David was twenty-eight years old when he was taken from the sheepfold, and anointed by Samuel in Bethlehem to be King over God's people. But there would not have been a king from the tribe of Judah or from the tribe of Benjamin if something had not happened long ago in that particular area of the Holy Land, because it was within a mile south of Bethlehem in the vicinity of a watchtower for the flocks, that Reuben the first-born son of Jacob lost his birthright to the crown promised long ago to the descendants of Abraham (Genesis 17:6,16).

We are told in the book of Genesis that soon after the death of Rachel, Jacob with his family and flocks set up camp south of Bethlehem 'beyond the tower [MIGDAL] of Eder' ('the flock') – Genesis 35:21–22. And there, a mile south of Bethlehem-Ephrathah, occured that incident with Bilhah, Jacob's concubine, which cost Reuben his birthright, and set in motion the course of events which resulted in the pre-eminence of Judah from whom 'came the chief ruler' (1 Chronicles 5:1–2). The area of Migdal-Eder, where Reuben lost the supremacy which was his by right of primogeniture, also plays a role in Jewish tradition concerning the Messiah, since it was there that the Messiah was to be revealed to Israel: 'And Jacob proceeded and spread his tent beyond Migdal-Eder, the place where it is to be that King Messiah will be revealed at the end of days' (Targum Jerusalem on Genesis 35:21). Thus, in the Gospel according to St. Luke (2:8), we are told that on the night the Messiah was born 'there were in the same countryside shepherds abiding in the fields (near Bethlehem) keeping watch over their flocks', and it was to them that the angel of the Lord revealed the birth of the Saviour 'in the city of David' (St. Luke 2:9–18). Since ancient times the vicinity of Migdal-Eder has been revered as the site of the angelic revelation to the shepherds. St. Jerome (c. A.D. 350), mentions that in his time the tower at Migdal-Eder was still extant: 'about a thousand paces from Bethlehem is the tower of Eder which means 'tower of the flock', a name which seems to be a prophetic allusion to the shepherds' future witness to the nativity of the Lord' (*Onomastikon* 43,62,68; see also Cyril of Scythopolis', *Life of St. Euthymius* chap. 86, 133; *Itinerary of the Pilgrim of Piacenza* p. 107, Edition Tobler et Moliniere).

The Son of Man did all things well, He was born in Bethlehem yet not in a house in the city called the 'House of Bread' but in a stable wherein just after He was born He was wrapped in swaddling cloths and laid in a manger. For He who is our Bread of Understanding was to commence His life where all bread making begins: in a grain bin. And though He came from the royal branch of the tribe of Judah, the blood of the priestly tribe of Levi also coursed in His veins, because His mother Mary was a cousin of Elizabeth who was 'of the daughters of Aaron' (St. Luke 1:5,36). Elizabeth was named after her ancestress Elisheba who married Aaron (in the Septuagint Greek Text of Exodus 6:23 'Elisheba' is rendered 'Elizabeth'), Mary's cousin was the mother of St. John the Baptist who went before the Messiah 'in the spirit and power of Elijah' (St. Luke 1:17). Thus, the royal and priestly blood lines were found in Yeshua, the King of kings, and the High Priest of high priests.

Simeon also played a part in the life of the Messiah from the tribe of Judah, for were not the two tribes closely associated in the history of Israel? Two Simeons (St. Luke 2:25–35; St. Matthew 16:15–17; Acts 15:14; 2 Peter 1:1) bore witness to Yeshua, 'the Lion of the tribe of Judah, the Root of David' (Revelation 5:5).

Knowing the importance of Bethlehem and its surroundings, later Jewish tradition says that when the time comes for the Messiah to be revealed in a great light, he shall be found in the outskirts of Bethlehem by Rachel's tomb (Zohar II. 8b).

Chapter 14

Nazareth

If we search the Holy Scriptures we shall find that the children of Judah were particularly blessed with the gift of understanding. We read in reference to 'Bezaleel the son of Uri, the son of Hur (the son of Caleb) of the tribe of Judah' who was 'filled . . . with the Spirit of God, in wisdom, and in great understanding [TEBUNAH] and in knowledge' (Exodus 31:2–3). And also concerning King 'David who was understanding [SAKAL] in all his ways . . . and had more understanding [SAKAL] than all the servants of Saul' (1 Samuel 18:14,30; see also 2 Samuel 14:20; 28:19), and of his son King Solomon who was also given 'a wise and understanding [BIN] heart' (1 Kings 3:12). For 'God gave Solomon wisdom and exceedingly great understanding' (1 Kings 4:29; 2 Chronicles 2:12), and when he was good, Solomon's grandson, King 'Abijah . . . dealt with understanding [BIN]' –2 Chronicles 11:23. And so did their descendant King Hezekiah of Judah for 'the Lord was with him and he understood [SAKAL] wherever he went forth' (2 Kings 18:7). Even 'David's uncle Jonathan, was a counsellor and an understanding [BIN] man' (1 Chronicles 27:32), and so were Daniel, Hananiah, Mishael, and Azariah for they had 'knowledge and understanding [SAKAL] in all learning and wisdom, and Daniel had understanding [BIN] in all visions and dreams' (Daniel 1:6,17,20; 5:11–12,14; 9:2,22; 10:1) because all four 'were of the children of Judah' (Daniel 1:6).

The royal line of the tribe of Judah was also enriched in understanding because of its close contacts and marital unions with non-Israelite peoples noted for their understanding. Have we not heard about the understanding of the Temanites (Jeremiah 49:7; Obadiah v. 8,9), and of 'the sons of Hagar who search for understanding on the earth'? (Baruch 3:23, RSV); and of the understanding of the Tyrians (2 Chronicles 2:11,13; Ezekiel 28:2,4), and the Arabians: Job from 'the land of Uz' (Job 1:1; 6:30; 13:1; 23:15; Lamentations 4:21), Eliphaz the Temanite (Job 15:1,9), Zophar the Naamathite (Job 20:1,3) and Elihu the Buzite? (Job 32:2,12). Being noted for its understanding, it was to be expected that the Messiah would choose to be born of a virgin from the tribe of Judah (St. Matthew 1:1–25; St. Luke 1:26–38; 2:1–12), for was He not Himself Understanding incarnate?

When God created Man, He formed him from the moistened dust of a *field,* and took him to live and work in His abundantly watered garden east of Eden. And we know that from the garden of Eden, the Lord God exiled Man *back* to the *field* where he was taken from (Genesis 3:23; see pp. 3–7, 8–10).

Thousands of years later on, Abraham made the same transition from field to garden and from garden to the same field, on the day he departed from the land of Canaan to go to Egypt which was compared to 'the garden of the Lord' (Genesis 13:10), and from Egypt back to the land of Canaan (Genesis 12:5 to 13:1–12). Many years later, Abraham's descendants also journeyed, en masse, from the land of Canaan to Egypt and were brought back to the Holy Land (Genesis 42–47; Exodus; Joshua), retracing the original journey of Man.

Was not the Messiah Himself to undergo the same passage? Thus, He was taken as an infant from the land where He was born into Egypt, and from there brought back to Israel (St. Matthew 2:1–22), so that it could be truly said of Him: 'Out of Egypt I have called My Son' (St. Matthew 2:15; Hosea 11:1).

In ancient times kings and princes were considered shepherds of their people (Isaiah 44:28; Jeremiah 2:8; 3:15; 23:4; Ezekiel 34:2,9; 37:24), providing sustenance and security for their flock. The Lord Himself is the Shepherd of His people (Psalm 23:1; 78:32; 79:13; 80:1; Isaiah 40:11; 49:9–10; Jeremiah 23:3; Ezekiel 34:11,12,23,24), feeding and watching over them. As a true son of the shepherd-King David, the Messiah was to be the 'great Shepherd of the sheep' (Hebrews 13:20; Zechariah 13:7; Micah 5:2,4; Psalms of Solomon 7:17), to feed, guard, and even lay down His life for them (St. John 10:15). If it was to be from Bethlehem-Ephrathah that the Messiah was to come who was to feed His people (Micah 5:2,4), it was in Nazareth that He would pray and watch over them.

Nazareth, the city where the Messiah lived until He 'was about thirty years of age' (St. Luke 3:23), was situated at the top of a hill (St. Luke 4:29) sixteen hundred feet above sea level. From the crest of the hill of Nazareth, the Messiah saw one of the most striking views in all of the Holy Land. Before His eyes were Mount Tabor with its rounded dome on the southeast; Mount Hermon with its white top in the distant north, Mount Carmel and the blue Mediterranean Sea to the west, and on the south, the whole broad plain of Esdraelon (the Valley of Jezreel) with Little Hermon and historic Mount Gilboa (2 Samuel 21:12) in the distance. The great high road—known in the days of Isaiah as 'the way of the sea'

(Isaiah 9:1)—ran across the plain just behind Nazareth from the port of Acre (Ptolemais) to Damascus. Another caravan road, from Damascus to Judea and Egypt, crossed Esdraelon not far from the base of the Nazareth hill, meeting a third from the North, at Megiddo, on the other side of the plain. The Roman road from Syria, moreover, after passing along the coast through Berytus, Sidon, Tyre and Acre, ran, by way of Sepphoris past the hills surrounding Nazareth, on to Samaria, Jerusalem, and to the South. Syrians, Phoenicians, Egyptians, Jews, Gileadites, Idumeans and Roman legions traversed those caravan roads not far from Nazareth.

The word Nazareth is derived from the Hebrew root NATSAR which means 'to watch', 'to observe', and 'to guard'. NOTSERAH, the Hebrew word for Nazareth means 'the watcher' or 'guardian'. Eliezer Hakkalir, a Jewish poet who lived in Galilee in the 7th century A.D., states in his Elegy on the Ninth Day of Ab that a 3rd century inscription found in Caesarea listed the priestly courses and their seats in Galilee. He mentions that the family of Happizzez (1 Chronicles 24:15) settled in Nazareth, a name derived in that Galilean source, from the root NATSAR 'to watch over' or 'to guard'. Truly, Nazareth is an appropriate name for the city with such a scenic vantage point. It was a good place for the Shepherd of Israel to live and watch over His sheep. Seven miles away, northwest of Nazareth, clearly visible from the top of the hill, was the other Bethlehem, the one belonging to the tribe of Zebulon (Joshua 19:15–16) which is called in the Talmud: Bethlehem Notseriyyah, i.e., 'Bethlehem of Nazareth' or 'House of Bread of the Watcher'.

'Nazareth of Galilee' (St. Matthew 21:11; St. Mark 1:9; St. Luke 1:26; 2:39) is as it were enclosed by fifteen gently rounded hills, the highest being the hill upon which the city of Nazareth was built. Quaresimus, who lived for a time in Nazareth, poetically described the city in these terms: 'Nazareth is a rose, and like a rose, it has the same rounded form, enclosed by mountains as the flower by its leaves' (*Elucidatio Terrae Sanctae* ii. 818). Although it was within easy reach and sight of the great caravan roads, the surrounding hills kept Nazareth protected and secluded from the commercial and military traffic below. There was no better place in Galilee for the Messiah to be a Watcher and yet remain hidden in the silent years before His ministry.

When we shall know that Yeshua the Son of Man is Understanding, we shall understand why He was humble and meek (St. Matthew 11:29; see pp. 68–70), and why He loved to remain hidden:

'For the nature of understanding is to be very deep, not superficial, it does not display itself openly but loves to hide itself in secrecy; it is discovered not easily but with difficulty and much labor' —Philo, *Som.* I. 6.

'Where is the place of understanding [BINAH]? Seeing that it is hidden [ALAM] from the eyes of all living, and kept hidden [SATHAR] from the birds of the heavens' —Job 28:20,21.

'There is no searching of His great understanding [TEBUNAH]', for it is hidden from us —Isaiah 40:28.

'Good insight shall hide itself, and Understanding shall withdraw himself into his secret chamber, and shall be sought by many, and yet not be found' —2 Esdras 5:9,10.

'Where has the multitude of understanding hidden itself?' —2 Baruch 48:36.

'The understanding [BINAH] of their men of understanding shall be hidden [SATHAR]' —Isaiah 29:14.

'Be unobtrusively modest [TSANA] in understanding [SAKAL]' — Sirach 32:3, Hebrew Text.

'He will hide his words until his time, and the lips of many shall declare his understanding [SUNESIS]' —Sirach 1:24.

And so it was that Yeshua 'hid Himself . . . and departed and did hide Himself from them' (St. John 8:59; 12:36), and would 'secretly withdraw Himself into the wilderness' (St. Luke 5:16; St. Matthew 8:18). And when they sought to make Him known before His time, 'He strictly charged His disciples that they should tell no man that He was Yeshua the Messiah' (St. Matthew 16:20; see also St. Matthew 9:30; 12:16; 17:9; St. Mark 1:43–45; 3:12; 5:43; 7:36; 8:30; 9:9; St Luke 5:14; 8:56). For although in Him 'are hidden all the treasures of wisdom and knowledge' (Colossians 2:2,3), they are held in the receptacle of His infinite yet unassuming understanding awaiting the day that we would recognize it to His exaltation.

A son of Man who truly understands knows that understanding is a gift from God: 'How can I understand unless You give me understanding?' (1QH 12:33, Dead Sea Scrolls). 'O Lord . . . give me understanding' (Psalm 119:33,34,73,125,130,144,169). Having received it, a son of Man knows that this great gift from God is formed as a vessel for him: 'by what means can I obtain understanding unless You form it (as a vessel) for me?' (1QH

10:6, Dead Sea Scrolls). By means of this wonderful vessel one is able to enclose and comprehend God's wisdom and knowledge, nevertheless, by itself the understanding is an empty vessel. What is the vessel of our understanding (see Philo, *Mig.* 193; *Deus* 42; *Q. Gen.* IV. 98; 2 Baruch 44:14; Sibylline Oracles III. 562; Corpus Hermeticum, *Lib.* IV. 4) compared to that of the Messiah? A greater thing than all the wisdom of Solomon is the understanding of the Son of Man (St. Matthew 12:42; St. Luke 11:31), which encompasses and contains all wisdom and knowledge. The understanding is not only likened to a vessel but also to a vigilant watchman standing and surveying all that is meant to be understood:

'The understanding . . . is not quiescent, but unsleeping' —Philo, *Abr.* 162; *Mig.* 222.

The unsleeping eyes of the understanding —Philo, *Spec.* I. 49.

'Be . . . understanding and vigilant' —Odes of Solomon 3:11.

'Thoroughly awaken your pure understanding' —2 Peter 3:1.

'Applying much watchfulness [AGRUPNIAN] and understanding [EPISTĒMĒN]' —Prologue to Sirach.

'Watchfulness [GRĒGORĒSIS] and understanding [SUNESIS] were found in him' —Daniel 5:11,14, Greek Text.

'Who is wise and will watch [SHAMAR] over these things? They will understand [BIN]' —Psalm 107:43.

'Those who understand it shall not sleep' —Enoch 82:3.

'They shall greatly understand [TEBUNAH] as the Watchers [i.e., angels] His works' —4Q Mess. II. 16 (Messianic Text Fragments, Dead Sea Scrolls).

'That this vermin that is man may be raised from the dust to Your secret of Truth, and from the spirits of perversity to Your understanding [BINAH], that he may stand up [AMAD] before You with the everlasting [angelic] host' [who watch and understand] —1QH 11:12,13, Dead Sea Scrolls.

'O Job, stand up [AMAD] and understand [BIN] the wonders of God' —Job 37:14.

'I stand up [AMAD] and You understand [BIN] me' —Job 30:20.

'Let the counsel of your own heart *stand up* [*STĒSON*], for there is no man more faithful to you than it' —Sirach 37:13, Greek Text.

'*Understand* [BIN] the counsel of your own heart for who is more faithful to you than it? A man's heart [i.e., his understanding; see pp. 45–46] sets before him [the counsel of] opportune action more than seven *watchmen* on a *watchtower*' —Sirach 37:13–14, Hebrew Text.

'The words of the Torah stand up [i.e., they let themselves be understood] for him who valorously gives them the labor they require to be understood' —Pesikta de Rab Kahana, Piska 12.5.

'O You *watcher* [*NATSAR*] of man' —Job 7:20, Hebrew Text.

'O You who *understand* [EPISTAMENOS] the understanding [NOUN] of man' —Job 7:20, Greek Text.

'Get *understanding* [BINAH] . . . do not forsake her and she will preserve you, love her and she will *watch* [NATSAR] over you' — Proverbs 4:5,6.

'Great *understanding* [TEBUNAH] will *watch* [NATSAR] over you' —Proverbs 2:11.

Should not Yeshua the Messiah who understands all things have lived in Nazareth, the city of the Watcher? And if a son of Man was to be a watcher: 'Son of Man, I have made you a watchman for the house of Israel' (Ezekiel 3:17; 33:7), shall not the Son of Man be the greatest Watcher of them all? For even as a young man from Nazareth, all the teachers 'who heard Him were astonished at His understanding' —St. Luke 2:47.

Chapter 15

Yeshua The Carpenter

We are 'God's cultivated field . . . and God's building' (1 Corinthians 3:9), for He sows His words in the ground of our hearts, and He resides in the temple of our souls if we are good (1 Corinthians 3:16–17; 6:19; 2 Corinthians 6:16; Leviticus 26:12). The Lord God related with Adam (Man) as a Gardener and a Husbandman; and with Noah (son of Man) as a Builder (Genesis 6:14–16). For God is indeed a divine Carpenter, and 'the sons of Man . . . built' (Genesis 11:5).

We know that the tribe of Judah was noted for its men of understanding (p. 105). Thus, it was to Bezaleel of the tribe of Judah and great-grandson of Caleb (1 Chronicles 2:19–20), that the building of the Sanctuary and all its furniture was delegated, because for that purpose the Lord had 'filled Bezaleel with the Spirit of God in wisdom, and in great understanding [TEBUNAH], and in knowledge and in all manner of workmanship' (Exodus 31:3; 35:31). The Lord also provided men of understanding to help Bezaleel in the carpentry of constructing the wooden 'tabernacle of the congregation, and the ark of the testimony, and the mercy seat that was upon it, and all the implememts of the tabernacle, and the table and its implements' (Exodus 31:7,8). For that reason the Lord told Moses: 'to every one understanding in heart I have given understanding, and they shall make . . . the tabernacle of witness, and the ark of the covenant, and the propitiatory that is upon it, and the furniture of the tabernacle, and the altars, and the table and all its furniture' (Exodus 31:6,7,8, Greek Text). Furthermore, it takes understanding to build a house for the Lord: 'Blessed be the Lord God of Israel who made heaven and earth, who has given David the king a wise son (Solomon), knowing in understanding [SAKAL] and insight [BINAH], so that he might (be able to) build a temple (literally 'house') for the Lord, and a royal palace (literally 'house') for his kingdom' (2 Chronicles 2:12). Truly, like a carpenter 'the pure understanding [NOUS] . . . builds a house [OIKODOMEI]' –Testament of Benjamin 8:3, Literal Translation. For 'if Understanding [PHRONESIS] works who is a greater artisan?' (Wisdom 8:6). Thus, the sons of Man 'built all sorts of houses . . . with understanding' (Sibylline Oracles I. 67–69). Let us not forget that 'as a man's understanding [SAKAL] so is his skill [TECHNĒ]' –

Testament of Naphtali 2:6, A Text. Nazareth, where the Messiah worked as a carpenter, was in the land of Zebulon the son of Jacob who said: 'I was the first to make a boat to sail upon the sea for the Lord gave me understanding [SUNESIN] in that' (work of carpentry) –Testament of Zebulon 6:1. Thus, the Lord Messiah lived in that district of land belonging to a skilled carpenter and seaman: Zebulon.

There are two 'fathers' or progenitors (pp. 14–15) of the human race: Adam (Man), and Noah (son of Man). The knowledge is ancient that our present generation stems forth from Noah, the 'father' of the sons of Man:

> Noah, after the destruction (of mankind) by the flood becomes the first beginning of the human race, with mankind again being propagated –Philo, *Q. Gen.* II. 17.

> Noah . . . the seed and spark of the new generation of men that was to be. And what favor is greater than that this same one [Noah] should be both the end and the beginning of mankind? – Philo, *Q. Gen.* I. 96.

> He, [God] considers Noah, who became, as it were, the beginning of a second genesis of man, of equal honor with him [Adam] who was first made in His image –Philo, *Q. Gen.* II. 56.

> Noah . . . the man called righteous and dear to God was preserved. Thus, he received two gifts of the highest kind—one that he did not perish with the rest, the other that he should be in his turn the founder of a new race of men –Philo, *Abr.* 46; 56.

> Noah's children 'became leaders of the regeneration . . . spared as embers to rekindle mankind' –Philo, *Mos.* II. 65.

Noah was the greatest carpenter the world has ever known, for he built the huge ark with all its compartments. Thus, Man (Adam) was a gardener and husbandman, but Noah (son of Man) was a builder. Yeshua the Messiah belongs to the generation of Noah. It was only fitting that He should have been a carpenter like His great ancestor Noah, the 'father' of the sons of Man. Moreover, rabbinic tradition commenting on Zechariah 1:20 (2:3 Hebrew Text), identified one of the 'four carpenters [CHARASHIM]' there as being the Messiah who was expected to rebuild the Temple (Sukkah 52b, Babylonian Talmud; Midrash Numbers Rabbah 14.1; Midrash Song of Songs Rabbah II. 13.4; Tanna debe Eliyyahu Rabbah 96). From Adam we received the knowledge of making bread (Genesis

3:19; see pp. 8–9), and from Noah the art of making wine (Genesis 9:20–21; Midrash Genesis Rabbah 36.3). Was it not right that the first miracle of the Carpenter-Messiah was to turn water into wine? (St. John 2:1–11).

Some training is required before anyone can build, but only an 'understanding man' (St. Matthew 7:24, Literal Translation) is able to build firmly and well. A good carpenter is called a 'joiner' because he can bring things together to make a perfect whole, but that takes understanding. For to understand is to be able to bring things together in such a way that the inward meaning is revealed as a result of their junction in a perfect fitting, much like the work of a master carpenter or joiner. The common Greek word for 'understanding': SUNESIS literally means 'to join together' or 'to unite'. Thus, Homer in his *Odyssey* (10.515) writes about 'the confluence [SUNESIS]' of two rivers. Understanding is like striking two flints together to produce the spark that enlightens. 'A text [of Holy Scripture] which is not fully explained in its own place is illuminated by another text' said Rabbi Eliezer ben Yose ha Gelili (Midrash Sheloshim uShetayim Middot). The rabbis knew that 'an understandng man is he who can deduce one thing from another' (Midrash in Libnath Hasappir). 'By stringing together proverb to proverb King Solomon drew out the secrets of the Torah' (Midrash Song of Songs Rabbah I. 1. Sect. 8). Like a joiner, Rabbi Simeon ben Azzai (c. A.D. 120) did the same with his understanding for 'he linked together the words of the Torah with those of the prophets and those of the prophets with those of the hagiographers, and therefore the words of the Torah rejoiced as on the day they were revealed in the flames of Sinai' (Midrash Song of Songs Rabbah I. 10.2; Midrash Leviticus Rabbah 16.2).

Knowing the necessity of understanding before being able to join texts together to clarify things, the rabbis had great respect for master carpenters because they were the artisans who were excellent joiners. If a difficult problem arose in their discussions they would ask: 'Is there a master carpenter [CHARASH] among us, or the son of a master carpenter who can solve the problem for us?' (Abodah Zarah 50b, Babylonian Talmud; see also Qiddushin I. 66a, Jerusalem Talmud). Consequently, the Hebrew word CHARASH ('master carpenter') and the Aramaic word for 'craftsman' [NAGGAR] became also the word for someone who really understood and could resolve mysterious things. A LIKKUD or TALMID was an ordinary 'scholar' but an exceptional scholar who could elucidate on puzzling problems was a CHARASH (literally 'carpenter'; TEKTON in Greek). Thus, 'an (enigmatic) expression which a master carpenter, or son of a master carpenter cannot justify' (Yebamot VIII. 9b, Jerusalem Talmud) was indeed a cryptic utterance! So great was the understanding of these 'carpenters [CHARASHIM]' that when they expounded or opened argument, all who heard them were dumbfounded (Gittin 88a; Sanhedrin 38a; Ḥagigah 14a, Babylonian Talmud; Yalkut to Daniel 1066). And so were all those who heard Yeshua, the Carpenter from Nazareth (St. Luke 2:47; 4:22; 13:10–17; 14:1–6; 20:20–40; St. Mark 2:18–22; 7:1–23; 11:27–33; St. Matthew 12:1–8,22–30; 21:23–27; 22:41–46), so that 'they did not dare to ask Him any more questions' (St. Mark 12:34; St. Luke 20:40). 'All bore witness to Him and marvelled at the gracious words that proceeded from His mouth' (St. Luke 4:22).

In the Hebrew language there is a relationship between the word for 'son [BEN]' and the word for 'to build [BANAH]', just as there is a relationship between the Hebrew word for 'daughter [BATH]' and the word for 'house [BAYITH, BETH]'. In the Mishnah and Talmud 'house' is a metaphor for 'wife' (Mishnah, Yoma 1.1; Shabbath 118b; Yoma 13c; Yebamoth 44a, Babylonian Talmud), and also for 'woman'. Perhaps, this is why the Lord God is said in Holy Scripture to have 'formed [YATSAR] Man from the [moistened] dust of the ground' (Genesis 2:7), but to have *'built'* Woman:

> From the rib which the Lord God had taken from man, He *built* [BANAH] a woman, and brought her to man — Genesis 2:22.

Among His people, women were considered 'houses' when they were with child or had brought forth children, but not when they were barren or had not yet conceived, for it was the child in them who built them up to be 'houses'.

When God rewarded the good midwives who did not kill the male children of the Jews, it is said that because the midwives reverenced God, 'He made them houses' (Exodus 1:21, Literal Translation), which means to say He blessed them with motherhood, and gave them children. In those days when a woman was sterile, the only way she had hope of being built up into a 'house' by a child, was through persuading her husband to have marital relations with her own slave girl or maid. The child born from that union would then be legally considered to be the child of the sterile mistress who would be able to say that she herself had been built up into a 'house' by the child of her slave. Thus, 'when Rachel saw that she bore Jacob no children, Rachel envied her sister, and said to Jacob, 'Give me sons, or else I die! . . . here is my maid Bilhah, go in to her, and she will bear a child on my knees, that I also may be built [BANAH] up from her.'

Then she gave him Bilhah her maid as wife, and Jacob went in to her, and Bilhah conceived and bore Jacob a son. Then Rachel said, 'God has judged my case and He has also heard my voice and given *me* a son.' Therefore she called his name Dan ('judge')' —Genesis 30:1,3–6; see also Genesis 30:9–13; 16:1–4. Thus the expression 'I shall be built up' means 'I shall have a son' because sons are the ones who are the 'builders', and who are supposed to understand (see pp. 13–14, 21–23, 46–47, 66–67, 81–83). A good son [BEN] can build [BANAH] well, because he understands [BIN] and has the insight [BINAH] to do so. The Son of Man was not only an understanding Carpenter but He was also the understanding Shepherd who watched in Nazareth over His people Israel, for the Messiah was a descendant of two kings noted for their understanding: the shepherd-King David and the builder-King Solomon.

Along with carpenters, shepherds were also noted for their understanding even from the time of the patriarch Abraham:

> A shepherd who understands —Sumerian Hymn no. 23, l. 10 in *Sumerische Konigshymnen.* Edited by W. P. Roemer, 1965.

> 'I will give you shepherds after My own heart who will feed you with knowledge and understanding' —Jeremiah 3:15.

> 'He also chose David His servant and took him from the sheepfolds; from the tending of the ewes with suckling lambs, He brought him to shepherd Jacob His people, and Israel His inheritance. So he fed them according to the integrity of his heart and guided them by the great understanding [TEBUNAH] of his hands' —Psalm 78:70–72.

> 'David, the [shepherd] son of Jesse was wise, and a light like the light of the sun, and literate and understanding and perfect in all his ways before God and men. And the Lord gave him an understanding [BINAH] and enlightened spirit' —11Q Ps^a col. xxvii.2–4 (Psalm 151) Dead Sea Scrolls.

> 'I am the good Shepherd' —St. John 10:11,14; St. Matthew 25:32; 26:31; Hebrews 13:20.

> 'All who heard Him were astonished at His understanding' —St. Luke 2:47; see pp. 82–83.

Thus, when His shepherds are rebuked they are censured for their unwatchfulness and their lack of understanding:

'His *watchmen* are blind, they know nothing, they are all dumb dogs unable to bark, sleeping lying down, loving to slumber. They are *shepherds* who cannot understand [BIN]' —Isaiah 56:10–11; see also Jeremiah 10:21.

Truly, it is the sons who do the carpentering. We know that the Lord gave King David all the plans for building the Temple, giving him also the necessary 'understanding [SAKAL]' to figure them out (1 Chronicles 28:11–19). But it was King David's 'wise *son* (Solomon) knowing in understanding [SAKAL] and insight' (2 Chronicles 2:12) who built the Temple of the Lord, helped by 'a wise [HAKAM] man knowing in understanding . . . the *son* of a woman of the daughters of Dan' (2 Chronicles 2:13,14) who because of his great understanding was able 'to figure out every device that was given to him' (v. 14) by the wise men of King David and King Solomon. It was also another son 'called by name Bezaleel, the *son* of Uri, the son of Hur of the tribe of Judah' (Exodus 31:2) who helped Moses build the Tabernacle with all its furnishings. After the destruction of the first Temple, it was 'the *sons* [BENIM] of the captivity who built the (second) Temple' (Ezra 4:1). And it is also said that in the future 'the *sons* [BENIM] of strangers shall build up' (Isaiah 60:10) the walls of the new Jerusalem. We should not forget that the first one who 'built a city' (Genesis 4:17) was Cain, a *son* of Man (Adam). And there was a time when 'the Lord came down to see the city and the tower which the *sons* [BENIM] of Man built' (Genesis 11:5) who were skilled in carpentering and bricklaying before they lost their understanding. Yeshua the Messiah is the Rock of our foundation for we are 'built up in Him' (Colossians 2:7; 1 Corinthians 3:9,11). But as 'Son' He is also our Builder (St. Matthew 16:18) for 'we are His house' and the 'Messiah is faithful as a *Son* over His *house,* whose house we are' (Hebrews 3:6). Good sons of Man not only build cities and houses but as 'sons' they also build up the 'house' of their mothers, and the glory of their fathers. The Son of man who became a Carpenter was fittingly born in a little town called the 'House of bread' (Bethlehem). For He is Himself our House and the Temple of God (St. John 15:5–7; 1 John 2:28; St. John 2:19–21), and also our Bread of Life and Understanding (St. John 6:35,48; Sirach 15:3; see pp. 82–83). Furthermore, in giving birth to Him, His mother Maryam may be truly said to be herself: the House of Bread.

Chapter 16

Galilee

When the Holy Land was divided by lot among the twelve tribes, the tribes of Zebulon, Issachar, Asher and Naphtali received as their portion the northern part of the land which was later on called Galilee. The Lord's Messiah dwelt in Nazareth which was in the portion of Zebulon whose name means 'Dwelling' (Genesis 30:20) in Hebrew. The prophet Jonah belonged to the tribe of Zebulon (Joshua 19:13; 2 Kings 14:25). The men of Zebulon were noted for their self-sacrificing courage (Judges 5:18; 1 Chronicles 12:33; Jonah 1:11–12), and it was the tribe of Zebulon along with the northern tribes of Naphtali and Issachar who came to the aid of King David bringing with them 'bread [LEHEM] on donkeys and camels, on mules and oxen, victuals, flour, cakes of figs, bunches of raisins, wine and oil and oxen and sheep abundantly' (1 Chronicles 12:40), and there was joy in Israel at their bounty. Zebulon, Naphtali, Asher and Issachar were considered to be humble tribes (Baba Kamma 92a, Babylonian Talmud; Midrash Genesis Rabbah 95.4; Targum Jerusalem on Genesis 47:2; 49:14–15). It was well known that the Lord dwelt in the land of Benjamin 'the beloved of the Lord' (Deuteronomy 33:12) because the Ark of the Covenant rested, and the Holy of Holies stood in the territory of the tribe of Benjamin (Midrash Genesis Rabbah 93.6,8; 99.1,3; Midrash Numbers Rabbah 2.10; Midrash Tehilim 68.14; Aboth Rabbi Nathan 35.3–4; 43.121; Sifre to Deuteronomy 352; Megillah I. 72 d, Jerusalem Talmud; T. Shebiith 7,10; Pesikta Rabbati, Piska 46.3; Midrash Tannaim 216–217; Midrash in Sechel Tob, *ad loc*; Zohar I. 247b). But there was also an old tradition that the divine Presence [SHEKINAH] would dwell in the midst of the tribe of Zebulon (Midrash Exodus Rabbah I.5), the land where the Messiah Yeshua lived for most of His life on this earth.

In the land of Israel, Galilee was the North, a region considered by those in Judea and Jerusalem to be way up and far away:

> 'The day will come when a word of Scripture will be sought here [in Judea] and not be found, when people will run back and forth from city to city for an explanation of a commandment and not find it. They will have to ride all the way up to Galilee with

regard to getting an answer' —Pirke Derek Eretz 14; Tanna debe Eliyyahu Zutta S, p. 14.

The North where the heavens are said to be (Job 26:7), is the place where God dwells (Ezekiel 1:4–5,28; Isaiah 14:13–14; Job 37:22; Psalm 48:2–3; Enoch 25:3), and where He works (Job 23:9). Thus, the sacrificial victims which were offered to God were slaughtered on the north side of the altar (Leviticus 1:11), and the constant North Star (Polaris) was a symbol of God (St. James 1:17). Even among the Sumerians and Babylonians, Enlil-Anu, the father of all the gods was enthroned in the North. Among the Jewish rabbis the North is the place of darkness (Midrash Numbers Rabbah 2.10; 3.12; Pirke Rabbi Eliezer III [2B ii]), and the place where God dwells because He has His habitation in the darkness (1 Kings 8:12; Job 22:13; Midrash Numbers Rabbah 33.4; Midrash Exodus Rabbah 20.8).

Zebulon, Naphtali, Issachar, and Asher were the northern tribes of Israel just as Judah and Simeon were the southern tribes. Being that it is 'from the North that darkness goes forth into the world' (Midrash Numbers Rabbah 2.10), it was the northern tribes of Galilee who were particularly in the shadow of darkness and were in most need of the Light of the Lord:

> 'They shall look on the earth below, and behold severe distress, and darkness, affliction, and anguish, and darkness so that no one can see. And he that is in anguish shall not be distressed but for a time. Drink this (cup of consolation) first, and do it [i.e., drink it] quickly O country of *Zebulon,* land of *Naphtali,* by way of the sea, and the rest who dwell by the sea-coast, and across the Jordan, *Galilee* of the Nations. O people who walk in the darkness, behold a great light! You who dwell in the land and in the shadow of death, a light shall shine upon you' —Isaiah 8:22–9:1–2, Greek Text.

Yeshua, 'the Light of the world' (St. John 8:12; 9:5; 12:46), lived for thirty years in Nazareth of Zebulon. And from there, as prophesied by Isaiah, He enlightened first the children of Zebulon and Naphtali who sat in the darkness (St. Matthew 4:13–17). The rabbis knew that 'the light of the Messiah' (Midrash Genesis Rabbah 85.1; Midrash Tehillim 21,179; Pesikta Rabbati [Friedmann] fol. 161a; Sanhedrin 99a, Babylonian Talmud) was going to enlighten those in the darkness: 'My true Messiah . . . will give light to the eyes of Israel' (Pesikta Rabbati, Piska 36.1).

The rabbis also knew that the Messiah would come from the North [i.e.,

Galilee], and to the Messiah they applied Isaiah 41:25: 'I have roused one up from the North, and he shall come from the rising of the sun (i.e., from the tribe of Judah whose place was in the East, see pp. 92–95) and he shall call upon My name.' They interpreted this to mean that 'when King Messiah who abides in the North will awaken, he will come and build the Temple' (Midrash Numbers Rabbah 13.2). They also said:

> 'The Messiah will appear in the land of Galilee' —Zohar I. *Bereshith,* 119a.

> 'The Messiah . . . will arise in the land of Galilee . . . the Messiah shall reveal himself in the land of Galilee because in this part of the Holy Land the desolation [Babylonian exiles] first began, therefore he will manifest himself there first' —Zohar III, *Shemoth* 7b, 8b, 220a; *Otzar Midrashim,* 466.

Some said that the Messiah would first manifest himself in the valley of Arbel in Galilee (Berakoth I.1; II.4; Yoma III.2, Jerusalem Talmud; Midrash Esther Rabbah 10.14; Midrash Song of Songs Rabbah 6.10). Others said that He would first appear in Ruma, another Galilean town (Targum Jerusalem on Exodus 12:42; Gittin 6, Jerusalem Talmud; Sanhedrin 98a, Babylonian Talmud). But they all agreed that it would be somewhere in Galilee that the Messiah would first manifest Himself and gather the peoples to lead them to Jerusalem (Mishnah, Sotah 9.15; Midrash Lekah Tob, *Balak* p. 258; *Beth haMidrash* [Jellinek] II: *Sepher Zerubbabel* p. 55; *Beth haMidrash* IV. p. 122; Maimonides, *Hilkhot Sanhedrin* 4.12; Saadia Gaon, *haEmunoth vaHadeot,* chapter 8; Sepher ha-Hezyonot p. 41; Ibid., [Shivhei] pp. 2b–3a; Rosh Hashanah 31b, Babylonian Talmud).

When we shall understand more about the South, we shall have good reason to know why Yeshua, the Son of Man lived and manifested Himself in the *northern* part of the Holy Land. For the people of the *southern* part were noted for their *wisdom*. We hear of the wisdom of King David (2 Samuel 14:20) of the southern tribe of Judah, and of 'the wisdom of King Solomon' (St. Matthew 12:42) his son, who 'was wiser than all men' (1 Kings 4:31). Wisdom was also found in the princes of Judah (Daniel 1:17,20; 1 Esdras 4:13,42), and in 'the wise men of the Negev' (Tamid 31b–32a, Babylonian Talmud), and in the wise men of Jabne (Rosh Hashanah 31a, Babylonian Talmud; Midrash Song of Songs Rabbah 8.9). Tekoah, a town in Judah, had not only 'a wise woman' (2 Samuel 14:2) but wise people as well (Menachoth 85b; Baba Bathra 145b; Pesachim 53a,

Babylonian Talmud). And we should not forget about the wise men of the southern tribe of Simeon (see p. 100). Further on south we hear about 'the wise men of Edom' (Obadiah vv. 8–9), and of Teman (Jeremiah 49:7) which in Hebrew also means 'South' [TEMAN, as in Exodus 26:18,35; Numbers 2:10; Deuteronomy 3:27; Job 9:9; 39:26; Psalm 78:26; Song of Songs 4:16; Isaiah 43:6, etc.]. South of Edom and Teman was the land of Egypt which was noted for 'the wisdom of the Egyptians' (Acts 7:22; Isaiah 19:11; Josephus, *Antiq.* I. 8.1; Zohar I. 81b) for in those days everyone heard about 'all the wisdom of Egypt' (1 Kings 4:30; Acts 7:22; Midrash Numbers Rabbah 19.3; Midrash Ecclesiastes Rabbah 7.23.1; Midrash Mishlei 27.101; Philo, *Mos.* I. 5–7). Even further down south from the wise Egyptians, was the land of 'the queen of Sheba' (1 Kings 10:1; 2 Chronicles 9:1) whom Yeshua the Messiah referred to as 'the queen of the South', saying that 'she came from the ends of the earth to hear the wisdom of Solomon' (St. Matthew 12:42). She must have been wise herself, for we are told that 'she came to test him (King Solomon) with riddles [CHIDDAH]': 'the riddles [CHIDDAH] . . . of the wise' (1 Kings 10:1; Proverbs 1:6). Was she not 'the queen of the South' where wisdom is found? In explaining why the seven-branched lamp (the Menorah) was placed on the south side of the Tabernacle, the ancient Palestinian Targum to Exodus 40:11 says that it was because 'on the south side . . . are the treasures of wisdom which resembles the light' (of the candelabrum). So proverbial was the wisdom of those who lived in the South that the rabbis said: 'he who desires to be wise should turn to the South' (Midrash Genesis Rabbah 16.4; Baba Bathra 158b, Babylonian Talmud).

If wisdom was to be found in the South, was it not proper that the Son of Man who understands all things should have lived in the North? For although Wisdom and Understanding long to meet, they are opposite and distinct (see pp. 77–83). If one were to be found in the South, the other one would be discovered in the North—heading—South:

'Is it by your understanding [BINAH] that the hawk flies, and spreads his wings toward the south [TEMAN]' to find wisdom? — Job 39:26.

Or 'is there no longer any wisdom in Teman?' —Jeremiah 49:7.

Chapter 17

Yeshua, The Hidden Messiah

'Truly, You are God who hide Yourself,
O God of Israel, the Saviour' —Isaiah 45:15

There was no better place for the Messiah to live a hidden life than to be up north in Galilee. The very word for 'North [TSAPHON]' in Hebrew is derived from the word TSAPHAN: to be 'hidden' and 'to hide'. 'King Messiah who abides in the north' (Midrash Leviticus Rabbah 9.6; Midrash Numbers Rabbah 13.2; Midrash Song of Songs Rabbah 4.16), lives there in concealment before his manifestation. His people knew that the Messiah would remain mysteriously hidden before he would be revealed. They also knew that it would require God's wisdom to reveal him to them when the time came for His glorious manifestation:

'King Messiah, David's Son . . . will remain hidden until the appointed time has come' —Midrash to Psalms 21.1.

'The Messiah who has been kept hidden all these years' —Pesikta Rabbati, Piska 34.2.

'This is the Messiah, whom the Most High has kept [hidden] for them' —2 Esdras 12:32; see also 2 Esdras 13:25,26,52; 14:9; Enoch 46:1–3.

'For this reason [see vv. 4–5] has he [the Messiah] been chosen and hidden before Him [God] . . . and the wisdom of the Lord of Spirits has revealed him [the Messiah] to the holy and righteous' —Enoch 48:6,7; 62:7.

There are many rabbinic references to the hiddenness of the Messiah before his revelation (Targum Jonathan re Jeremiah 30:21; Micah 4:8; Zechariah 3:8; Midrash Numbers Rabbah 11.2; Midrash Ruth Rabbah 5.6; Midrash Song of Songs Rabbah 2.9.3; Pesikta R. Kahana, Piska 5.8; Pesikta Rabbati, Piska 15.10,14; Yalkut Shimoni 518, 581, 986; Sukkah 52b, Babylonian Talmud; *Beth haMidrash* [Jellinek] vol. III. 80; V. 189–190; Zohar II. 7b, 8a, 172b; *Otzar Midrashim,* 555–557. etc.; see also 2 Baruch

29:3; 39:7; 3 Enoch 48:10A; Sanhedrin 97a–97b, Babylonian Talmud re Isaiah 49:1–7). It may well be that men will see the Messiah before he is acknowledged; but they will not see him as he really is, until he is revealed (Rabbi Tarphon in Justin's *Dialogue with Trypho*, chapters 8 and 10).

We have seen (pp. 107–108, 65–71) how Understanding hides before its exaltation, and wears the garments of humility and meekness before it is clothed in glory. It may live in poverty, suffer and be despised but in the end the Lord enthrones Understanding by His side. Joseph, the righteous son of Jacob languished in jail despised and forgotten until the time came for his understanding to be revealed before Pharaoh who then exalted him and made him ruler over all Egypt (Genesis 40–41). Daniel, one of 'the captives of Judah' (Daniel 2:25) exiled in Babylon, lived a hidden life until he was also exalted and made 'ruler over the whole province of Babylon' (Daniel 2:48) when his wisdom and understanding were made manifest before the King (Daniel chap. 2; see also 1 Esdras 3–4). The Servant, in the book of Isaiah, who is exalted by his understanding (Isaiah 52:13,15) is before his exaltation a despised and suffering Servant (Isaiah 52:14; see also Isaiah 53:11–12, 1–10). The chosen Servant hidden in the shadow of God's hand and in His quiver (Isaiah 49:2) is also despised and abhorred (Isaiah 49:7) yet He is nevertheless 'a light to the Gentiles' (Isaiah 49:6) and the liberator of those imprisoned by the darkness (Isaiah 49:9; St. Luke 2:30–32; 1:78–79).

A seed is hidden when it is sown, but it does not remain concealed because the ground that holds it fast causes it to open so that it may sprout forth the plant that shall be seen by all. Yeshua the Messiah is the Word of God (St. John 1:1–3,14) given to us as a Seed (St. Luke 8:11): a Grain of wheat (St. John 12:24) that was to become our Bread of life (St. John 6:35,48; 1 Corinthians 10:16; 11:23–24). He is also the Sower (St. Matthew 13:37) who sows Himself (St. John 8:5,11; St. Mark 4:14) in us, for we are the ground of His field. The seed has a humble beginning but it brings forth fruit in the golden ear of grain in the end. Sorrow and uncertainty accompany the sowing, nevertheless, there is great joy at harvest time (Psalm 126:5–6; Isaiah 9:3). The same humble Son of Man who sows in the beginning becomes the *crowned* Lord of the harvest ready to reap at last (Revelation 14:14–16).

Shall there be bread without the stage of the hidden seed and the hidden leaven? And shall the crowned Harvestman be sent before the humble Sower? God in His wonderful wisdom does all things exceedingly well. His people expected an immediate reaping by an all-conquering Messiah who would set things right for them through swift retributive judgment against the wicked and the enemies of their nation. Thus, St. John the Baptist preached that the Lord's ax was laid to the root of the fruitless trees in readiness for their cutting, and that the winnowing fan was in the hand of Him who was prepared to thoroughly purge His threshing floor and burn all the chaff (St. Matthew 3:10,12). But the Lord is good, He calls to repentance before He condemns, and He redeems before He judges. 'The Lamb of God' (St. John 1:29, 36) who was slain for our good (Revelation 5:6,8–9; 12:10–11; 1 Peter 1:19; Isaiah 53:7–8), is the same 'Lamb' who is glorified and enthroned in the end as the all-conquering 'Lord of lords and King of kings' (Revelation 17:14; 22:1–3).

The prophets knew that the founders of the two royal houses of Israel: King Saul of the royal house of Benjamin, and King David of the royal house of Judah were both in lowly occupations at the very commencement of their kingship. One was sent with a servant to look for the lost donkeys of his father (1 Samuel 9:2–3), and the other was tending his father's sheep (1 Samuel 16:10–13; Psalm 78:70–72) just before they were anointed kings. And both were humble of heart in the beginning of their reign, for Saul said to Samuel: 'Am I not a Benjamite of the smallest of the tribes of Israel? and my family the least of all the families of the tribe of Benjamin? Why then do you speak like this to me?' (1 Samuel 9:21). And did he not hide himself from the people when they sought to make him king? (1 Samuel 10:21–24). In the supernumerary Psalm found in the ancient Septuagint (Greek) version of the Bible, King David also says:

> 'I was small among my brothers, and youngest in my father's house. I tended my father's sheep . . . He sent forth His minister [Samuel], and took me from my father's sheep, and he anointed me with the oil of His anointing. My brothers were handsome and tall, but the Lord did not take pleasure in them.' —Psalm 150 (151):1,4–5; see also 2 Samuel 6:21–22.

And although he was the Lord's anointed one, did he not humbly return to tending his father's sheep, and carrying provisions to the place where his brothers were encamped? (1 Samuel 17:15,17–18). David's son, King Solomon of great fame and glory, shortly after he became king and was married, also humbled himself before the Lord and said to Him: 'O Lord my God, You have made Your servant king in place of David my father, although I am but a little child, I do not know how to go out or come in' (1 Kings 3:7). Thus, through the prophet Zechariah, the Lord promised to send King Messiah to His people not as a proud all-conquering hero riding on a white charger, but as someone righteous and humble riding upon an ass, and bringing salvation and peace to the ends of the earth:

> 'Rejoice greatly, O daughter of Zion! Shout, O daughter of Jerusalem! Behold, your king is coming to you, he is righteous and bringing salvation, humble and riding on an ass: a colt the foal of an ass . . . he shall speak peace to the nations; his dominion shall be from sea to sea, and from the River to the ends of the earth' —Zechariah 9:9,10.

Such was the extent of this promised King's sovereignity that the rabbis overwhelmingly acknowledged that he was no one else but the Messiah (Sanhedrin 98a, 99a; Berakoth 56b, Babylonian Talmud; Midrash Genesis Rabbah 75.11,6; 98.9; 99.9; Midrash Ecclesiastes Rabbah I.9; Midrash Song of Songs Rabbah I.4.2; Pesikta Rabbati 34.1–2; Pesikta Rab Kahana 22.3; Pirke Rabbi Eliezer 31; Midrash on Psalms 60.3; Tanchumah on Genesis 32:5; Sekel Tob on Genesis 32:5; Yalkut Shimoni, folios 130, 575; Midrash Haggadol on Genesis 32:6; 41:1; 49:10; Zohar I. 238a; III. 238a, 275b, 278b). As the great rabbi Rashi (Solomon ben Isaac) said concerning this verse (Zechariah 9:9): 'It cannot be explained any other way but referring to the Messiah'.

This righteous and humble King Messiah riding upon an ass was to bring salvation and peace to His people, not by force of arms (see v.10), but through the knowledge of God, a knowledge acquired through obedience to His will and the perfect keeping of His commandments (see pp. 5–7, 13, 24, 27). There is salvation in the knowledge of God, and there is also peace. Knowledge brings deliverance: 'Through knowledge shall the righteous ones be delivered' (Proverbs 11:9; 2 Peter 2:20; Ephesians 4:13–14), because with knowledge we can know what is good, and what is evil, so that we may depart from evil and choose the good so that we may live (Deuteronomy 30:15–19). Thus, 'the excellency of the knowledge of wisdom is that it will give life to him who has it' (Ecclesiastes 7:13–14, Greek Text). Where there is no knowledge there is no deliverance; that is why the Lord said: 'My people are destroyed for lack of knowledge' (Hosea 4:6); 'My people have gone into captivity because they have no knowledge, their honorable men are famished, and their multitude dried up with thirst' (Isaiah 5:13). For 'they (the wicked) have stopped the thirsty from drinking the liquor of knowledge, and when they were thirsty they made them drink vinegar so that their straying might be gazed on and that they might be foolish concerning their feasts and that they might be taken in their nets' (1QH 4:11,12, Dead Sea Scrolls). Jerusalem was destroyed because the leaders of the people did not know the time of their visitation by the Messiah (St. Luke 19:41–45). The knowledge of God also brings peace. In the days when 'the wolf shall dwell with the lamb, and the leopard shall lie down with the young goat, and the calf and the young lion and the fatling shall be together and the cow and the bear shall graze and their young ones shall lie down (in peace) together and . . . the nursing child shall play by the cobra's hole, and the weaned child shall put his hand in the viper's den. And they shall not hurt or destroy' each other again. It will be because 'the earth shall be full of the knowledge of the Lord as the waters cover the sea' (Isaiah 11:6–9): in the day of the Messiah (Isaiah 11:10). And when the time shall come that 'they shall beat their swords into plowshares, and their spears into pruning hooks, and nation shall not lift up sword against nation, neither shall they learn war anymore' (Isaiah 2:4), it will be because again, 'the teaching [TORAH] shall go forth out of Zion, and the Word of the Lord from Jerusalem' because 'the God of Jacob will teach us His ways, and we shall walk in His paths' (Isaiah 2:3) full of the knowledge of God. When 'knowledge shall fill the world, then foolishness shall be no more' (1Q Myst. I:7 [Book of Mysteries], Dead Sea Scrolls).

Just as the Messiah is hidden at first, so is knowledge. And 'knowledge shall be increased' (Daniel 12:4; Colossians 1:10) the same way a seed is increased within the fruit: by first placing and keeping that seed in the heart of the ground. For there is a hidden stage in knowledge wherein it is guardedly kept until it bears fruit. Thus, 'knowledge is hidden from men' (1QS 11:6, Dead Sea Scrolls) and 'the eyes of the Lord watch over (hidden) knowledge' (Proverbs 22:12) until it shall become manifest in the fruit of knowledge brought forth. 'A prudent man conceals knowledge' (Proverbs 12:23), 'concealing the mysteries of knowledge for the sake of Truth' (1QS 4:6, Dead Sea Scrolls) until the time is ripe. Remember that hidden in the seeds of His commandments which the Lord bids us to keep, are His good counsels full of wisdom, understanding and knowledge to guide, protect and enliven us (see pp. 57, 65–66, 73–74). We shall understand the wisdom and knowledge of God hidden within His commandments if we obey them but 'they who do not obey . . . shall die without knowledge' (Job 36:12).

The aim of His commandments is to perfect us into being children of God having a filial knowledge of Him and able to share His holy knowledge with others. Truly 'the lips of the wise sow [ZARAH] knowledge but not the heart of fools' (Proverbs 15:7) because those who are righteous and wise have brought forth the fruit of knowledge from their hearts and are able to sow its seeds into the hearts of others. But the heart of the foolish is barren of His knowledge. 'Go from the presence of a fool when you know that the lips of knowledge are not in him' (Proverbs 14:7), for he has nothing good to sow in your heart. 'The heart of him who understands seeks knowledge' (Proverbs 15:14) because he knows that 'for the soul to be without knowledge is not good' (Proverbs 19:2). Life, salvation and peace come with the knowledge of God.

The peace that comes with the knowledge of God is brought to us by righteousness. The knowledge of God converts us to a life of righteousness:

> 'I will lead the blind in a way they do not know, and in paths they have not known I will guide them. I will turn the darkness before them into light, and make crooked things straight. These things will I do for them, and will not forsake them. They shall be converted, they shall be greatly ashamed' —Isaiah 42:16,17.

> 'He shall instruct them [by his knowledge] in all that has been found . . . so that they may separate themselves from all those who have not departed from all perversity' —1QS 9:20, 21, Dead Sea Scrolls.

> 'I have knowledge through the abundance of Your goodness . . . I have bound myself not to sin against You, and not to do anything that is evil in Your eyes' —1QH 14:17,18, Dead Sea Scrolls.

> 'By His knowledge shall My righteous Servant make the many to be righteous' —Isaiah 53:11.

> 'He shall guide each man in knowledge . . . he shall make them understand the marvelous and true mysteries . . . so that they may walk with one another in perfection in all that has been revealed to them' [for righteousness] —1QS 9:18,19, Dead Sea Scrolls.

> 'You have taught him understanding of Your mysteries that he may not sin against You' —1QH 17:21,22, Dead Sea Scrolls.

> 'Filled with all knowledge to admonish' —Romans 15:14.
> 'According to his unfaithfulness shall the men of knowledge admonish him until the day when he returns [to righteousness] to take his place among the men of perfect holiness' —CD [Zadokite Fragment MS.B1] II. 4,5 [XX. 4,5, Rabin].

'Desire that you may be filled with the knowledge of His will in all wisdom and spiritual understanding, so that you may walk worthy of the Lord, fully pleasing to Him' —Colossians 1:9,10.

'Do Thou teach me what I do not see [and know, note pp. 19–21]; if I have done iniquity, I will do it no more' —Job 34:32.

'You have favored me, Your servant, with the Spirit of knowledge to love truth and righteousness and to loathe all the ways of perversity' —1QH 14:25,26, Dead Sea Scrolls.

'Out of His mouth comes knowledge and understanding' —Proverbs 2:6.
'They shall be converted by Your glorious mouth' —1QH 6:14, Dead Sea Scrolls.

'Grace and peace be multiplied to you through the knowledge of God' (2 Peter 1:2). For those who have been converted to righteousness by the knowledge of God have peace: 'the peace of righteousness' (Baruch 5:4). Because 'the work of righteousness shall be peace, and the effect of righteousness, quietness and assurance forever' (Isaiah 32:17; see also Isaiah 48:18; 60:17; Psalms 72:3; 85:8; 119:165; Romans 2:10; 8:6; 14:17; Philippians 4:9; St. James 3:18). 'The righteous . . . shall enter into peace' (Isaiah 57:1,2) for 'righteousness and peace' (Psalms 85:10; 72:7) go together. 'Behold the upright: for the future of that man is peace' (Psalm 37:37). But 'there is no peace,' says the Lord, 'for the wicked' (Isaiah 48:22; 57:21; Enoch 5:4; 94:6; 98:11,15–16; 99:13; 101:3; 102:3; 103:5,8), because 'the wicked . . . do not know' (Psalm 82:4,5) and 'the wicked do not understand knowledge' (Proverbs 29:7b). Therefore 'they (the wicked) do not know the way of peace' (Isaiah 59:8; Romans 3:17) which is entered by 'the gates of righteousness' (Psalm 118:19).

God gave His shepherds knowledge and understanding (Jeremiah 3:15) for the sake of His people, to warn sinners (Ezekiel 3:17; Jeremiah 36:3) and turn them from their evil ways (Jeremiah 23:22; 25:5; 35:15; Ezekiel 18:30; Zechariah 1:4; Acts 26:18–20). The knowledge of God that converts us to a life of righteousness and peace, comes from good teaching. Thus, King David says to the Lord: 'I will teach transgressors Your ways, and sinners shall be converted to You' (Psalm 51:13), for to know the ways of God is to know Him (Exodus 33:13), and to be drawn to a life of righteousness and peace by the knowledge of God. 'Through His (the Messiah's) teaching, peace shall be greatly increased upon us' (Targum to Isaiah 53:5) for when 'all your children shall be taught by the Lord, great shall be the peace of your children' (Isaiah 54:13). Truly, 'great peace have they who love Your teaching [TORAH], and nothing shall cause them to stumble' (Psalm 119:165). It is when the shepherds are delinquent and have lost their knowledge and understanding that the sheep become confused and are scattered (Isaiah 56:10–12; Jeremiah 23:1–2; 50:6; Ezekiel 34:2–6). When Yeshua the Messiah saw that the people were 'harassed and scattered' (St. Matthew 9:36), 'He was moved with compassion for them, because they were like sheep without a shepherd. So He began to teach them many things' (St. Mark 6:34), because He is the good Shepherd (St. John 10:11).

He taught us that great things have small hidden beginnings; and from the tiny seed shall spring forth 'a *great* tree' (St. Luke 13:19, Literal Translation). For 'there is nothing hid except to be made manifest; nor is anything secret except to come to light' (St. Mark 4:22). The Omnipresent hides Himself so that we may seek and find Him, and having found Him reveal Him to the rest. And He who is the Almighty One was born to us a helpless Babe to disarm us by the power of our aroused compassion and lovingkindness. He told us that only by dying to ourselves shall we be born again in Him to life everlasting, and that in keeping the least of His things we shall have great fruits to give from that which was kept. The Saviour of Israel hides Himself in our hearts so that we may hold and bring Him forth in our lives, to His glory and our salvation.

Chapter 18

Witnessing The Son Of Man

When the time comes for the Lord to be revealed, He shall call upon His witnesses:

> 'Ye are My witnesses,' says the Lord, 'and My servant whom I have chosen, that ye may know and believe Me, and understand that I am He. Before Me there was no God formed, nor shall there be after Me. I, even I, am the Lord, and besides Me there is no saviour' —Isaiah 43:10–11.

The hidden Saviour (Isaiah 45:15) reveals Himself through His witnesses because 'God is Truth' (Horeb, *Mitzvoth,* V. 482). 'Truth is the name of God' (Sanhedrin I.18, Jerusalem Talmud; Alphabet de Rabbi Akiba, Prologue), and it takes two to bear witness and reveal the Truth (Deuteronomy 17:6; 19:15; St. John 8:17; St. Matthew 18:16; 2 Corinthians 13:1; Revelation 11:3). It is possible for one to bear witness to the Word of God before it is revealed, but it takes two to bear witness to the Truth of His Word in all its glory.

There was a time when Aaron went into the tabernacle of the congregation and lifted up his hands and blessed the people but the glory of the Lord did not appear before them until both 'Moses and Aaron went into the tabernacle of the congregation and came out, and blessed the people, then the glory of the Lord appeared to all the people' (Leviticus 9:23; see Targum Jerusalem on Leviticus 9:22–23).

St. John the Baptist bore witness to Yeshua the hidden Messiah (St. John 1:6–8,15,29,32–34,36; 3:26,28,36; Acts 19:4), but he did not manifest Him in all His glory. A preview of that glory was given to three of the Messiah's disciples when they saw Him transfigured and shining like the sun before *two* witnesses: Moses and Elijah (St. Matthew 17:1–3; St. Mark 9:2–4; St. Luke 9:28–30). The Law and the Prophets bear witness to Him (Romans 3:21; Sanhedrin 99a, Babylonian Talmud). This Truth was made known to *two* of His disciples (St. Luke 24:13,27) who walked with Him. St. John the Baptist was sent before Him 'in the spirit and power of Elijah' (St. Luke 1:17) to bear witness to the Word. We may be sure that when the time comes for the Truth of that Word to be made known, 'a *double* portion' of the 'spirit' of Elijah (2 Kings 2:9) shall do the work of revealing it.

In the ancient Greek text, the prophet Habakkuk rightly says:

'O Lord, I have heard Your report and was afraid, I have observed Your works, and was amazed. You shall be *known* between the *two* living creatures, You shall be acknowledged when the years draw near. You shall be manifested when the time has come' – Habakkuk 3:2, Septuagint Text.

'For there is nothing hid, except to be made manifest; nor is anything secret, except to come to light' (St. Mark 4:22; St. Matthew 10:26; St. Luke 8:17; 12:2; 1 Corinthians 4:5; Ecclesiastes 12:14).

When the Messiah said that His time had not yet come (St. John 7:6), He spoke not only concerning the time of His suffering and death, but also of His glory and exaltation. Yeshua the Messiah spoke of Himself as the Son of Man who was to suffer and be put to death as a ransom (Isaiah 53:8) for many (St. Matthew 16:21; 17:12,22; 20:18–19,28; St. Mark 8:31; 9:12,31; 10:33–34,45; St. Luke 9:22,44; 18:31–33; 22:21–22). His people knew that the one called the Son of Man was the Messiah:

'O God of Hosts, look down from heaven and see, and visit this vine and the vineyard which Your right hand has planted, and the *son* [*BEN*] whom You made strong for Yourself. . . . Let Your hand be upon the man of Your right hand: upon *the son of man* whom You made strong for Yourself' –Psalm 80:14–15,17, Hebrew Text.

'O God of Hosts, look down from heaven and see, and remember this vine in mercy, and the stock which Your right hand has planted and upon the *King Messiah* whom You made strong for Yourself. . . . Let Your hand be upon the man whom You have established with Your right hand, upon *the son of man* whom You made strong for Yourself' –Targum to Psalm 80:14–15,17.

The 'Son of Man' who came with 'the clouds of heaven' in Daniel 7:13–14 was none other than the Messiah according to the rabbis (see Midrash on Psalms 2.9; 21.5; Midrash Numbers Rabbah 13.14; Midrash Haggadol re Genesis 41:1; Tanchumah on Genesis 27:30–32; Yalkut Shimoni fol. 571; Tanchumah Toledoth 20.4; Sanhedrin 38b; 98a, Babylonian Talmud; Seder Rab Amran [Sepher Hechaloth] i.13a in Jellinek's *Beth haMidrash* vol. V, p. 168; VI, pp. 150 ff.; Rashi and Saadia Gaon *ad loc.*; see also Rabbi S. Cohen's, *La Bible* vol. 17, p. 38 and Rabbi Z. Kahn's, *Bible Rabbinique* vol. 2, p. 492, n. 4 re Daniel 7:13 Messianically interpreted). In the Judaica section of the British Museum Library there is an old Hebrew manuscript (MS. 1048–Harley 5686) which states in folio 128a: 'These are the glad tidings of the Messiah ben David, that is, the Son of Man.'

The Lord Himself identified the Son of Man as being the Messiah:

'The *Son of Man* must suffer many things, and be rejected by the elders and chief priests and scribes, and be killed, and be raised on the third day' –St. Luke 9:22; St. Matthew 17:12; St. Mark 8:31; 9:12.

'Ought not the *Messiah* to have suffered these things, and to enter into His glory?' –St. Luke 24:26.

'Are You the *Messiah* the Son of the Blessed?' And Yeshua said, 'I am. And you will see the *Son of Man* sitting at the right hand of the Power, and coming with the clouds of heaven' –St. Mark 14:61,62; St. Matthew 26:63,64.

He [Yeshua] asked them, 'Who do you say that I am?' Peter answered Him, 'You are the *Messiah*'. And He charged them to tell no one about Him. And He began to teach them that the *Son of Man* must suffer many things and be rejected by the elders and the chief priests and the scribes and be killed and after three days rise again –St. Mark 8:29–31.

The Gospels tell us that this rejected and suffering Messiah-Son of Man was to be glorified and exalted some day, and that His message would be preached to the ends of the earth by His followers. We know now that His coming divided Time in half, and that His adherents are more than a billion and a half people on this earth. But we had not known who the Son of Man was, for we were still waiting for Knowledge and Understanding to reveal Him and bear Him witness.

In Yeshua the Messiah are 'hidden all the treasures of wisdom and knowledge' (Colossians 2:3) waiting for us to bring them forth to His exaltation. The Son of Man shall be glorified when these treasures are revealed, for they are 'hidden' in Him to be made manifest. The finding out of His hidden wisdom and knowledge depends on our understanding and above all on our desire to make Him known and loved by His own, because these treasures are reserved for them.

Without understanding, there is no searching and finding of His hidden wisdom and knowledge. 'The heart is deep beyond all things' (Jeremiah 17:9, Greek Text), and we 'cannot fathom the depths of the human heart' (Judith 8:14). But 'the Lord searches all hearts and understands the inclinations of the thoughts' (1 Chronicles 28:9). 'He (God) searches out the deep and the heart because He has understanding' (Sirach 42:18, Hebrew Text). It is our understanding which motivates us to seek what is hidden because the 'understanding loves to learn and advance to full understanding, and its way is to seek the hidden meaning rather than the obvious'—Philo, *Decal.* 1. Thus where 'there is no one who understands, there is no one who seeks after' (Romans 3:11). Moreover, to say that 'Wisdom . . . takes hold of those who *seek* her' (Sirach 4:11, Greek Text), is to say that 'Wisdom . . . takes hold of those who *understand* her' (Sirach 4:11, Hebrew Text). And when it was said of some men that 'by their *searchings out* they were rulers of the people' (Sirach 44:4, Hebrew Text), it was meant that 'by their *understanding*' they were 'rulers of the people' (Sirach 44:4, Greek Text). Likewise, because it also takes understanding to find out what is hidden, the word 'to find' became synonymous with the word 'to understand':

> 'They who fear the Lord shall *find* judgment' —Sirach 32:16, Greek Text.

> 'They who fear the Lord shall *understand* judgment' —Sirach 32:16, Hebrew Text.

> 'Despise me not and in the end you shall *find*' —Sirach 31:22, Greek Text.

> 'Despise me not and in the end you shall *understand*' —Sirach 31:22, Hebrew Text.

Just as it takes two to bear witness to the Truth, it also takes the combined effort of two to be able to understand the hidden things of the Lord. For there must be one praying for the necessary wisdom and understanding (Wisdom 7:7) while the other one searches out the secret things (see Daniel 2:16–19). Thus, he who has found a true friend has found understanding:

> 'Happy is he who finds a *true friend*' —Sirach 25:9, Latin Vulgate Text.

'Happy is the man who finds *understanding*' –Sirach 25:9, Greek Text.

It was said by the rabbis that if someone saw a solitary reed in a dream he could hope for wisdom, but if he saw two reeds he could hope for understanding (Berakoth 56b, Babylonian Talmud). For we 'see and know and consider and understand *together*' (Isaiah 41:20). When God wants us to really understand, He shall make us to be 'perfectly joined together in the same understanding [NOI]' –1 Corinthians 1:10. Did not Elihu say: 'Let men [plural] of understanding tell me, and let a wise man [singular] hear me'? (Job 34:34). We can now understand why it is written in the book of Proverbs that:

> 'The righteous one searches [TUR] for his friend [REA], but the way of the wicked causes them to err [TAAH]' –Proverbs 12:26.

The wicked err and get confused, first of all, because 'the wicked do not understand' (Proverbs 29:7; 4:19; Daniel 12:10; Wisdom 2:21,22; 10:8; Proverbs 13:19, Greek Text; 2 Timothy 3:7), and secondly because they do not have the insight to seek the help of a righteous companion to obtain good understanding: 'the understanding [PHRONĒSEI] of the just' (St. Luke 1:17; see Proverbs 12:5,15) which would have prevented them from erring.

When Yeshua the Messiah began His ministry, His first followers were two disciples of St. John the Baptist (St. John 1:35–37) who in turn called to themselves companions to also follow Him (St. John 1:40–51). And when the Messiah sent forth His own disciples, He sent them by twos (St. Mark 6:7; St. Luke 10:1). And He told them, 'If two of you agree on earth concerning anything they ask, it will be done for them by My Father in heaven' (St. Matthew 18:19).

Great things happen when two hearts are joined as one in a work of God, for if someone may cause a thousand to scatter, two people can put ten thousand adversaries to flight (Deuteronomy 32:30). When Jonathan and his armorbearer were of one heart (1 Samuel 14:7) the Lord caused an entire encampment to scatter before them (1 Samuel 14:6–16). And it was after 'the soul of Jonathan was knit to the soul of David' (1 Samuel 18:1) that the women sang, 'Saul has slain his thousands, and David his ten thousands' (1 Samuel 18:7). Watch out and beware if you see *two* men riding in *one* chariot (Isaiah 21:8–9; 2 Kings 10:15–28) because judgment is imminent. 'O that a man [GEBER] might plead with God as a son of man (intercedes) for his friend' (Job 16:21, Literal Translation) because then two hearts would desire the same thing, and the Lord would grant it (St. Matthew 18:19).

The Maccabean and Herodian epoch (c. 174 B.C.–A.D. 10) before the coming of the Messiah was noted for the quality of Scriptural exposition, because the leading rabbis of that period of time worked in pairs. It was the age of the Zugoth ('pairs') which preceded the era of the Tannaim (Mishnah, Peah 2:6; Tosefta Yadaim 2:16). The rabbis of that time knew the importance of concerted effort in a work of God, for they knew that 'two are better than one because they have a good reward for their labor' (Ecclesiastes 4:9). The first Zug ('pair') were Yose ben Joezer and Yose ben Yohanan of Jerusalem (174–164 B.C.) who were followed by Joshua ben Perachya and Nittai of Arbel. After them came Judah ben Tabbai and Simeon ben Shetah who were succeeded by Shemaiah and Avtalyon, and lastly by Hillel and Menahem (Mishnah, Hagigah 2:2; Pirke Aboth 1:4–12). Hillel died at a ripe old age and left eighty paired disciples (Negaim V.7, Jerusalem Talmud; Negaim 39a, Babylonian Talmud) who were also famous as their teacher was, for their wisdom and learning (Sukkah 28a, Babylonian Talmud). Among the Zugoth it was said of Shemaiah and Avtalyon that they were the greatest men of their generation for they were 'great sages and great interpreters' (Pesachim 70b, Babylonian Talmud). Hillel, the last of the Zugoth is considered by all to be the greatest rabbi (Introduction to Sifra, *Baraita* of Rabbi Ishmael; Tosefta Sanhedrin 7:11; Aboth Rabbi Nathan 37,110; Sotah 48b, Babylonian Talmud).

In both the Old and the New Testaments, when the Lord calls someone concerning a matter of importance, He calls the name of that person twice, thereby gaining special attention: 'Abraham, Abraham', 'Moses, Moses', 'Samuel, Samuel' 'Simon, Simon', 'Saul, Saul' (Genesis 22:11; Exodus 3:3; 1 Samuel 3:10; St. Luke 22:31; Acts 9:4). The doubling of a dream establishes the certainty of its coming to pass (Genesis 41:32; Berakoth 55b, Babylonian Talmud; Sippar Text 55; Nippur Fragment III. 3–8; see also Sirach 42:24–25). And the repetition of a thing establishes the certainty of a matter:

'Dying, you shall die' —Genesis 2:17, Literal Translation.

'Behold, I, even I do bring the flood of waters upon the earth to destroy all flesh' —Genesis 6:17.

'In blessing, I will bless you, and in multiplying, I will multiply your seed as the stars of the heavens, and as the sand which is on the seashore' —Genesis 22:17.

The Lord said, 'I have seen, I have seen the affliction of My people' —Exodus 3:7, Literal Translation.

The Lord passed before him [Moses] and proclaimed, 'the Lord, the Lord God' —Exodus 34:6.

'Amen, Amen, I [Yeshua] say to you' —St. John 1:51; see also John 3:3,5,11; 5:19,24,25; 6:26,32,47,53; 8:34,51,58; 10:1,7; 12:24; 13:16,20,21,38; 14:12; 16:20,23; 21:18.

When the time comes for the hidden Messiah to be revealed and exalted, two shall be called to do that glorious work for Him. We have seen how Yeshua gave us a preview of that day when He was transfigured on a high mountain before two, and when He sent two of His disciples (St. Matthew 21:1; St. Mark 11:1; St. John 19:29) as a sign to fetch two asses that He 'needed' (St. Matthew 21:1–9) for the brief moment of His triumphal entry through the gates of Jerusalem. Thus He fulfilled what the prophet Zechariah had spoken:

Tell the daughter of Zion, 'Behold, your King is coming to you, humble and mounted on an ass, *and* on a colt, the foal of an ass' —St. Matthew 21:5; Zechariah 9:9, Septuagint.

And 'the Lord' shall have 'need of *them*' asses (St. Matthew 21:3) when the time comes for the understanding of the Son of Man to be revealed and exalted. For it is written: 'Be not like a horse or a mule, without understanding' (Psalm 32:9), but rather be like a donkey that understands (Numbers 22:21–32; Job 28:28). For 'a stupid man will get understanding when a wild ass's colt is born a man' (Job 11:12, RSV) able to teach him. The work of revealing and exalting the hidden Messiah-Son of Man so that He may be known and understood by all, is a task for two witnesses. 'The Word became flesh' (St. John 1:14) may be announced by one coming 'in the spirit and power of Elijah' (St. Luke 1:17), but the Truth of that Word requires that it be revealed and witnessed by two who shall be joined in the 'double spirit' and power of Elijah. For the same Lord who said:

'Ye [plural] are My witnesses . . . and My servant [singular] whom I have chosen, that ye may know and believe Me, and understand that I am He [the Saviour]' —Isaiah 43:10,

also said:

'If ye [plural] are willing to receive it [the work of Elijah is to make the Messiah known], he [singular] is Elijah, the one who is to come. He who has ears to hear, let him hear!' —St. Matthew 11:14–15.

'For indeed Elijah is coming and will restore all things' —St. Matthew 17:11.

Chapter 19

Yeshua The Son Of Man, And Noah

*'For as the lightning comes from the
east and shines as far as the west, so
will be the manifestation of the Son of Man.'
—St. Matthew 24:27*

Just as Adam the original Man was the Father of all mankind before the Flood, so is Noah the Father of all the generations that repopulated the earth after the Deluge. We are all children of a son of Man: Noah. The generation of Man was swept away by the waters of the Flood; the regeneration that came forth from a son of Man continues. 'The world was replenished from one (son of) man: Noah' (Midrash Leviticus Rabbah 5.1), the seventy nations that are spread throughout the earth proceeded from him (Noah) —Midrash Numbers Rabbah 14.12.

If we want to understand the mysterious imageries found in the Holy Scriptures and Apocalyptic writings that depict the Messiah ascending from the heart of the sea, and coming with the clouds, we must not forget that the Messiah-Son of Man is a descendant of that son of Man: Noah, who came forth from the waters of the Flood to regenerate mankind. Furthermore, if *Man* (Adam) who was directly created and formed from the dust of the ground may be said to be truly an *Earthman,* then the *sons of Man* may be said to be in a certain sense: *Watermen.* For God 'gives to a Man [ADAM] a son (of Man) out of a drop of water' (Mekilta on Exodus 15:11, Tract *Shirata* 85–89; Pirke Aboth 3:1; Sotah 5a, Babylonian Talmud; Yebamoth IV. 5c, Jerusalem Talmud; Tanchumah, *Pikkude* 3; Wisdom 7:2; 1QS 11:21–22, Dead Sea Scrolls; see also Koran, Suras 21:31; 22:5; 23:12 ff.; 24:44; 32:6 ff.; 35:12; 86:6; and Muslim commentators Tabari and Zamakshari *ad loc.*). Thus, symbolically as a 'waterman', the Messianic Son of Man in 2 Esdras rises from the heart of the sea:

> 'I saw a wind rising from the sea that stirred up all its waves. As I kept looking that wind brought up out of the depths of the sea something resembling a son of man [BAR NASHA] and that son of man was flying with the clouds of heaven. Whenever he turned his face to look, everything he looked upon trembled, and whenever the voice of his mouth sounded, all who heard it melted as wax melts when it comes in contact with fire. Afterwards I saw an innumerable host of men gathered together from the four winds of heaven to wage war against the son of man who had risen out of the sea' —2 Esdras 13:2–5, Syriac Text.

And in the book of the prophet Daniel:

> 'I saw in the night visions, and behold, One like the Son of Man
> [BAR ENASH], coming with the clouds of heaven. He came to the
> Ancient of Days, and they brought Him near before Him. Then
> to Him was given dominion and glory and a kingdom, that all
> peoples, nations and languages should serve Him. His dominion
> is an everlasting dominion, which shall not pass away. And His
> kingdom is one that shall not be destroyed' — Daniel 7:13–14.

Similarly in 2 Baruch 53:1–12, a cloud originally arising from the great
sea and raining throughout Time, finally contains the Messiah in the imagery of bright waters and lightning on top of that cloud which in the end
has dominion over all (2 Baruch 72:1–6). Calling Himself the Son of Man,
Yeshua the Messiah was born of a virgin named Maryam ('bitter sea'), and
when He first manifested Himself, the crowds saw Him ascending from
the waters of the Jordan river just after being baptized by St. John the
Baptist:

> When Jesus was baptized He arose [ANEBĒ] from the water, and
> behold, the heavens were opened to Him, and he [St. John the
> Baptist; see St. John 1:32–34] saw the Spirit of God descending
> like a dove and alighting upon Him. And suddenly a voice came
> from heaven, saying, 'This is My beloved Son in whom I am well
> pleased' — St. Matthew 3:16–17.

We know that as a descendant of Noah, the 'Father' of the sons of man,
the first miracle of Yeshua the Messiah was to change water into wine (see
p. 113) showing His power over that element. Moreover, as the Son of Man,
He displayed His mastery over the waters by walking on them (St. Matthew 14:25–33; St. Mark 6:48–50; St. John 6:19–20), and by commanding
the winds and the sea to be still when there was 'a great storm in the sea'
(St. Matthew 8:24–27; St. Mark 4:37–41; St. Luke 8:23–25). And His disciples saw that the winds and the sea obeyed Him. Let us not forget that
Yeshua the Son of Man lived for the most part of His life in the territory
of Zebulon, the seafaring tribe.

Furthermore, because the term 'son of Man' connotes not only a 'waterman' but also someone who understands (see pp. 13–14, 21–23, 46–47,
66–67, 81–83), we may expect the words 'water', 'springs', 'rivers', 'sea',
'clouds' and 'rain' to have associations with 'understanding':

'Wisdom shall . . . give him the waters of great understanding [TEBUNAH] to drink' —Sirach 15:3, Hebrew Text.

'The Creator freely gave man the Word, but the Understanding He sent down to earth as waters in a great basin' —Corpus Hermeticum, *Libellus* IV. 4.

'In the first place our understanding [NOUS] is called a spring' — Philo, *Fug.* 177.

'Understanding [SAKAL] is a wellspring of life to him who has it' —Proverbs 16:22.

'Those . . . athirst as they are for instruction settle down beside springs of understanding [EPISTĒMAIS] which are able to water their souls and give them to drink' —Philo, *Fug.* 187; *Mut.* 69; *Q. Gen.* III. 27.

'The wise among the people . . . in them is the spring of understanding' —2 Esdras 14:46,47.

'The understanding of a wise man shall abound like a spring' — Sirach 21:13, Syriac Text.

'Thou hast hidden the spring of understanding [SAKAL]' —1QH 5:26, Dead Sea Scrolls.

'He makes understanding [SUNESIN] abound like the Euphrates, and like the Jordan at harvest time' —Sirach 24:26.

'O Solomon . . . how wise you were in your youth! You overflowed like a river with understanding' —Sirach 47:13,47.

'Your understanding is like a river whose spring never fails, an immense sea which knows no decrease' —Babylonian Tablet no. 35405, lines 23–24, British Museum.

'Man . . . his understanding is from the swiftness of the angels and from clouds' —2 Enoch 30:8.

'Wisdom rains down insight [EPISTĒMĒN] and knowledge of understanding' —Sirach 1:19.

'He [the Lord] will fill him with the spirit of understanding, and

he will pour forth the words of His wisdom as showers' —Sirach
39:8,9, Latin Vulgate.

Good teaching is as rain upon parched earth for it causes the seed of His
Word to open up and spring forth from the ground of our hearts bearing
for us the fruits of understanding. Thus Moses said:

'My teaching shall drop down as the rain, and my choice words
[IMRAH, plural] shall distill as the dew, as the droplets upon the
tender grass, and as showers upon the herb' —Deuteronomy 32:2.

'The words of the teaching [TORAH] are likened unto water' —
Taanith 7a, Babylonian Talmud.
'For as waters give life to the world, so do the words of the Torah
give life to the world' —Sifre 84a; 37cd; see also Berakoth
24a,61b; Sukkah 55a; Erubin 54a; Moed Katan 25b; Sanhedrin
7a; Abodah Zarah 3b, Babylonian Talmud; Midrash Genesis Rabbah 70.8; Midrash Song of Songs Rabbah 1.2,3; Pesikta de Rab
Kahana, Piska 5.6; Pesikta Rabbati, Piska 5.6; Tanna debe Eliyyahu p.105.

'The righteous . . . their teaching shall be received quickly as
streams of water that flow in a thirsty land' —Targum to Isaiah
32:2.

'Thou [Solomon] . . . didst overflow like the Nile with thy instruction' —Sirach 47:14, Hebrew Text.

'You, O my God, have put in my mouth as it were an abundant
rain for all, and a spring of living waters which shall not run dry'
—1QH 8:16,17, Dead Sea Scrolls.

'My speech dropped upon them, and they waited for me as for the
rain and opened wide their mouth' —Job 29:22,23.

Thus, when St. Paul said to the Corinthians, 'I have planted and Apollos
watered' (1 Corinthians 3:6) he meant that he (Paul) preached the Gospel
and Apollos by his great understanding in the Holy Scriptures eloquently
elaborated and proved by his teaching that Yeshua was the Messiah (Acts
18:24,28) because 'to water' is 'to teach'. When the rabbis said of another,
'we drink of your water' (Hagigah 3a, Babylonian Talmud) they intended
to say 'we assimilate your teaching'. Thus, Rabbi Eleazar ben Arach, a
good teacher, was said to be 'as a full flowing spring' (Pirke Aboth 2:10).
We can understand why an Essene teacher said of himself: 'You (God) have

opened a spring in the mouth of Your servant . . . that he may proclaim them ('the precepts') to creatures because of his understanding [BINAH], and be an interpreter of these things' (1QH 18:10–11, Dead Sea Scrolls) through the same waters of understanding that the Lord opened for him. Was it not said of Simeon ben Yeshua ben Eleazar ben Sirach that 'out of his heart . . . poured forth great understanding [TEBUNAH]'? —Sirach 50:27, Hebrew Text. 'My son, keep my counsel and understanding, and do not let them flow by [PARARRUĒS] you' (Proverbs 3:21, Greek Text).

All wisdom, understanding and knowledge come from the Lord. Therefore, 'the Lord (Himself) is the fountain of living waters' (Jeremiah 17:13; 2:13), and He said through His prophet Isaiah: 'Ho, everyone who thirsts, come to the waters . . . come to Me' (Isaiah 55:1,3). Moreover, the Lord gives us His Word not only as a Seed (St. Luke 8:11) but also as a fructifying rain of understanding that shall make that Seed bear fruit:

> 'As the rain comes down and the snow from heaven . . . waters the earth and makes it bring forth and bud that it may [bear fruit and] give seed to the sower and bread to the eater, so shall My Word be that goes forth [as rain] out of My mouth' —Isaiah 55:10,11.

Consequently, we should thirst for the Lord, and for His Word, and for His understanding:

> 'As the deer longs for the water brooks, so my soul longs for You, O God. My soul thirsts for God, for the living God' —Psalm 42:1,2.

> 'O God . . . my soul thirsts for You, my flesh longs for You as in a dry and thirsty land where there is no water' —Psalm 63:1; Psalm 143:6.

> 'I opened my mouth, and panted [with thirst] for I longed for Your commandments' —Psalm 119:131.

> 'The soul which is thirsty for understanding' (Philo, *Q. Gen.* III. 27) thirsts for it as for water which comes from the rain clouds and springs, streams, rivers, and 'the well of understanding [EPISTĒMĒS]' —Philo, *Plant.* 168.

Rabbinic tradition states in many passages that the Messiah will come as a great Teacher and Revealer of hidden things for he is the one endowed with the seven gifts (Isaiah 11:2) of the Holy Spirit (see Targum Isaiah

11:2; Midrash Numbers Rabbah 13.11; Midrash Ruth Rabbah 3.14; Targum Ruth 3:15; Sanhedrin 93b Babylonian Talmud), and he has perfect knowledge of God directly acquired by himself (Midrash Numbers Rabbah 14.2). Moreover, seated at the right hand of God, the Holy One reveals all the secret meanings of the Torah to him (Pesikta Hadta p.47 [in Jellinek's, *Beth haMidrash,* vol. VI, pp. 36–70]). Thus, the Messiah will teach a new Torah (Alphabet de Rabbi Akiba 27–28 [Jellinek's *Beth haMidrash,* vol. III, pp. 12–64]). 'The Holy One will give the new Torah through the Messiah. The 'New Torah' means the secrets and mysteries of the Torah which have remained hidden until now' (Midrash Talpiyot 58a; see also Yemenite Midrash, pp. 349–350 found in Yehuda Ibn Shemuel's, *Midrash Geulah*). 'The Torah which a man learnt in this world is vanity compared with the Torah of the Messiah' (Midrash Ecclesiastes Rabbah 11.1). 'In the days of the Messiah, the Torah shall return to its renewal' (Pesikta Rabbati fol. 75a) because 'the Messiah will make clear for them the words of the Torah' (Midrash Genesis Rabbah 98.9; Sanhedrin 97a, Babylonian Talmud). The knowledge of God (see pp. 125–128) received from the great teaching of the Messiah will lead his hearers to a life of righteousness. Thus, 'the Messianic time will be an era of purity and perfect knowledge' for mankind (Zohar, *Mathnitim* [found in section Toldoth following *Midrash Haneelam*]). And for the same reason it will be an era of perfect peace because 'through the Messiah's teaching peace shall be greatly increased upon us' (Targum on Isaiah 53:5; Ibid., 54:13), and there will even be great peace between man and beast (Sifre to Numbers 1; Sifre to Deuternomy 50; Sifra 26.6; Tosefta Shabbath [end]; Tosefta Berakoth 3.20; Pesikta Rab Kahana fol. 5,44b; Pesikta Rabbati fol. 15,68b; Midrash Shemuel 18,97; Midrash Song of Songs Rabbah fol. 29a; Midrash Ecclesiastes Rabbah 5.10, etc.). 'Behold My Servant the Messiah . . . the coastlands eagerly await for his teaching' (Targum on Isaiah 42:1,4 Codex Reuchlinianus and Nuremberg MS; see also Midrash Tehillim 2.9; Yalkut ii. p. 104d) for 'the Messiah . . . will give light to the eyes of Israel' (Pesikta Rabbati, Piska 36.1), and when He comes 'the things which are concealed from you, you will see' (Midrash Numbers Rabbah 19.6). Yes, 'when the Righteous Messiah comes we shall also understand the blank spaces in the Torah' for 'he will reveal to us even the meaning of the blank spaces in the Torah' (Levi Yitzchak's, *Imre Tzaddikim,* p.10[5b]). And this Messiah 'is the Son of Man who has righteousness, and with whom dwells righteousness, and who reveals all the treasures of that which is hidden' (Enoch 46:3; 49:1–3; 51:3).

Knowing that understanding is portrayed as waters, we may expect that when the Messiah shall come to teach us hidden things and make us understand, He shall be depicted as a wonderful rain:

'He [the Messiah] shall come down like rain upon the mown grass, and like showers that water the earth' —Psalm 72:6.

His people have always interpreted Psalm 72 Messianically (see Targum on Psalm 72; Midrash Tehillim 72.3–6; 93.3; 119.16; Midrash Genesis Rabbah 78.12; Midrash Numbers Rabbah 13.14; Midrash Ecclesiastes Rabbah I.9,1; Midrash Mishlei on Proverbs 19:21; Mekilta on Exodus, Tract *Amalek* II. 188–192; Sifre on Deuteronomy fol. 310; Yalkut Shimoni, fols. 133, 267, 942; Lekah Tob 120, 172; Shekel Tob re Genesis 33:11; Midrash Haggadol re Genesis 1:1; 33:11; Midrash Tanchumah on Deuteronomy 25:19; Pirke Rabbi Eliezer, pereq 3; Pesikta de Rab Kahana, Piska 3.16; 18.6; 22.5a; Sanhedrin 98b, 99a; Pesachim 54a; Nedarim 39b, Babylonian Talmud; and Rabbi Kimchi's, Ibn Ezra's, and Rashi's commentaries on Psalm 72).

And since rain comes from the clouds, it is not surprising that one of the names given to the Messiah is Anani ('the one from the clouds'; see Targum on 1 Chronicles 3:24 and Tanchumah on Genesis 27:30 re Daniel 7:13). Another name given to the Messiah is Bar Nepheli ('the son of the cloud'; see Sanhedrin 96b, Babylonian Talmud). In the Pesikta de Rab Kahana, Piska 4.7, the clouds are said to bear within them the precious hidden things of the Torah which are to be revealed. And in the Cabbalistic writings, rain is symbolical of the bestowal of spiritual gifts upon man from above (Yalkut Reubeni ii.56b, Warsaw 1901). Is not all flesh as the grass? (Isaiah 40:6; 44:4). Therefore, the Messiah and the blessings of the Lord come down as rain 'to everyone (who is as) grass in the field' (Zechariah 10:1, Literal Translation).

In the Syriac version of 2 Esdras, the Son of Man who ascended from the heart of the sea (2 Esdras 13:1–3,25,51), remains hidden (2 Esdras 13:26,52; see also Enoch 48:6–7; 62:7) until the time comes for Him to be revealed and glorified (2 Esdras 13:26,52). In the meantime, 'He gathers strength with the clouds of heaven' (2 Esdras 13:3, Syriac) waiting until the day comes for Him to sally forth with them in power, to receive His due:

'I saw . . . One like the Son of Man, coming with the clouds of heaven . . . to Him was given dominion and glory . . . His domini-

on is an everlasting dominion, which shall not pass away. And
His kingdom one that shall not be destroyed' —Daniel 7:13,14.

'They shall see [Yeshua] the Son of Man coming on the clouds of
heaven with power and much glory' —St. Matthew 24:30.

'You will see the Son of Man sitting at the right hand of the Power, and coming on the clouds of heaven' —St. Matthew 26:64.

Being a descendant of Noah the 'waterman', it is only fitting that the Son
of Man should come in triumph with His retinue of clouds: the source of
rain, understanding, teaching and power. 'His power is in the clouds'
(Psalm 68:34) because 'by His mighty power He made the clouds strong'
(Sirach 43:15), 'He strengthened [AMATS] the clouds' (Proverbs 8:28) by
His power. 'I wish to show you their power in order that you may understand' (Shepherd of Hermas, *Mand.* VI. 35.1) that in the clouds is the
lightning to make us see and know: 'the lightnings that are in the clouds'
(Story of Ahikar 6:16, Syriac Text). For there is a relationship between
light and knowledge: 'the *light* of *knowledge*' (Testament of Levi 4:3; 18:3;
Testament of Benjamin 11:2, B Text; Hosea 10:12, Greek and Syriac Texts;
Targum Jonathan on Hosea 10:12). And in the same clouds is 'the voice
of' His thunder (Psalm 77:18; 104:7) to make us 'hear and understand' (St.
Matthew 15:10; see pp. 19–21). For there is a connection between hearing
and understanding. 'To hear is to understand' (Clement of Alexandria,
Strom. II. 4) provided we really listen for 'there is no understanding to
him who hears' (Isaiah 33:19, Greek Text) without paying close attention.
'The understanding hearer' (Isaiah 3:3, Greek Text) is the one who really
gives heed to what is said. 'If you love to hear, you shall receive understanding' (Sirach 6:33, Greek Cursives 248, 253, Aldine Septuagint, Syriac and Old Latin Texts). 'All who could hear with understanding'
(Nehemiah 8:2) were those who really listened. Such is the verbal affinity
between 'hearing' and 'understanding', that the Hebrew word 'to hear'
[SHAMEA] also means 'to understand':

'I have *heard* [SHAMEA] said of you [Joseph], that you can *understand* [SHAMEA lit. 'hear'] a dream to interpret it' —Genesis
41:15; see also Literal Translations of Genesis 44:23; Deuterononmy 28:49.

'Please speak to your servants in the Aramaic language for we
understand [SHAMEA lit. 'hear'] it' —2 Kings 18:26; Isaiah 36:11.

'An ancient nation whose language you do not know, nor understand [SHAMEA lit. 'hear'] what they speak' —Jeremiah 5:15; Ezekiel 3:6.

'Of deeper speech than you can understand [SHAMEA lit. 'hear']' —Isaiah 33:19.

Thus, the rabbis declared: 'Do not say that a thing which cannot be heard will be understood' (Pirke Aboth 2:5). And Solomon was wise when he prayed to the Lord: 'Give Your servant a heart that hears [SHAMEA] . . . so that I may understand [BIN]' —1 Kings 3:9.

'Now, men do not see the bright light which is in the clouds' (Job 37:21), but when the time comes for the Messiah to be revealed, the bright light of knowledge will flash forth from them with a loud sound of thunder to make people also understand that the One who shall come with the clouds of the heavens is the Messiah-Son of Man (Sanhedrin 98a, Babylonian Talmud). The clouds are with him to bear witness to Him (Hebrews 12:1). In the meantime, 'who can understand the thunder of His power?' (Job 26:14). We have to wait until that thunder shall give forth its voice so that it may be understood. For if thunder is said to have a 'voice' (Psalms 77:18; 104:7; Revelation 10:3,4), it is so that it can give us understanding. 'Does not Wisdom *cry* out? and great understanding [TEBUNAH] put forth her *voice*?' (Proverbs 8:1). 'Hear my *voice* and understand' (2 Esdras 8:19). 'If you have understanding hear this: give ear to the *voice* [QOL] of my words' (Job 34:16), because they will be telling you to 'lift up your *voice* [QOL] for great Understanding' (Proverbs 2:3) so that she may come to you and help you understand that 'a *voice* will cry out at night which many will not understand but all will hear' (2 Esdras 5:7, Syriac Text). Yes, all will hear but some will understand (St. John 12:28–30) that there is a relationship between 'voice', and 'understanding'. For 'God thunders with His *voice* marvelously' (Job 37:5) to make us understand. But until He puts His *voice* into it, 'who can understand the thunder of His power?' (Job 26:14).

Thus, symbolically within the clouds is the knowledge and understanding that shall exalt the Messiah-Son of Man, and give glory to Him. For it is written that 'from the North come the clouds shining like gold: in these are the great glory and honor of the Almighty' (Job 37:22, Greek Text; see p. 30). And in the same clouds that come with the Messiah-Son of Man is the teaching and learning rain that He shall cause to descend upon us. Long ago, the prophet Joel spoke concerning the coming of the Messiah as a marvelous Teacher:

> 'Be glad then, you children of Zion, and rejoice in the Lord your
> God; for He has given you the Teacher [YARAH] of righteousness
> [LITZEDAKAH], and He will cause to come down for you the rain:
> the former rain and the latter rain in the first month' – Joel 2:23.

There are two rainy seasons in the Holy Land: the late fall rain, and the
spring rain. The fall rains commence in mid-October to the end of Novem-
ber, and they come after the long hot summer to soften the hard dry
ground for plowing and sowing. The spring rains come between March
and April just before the harvest, to help bring the grain to maturity.
Since the *agricultural* year begins at plowing and sowing time, the fall
rain is called the 'former rain [YARAH]' or 'early rain [YARAH]'. And the
spring rain which falls in the latter part of the agricultural year, is called
the 'latter rain [MALQOSH]'. The 'first month' of the calendar is the month
of Nisan (March-April). Before the first month was called Nisan by the
Jews, it was known to them as the month of Abib ('ears of grain' month;
see Exodus 13:4; 23:15 and Deuterononmy 16:1). Interestingly, the
Hebrew word for 'teacher [YARAH]' or 'to teach [YARAH]' is the same as
the Hebrew word for 'former rain' or 'early rain': [YARAH]. In turn, MAL-
QOSH [the Hebrew word for 'latter rain'] is closely related through the
common root LAQOSH, to the Hebrew word LEQACH which means 'learning' or the actual thing which is taught and learned:

> 'Teach a righteous man and he will increase in learning [LE-
> QACH]' –Proverbs 9:9.

> 'My teaching [LEQACH] shall drop down as the [latter] rain [MAL-
> QOSH]' –Targums Onkelos and Jerusalem on Deuteronomy 32:2.

Thus, in Joel 2:23 the 'Teacher of righteousness' will cause the 'Teaching
rain' and the 'Learning rain' to come down together at the same time in
'the first month' which is when the ripening ears of grain are ready to
hear and understand. Therefore, we are to 'ask the Lord for rain in the season of the latter rain' (Zechariah 1:10) because then the time is ripe for
understanding. And we shall see the Son of Man coming with the clouds
of heaven to rain upon us. For 'His going forth is certain as the dawn, and
He shall come down to us as rain, as the latter rain and the former rain
to the earth' (Hosea 6:3). 'In His day the righteous shall flourish and abundance of peace until the moon is no more' (Psalm 72:7). For when He gives
us the teaching and the learning rain He shall also 'rain righteousness'
(Hosea 10:12; see also Ḥagigah 12b, Babylonian Talmud) upon us, and the

'Truth shall spring up from the earth' (Psalm 85:11) of our hearts to His glory.

> 'O Lord . . . Your lovingkindness is great unto the heavens, and Your truth unto the clouds' —Psalm 57:9,10.

Chapter 20

Yeshua The Messiah And The Right Hand

The Messiah-Son of Man who is to come with the clouds of heaven is seated at the right hand of God:

> 'You will see the Son of Man sitting at the right hand of the Power' —St. Matthew 26:64; St. Mark 14:62.

> 'From now on the Son of Man will be seated at the right hand of the power of God' —St. Luke 22:69; Romans 8:34; Colossians 3:1.

> While the Pharisees were gathered together, Yeshua asked them a question, saying, 'What do you think about the Messiah, whose Son is He?' They said to Him, 'The Son of David'. He said to them, 'How then does David in the Spirit call Him 'Lord', saying: The Lord said to my Lord, 'Sit at My right hand, till I make Your enemies Your footstool'? If David then calls Him 'Lord' how is He his Son?' And no one was able to answer Him a word, nor did anyone dare from that day on to ask Him another question —St. Matthew 22:41–46; Psalm 110:1.

> 'Prepare the way! the King Messiah comes . . . may the mountains abase themselves, may the valleys be filled, may the cedars incline to render him homage. Prostrate yourselves all of you before the Messiah King, and bend your knees before him who is seated at the *right hand* of the Holy One' —Zohar I. 4b.

His people knew that the highest honor was to sit at God's right hand (Nedarim 32b, Babylonian Talmud; Zohar I. 47b, 53b, 169b, 174b). Thus, the 'Lord' seated at the right hand of God in Psalm 110 was interpreted messianically by the Jews (Midrash Genesis Rabbah 85.9; Midrash on Psalm 110.4; Shabbath 63a, Babylonian Talmud; Aboth Rabbi Nathan chap. 34; Yalkut Shimoni fol. 869; Yalkut ha Makiri on Psalm 110; Zohar I. 39a; Rabbis Huna ben Hanina, Eleazar ben Pedat, Levi, Abbahu, Obadiah ben Joseph Sforno, Isaac ben Moses Arama, and Ibn Ezra re Psalm 110; see also rabbinic citations in Strack-Billerbeck vol. IV, 452–460; Justin Martyr, *Dial.* 33, 83; Tertullian, *Marcion* 5.9).

The firstborn's position was at the right hand of his father (Genesis 48:13–19; Josephus, *Antiq.* 6 [11.9] 235), and the queen sat at the right hand of the king (Psalm 45:9; 1 Kings 2:19; 1 Esdras 4:29), for it was the place of honor. Only true friends were to sit at one's right hand (Sirach 12:12). The pagans also knew that the highest honor was to be seated at the right hand of the deity (Baal Text 2.5.46–48; Hymn 2 to Apollo, l. 29; Callimachus Fragment 133).

The right hand of God is 'glorious in power' (Exodus 15:6), and 'glory and splendor are at the right hand of God' (Testament of Job 32.12 [vii.36]). Therefore, he who sits at the right hand of the Most High shares in His power and glory. But before the Lord reveals (Sirach 36:6) the glory of His right hand and 'His glorious arm' (Isaiah 63:12), He conceals it (Psalm 74:11; Lamentations 2:3; 3 Enoch 44:7; 48A:5), just as He keeps His Messiah hidden (see pp. 121–122) until it is time for Him to be revealed in all His glory. And just as the Suffering Servant-Son of Man is exalted in the end through His understanding (see pp. 70–71, 90–94, 131–132), so is it promised that the right hand of God shall be exalted (Psalms 89:13; 118:16; 3 Enoch 48A:5) for there is the place where His understanding is found.

Long ago, wise men and prophets knew that understanding is found in the right hand:

'A wise man's *understanding* is at his *right hand*' —Ecclesiastes 10:2.

'In length of days: *understanding*' —Job 12:12.

'Length of days are in wisdom's *right hand*' —Proverbs 3:16.

'My *right hand* has stretched out the heavens' —Isaiah 48:13.

'He . . . has stretched out the heavens by His great *understanding* [TEBUNAH]' —Jeremiah 10:12; 51:15.

'Extending to them *understanding* as it were a strong *right hand*' —Clement of Alexandria, *Exh.* I. 2.3.

'I am Understanding, I have strength' —Proverbs 8:14.

'My understanding being confused, he [the angel] grasped my right hand and strengthened me' −2 Esdras 10:30.

'Your *right hand* O Lord, has dashed the enemy in pieces' − Exodus 15:6.

'Awake, awake, put on strength O *arm* of the Lord . . . was it not You ['O *arm* of the Lord'] who did cut Rahab [i.e., Egypt] into pieces?' −Isaiah 51:9.

'By His great *understanding* [TEBUNAH] He smites through Rahab' −Job 26:12b, Literal Translation.

'He [King David] fed them according to the integrity of his heart and guided them by the great understanding [TEBUNAH] of his hands' −Psalm 78:72.

Even the ancient Egyptians knew that Understanding is found at the right hand of the deity:

'Sia [god of understanding] who is at the right hand of Re [the principal deity]' −*Ancient Egyptian Pyramid Texts,* edited by R.O. Faulkner, Oxford, 1969, Utterance no. 250.

'It is Sia who says what is in the heart of the great one at the feast of the red garment, for he is Sia [Understanding] at the right hand of Re' −Ibid., Utterance nos. 267−268.

'I am Sia [Understanding] at the right hand of Re, who establishes the heart of him who stands before the Tephet of Nu' − *Egyptian Book of the Dead* 174.18.19. Found in E. Naville's *Das Agyptische Todtenbuch der XVIII bis XXX Dynastie,* 2 vols.

'God is mighty . . . He is mighty in the power [KOACH] of understanding' (Job 36:5). 'Great is our Lord, and of great power: His great understanding [TEBUNAH] is infinite' (Psalm 147:5) and powerful. For there is power in understanding, and if understanding is in the right hand, we may be sure that the right hand has power. Thus, we hear about 'the right hand of Your power' (1QH 18:7, Dead Sea Scrolls), and 'the right hand of the power of God' (St. Luke 22:69). And the declaration: 'My *right hand* has stretched out the heavens' (Isaiah 48:13) becomes 'by My *power* I have stretched out the heavens' (Targum on Isaiah 48:13; see also Targum Sheni on Esther chap. 13). Yes, 'He . . . has stretched out the heavens by His great [and powerful] *understanding*' (Jeremiah 10:12; 51:15). 'Understanding has mighty power' (Corpus Hermeticum, *Libellus* IX. 10). 'Have you gained power for yourself by your insight [EPISTĒMĒ] and understanding?' (Ezekiel 28:4, Greek Text). There are many texts in Holy Scripture that tell about the power of understanding:

'Why is the power of understanding given to me?' −2 Esdras 4:22.

'The understanding [SUNESEI] of the powerful [DUNASTŌN]' − Sirach 10:3.

'All [angelic] beings powerful in understanding' −4QSl 39.1.21 (Angelic Liturgy, Dead Sea Scrolls).

'You alone . . . are powerful in understanding' −Judith 11:8.

'A mighty man [GIBBOR] of understanding [SAKAL]' −Jeremiah 50:9.

'Give your daughter . . . to a mighty man [GEBER] of understanding' −Sirach 7:25, Hebrew Text.

'The Lord . . . by [His] great *understanding* [TEBUNAH] He has established the heavens' −Proverbs 3:19.

'By His transcendent *power* He established the heavens' −First Clement to the Corinthians 33:3; see also Shepherd of Hermas, *Visions* I.3.3:4.

'To whom has He given *power* to declare His works?' −Sirach 18:4, Greek Cursives 248, 106.

'To declare His works with *understanding*' −Sirach 17:9, Greek Cursives 248, 106.

Thus, Philo Judaeus wrote about being 'endowed in the understanding, the divinest part of us, with power [DUNAMEI] such as athletes possess' (Philo, *Det.* 29). Knowledge about the power of understanding is ancient; in the Accadian language related to Hebrew, the word for 'understanding' and 'strength' was the same word UZNI, and in that tongue the word EMER means both 'to have understanding' and 'to be strong':

'O Lord Bel, thou prince, who art *mighty in understanding*' –
Hymn to Marduk, no. 10.

'*Powerful* one of wide *understanding*, director of gods and men' –
Hymn to Marduk, no. 9.

We have seen (pp. 30–34) how God as '*The Almighty*' understands and is
the Giver of understanding. He is also addressed as 'the Power' when attention is drawn to His right hand: 'You will see the Son of Man sitting
at the right hand of the Power' (St. Matthew 26:64; St. Mark 14:62). Knowing that the 'right hand' of God is synonymous with His 'understanding',
God's 'power' is also equivalent to His 'understanding':

'In much *understanding* [EPISTĒMĒS] the Lord divided them' –
Sirach 33 [36]:11.

'You have divided these things through the Mysteries of Your *understanding* [SAKAL]' –1QH 13:13, Dead Seas Scrolls.

'By His *power* dividing holy things among them from the profane'
–Sirach 18:3.

'I will give you shepherds after My own heart who will feed you
with knowledge and *understanding*' –Jeremiah 3:15.

'The Lord . . . shall feed His flock with *power*' –Micah 5:4, Greek
Text.

Conversely, to be without power is to have no understanding because the
power to understand is gone:

'I am completely without power [DUNAMAI] to understand' –
Shepherd of Hermas, *Similitude* IX. 14.91:4.

'I have no power [A-DUNATA] to understand [NOĒSAI]' –Proverbs
30:18, Greek Text.

'We have not the power to understand its true interpretation' –
Sifre to Deuteronomy 306.

'They have no power to understand this themselves' –Epistle of
Jeremy v. 42 (Baruch 6:42), Literal Translation.

Thus, we hear about 'a man weak and shortlived and of small power [ELASSŌN] to understand' (Wisdom 9:5), and of others who were powerless because 'their understanding has fainted' (Ps. Philo, *Biblical Antiquities* XV. 6). No wonder, Philo prayed: 'O my Understanding, never show weakness or slacken' (Philo, *Mig.* 222). We can understand why Yeshua the Messiah said:

> 'Why do you not know My speech? Because you have no power [i.e.,'understanding'] to hear [i.e., 'understand', see pp. 19–21] My word' –St. John 8:43.

> 'I have yet many things to tell you but you have no power [i.e., 'understanding'] to bear them now' –St. John 16:12.

> Yeshua answered and said to them, 'You are mistaken because you do not know the Scriptures nor the power [i.e., 'understanding'] of God'   –St. Matthew 22:29; St. Mark 12:24.

> They were amazed at His understanding and answers –St. Luke 2:47.

> They were amazed at His teaching for His word was with power [i.e., 'understanding'] –St. Luke 4:32.

> For He 'had power to explain to others what he understood' –J. Stobaeus, *Hermetica,* Exh. 23.5.

'The power of understanding' (2 Esdras 4:22; Enoch 14:3) is in Yeshua the Son of Man, because He is: 'Messiah, the power [i.e., 'understanding'] of God, and the wisdom of God' (1 Corinthians 1:24). And it is because Yeshua the Son of Man is Understanding personified that we 'will see the Son of Man sitting at the *right hand* of the Power' (St. Matthew 22:64; St. Mark 14:62) for that is the place where Understanding belongs. When Gabriel, the angel who gives us understanding (see p. 94) was sent to Zacharias, he appeared to him 'standing on the *right side* of the altar of incense' (St. Luke 1:11), the place of understanding. That is why Yeshua the Messiah told His disciples to 'cast the net on the *right side* of the boat' (St. John 21:6) when He wanted them to catch a lot of 'great fishes' and not break their net (St. John 21:11). O Solomon 'you did gather parables [in your net] like the sea through your understanding' (Sirach 47:15, Syriac Text). If you are like him 'you shall rejoice in Wisdom, and her *net* [of understanding] shall become the foundation of your power' (Sirach

6:28,29, Syriac Text). For where there is understanding, there is strength: 'I am Understanding, I have strength' (Proverbs 8:14).

Just as Wisdom and Understanding are hypostatized in the books of Proverbs, Wisdom and Sirach; so is the right arm and even the right hand of the Lord personified:

> 'Awake, awake, put on strength [as a warrior] O Arm of the Lord! Awake as in the ancient days, in the generations of old. Was it not You ['O Arm of the Lord'] who did cut Rahab into pieces?' — Isaiah 51:9.

> 'To whom has the Arm of the Lord been revealed?' —Isaiah 53:1 (applied to the Messiah in St. John 12:37–38; see also Deuteronomy 7:19; Acts 7:36–38).

> 'His arm shall rule for Him' —Isaiah 40:10.

> 'He made His glorious arm go at the right hand of Moses' —3 Enoch 48A:3; Isaiah 63:12.

> 'Your right hand shall find out those who hate you' —Psalm 21:8.

> 'Your right hand shall teach you awesome things' —Psalm 45:4.

> 'The right hand of the Omnipresent One wept, and five rivers of tears flowed from its five fingers' —3 Enoch 48A:4.

Knowing that Understanding is hypostatized in the Holy Scriptures and other ancient writings, we can see it take form in the personified right arm and hand of God. And because the Son of Man is Understanding, He is in a special sense the Right Hand of God: 'the Man of Your right hand . . . the Son of Man whom You made strong [as Your right hand] for Yourself' (Psalm 80:17). Moreover, as the Messiah-Son of Man was hidden from the eyes of His people (St. John 12:34–41; 7:4,6) so is God's glorious right arm and hand concealed (Psalm 74:11; Lamentations 2:3; 3 Enoch 44:7; 48A:5) until the time comes for His great understanding to be revealed. His people longed for the sight of His right hand:

> 'Lord of the Universe, how long will You sit upon Your throne as a mourner sits in the days of his mourning, with Your right hand [hidden] behind You, and not redeem Your sons and reveal Your kingdom in the world? . . . Do You not pity Your right hand be-

hind You, by which You stretched out the heavens?' —3 Enoch 44:7; see Jeremiah 10:12; 51:15.

They yearned for His great right arm and hand to be revealed (Isaiah 53:1; Sirach 36:6), because they knew that on the day it would be made manifest, *the Messiah would be revealed* for 'then the Holy One, blessed be He, will reveal His great arm in the world, and show it to the Gentiles . . . and the glory of its splendor shall be like the brilliant light of the noonday sun at the summer solstice. At once Israel shall be saved from among the Gentiles, and *the Messiah shall appear to them* and bring them up to Jerusalem with great joy. Moreover, they shall eat with the Messiah and the Gentiles shall eat with them, as it is written: 'The Lord has made bare His holy arm in the eyes of all the nations, and all the ends of the earth shall see the salvation of our God'' —3 Enoch 48A:9–10; Isaiah 52:10.

Chapter 21

Yeshua The Son Of Man And Suffering

We have seen how the revelation of the great and glorious right arm of God is equated with the appearance of the Messiah: the Right Arm and Hand of God (3 Enoch 48A:9–10; St. John 12:34–41). And just as the great understanding of God is found in action in His right hand, so it is also operative in His Messiah 'in whom are hidden all the treasures of wisdom and knowledge' (Colossians 2:3. See pp. 141–142). Moreover, the Messiah-Son of Man was to come as a Saviour (Enoch 48:7; Psalms of Solomon 17:23–27; Midrash Numbers Rabbah 11.2; Midrash Ruth Rabbah 5.6; Midrash Ecclesiastes Rabbah I. 9.1; Midrash Song of Songs Rabbah II. 8.3; V. 2; Pesikta de Rab Kahana, Piska 5.7,8; Pesikta Rabbati, Piska 15.10; Yalkut Shimoni, fols. 518, 603, 986). And as Saviour-Redeemer, the Messiah could also be likened to the right arm and hand of God, for it is well known that it is the arm and hand by which the Lord works salvation (Exodus 15:6; Psalms 17:7; 18:35; 20:6; 63:8; 77:15; 89:10,13; 136:11–12; Isaiah 30:30–31; 33:2; 51:9 [Psalm 89:10]; 59:16; 63:5).

But the Messiah was to be not only 'Messiah, the Saviour of the world' (St. John 4:42) but also the Vanquisher of Satan, the evil instigator of all sin (Pesikta Rabbati, Piska 36.1; Yalkut Shimoni fol. 499). Thus, He was to be named Yeshua, which means: 'Saviour' for 'He shall save His people from their sins' (St. Matthew 1:21), and break their bondage to the evil one. This type of salvation, which the Messiah would bring, was won by His own righteousness, the evil one has no hold on the Messiah, because He is the perfect Righteous One, able to vanquish Satan by His righteousness:

'This is the Son of Man who is born to righteousness and righteousness abides over him and the righteousness of the Head of Days does not forsake him' —Enoch 71:14.

'This is the Son of Man who has righteousness, with whom righteousness dwells' —Enoch 46:3.

'A man shall arise from my [Judah's] seed, like the sun of righteousness, walking with the sons of Man in meekness and righteousness; and no sin shall be found in him' –Testament of Judah 24:1.

'The Son of David . . . shall judge peoples and nations in the wisdom of his righteousness . . . he shall be a righteous King taught by God, over them, and there shall be no unrighteousness in his days in their midst' –Psalms of Solomon 17:23,31,35.

'What is the name of the King Messiah? Rabbi Abba Bar Kahana said, "His name is the Lord our Righteousness" ' –Midrash Lamentations Rabbah I.16.51; Pesikta de Rab Kahana 22.5a; Midrash on Psalms 21.2; Baba Bathra 75b, Babylonian Talmud; Yalkut Shimoni, fol. 384: all referring to Jeremiah 23:6.

'He [Yeshua] committed no sin, no guile was found in His lips' –1 Peter 2:22.

'He [Yeshua] is pure . . . in Him is no sin' –1 John 3:3,5.

'Him [Yeshua] . . . who knew no sin' –2 Corinthians 5:21.

'One [Yeshua] who in every respect has been tempted as we are, without sinning' –Hebrews 4:15.

'Which of you convicts Me of sin?' –St. John 8:46.

'The ruler of this world [Satan] . . . has no power over Me [Yeshua]' –St. John 14:30.

'Messiah [Yeshua] is the fulfillment of the law for righteousness' –Romans 10:4.

'Yeshua Messiah the righteous' –1 John 2:1.

It is in [Yeshua] the Messiah-Son of Man, that all righteousness is personified (Romans 10:3–4). Therefore, it is fitting that as God's righteousness, His place is at the right hand for it is written of the right hand of God:

'The right hand of My righteousness' –Isaiah 41:10.

'Thy right hand is full of righteousness' –Psalm 48:10.

His people expected the Messiah to come as a conquering hero to drive out their enemies and crush the power of their oppressors. But the Lord knew that what had to be conquered first was the hate and greed within the heart of the oppressor. His people also had to be cleansed of their sins, otherwise the promised Messianic reign of peace could not be established, for others would rise to take the place of those vanquished by force of arms alone, because the same evil motives would be there. God had to reign first in the heart of Man before His kingdom would be established throughout the earth.

It is through repentance and righteousness that salvation comes (2 Corinthians 7:10; St. Luke 1:77; Psalms 37:39; 50:23; 85:9; Isaiah 45:8; 2 Thessalonians 2:13). When God sends forth His righteousness, He sends forth His salvation (Isaiah 51:5; 46:13; Psalm 98:1–2), and where we find His righteousness, we find His salvation side by side (Psalms 24:5; 40:10; 51:14; 70:15; 119:123; Isaiah 51:8; 59:16–17; 61:10; 62:1; Zechariah 9:9). Conversely, 'salvation is far from the wicked' (Psalm 119:155), and 'the wicked do not understand' (Proverbs 29:7; 28:5; Daniel 12:10; Psalm 82:4,5), because along with God's righteousness and salvation we are also given His understanding. For He is 'a God of righteousness and understanding' (1QH Fragment 7:8, Dead Sea Scrolls) and it is written of Him that 'by Your righteousness You make them understand' (11Q Ps^a xix.3 [Plea of Deliverance], Dead Sea Scrolls).

To have the Messiah-Son of Man revealed, is to have the righteousness, understanding and salvation of God made manifest in Him. In turn, the right arm and hand of God has the same correlation with His righteousness, understanding, and saving power as the Messiah-Son of Man does. Hence, to have the *personified* Right Arm and Hand of God revealed, is to have His righteousness, understanding and salvation made manifest as it is in His Messiah. In 3 Enoch 44:7, the Jewish people equated the delay of their redemption to the fact that the Lord was still keeping His right hand hidden behind Him. They asked Him to reveal it so that they would be redeemed, for in the day that 'the Holy One, blessed be He, will reveal His great [right] arm in the world . . . Israel shall be saved . . . and the Messiah shall appear . . . and all the ends of the earth shall see the salvation of our God' (3 Enoch 48A:9,10; see also Sepher Hekhalot [Jellinek's *Beth haMidrash,* Vol. V, pp. 189–190]).

The Lord may keep His right hand temporarily hidden, but He does not keep it idle. Before He shall reveal 'the saving strength of His right hand' (Psalm 20:6) on behalf of His people, He conceals it so that it may do the hidden work of first saving them from their sins. For 'He shall redeem Israel from all his iniquities' (Psalms 130:8) before He shall redeem him from all his foes, by the power of His right hand.

The Messiah's secret first coming was to do the hidden work of salvation, to call sinners to repentance, to atone for them, and enable them to become true children of God. He was to sow righteousness in us so that salvation would be able to spring forth from the ground of our hearts to His praise. For the Lord had said through His prophet Isaiah, 'Let the clouds pour down *righteousness,* let the earth open, and let them bring forth *salvation*' (Isaiah 45:8): because the rain of 'righteousness' has penetrated the ground of their hearts. Consequently, He 'who sows righteousness' (Proverbs 11:17; Hosea 10:12) brings forth life (Proverbs 11:30), salvation (Odes of Solomon 1:5, Syriac Text), and peace (St. James 3:18), from the hearts of those who have kept the seeds of righteousness. They, in turn, shall bring forth from those seeds: 'the fruits of righteousness' (Philippians 1:11). It is through His Messiah Yeshua, the Son of Man, that we shall be able to bring forth fruits of righteousness because He is the One who sowed the seeds of righteousness in the redeemed ground of our hearts. 'The fruits of righteousness come through Yeshua Messiah to the glory and praise of God' (Philippians 1:11). We should always remember that we are truly earthpeople, and that our relationship with the Lord is that between earth and Sower, field and Farmer, ground and Seed, matter and Life (see pp. 3–4, 57–58). God sows before He reaps, and He prepares the ground before He plants in it, for He does all things well (Isaiah 28:23–29). From the very beginning of His ministry, Yeshua the Son of Man came 'to fulfill all righteousness' (St. Matthew 3:15) and 'to call . . . sinners to repentance' (St. Matthew 9:13; St. Mark 2:17; St. Luke 5:32) so that the ground of their hearts would be ready for the sowing of His own righteousness. It was not as crowned Reaper that the Messiah came, but as a humble Sower (St. Matthew 13:37) 'to give repentance to Israel and forgiveness of sins' (Acts 5:31) so that we might bring forth from the seeds of His exhortations: 'fruits worthy of repentance' (St. Matthew 3:8). Truly, the day shall come when 'infidelity is cut off' (2 Esdras 7:44) and all 'the wicked shall be cut off from the earth and the transgressors shall be rooted out of it' (Proverbs 2:22; see also Psalms 37:28,34,38; 52:15; 104:35; 145:20 etc.). For indeed, 'the wicked are reserved for the day of doom; they shall be brought forth on the day of wrath' (Job 21:30).

In the meantime we must wait until 'righteousness is grown, and truth is sprung up' (2 Esdras 7:44) from the sowing of Yeshua the Messiah, for He is Himself 'the implanted Word which is able to save your souls' (St. James 1:18). On the day the crowned Reaper is sent, the good ground will cry out to Him: 'Your fruits are full and complete, they are full of Your salvation!' (Odes of Solomon 1:5), and Your truth. The fruits of righteousness are the perfected seeds of righteousness because all seeds reach perfection in the fruit brought forth full of children seeds. 'He who sows the good seed is the Son of Man,' 'the [Son of Man] Sower sows the Word:' 'His Seed' (St. Matthew 13:37; St. Mark 4:14; St. Luke 8:5,11). He sows the Word in the ground of our hearts to transform us, and to have us bring forth the fruit of the seed of His Word, for we are the ground. 'The perfection of the Word is Truth' (Philo, *L.A.* III. 45). It is left for us to bring forth the Truth of His implanted Word. We bring His Word to fruit through obedience, along with the patient tilling of the ground of our hearts so that the seed of His Word may flourish and bear fruit. Faith in the Word enables us to persevere in keeping it and holding it fast so that it may complete the work it was sent to do which is to free us who are earthbound, and give us 'the glorious liberty of the children of God' (Romans 8:21). They who bring forth the children seeds of the sown Word bring forth the 'saving Truth' (Psalm 69:13 NASB) that was hidden in it and are thereby freed. It is they who truly know that 'the Truth shall make you free' (St. John 8:32), for we are sanctified and saved by the Truth (St. John 17:17,19; Psalms 19:7; 118:9,11; 1QS 4:18–22, Dead Sea Scrolls; St. Luke 8:11,15; Ephesians 5:26; 2 Thessalonians 2:13; St. James 5:19–20; 1 Peter 1:22; St. James 1:18,21; 1 Peter 1:23; 1 Corinthians 15:1–2; Ephesians 1:13; 1 Timothy 2:4; conversely: 2 Thessalonians 2:10).

Just 'as through the disobedience of one man (Adam) many were made sinners, so also through the obedience of one Man (the Messiah) many shall be made righteous' (Romans 5:19). The Messiah was sent to redeem us, and to teach us perfect obedience. He 'did not come to judge the world but to save the world' (St. John 12:47), He 'came not to destroy men's lives but to save them'–'from their sins' (St. Luke 9:56; St. Matthew 1:21). He 'came that they may have life, and that they may have it more abundantly' (St. John 10:10). He told them, 'I have come as a light into the world that whoever believes in Me may not remain in the darkness' (St. John 12:46) for He was 'the true Light which gives light to everyone who comes into the world' (St. John 1:9).

We know that the holy right arm and hand of God represents His saving power, great understanding, righteousness, and holiness. For when it is said that 'the Lord has sworn by His *right hand*' (Isaiah 62:8), it is meant that 'the Lord has sworn by His *holiness*' (Amos 4:2; Psalm 89:35). Thus, that arm and hand of the Lord is known as 'His right hand and His *holy* (right) arm' (Psalm 98:1; Isaiah 52:10). And knowing that it is through His truth that we are made holy and saved, we may be sure that we shall find His Truth also at the right hand of God. Because if it is said of the wicked that 'their right hand is a right hand of falsehood' (Psalm 144:8,11), and of an idolater that it is not possible for him to say: 'there is not a lie in my right hand' (Isaiah 44:20), then the right hand of the Lord and of the children of God must be a right hand full of Truth. Yeshua, the Messiah-Son of Man is seated at the right hand of God, because He is not only the Saviour, the Understanding of God, and the All-Righteous One, but also the Truth incarnate (St. John 14:6; 1:14,17; 8:31–32; 18:37; 1 John 5:20).

It is what is hidden that shall be revealed 'for there is nothing hidden which will not be revealed, nor has anything been kept secret but that it should come to light' (St. Mark 4:22). And it is the humble who shall be exalted, because 'humility goes before honor' (Proverbs 15:33; 18:12; 25:6–7; 29:23; St. Luke 14:11; St. James 4:10). The right arm and hand of God shall be revealed in the person of His hidden Messiah (Isaiah 52:10; 3 Enoch 48A:9; St. Matthew 24:27; St. Luke 17:24,30). And the right arm and hand of the Lord shall be exalted in His Messiah, because the greatest saving act of the arm of the Lord was done for us in the guise of His humble and suffering Servant: the Messiah.

God is exalted in His saving acts (Exodus 15:2,6; Psalms 18:46; 108:5,13; Isaiah 33:3–5), and when He abases the proud (Isaiah 2:11,17; Ezekiel 38:18–19,21–23) and executes judgment (Isaiah 5:16). His servants are exalted when His righteousness is found in them (Deuteronomy 4:6,8; 28:1; Proverbs 14:34) and when their wisdom and understanding are brought to light (see pp. 64–65, 70–71, 90–92).

In the rich imagery of the Holy Scriptures a son is a 'branch':

> 'O God of hosts, look down from heaven and see, and visit this vine and the vineyard which Your right hand has planted, and the Branch [literally BEN = 'son'] that You made strong for Yourself' —Psalm 80:14,15.

> 'Joseph [son of Jacob] is a fruitful bough [literally BEN = 'son']' —Genesis 49:22.

> 'Behold, the day will come,' says the Lord, 'That I will raise to David a righteous Branch [i.e., a son]' —Jeremiah 23:5; 33:15.

It is in the 'son-branch' that the tree bears fruit, and that the tree is served. Therefore, the Servant of the Lord is also called a 'branch':

> 'Behold, I am bringing forth My Servant the Branch' —Zechariah 3:8.

We know that good sons of Man (see pp. 13–14, 32, 46–47, 81–83), and servants (see pp. 64–65, 66–71) are noted for their understanding and that both are compared to branches. Consequently, understanding *per se* may also be compared to a fruitful branch. There are dire consequences if the branches have no understanding:

> 'When its [the people's] branches are withered, they will be broken off; the women come and set them on fire, because it is a people of no understanding' —Isaiah 27:11.

Before they have become hopelessly 'withered', the branches of understanding that have not borne fruit are pruned: 'O Lord . . . give seed to our heart and cultivation to our (branches of) understanding so that fruit may come from it' (2 Esdras 8:6). Thus, if 'Wisdom's branches are length of days' (Sirach 1:20) and 'in length of days: understanding' (Job 12:12), then Wisdom's branches are branches of understanding.

Just as good sons of Man and servants are expected to have understanding, so are the disciples of a wise teacher. The Lord's Messiah referred to His disciples as 'branches':

> 'I am the Vine and you are the branches' —St. John 15:5.

> 'Every branch in Me that does not bear fruit He takes away, and every branch that bears fruit He prunes, that it may bear more fruit' —St. John 15:2.

> 'By this is My Father glorified, that you bear much fruit, and so prove to be My disciples' —St. John 15:8.

Ultimately, an *arm* is like a *branch*. Thus, to have the arm of the Lord revealed while doing its hidden saving work can also be a way of having His Servant the Branch revealed while He is doing His hidden work of salvation. His people knew that the Servant of the Lord called by Him, 'the Branch' (Zechariah 3:8) was none other than the Messiah:

> 'I will bring forth My Servant the *Branch*' —Zechariah 3:8.

> 'I will bring forth My Servant the *Messiah*' —Targum Jonathan to Zechariah 3:8.

> 'Behold the [Servant] Man whose name is the *Branch*' — Zechariah 6:12.

> This [re Zechariah 6:12] refers to the *Messiah* of whom it also
> says, 'I will raise to David a righteous Branch' [Jeremiah 23:5]
> —Midrash Numbers Rabbah 18.21; Midrash Lamentations Rab-
> bah I. 16.51; Midrash Mishlei on Proverbs 19:21, sect. 19.

The rabbis knew that 'the Branch of the Lord', in all the references to
Him was the Messiah (see Targum Jonathan on Isaiah 4:2; 11:1; Jeremiah
23:5; 33:15; Zechariah 6:12 and other rabbinic references; see also pp.
88–90). This Servant-Branch of the Lord was to 'reign as king and understand [SAKAL-SUNESEI]' —Jeremiah 23:5, Hebrew and Greek Texts. It
was also promised that this now King-Branch of the Lord would in the end
'execute judgment and righteousness in the earth' (Jeremiah 23:5), but
before that He would be unnoted, coming in humility and meekness, bearing salvation to those who received Him:

> 'Rejoice greatly, O daughter of Zion! Shout, O daughter of Jerusa-
> lem! Behold your King is coming to you; He is righteous and *hav-
> ing salvation,* humble and riding on an ass, a colt, the foal of an
> ass' —Zechariah 9:9, Hebrew Text.

> 'Rejoice greatly, O daughter of Sion! Proclaim it aloud, O daugh-
> ter of Jerusalem! Behold, the King is coming to you, righteous
> and *saving,* He is meek and riding on an ass, and a young foal
> [of an ass]' —Zechariah 9:9, Greek Septuagint Text.

The Servant-Branch in the book of Zechariah (3:8; 6:12) was identified
by the teachers of His people as being the Messiah. They also knew that
in the same book of the prophet Zechariah, the meek and humble King
formerly referred to as 'My Servant the Branch' was no one else but the
Messiah (see rabbinic references concerning Zechariah 9:9 on p. 124). For
the teachers remembered that long ago, in the book of the prophet Isaiah,
the Lord had described His Messiah as a wonderful plant springing forth
from the stock of Jesse:

> 'There shall come forth a shoot from the stock of Jesse, and a
> Branch shall grow out of his roots. And the Spirit of the Lord
> shall rest upon him, the spirit of wisdom and understanding, the
> spirit of counsel and might, the spirit of knowledge and of the
> fear of the Lord. And his delight shall be in the fear of the Lord.
> He shall not judge by what his eyes see, nor decide by what his
> ears hear; but with righteousness he shall judge the poor, and de-
> cide with equity for the meek of the earth. And he shall smite
> the earth with the rod of his mouth, and with the breath of his

lips he shall slay the wicked. Righteousness shall be the girdle of his loins, and faithfulness the girdle of his waist' —Isaiah 11:1–5.

Many are the rabbinic references interpreting Messianically this wonderful Branch from the stock of Jesse (Targum on Isaiah 11:1–10; Midrash Genesis Rabbah 2.4; 97 [NV]; Midrash Ruth Rabbah 7.2; Midrash on Psalms 2.3; 21.1,3; 72.3–4; Midrash Song of Songs Rabbah 6.10.1; Midrash Lamentations Rabbah I. 16.51; Pesikta Rabbati, Piska 33.6; 37.1; Pirke Rabbi Eliezer, chap. 3; Yalkut Shimoni, fols. 4, 145, 415, 725, 805; Zohar II. 172b; III. 130b, 203b; III. 289 [Idra Zutta Hadisha section]; Berakoth 5a, Jerusalem Talmud; Sanhedrin 93a, Babylonian Talmud; Ibn Ezra and Abarbanel on Isaiah 11; see also Enoch 49:3 [Isaiah 11:1,2]; 49:4 [Isaiah 11:3,4]; 62:2 [Isaiah 11:1–4]; Sibylline Oracles III. 286; 2 Esdras 13:10,37–38 [Isaiah 11:4]).

By tracing the references to the Branch of the Lord through the books of the prophets, we are able to understand that he sprung forth from the house of David, and was endowed by God with great wisdom, understanding, knowledge, counsel, might and reverence for Him. We are told that the Servant-Branch of the Lord is truly righteous and faithful in an extraordinary way, for he was to be called 'the Lord our Righteousness' (Jeremiah 23:5–6). And although he was a King by virtue of his royal lineage, he did not come in glory but in meekness and humility ready to do the will of God at all costs in perfect obedience. He was to be called the Servant of the Lord just as the Lord called King David His servant (2 Samuel 7:5,8; 1 Kings 3:6–9; 8:24–26; 11:13,36,38; 14:8; 2 Kings 8:19; Psalm 89:3,20; Ezekiel 34:24; 37:23), and King David referred to himself as a servant of the Lord (1 Samuel 23:11; 2 Samuel 7:19–21,25–29; 24:10; Psalms 18 and 36; titles and Psalms 19:11,13; 27:9; 31:16; 69:17; 86:2; 143:12; 144:10). Being a Servant and a Servant-King as was his ancestor King David, the Branch of the Lord possesses good understanding and is to be exalted in the end by his understanding (Isaiah 52:13–15; Jeremiah 23:5; 1 Samuel 18:30, Literal Translation). It was to be through the Servant-Branch of the Lord that the Arm of the Lord would perform the greatest act of salvation, for as His truly righteous Servant, the Branch of the Lord was able to atone for, and redeem the people from their sins.

The Lord dwells in the highest heavens and in the simple and lowly ones. 'For thus says the High and Eminent One who lives forever, whose name is Holy: 'I dwell in the high and holy place, and also with him who is of a contrite and humble spirit" (Isaiah 57:15). 'Though the Lord is on high, yet He sees the lowly; but the proud He knows from afar' (Psalm 138:6). 'God resists the proud, but He gives grace to the humble' (St. James 4:6; 1 Peter 5:5; Proverbs 3:34). We may be sure that the Servant whom the Lord would choose to do the saving work of His right arm would be someone pleasing to Him because of his humility, meekness, and righteousness. 'The Lord loves the righteous' (Psalms 146:8; 147:11; Proverbs 15:9; Testament of Joseph 11:2), because 'the righteous Lord loves righteousness' (Psalms 11:7; 33:5; 45:7; 1 Chronicles 29:17). And 'the Lord has set apart for Himself him who is godly' (Psalm 4:3) and blameless, for 'He loves holy hearts and all blameless persons are acceptable to Him' (Proverbs 22:11, Greek Text). Just as the animals used for the atoning sacrifices of the Temple had to be perfect:

> Whoever offers a sacrifice . . . it shall be perfect to be accepted, there shall be no blemish in it —Leviticus 22:21; Ibid., 1:3,10; 3:1,6; 4:23,28,32; 5:15,18; 6:6; 9:2,3; 14:10; 22:19; 23:12,18, etc.

> A sacrifice is not acceptable when it is not perfect —Sifre Vayikra N'dab III.3; Leviticus 22:20; Deuteronomy 15:21;

so does a servant of the Lord have to be perfect to be acceptable to the Lord should he desire to offer up his life in atonement for the sins of the people.

When His people sinned they had to make an atonement for their sins by sacrificing an animal before the Lord in His Temple. The blood of the animal had to be shed 'because the life of the flesh is in the blood, and I [the Lord] have given it to you on the altar to make atonement for your souls; for it is the blood that makes an atonement for the soul' (Leviticus 17:11). The life of the animal was shed when its blood was shed. The mercy of God provided as a substitute for the sinner an animal victim on which the guilt and the punishment of the sinner were laid. Did not the Lord provide just such a substitute in the ram which was offered instead of Isaac? (Genesis 22:1–13).

Thus, in bringing the sacrificial animal [a perfect lamb, sheep or goat] to the priest in the Temple, the sinner 'laid his hand on the head of the [animal to be sacrificed as a] burnt offering, that it may be accepted for him to make atonement on his behalf' (Leviticus 1:4). It was a very solemn moment for the sinner because he knew 'that in all justice it is the offerer's own blood that should have been shed and his body burnt but the Creator in His great mercy has accepted the animal victim from him as a vicarious substitute [TEMURAH] and an atonement [KEPHER] that its blood should be poured out instead of his (the sinner's) life' (Nachmanides

[Rabbi Moses ben Nachman], *Commentary on the Five Scrolls,* Section on Leviticus 1). 'The offender when he beholds the victim on account of his sin, slain, skinned, cut in pieces and burnt with fire upon the altar, should reflect that thus he would have been treated had not God in His clemency accepted this expiation for his life' (Rabbi Isaac ben Moses Arama, *Commentary on Leviticus;* see also Abarbanel's *Preface to Leviticus* and David de Pomis ad loc.). What also moved the offender was the pitiful sight of his innocent, perfect and unblemished lamb about to be killed in atonement for his sins.

His people knew that the death of innocent children had an atoning efficacy (Shabbath 33b; Berakoth 5a end, Babylonian Talmud; Midrash Ecclesiastes Rabbah 4.1.1). The death of children is still considered as an atonement for the sins of the parents and their older contemporaries (Shabbath 119b, Babylonian Talmud; Midrash Genesis Rabbah 58.2; Midrash Zutta 47 [2 Samuel 12:13–23; Micah 6:7]), because sinlessness atones (Midrash Tanchumah 6).

'The Lord alone is righteous' (Sirach 18:2), and 'to the Lord our God belongs all righteousness' (Baruch 1:15; 2:6) for He is our righteousness (Jeremiah 23:5) and by His lovingkindness and righteousness we are cleansed of our sins:

> 'You pardon iniquity and cleanse man from sin through Your righteousness' −1QH 4:37, Dead Sea Scrolls.

> 'Through His righteousness are my rebellions blotted out' −1QS 11:3, Dead Sea Scrolls.

> 'From the fount of His righteousness comes my justification' −1QS 11:5; Ibid., 11:12,14a, Dead Sea Scrolls.

> 'By His immense goodness He will pardon all my iniquities and by His righteousness He will cleanse me of the defilement of Man and of the sins of the sons of Man that I may acknowledge His righteousness unto God and His majesty unto the Most High' −1QS 11:14–15, Dead Sea Scrolls.

Only because of the righteousness of God which is found in the righteous, could His people place any hope in the atoning efficacy of the sufferings and death of the just. They thought that Abraham's heroic righteousness and fidelity, and Isaac's obedience and meekness on Mount Moriah (Genesis 22:1–13) atoned for all time for the sins of Israel (Midrash Genesis Rabbah 56.9–10; Midrash Exodus Rabbah 35.4; Midrash Leviticus Rabbah 29.9,3; Midrash Tanchumah [ed. Buber] I. 115; Tanchumah Wa-Yera 40, 23; Tanchumah, Shelah 14; Pesikta de Rab Kahana 23.9, [154a,b, 167a, 200b]; Pesikta Rabbati 40.5 [171b]; Mekilta Bo, 8a, 12a [Lauterbach]; Rosh ha Shanah 16a, Berakoth 7a, Shabbath 89b, Babylonian Talmud; Midrash Haggadol I. 325–326; Midrash Tehillim 47; Taanith II.4, 65d, Jerusalem Talmud; Targum Jerusalem on Genesis 22; Yalkut Genesis 99, 479, 645, 782; Yalkut Joshua 12; Yalkut Micah 555; Yalkut Isaiah 508). Thus, according to them, 'Isaac, who was tied up like a bundle upon the altar . . . atones for the sins of Israel' (Midrash Song of Songs Rabbah I.14.1). The rabbis would say, 'As the Day of Atonement atones, so does the death of the righteous' (Midrash Leviticus Rabbah 20.12). Furthermore, 'As the Red Heifer makes atonement, so, too, does the death of the righteous' (Moed Katan 28a, Babylonian Talmud; Yoma I.1,38b, Jersualem Talmud). Yes, 'the death of the righteous atones for Israel's sins' (Pesikta de Rab Kahana, Piska 26.11 end). And because the martyrs died for the sake of the Law of the God of Israel, the rabbis also said that 'the Jewish martyrs by their death make atonement for the rest of their brethren' (Sifre to Deuteronomy, sec. 333 [fol. 140a]; see also *Hekhalot Rabbati,* chaps. 5 and 6 [in Jellinek's, *Beth haMidrash,* vol. III. pp. 83–108]). Thus, in the books of the Maccabees, the martyrs themselves prayed:

> 'I . . . offer up my body and life for the laws of our fathers beseeching God that He would speedily be merciful to our nation . . . and that in me, and my brothers (all of whom died as martyrs) the wrath of the Almighty, which is justly brought upon all our nation may cease' —2 Maccabees 7:37,38.

> 'Be merciful to Thy people, and be satisfied with the punishment of me on their account. Let my blood be a purification for them, and take my life in recompense for theirs.' Thus speaking, the holy man departed, noble in his torments, and even to the agonies of death' —4 Maccabees 6:28–30; Ibid., 1:10–11; 17:20–22; see also Exodus 32:31–35.

Nevertheless, they had no real assurance that the Lord would accept their sacrificial offering of themselves in atonement for the sins of the people. For if the Lord did not accept any animals except the 'perfect [TAMIM] . . . and without blemish' (Leviticus 22:21) to make atonement for them (Leviticus 22:20; Malachi 1:6–14), what certitude could the 'righteous' have of being accepted by the Lord as a perfect and unblemished offering? And if 'there is not a righteous man upon the earth who does good and does not sin' (Ecclesiastes 7:20; 1 Kings 18:46; 2 Chronicles 6:36; Psalms 14:3; 130:3; Proverbs 24:16), 'how can a man be (considered) righteous before God?' (Job 9:2; 25:4). 'We are all an unclean thing, and all our righteous deeds are as filthy rags' (Isaiah 64:6; Job 15:14–16; Psalm 51:5) before Him. 'Who can say 'I have made my heart clean, I am pure from my sin?'' (Proverbs 20:9). 'If we say we have no sin, we deceive ourselves and the truth is not in us' (1 John 1:8,10). 'Who can bring a clean thing out of an unclean? No one!' (Job 14:4), or who can redeem others who is himself in need of redemption? 'Truly, no man can redeem his brother, nor give to God a ransom for him' (Psalm 49:7) unless he is able to do so because he is Someone called 'the Lord our righteousness': the Messiah (Jeremiah 23:6; see pp. 156–157).

The marvelous acts of salvation performed by the right Arm and Hand of God are both seen and hidden. The people saw His right Arm in action when the Lord routed their enemies, but the most wonderful saving work done by *His right Arm* for them was hidden from their eyes. Because that work of redemption and salvation was done in the heart through the atoning death of His perfectly righteous Messiah: the meek and humble Servant-Branch, and hidden *Arm of God:*

> Who has believed what we have heard? And to whom has the Arm of the Lord been revealed? For He grew up before Him as a tender plant, and as a root out of dry ground. He had no stately form or majesty [HADAR] that we should behold Him, nothing in His appearance that we should desire Him. He was despised and rejected by men, a Man of sorrows and knowing grief. And as One from whom men hide their faces. He was despised and we did not esteem Him.

> Surely, He has borne our griefs and carried our sorrows; yet we esteemed Him stricken, smitten by God and afflicted. But He was pierced [CHALAL] through for our transgressions, He was bruised for our iniquities; the chastisement for our peace was upon Him, and by His stripes we are healed. All we like sheep have gone astray; we have turned every one to his own way; and the Lord has lain on Him the iniquity of us all.

> He was oppressed, and He was afflicted, yet He did not open His mouth; like a lamb that is led to the slaughter, and like a sheep that is silent before its shearers, so He did not open His mouth. By oppression and judgment He was taken away; and as for His generation, who considered that He was cut off out of the land of the living, stricken for the transgression of My people? And He

was assigned a grave with the wicked and with a rich man in His death, although He had done no wrong, and there was no deceit in His mouth.

Yet it was the will of the Lord to bruise Him, and put Him to grief, and though He made Himself a guilt offering, He shall see His offspring, He shall prolong His days; and the good pleasure of the Lord shall prosper in His hand. He shall see the travail of His soul and be satisfied. By His knowledge shall My righteous Servant make the many to be accounted righteous; and He shall bear their iniquities. Therefore I will allot Him a portion with the great, and He shall divide the spoils with the strong, because He poured out His soul to death, and was numbered with the transgressors; yet He bore the sin of many, and made intercession for the transgressors —Isaiah 53:1–12.

No one else but He who was called 'the Lord our righteousness' (Jeremiah 23:6) would be able to 'save His people from their sins' (St. Matthew 1:21) by His atoning death. For He alone is 'the Lamb of God who takes away the sin of the world' (St. John 1:29,36; Revelation 5:6,12; 7:14; 12:11; 21:14).

Chapter 22

Son Of Suffering – Son Of Strength

'To whom has the Arm of the Lord been revealed?' —Isaiah 53:1
'To whom has the understanding of wisdom been revealed?'
—Sirach 1:7, Syriac and Sahidic Texts

The perfect righteousness of the Messiah is acknowledged by the rabbis (Midrash Lamentations Rabbah I.16.51; Midrash on Psalms 21.2; Pesikta de Rab Kahana, Piska 22.5a; Baba Bathra 75b, Babylonian Talmud; Yalkut Shimoni, fol. 384; see also citations on p. 156–157). And when the prophet Isaiah spoke concerning the personified right arm and hand of God, the rabbis knew that he was referring in a hidden sense to the Messiah in certain instances:

> In the times of the Messiah, 'the Lord shall manifest a second time His hand' (Isaiah 11:11). He [the manifested personified Hand of the Lord] shall be the Redeemer [i.e., the Messiah] in person so that 'Israel shall be saved in the Lord with an everlasting salvation' (Isaiah 45:17). And 'his [the King Messiah's] rest shall be glorious' (Isaiah 11:10) . . . All the world shall say, 'It is fitting that his rest shall be glorious, for while ordinary kings acquire glory for themselves through victorious wars, and do not believe themselves to be esteemed when they are at rest, he [the King Messiah], on the contrary, without waging war makes everyone subject to him, and all render him homage' —*Commentary Minha-Ghedola,* found in the Grand Rabbinic Bible of Amsterdam, 1700–1705 [Rabbinic Bible of Bomberg].

Many of the qualities of the right arm and hand found in the Holy Scriptures can also be applied to the Messiah. For it is full of righteousness, holiness and truth (Psalm 48:10; Isaiah 41:10; Psalm 98:1; Isaiah 52:10; see p. 178), and it is hidden but shall be revealed and exalted (3 Enoch 44:7; 48A:1,9–10; Psalms 89:13; 118:16). It is the arm and hand of salvation (see p. 156), redemption (Psalms 77:15; 89:10,13; 136:11–12; Isaiah 51:10) and upholding (Psalms 18:35; 63:8; Isaiah 41:10). It teaches (Job 27:11; Psalm 45:4) and from it we have received the Law of God (Deuteronomy 33:2; see also Midrash Numbers Rabbah 22.9; Midrash on

Psalms 18.28; Shabbath 63a, 88b, Babylonian Talmud; 1Q34, II.7, Dead Sea Scrolls). It is full of understanding (see pp. 149–151) so it is able to search out (Psalm 21:8) and guide (Psalm 78:22; Isaiah 63:12; 3 Enoch 48A:3). It is mighty and strong (Exodus 6:1; 13:9; Psalm 136:12; Isaiah 40:10; 51:9; Jeremiah 21:5; 32:21) but yet compassionate (3 Enoch 48A:4) because love is in the right hand (Sanhedrin 107b; Sotah 47a, Babylonian Talmud; see Song of Songs 2:6; 8:3). 'O Lord . . . You are the right hand of my salvation and my Helper' (Odes of Solomon 25:1,2; 8:6, Syriac Text), and 'Your right hand has exalted me' (Odes of Solomon 25:9). 'You became for me a right hand by which You saved me' (Odes of Solomon 25:2, Coptic Text).

The early Christians knew that Yeshua the Saviour was the personified Arm and Hand of the Lord prophecied by Isaiah:

'Christ . . . is the Arm of the Lord' –Clement of Alexandria, *Exh.* XI. 120.4.

'Christ is the Hand of the Lord' –St. Jerome, *Commentary on Isaiah* 66:14.
'Christ is the Hand and Arm of God' –Cyprian, *Treatises* XII. Lib.ii. Test. iv.

'The Son is the Arm of the Lord and the Right Hand of the Lord' –Melito of Sardis; see also Tertullian, *Praxeas,* Chap. XIII; *Apostolic Constitutions,* Book V. sect. III. xvi. [Constantinople Codex].

For if Israel was saved from her foes by 'the right arm and hand of the Lord' (Exodus 15:6; Psalms 17:7; 18:35; 20:6; 63:8; 77:15; 89:10,13; 108:6; 136:11–12; Isaiah 30:30–31; 32:2; 51:9; 59:16; 63:5; Jeremiah 21:5; 32:21), then who else but the personified right arm and hand of God would deliver the people from the evil one and save them from their sins? The Saviour-Messiah is the Arm of the Lord.

Notwithstanding later rabbinic commentaries interpreting non-Messianically the fifty-third chapter of the book of the prophet Isaiah, early Jewish tradition held that the Messiah was the Arm of the Lord and Suffering Servant in Isaiah 53:1–12. Isaac Abarbanel (1437–1508) said concerning this chapter: 'Jonathan ben Uzziel interprets it in the Targum as being the future Messiah, and this is also the opinion of our learned men in the majority of the Midrashim' (exegetical works). Rabbi Moshe el Sheikh of Safed who was the Chief Rabbi said: 'Our rabbis with one voice accept and affirm the opinion that the prophet [Isaiah 53] is speaking of King Messiah, and we shall ourselves also adhere to the same view'. Rabbi Elijah de Vidas who wrote the *Reshit Hokmah* (Venice 1579) stated: 'Since the Messiah bears our iniquities, which produce the effect of his being bruised (Isaiah 53:4–5,10), it follows that he who will not admit that the Messiah thus suffers for our iniquities must endure and suffer for them himself.' He reiterated what Rabbi Moshe Kohen Ibn Crispin of Cordoba and Toledo said two hundred years before him, when he wrote that those who for controversial reasons apply the prophecy of the Suffering Servant in Isaiah 53 to Israel find it impossible to understand the true meaning of this prophecy, 'having forsaken the knowledge of our teachers, and inclined after the stubbornness of their own opinions [they] distort the passage from its natural meaning . . . for it was given by God as a description of the Messiah.' Rabbi Moshe Ibn Crispin had undoubtedly read what the eleventh century Rabbi Moshe ha-Darshan said in his commentary on Genesis: 'The Holy One gave the Messiah the opportunity to save souls but to be severely chastised, and straightway the Messiah accepted the chastisements of love as it is written, 'He was oppressed and he was afflicted' [Isaiah 53:7]. And when Israel is sinful, the Messiah seeks mercy upon them as it is written: 'By His stripes we were healed' [Isaiah 53:5] and 'He carried the sins of many and made intercession for the transgressors' ' [Isaiah 53:12]—*Genesis Rabbati* sect. on Genesis 24:67 (*Midrash Bereshith Rabbati*, edited by H. Albeck, Jerusalem, 1940). Thus in the Yalkut to Isaiah 60:1, the Messiah cries out: 'King of the Universe, I accept these sufferings with joy in my heart on condition that none in Israel be lost . . . and that all may be saved in my days. On this condition I accept all.' In an ancient hymn-prayer composed by Eliezer Hakkalir (see p. 107) which is sung during the Musaf Service in the Day of Atonement there is the lament that:

> 'Our righteous Messiah has departed from us. We are horror-stricken and have no one to justify us.
> Our iniquities and the yoke of our transgressions he carries [Isaiah 53:4,12], and he is wounded because of our transgressions [Isaiah 53:5].
> He bears on his shoulder the burden of our sins, to find pardon for all our iniquities. By his stripes we are healed. O Eternal One, it is time that You should create him anew! O bring him up from the land of Seir to announce salvation to us from Mount Lebabon.'

They knew in those days that 'the Messiah bears the sins of Israel' (*Sefer*

Chasidim p. 60, Venice and Basle editions, 1581), and that he suffered for them: 'When the Holy One, blessed be He, sees David and the Messiah, He calls David and says to him, "My son . . . I have brought sufferings upon him [the Messiah]" ' –Pesikta Hadta [In Jellinek's *Beth haMidrash* Vol. VI, p. 47]. For 'the Messiah takes upon himself the sins of the people' (Zohar II fol. 85, Edition Solisbac), and their sufferings: 'While Israel dwelt in the Holy Land and offered sacrifices [in the Temple] he was preserved from all maladies and sufferings by merit of the sacrifices. Now it is the Messiah who bears the pains and sufferings of all the world' (Zohar II fol. 211b re Exodus 33:23). The Messiah bore these sufferings gladly because they obtained forgiveness from God for His people:

> 'The Holy One, blessed be He, will tell him [the Messiah] in detail what will befall him . . . , their sins will cause you to bend down as under a yoke of iron and make you like a calf whose eyes grow dim with suffering and will choke your spirit as with a yoke, and because of their sins your tongue will cleave to the roof of your mouth. Are you willing to endure such things? . . . The Messiah will say: "Master of the universe with joy in my soul and gladness in my heart I take this suffering upon myself provided that not one person in Israel shall perish, so that not only those who are alive be saved in my days, but also those who are dead, who died from the days of Adam up to the time of redemption" ' –Pesikta Rabbati, Piska 36.1; Zohar II. 212a.

> 'The Patriarchs will arise and say to the Messiah, " . . . our righteous Messiah, even though we are your ancestors, you are greater than we because you did suffer for the iniquities of our children, and terrible ordeals befell you, such ordeals as did not befall earlier generations or later ones for the sake of Israel" ' –Pesikta Rabbati, Piska 37:1.

> 'Dip your morsel of bread in the vinegar [Ruth 2:14]: this refers to the Messiah's sufferings, for it is said in Isaiah 53:5: "He was pierced through for our transgressions, he was bruised for our iniquities" ' –Midrash Ruth Rabbah, 2.14.

There are many other rabbinic references identifying the Messiah as being the Suffering Servant in the fifty-third chapter of Isaiah (see Genesis Rabbati 1:3; 24:67; 37:22 [re Isaiah 53:3,5–12]; Yalkut Shimoni, fols. 499 [Isaiah 53:4–6,8]; 476 [Isaiah 53:5]; Midrash Haggadol on Genesis 49:10 [Isaiah 53:4]; Midrash Samuel, Parashah 19 [Isaiah 53:5]; Zohar II, 115b, 212a; III, 276b [Isaiah 53:5]; Sanhedrin 98b, Babylonian Talmud [Isaiah

53:4]; Midrash Konen 29 [In Jellinek's *Beth haMidrash* II, pp. 23–29]; Maaseh Rabbi Joshua 50 [In Jellinek's *Beth haMidrash* II, pp. 48–51]; Rabbi Tobias ben Eliezer's, *Lekah Tob* re Isaiah 53:3–5; Rabbi Simeon bar Yohai on Isaiah 53; Rabbi Saadia Ibn Danan's, Commentary on Isaiah 53; and Maimonides on Isaiah 53:2). Concerning the fifty-second and fifty-third chapters of Isaiah, Rabbi Naphtali ben Asher Altschuler wrote: 'I will proceed to explain these verses [Isaiah 52–53] of our Messiah, who God willing will come speedily in our days. I am surprised that Rashi and Rabbi David Kimchi have not with the Targums applied it to the Messiah likewise.' Jewish Karaite commentators, among them Japheth ben Eli, Benjamin al-Nahawandi and Salmon ben Jeroham also interpreted the Suffering Servant in Isaiah 53:1–12 messianically.

Remembering that King Saul and King David were both chosen and anointed by the Lord [1 Samuel 9:15–16; 10:1; 16:1,12–13] to rule over His people, the rabbis concluded that in the future the Lord would send His people two Messiahs, a warrior Messiah (Messiah ben Joseph or ben Ephraim) who would suffer and die in battle (as King Saul did), and a conquering Messiah (Messiah ben David) who would resurrect the fallen Messiah (Daniel 9:26), then triumph over his enemies and usher in a long reign of peace. The first Messiah was to be a descendant of Joseph the son of Jacob and Rachel, and the second Messiah was to come from the stock of Judah, the son of Jacob and Leah. We first hear about Messiah ben Joseph in the Babylonian Talmud, Sukkah 52a,b [Jerusalem Talmud, Sukkah V. 2] in a saying attributed to Rabbi Kalafta ben Dosa of the second century A.D. There are also numerous references to Messiah ben Joseph or Messiah ben Ephraim in the Targums, Midrashes and other rabbinic writings (see Targums to Exodus 40:11; Song of Songs 4:5; 7:4; Midrash Genesis Rabbah 75.6; 95.1; 99.2; Midrash Exodus Rabbah I.5; Midrash Numbers Rabbah 14.1; Midrash Exodus Rabbah I.5; Midrash Numbers Rabbah 14.1; Midrash Song of Songs Rabbah II. 13.4; Midrash on Psalms 60.3; 87.6; Pesikta Rabbati, Piska 34.2; 36.1; 37.1,2; Midrash Lekah Tob, folio 126b; Tanna Debe Eliyyahu Rabbah 98; Sepher Zerubbabel [In Jellinek's, *Beth haMidrash* Vol. II, pp. 54–57]; Agadath Mashiah [In Jellinek's, *Beth haMidrash* Vol. III, pp. 141–143]; Revelations of Rabbi Simeon ben Yohai [In Jellinek's, *Beth haMidrash* Vol. III, pp. 78–81]; Midrash Vayosha [In Jellinek's, *Beth haMidrash* Vol. I, pp. 55–57]; Wars of the King Messiah [In Jellinek's, *Beth haMidrash* Vol. II, pp. 58–63]; Yelammedenu 20 [In Jellinek's, *Beth haMidrash* Vol. VI, pp. 79–90]; Pirke Rabbi Yoshiyyahu 115 [In Jellinek's, *Beth haMidrash* Vol. VI, pp. 112–116]; Zohar Vol. I, 38a,b; 267b; Vol. II, 8a; 211a,b, 212a; Vol. III, 166a;

203b; 278b; Sepher Zohar Chadash sect. Balak [end]; Midrash Geulah of Yehuda Ibn Samuel p. 103 [Mosad-Bialik-Masada Edition, Jerusalem, 1954]; Midrash of the Ten Kings [In Horowitz's, *Sanlung Kleiner Midraschim* Vol. I, pp. 37–55]).

In those and other texts concerning the first Messiah (Messiah ben Joseph), there is the imagery of his submission to suffering (Pesikta Rabbati, Piska 36.1; 37.1–2; Zohar I.38b; II.8a, 212a; Midrash Konen [In Jellinek's, *Beth haMidrash* Vol. II, pp. 23–29] etc.), his lowliness (Tanna debe Eliyyahu 98; Sukkah 52 a,b, Babylonian Talmud; Idem. V. 1–2, Jerusalem Talmud; Yalkut Jonah, 550), and hiddenness before his appearance in upper Galilee (Lekah Tob ii, p. 258 [Edition Wilna, 1880]; Midrash Geulah p. 103; Bacher's *Die Agada der palestinischen Amoraer,* ii, p. 432, note 4; Strack-Billerbeck, i, p. 161). We are told of his gathering followers to himself and of his advance to Jerusalem and temporary triumph over his enemies before being slain by them. The second Messiah (Messiah ben David) comes and resurrects him and goes on waging war and overcoming all the enemies of Israel. Messiah ben David is the one who ushers in the wonderful promised messianic era.

Nothing is heard about Messiah ben Joseph after his resurrection by Messiah ben David. In the Zohar we are given the insight that Messiah ben Joseph and Messiah ben David are but one and the same Messiah. (See Zohar I. 267b, section Sefer Habahir re Genesis 1:2).

If we search the Holy Scriptures we shall see that there is a final exaltation of those who are good. They may have been despised, persecuted, slandered and slain, but in the end they are vindicated and sit in judgment against their former oppressors. It is they who receive the kingdom, power and dominion from the Lord. We have seen how Joseph of Egypt and Daniel of Babylon came forth from dungeons to be given rule by the kings, and how Gideon came forth from concealment to lead the tribes (Judges 6:11–8:28). The Lord's anointed ones were at lowly occupations when they received their commissions to reign (see pp. 123–124). Thus, the teachers of His people knew that when the Messiah would first appear he would come in humility because 'humility goes before honor' (Proverbs 18:12), and meekness before exaltation. Later on they had the further insight that a life of suffering was entailed for the first Messiah, and that after initial successes in battle there would be defeat and death for the warrior Messiah known as Messiah ben Joseph or Messiah ben Ephraim. It was to be Messiah ben David (the second Messiah), who would restore all things, establish the Kingdom and introduce a long reign of peace and prosperity throughout the world. Just as it was not Moses, the original saviour, but Joshua, who led the people to the Holy Land; and not King Saul, but his successor King David, who established the Kingdom.

They remembered that among all the adults of the twelve tribes who left Egypt, only Joshua of the tribe of Ephraim (son of Joseph), and Caleb of the tribe of Judah entered and possessed the promised land (see pp. 97–98). Later on, the one great Kingdom of Israel under King Solomon was split in two portions, the northern kingdom given to King Jeroboam of the descendants of Joseph, and the southern part kept by King Rehoboam of the tribe of Judah, so that the land had two capitals, one in the territory of Ephraim (Shechem-Samaria), and the other in Judah (Jerusalem). The rabbis must have noted that after the Babylonian exile the Kingdom of Judah was reestablished but not the northern Kingdom of the Ephraim kings; it suffered the same fate as the sanctuary in Shiloh (in the territory of Ephraim) which was completely destroyed (Jeremiah 7:12; 26:6,9), but Jerusalem still remains the holiest of cities and shrines. Is it any wonder that the rabbis surmised that the Lord would send His people two Messiahs, a transitory one from the house of Joseph, and one who would live and reign forever: Messiah ben David from the house of Judah?

But the truth is that the Messiah was to be sent as the Son of Man to live among the progeny of the generation of a son of Man: Noah (see chapter 19). And as the Son of Man, Yeshua Messiah ben David took upon Himself the lot of the sons of Man which is to suffer, 'for the generation of Man [Adam] before the flood was hopelessly corrupt and rebellious because they did not have much suffering' (Midrash Genesis Rabbah 26.6). But since the deluge the sons of Man have to suffer:

> 'Great labor God apportioned and a heavy yoke upon the sons of Man, from the day they came forth from their mother's womb till the day they return to the mother of all' [i.e., the earth] –Sirach 40:1, Hebrew Text.

> 'I have seen the travail which God has given to the sons of Man' –Ecclesiastes 3:10.

> 'Grievous task has God given to the sons of Man, by which they may be exercised' –Ecclesiastes 1:13b.

The sons of Man are tried on this earth because it is they who are expected to be righteous (see pp. 15–17, 46–47). 'God tries only the righteous' (Midrash Genesis Rabbah 34.2). The Lord makes His servant-sons of Man undergo tribulations in order to perfect them. For He desires that His faithful servant-sons of Man be worthy to receive His holy knowledge (see pp. 51–55), and be given 'the glorious liberty of the children of God' (Romans 8:21).

His people knew about the pre-existence of the Messiah, and that he was with God in the heavens before coming down to earth (Enoch 39:7a; 46:1–3; 48:3–6; 49:2b; 62:6–9; Pesachim 54a; Nedarim 39 a,b, Babylonian Talmud; Midrash Genesis Rabbah 1.4; 2.4; Midrash on Psalms 2.10; 21.4; 93.3; Pesikta Rab Kahana, Piska 6.5, 5.5,9; Pesikta Rabbati, Piska 33.6; 34.2; 36.1; Pirke Rabbi Eliezer, Perek 3; Midrash Mishlei on Proverbs 8:9; Tanchumah on Numbers 7:1; Yalkut Shimoni, folios 298, 806, 942; Midrash Haggadol on Genesis 1:1; Zohar I. 4b, 38b, 231b [re Genesis 49:11]; III. 164a,b, 167a; Revelations of Rabbi Joshua ben Levi in Midrash Konen [In Jellinek's, *Beth haMidrash,* Vol. II. 29]; Seder Gan Eden [In Jellinek's, *Beth haMidrash,* Vol. III. 132, 195] etc; see also Sibylline Oracles V. 108, 256–259, 414–428). When it is said in Pesachim 54a and Nedarim 39a,b (Babylonian Talmud) that the name of the Messiah existed before creation, it is meant that he existed personally then, just as it is said of the personified name of the Lord: 'Behold, the name of the Lord comes from afar, burning with His anger, and His burden is heavy; His lips are full of indignation, and His tongue like a devouring fire' (Isaiah 30:27), for the name can be as the person himself. They knew that in the heavens, the Messiah was an exalted being who was given to wear God's crown (Midrash Exodus Rabbah 8.1; Midrash on Psalm 21.1), and clothed in His own vestments (Midrash Numbers Rabbah 14.3), and given to sit on God's throne (Enoch 51:3), for was he not named as the Lord Himself? (Jeremiah 23:6; Isaiah 9:6). 'God will call the King Messiah after His own name' (Midrash on Psalms 21.2; Midrash Mishlei on Proverbs 19:21). Nevertheless, the Messiah does not repose in comfort and glory in the heavens, but grieves for his people Israel (Midrash Konen 29 [*Beth haMidrash,* Vol. II. 48–51]), and he willingly takes upon himself their tribulations in atonement for their sins (Pesikta Rabbati, Piska 36.1; 37.1; Yalkut to Isaiah 60:1). So great is the Messiah's love for his people that it may be truly said of him that 'in all their affliction he was afflicted' (Isaiah 63:9).

We know that the Messiah-Son of Man is the embodiment of true righteousness, and that he is full of compassion towards his people Israel. If it is said that 'the Lord tries the righteous' (Psalm 11:5; Jeremiah 20:15), would the Messiah who came 'to fulfill all righteousness' (St. Matthew 13:15), have exempted himself from the trials and sufferings of the righteous? Immediately after 'Yeshua Messiah the righteous' (1 John 2:1) manifested Himself in the waters of the river Jordan (St. Matthew 3:13–17; St. Mark 1:9–11; St. Luke 3:21–22), He was led by the Holy Spirit into the wilderness (see Pesikta Rabbati, Piska 15.10), to be tested there by the devil (St. Matthew 4:1–11; St. Mark 1:12–13; St. Luke 4:1–13). Did not a Voice from heaven call Yeshua: 'My beloved Son in whom I am well pleased'? (St. Matthew 3:17; 17:5; St. Mark 1:11; St. Luke 3:22). And though 'the Lord loves the righteous' (Psalm 146:8; Proverbs 15:9), He nevertheless made Yeshua the Son of Man undergo trials because 'whom the Lord loves, He disciplines as a father the son in whom he delights' (Proverbs 3:12). He was also called 'My Son, the Chosen One' (St. Luke 9:35, Sinaiticus and Vaticanus Texts, etc.) for was not the 'Messiah, the Chosen One of God'? (St. Luke 23:35). Therefore He was tried in adversity as are all God's chosen ones (Isaiah 48:10; Daniel 12:10, Greek Text; Proverbs 17:3, Greek Text; Tobit 12:13, Latin Vulgate Text; Wisdom 3:1,5–6; Sirach 2:5; Psalms of Solomon 13:10). 'Was not Abraham found faithful in the trial?' (1 Maccabees 2:52). Indeed, for 'when he (Abraham) was proved he was found faithful' (Sirach 44:20), because the trial brings forth the proof of fidelity and truth. Thus, He who is 'called Faithful and True' (Revelation 19:11) went through the trials of the righteous to be found faithful, for He came 'to fulfill all righteousness' (St. Matthew 13:15) and to do all things well. It is because He is the truly compassionate Messiah, that Yeshua the Son of Man labored and suffered as all the sons of Man do, and that He willingly underwent the trials and adversities which are the lot of the righteous and chosen ones of God on this earth.

'His holy Messiah' (Zadokite [Geniza] Fragment 8:2) is holy. 'The Lord purifies every man who is holy' (Psalms of Solomon 13:10). And if it is said that the Lord's holy ones 'were chastened so that they might be made holy' (2 Baruch 13:10), shall Yeshua the Messiah: 'the Holy One of God' (St. Mark 1:24; St. Luke 4:34; Revelation 3:7) have exempted Himself from the chastening of His holy ones on this earth? He is 'Messiah the Chosen One of God' (St. Luke 23:35; 9:35), and 'the man whom the Lord does choose he shall be holy' (Numbers 16:7) by accepting the discipline of the Lord, just as 'He chastened us . . . for our own profit that we may be partakers of His holiness' (Hebrews 12:10).

We know that Yeshua the Son of Man called attention to His servanthood (St. Luke 22:27; 12:37; St. Matthew 20:28; St. Mark 10:45; St. John 13:4–5,12; Philippians 2:7–8), and to His meekness and humility (St. Matthew 11:29). And we have seen that it is the meek, humble and patient servants who understand, for the Lord rewards them with the gift of understanding (see pp. 65–66, 68–71) which shall exalt them (pp. 64–65, 70–71, 90–92).

Furthermore, Yeshua, 'the Lamb of God' (St. John 1:29,36) did not die the relatively painless death of the sacrificial victims because it was the will of God that His atoning death would involve great suffering, for in the eyes of His people suffering itself has an atoning effect. They said that 'suffering has a greater atoning effect than sacrifice inasmuch as sacrifice affects only man's property while suffering touches his very self' (Sifre 73b). 'Suffering under chastisements makes atonement' (Midrash on Psalms 94.2). 'He who gladly bears the sufferings that befall him brings salvation to the world' (Taanith 8a, Babylonian Talmud). 'Beloved is suffering, for as sacrifices are atoning, so is suffering atoning'; 'sufferings wash away all the sins of a man' (Berakoth 5b,a; Erubin 41b; Kiddushin 39, Babylonian Talmud; Sotah 17a, Jerusalem Talmud). 'The Lord exacts man's debt through suffering' ([re Genesis 3:16–17] Pesachim 118a, Babylonian Talmud; see also Yoma 23a; Baba Metzia 85a; Sanhedrin 101a,b, Babylonian Talmud; Sifre to Deuteronomy 4,5,32; Midrash Leviticus Rabbah 36.4–6). By command of the Lord, Ezekiel lay down on his left side for three hundred and ninety days bearing the iniquity of the house of Israel which the Lord placed upon him. And when he had completed that penance, the Lord commanded him to lie down on his right side for forty days bearing the iniquity of the house of Judah which the Lord also placed upon him. When Yeshua the Messiah was delivered to the soldiers to be crucified (St. John 19:16–17), he bore 'the iniquity of us all' (Isaiah 53:6) in bearing the heavy cross to the place of execution. Long ago, in the same area, 'Abraham took the wood of the burnt offering and laid it on Isaac his son (Genesis 22:6) so that his son became like a man carrying his stake on his shoulder' to the place of execution (Midrash Genesis Rabbah 56.3; Pesikta Rabbati, Piska 31.2 [143b]; Yalkut 101; Yelammedenu in Yalkut Torah [Mann] p. 308; Tanchumah Wa-Yera [Buber] 46, p. 114).

Sufferings not only atone but also give knowledge and understanding to the righteous who suffer (see pp. 51–55, 68–71). In the Menachoth (29b) tractate of the Babyloninan Talmud, the rabbis said that the understanding of Rabbi Akiba and his knowledge of the letters of the Law was greater than that of Moses, because Rabbi Akiba was destined to suffer a painful martyrdom. In the days of old, they knew that 'the rod and reproof give wisdom' (Proverbs 29:15), and that 'lashes and chastisement are at all times wisdom' (Sirach 22:6) for 'such is the discipline of wisdom, causing pain to produce understanding' (Clement of Alexandria, *Stromata* II, chapter 2). Thus, 'to whom has the *understanding* [EPISTĒMĒ] of wisdom been made manifest' (Sirach 1:7, Greek Cursives 23,55,70,106,253 and Old Latin Texts) was rendered: 'to whom has the *discipline* of wisdom been revealed and made manifest?' (Sirach 1:7, Latin Vulgate Text). Hence, the Jewish scribes in Alexandria who translated the Hebrew Scriptures into Greek rendered: 'He made him [Jacob] *understand*' (Deuteronomy 32:10, Hebrew Text, Literal Translation) into: 'He *chastised* him' (Deuteronomy 32:10, Greek Septuagint Text), for they knew in those days that 'all undisciplined people [are] void of understanding' (Sibylline Oracles III. 670). As the angel said to Tobias: 'they . . . who give themselves to their lusts are as the horse and mule which do not have understanding' (Tobit 6:17, Latin Vulgate) for 'there are no two things so utterly opposed as understanding [EPISTĒMĒ] and pleasures of the flesh' (Philo, *Deus.* 143), 'the understanding of the pleasure-loving man is blind' (Philo, *Q. Gen.* IV. 245). The prophet Isaiah excoriated the shepherds of His people for leading lives of debauchery which deprived them of understanding: 'they are greedy dogs who do not know satisfaction. And they are shepherds who do not know [YADA] how to understand [BIN], they all look to their own way, every one after his own gain, each to his own quarter. "Come", one says, "I will bring wine, and we will fill ourselves with intoxicating drink; tomorrow will be as today even much better"' (Isaiah 56:11–12). The shallow sybarites who have never experienced the sufferings and cares of this world do not know nor understand that:

> 'The delightful experience of abounding pleasure is the ruin of the understanding' –Philo, *Agr.* 108.

> 'Pleasures . . . bewitch the understanding' –Philo, *Spec.* I. 9.

> 'Nothing else so constrains and oppresses the understanding as do desires for sensual pleasures' –Philo, *Q.Gen.* IV. 177.

> 'Pleasure endeavors to break up and destroy the way of life of the wise understanding' –Philo, *L.A.* III. 189.

> 'Wine bibbing . . . gluttony . . . delicate living and excessive indulgence in food . . . mulct the most vital element: the understanding' –Philo, *Ebr.* 22,33.

> 'The fascination of vice obscures the things that are good, and the wandering allurements of concupiscence pervert the innocent understanding' –Wisdom 4:12.

> 'Men who have lived dissolutely and unrighteously . . . they went

far in the ways of error . . . being deceived as babes without understanding [APHRONŌN]' —Wisdom 12:23,24.

'Lovers of pleasure rather than lovers of God . . . this sort are . . .
ever learning and never able to come to the full knowledge of the
Truth' —2 Timothy 3:4,6,7.

'Understanding [PHRONĒSIS] and indulgence of the body cannot
occupy the same quarters' —Philo, *L.A.* 151.

'Understanding starves when the senses feast, on the other hand
it rejoices when they are fasting' —Philo, *Mig.* 204; Idem. *De
Providentia* 67.

'Understanding [EPISTĒMĒ] comes into being through estrange-
ment from sensuality . . . it follows that the lovers of wisdom reject rather than choose sensuality' —Philo, *Cher.* 41.

'O Understanding, if you do not prepare yourself, excising desire,
pleasures . . . , follies, injustices and related evils, and if you do
not adapt yourself to the vision of holiness, you will end your life
in blindness unable to see the sun of understanding' —Philo, *Q.
Exod.* II. 51.

His people knew, indeed, that understanding is found in the poor and
humble, in faithful servants, in those who suffer, and in those who are oppressed. But that insight is lacking in the wealthy ones living in the
midst of luxury and delights, basking in the adulation of sycophants:

'One who lives in luxury . . . does as he pleases . . . and does not
understand what he is doing' —Shepherd of Hermas, *Sim.* VI. 5.
65:3.

'Man who is held in honor [for his riches] . . . does not understand' —Psalm 49:20.

'See your kings and your great ones, those who are clothed in soft
garments, they shall not be able to understand the Truth' —
Gospel of Thomas, Logion 78.

'Their riches concealed from them the Truth and darkened them'
—Shepherd of Hermas, *Sim.* IX, 30.107:4.

'Wealth has led astray the hearts [i.e., understanding; see pp.
45–46] of princes' —Sirach 8:2, Hebrew Text.

'They [the rich] became insolent in their prosperity and they were without understanding' —Psalms of Solomon 1:6, Syriac Text.

Thus, when Job asked: 'Where is the place of understanding? Man does not know the price thereof, neither is it found in the land of those who live in delights' (Job 28:12,13, Latin Vulgate Text), he knew that it would not be found in places where all bodily desires are catered to. 'Choice things [luxuries, delicacies] bestowed are a pollution for the soul, and for a man of knowledge [the delicacies are] a suffering in the inward parts' (Sirach 40:29,30, Hebrew and Syriac Texts) because that man of knowledge knows that those dainties dull his knowledge and understanding. 'Those who cram themselves with food and drink are most wanting in wisdom because the reason is drowned by the stuff brought in' (Philo, *De Providentia,* 67). Long ago they knew that fasting and afflicting one's self aided in gaining understanding and knowledge from God into His mysteries:

'From the first day you [Daniel] set your heart to understand by afflicting yourself before God' —Daniel 10:12.

'I fasted seven days mourning and weeping . . . then my soul recovered the spirit of understanding' —2 Esdras 5:21,22.

'My heart anguished forth [CRUCIABATUR] understanding' —2 Esdras 14:40.

'Fifteen days after I had fasted and prayed much to the Lord, the knowledge of the writing was revealed to me' —Shepherd of Hermas, *Vis.* II. 2.6:1.

'This is the way that is good for the study of the Torah: a morsel of bread with salt you must eat, and water by measure you must drink, and you must sleep upon the ground, and live a life of affliction while you are toiling in [trying to learn and understand] the Torah. If you do so, happy shall you be' —Pirke Aboth 6:4; Sanhedrin 99, Babylonian Talmud.
For 'happy is the man . . . who gets understanding' (Proverbs 3:13) from toiling in the Torah.

'A man does not become worthy to acquire Torah unless he gives his life in its behalf, and unless he dispenses with all comforts and pleasures while he strives to attain [understanding in] it' — Tanna Debe Eliyyahu Rabbah, 21.

'Understanding of the Torah is given only to one who has undergone suffering for its sake' –Tanna Debe Eliyyahu Rabbah, p. 156.

Those who led ascetic lives to acquire understanding and knowledge in the Torah were said to have taken upon themselves 'the yoke of the Torah' (Abodah Zarah 5; Tanna Debe Eliyyahu Rabbah 8; Ibid. Zutta 198) and 'labored in the Torah' (Hullin 7, Babylonian Talmud; Midrash Genesis Rabbah 63; Midrash Leviticus Rabbah 31.4; Midrash Ecclesiastes Rabbah 11.1; Midrash Song of Songs Rabbah 1.1,3; Zohar I.243a; III.35a), as 'a slave to the Torah' (Baba Metzia 85, Babylonian Talmud), 'toiling to acquire knowledge' (Sanhedrin 92, Babylonian Talmud) in it. The rabbis said: 'The study of the Torah is a work which has no end' (Aboth de Rabbi Nathan 27.3) therefore 'the words of the Torah should be studied mornings and evenings' (Midrash Samuel 5.2). It was the meek and humble who labored in the Torah and who understood the most because 'the words of the Torah find a resting place only in a man of lowly spirit' (Taanith 7, Babylonian Talmud, Derek Eretz Zuta 1:1). 'Learn from Me for I am meek and humble of heart' said Yeshua the Messiah (St. Matthew 11:29), for as the Servant-Son of Man He understood and knew all things in His meekness and humility.

It is 'the poor man who knows' (Ecclesiastes 6:8), and it is 'the poor man who has understanding' (Proverbs 28:11; Sirach 10:29, Hebrew Text). 'More lordly is the poor man who understands than the rich man without understanding' (Philo, *Q. Gen.* III. 22). 'A rich man who is void of understanding' (Sirach 22:23, Greek MSS 248, 106), has become that way by being overly occupied with worldly goods forgetting that 'the Torah is truly the best merchandise' (Taanith 21 with additions, Babylonian Talmud); 'Torah is the best Sechorah ['merchandise']' –Paraphrase of Tanchumah to Terumah.

As for ordinary merchandising, 'he who has much business does not become wise' (Pirke Aboth 2:6) because 'the study of the Torah is not found among merchants' (Ibid.). 'What has a man to do to become wise? Study much and trade little' (Niddah 70, Babylonian Talmud) for with much business comes covetousness. For 'he who is grasping, even though he possesses many things, is nevertheless dull in understanding' (the Story of Ahikar 2:92, Armenian Text) and blind, 'like blind men whose understanding through covetousness has lost the power to see' (Philo, *De Providentia* Fragment 2.12); and like the lukewarm whom the Lord excoriated in these words: 'Because you say, 'I am rich, and become wealthy, and have need of nothing'–you do not know that you are . . . blind' (Revelation 3:17). Those who are spiritually blind cannot see and know. Thus, 'he who strives to be rich . . . does not know' (Proverbs 28:22); 'the newly rich . . . know nothing' (Philo, *Spec* II. 23). Therefore His people were advised: 'be not much engaged in business, and busy yourself with the Torah' (Pirke Aboth 4:10). Did not the Son of Man who understands all things say:

> 'Watch, and beware of all covetousness, for a man's life does not consist in the abundance of his possessions' –St. Luke 12:15.

> 'The cares of this world, and the deceitfulness of riches, and the lusts of other things entering in [the heart], choke the Word, and it becomes unfruitful' –St. Mark 4:19.

> 'You cannot serve God and riches [MAMMON]' –St. Matthew 6:24.

> 'The Son of Man has nowhere to lay His head' –St. Matthew 8:20.

Throughout the history of Israel, whenever His people in prosperity became wicked and forgot the Lord, they would as a result lose His knowledge and understanding. The Lord would then afflict them so that through their sufferings they would once more come to understand and know Him:

> 'I [the Lord] will take away all her [Israel's] gladness . . . I will . . . make her desolate . . . to open her understanding' – Hosea 2:11,14,15, Greek Text.

> 'Affliction ['fearful trembling', Hebrew Text] alone will make you understand what you hear' –Isaiah 29:18, Old Latin and Latin Vulgate.

> 'From desolation to ruin and from pain to the blow and from travail to the billows ['of death' v. 4] my soul [as a result] understood Your marvels' –1QH 9:6,7, Dead Sea Scrolls.

> 'He opens the *ears* of men' –Job 33:16, Hebrew Text.

> 'He opens the *understanding* of men' Job 33:16, Greek Text.

> 'If they be bound in fetters and held in the cords of affliction, then . . . He opens their ears to instruction' –Job 36:8,10.

'It is good for me that I have been afflicted so that I may learn'
—Psalm 119:73.

'He who has learned many things shall show forth understanding' —Sirach 34:9, Latin Vulgate.

'Lack of understanding is only cured by fear' —Philo, *Spec.* II. 239.

'He learned understanding from fear' —Philo, *Mos.* II. 272.

'I [the Lord] will reprove you and set in order before your eyes, now understand this' —Psalm 50:21,22.

'He who hears reproof gets understanding' —Proverbs 15:32.

'Admonition . . . produces understanding' —Clement of Alexandria, *Paed.* I. IX. 76.1; X. 94.2.

'Reprove one who has understanding and he will understand knowledge' —Proverbs 19:25.

'I will execute great vengeance upon them, with furious rebukes and they shall know' —Ezekiel 25:17.

'I will pour out My wrath on you, and spread My anger against you . . . I will punish you . . . My eye will not spare you nor will I have pity. I will punish you according to your ways . . . then you will know' —Ezekiel 9:8,9; Ibid. 5:11–13; 6:6–7; 38:22–23 and texts on pp. 51–55.

Moreover, the good among His people knew that 'there is no limit to trials, but the man of understanding increases his knowledge by their means' (Ibn Gabirol, *Mibchar ha Peninim*). Thus, 'the man who has understanding [EPISTĒMŌN] will not murmur when he is disciplined' (Sirach 10:25, Greek MS 248 and Syriac Texts), for 'the godly man . . . makes his sufferings contribute to the increase of his knowledge' (Corpus Hermeticum, *Lib.* IX. 4b). The righteous Servant in the fifty-third chapter of Isaiah, suffered greatly in behalf of His own (Isaiah 53:1–10), and what He suffered gave Him the great knowledge (Isaiah 53:11) that shall justify Him in the end before the eyes of His people. For all good servants are justified and exalted by their knowledge and understanding gained through suffering. Even the ancient Egyptians knew that suffering gives knowledge to the righteous, because the old Egyptian word SUN means 'to suffer pain' or 'to be in distress' and it also signifies 'to know' or 'to have knowledge'. The early Christians also knew that suffering is the door through which the righteous enter the realm of knowledge and understanding. Thus, 'the Lord [Yeshua the Messiah] having come alone into the world of understanding, enters by His sufferings' (Clement of Alexandria, *Stromata* V. c.6).

Suffering is also the door through which the righteous enter the realm of perfection (see p. 51–52) for we are 'made perfect through sufferings' (Hebrews 2:10), and it is in tribulations that we are to be 'tried and found perfect' (Sirach 31:10). The Messiah 'through what He suffered . . . being made perfect' (Hebrews 5:8,9) for our sake, became for all time the peerless example of perfect righteousness. We are made 'perfect in Messiah Yeshua' (Colossians 1:28) who is our righteousness (1 Corinthians 1:30; 2 Corinthians 5:21; Romans 5:25; Philippians 3:9; 2 Peter 1:1), and who suffered and died to redeem and perfect us (1 Peter 5:10). The rabbis knew that 'the latter Abraham differed from the former in that the latter was Abraham made perfect [through his fidelity in sufferings], whereas the former was still imperfect' (Zohar I. 120b; see also Midrash Numbers Rabbah 18.21). Abraham had to go through ten trials (Jubilees 17:17,18; 19:8; Pirke Aboth 5:4; Midrash Exodus Rabbah 15.2; 30:16; 44:5) before he was perfected. 'Abraham [through his trials] . . . acquired knowledge' (CD 16:6 MS. B [Cairo Genizah Zadokite Fragments]) because perfection gives us true knowledge of God. It is when 'Enoch was found perfect [TAMIM]' that he 'was taken as a sign of knowledge [DAATH] to all generations' (Sirach 44:16, Hebrew Text).

'Job was a plain [TAM = 'plain', 'simple', 'open'] and upright man' (Job 1:1a,8) who was also wise and understanding because he was 'one who feared God and departed from evil' (Job 1:1b,8; 28:28), but he did not have true knowledge of God until he was tried with suffering and made perfect [TAMIM] so that in the end, purified by his sufferings, Job was able to 'see' God whom he had only 'heard' about previously (Job 42:5). Until they have been perfected through trials and sufferings, the 'simple' [TAM] do not 'know' they are like those who 'went about in their simplicity [TAM] and they did not know anything' (2 Samuel 15:11). Likewise 'Jacob . . . a simple [TAM] man' (Genesis 25:27) when he was purified by his trials and conflicts, became at last 'Israel': 'the man who saw God' (see p. 63–64) for we are told that 'Jacob was perfected as the result of discipline' (Philo, *Agric.* 42) so as to be able to see God and know Him as Job did in the end. It is the goal of Man and all the children of Man to see and know the Lord. 'The full knowledge [EPIGNOSIN] of the truth is according to godliness' (Titus 1:1). 'Pure as regards corporeal lusts and pure in holy thoughts are those who attain to the knowledge of God' —Clement of Alexandria, *Stromata* IV. chap. 6.

Long ago, the birth of Benjamin (Genesis 35: 16–18) taught us the important lesson that just as understanding comes forth from suffering, 'strength' [ON as in Genesis 49:3; Deuteronomy 21:17; Hosea 12:3] is born of 'affliction' [ONI as in Genesis 41:52; Exodus 3:7; 4:31; 2 Kings 14:26; Psalm 25:18 etc.]. Before she died at childbirth, Rachel named her newborn babe: Ben Oni ('son of my suffering') but after she expired, his father renamed him Benjamin ('son of my right hand'). The child could just as easily have been called 'son of strength' or 'son of understanding' because we know that the right hand is not only the hand of strength but also of the power of understanding. Little Benjamin, the only son of Israel (see p. 96), and his descendants are destined to be the true heirs of all the treasures of Understanding which are the infinite wisdom and knowledge of God. And the day is near when Benjamin-Israel shall see his inheritance in Yeshua the Son of Man and the Redeemer Messiah 'in whom are hidden all the treasures of wisdom and knowledge' (Colossians 2:2,3).

Chapter 23

Shiloh

'The scepter shall not depart from Judah, nor a lawgiver from
between his feet until Shiloh comes [or: until he comes to Shiloh]
and to him shall be the obedience of the peoples' –Genesis 49:10.

When Reuben was deprived of his birthright because of the incident with
Bilhah (Genesis 35:22; 49:3–4; 1 Chronicles 5:1), and Simeon and Levi
lost theirs because of their ruthless massacre of Hamor, Shechem and the
Hivites (Genesis 34:1–31; 49:5–7), the leadership over Jacob's sons fell
upon the shoulders of Judah and his descendants, for as the fourth son he
was next in line. It was Judah who was the spokesman for his brothers
(Genesis 43:3–4,8–9; 44:16,18–34) and to his brothers (Genesis 37:26–27).
Judah was made the chief delegate by Jacob (Genesis 46:28) and his
descendants were first in the order of the tribes in their tents (Numbers
2:3), and in the march through the wilderness (Numbers 2:9). The tribe
of Judah was the first to offer the offering on the first day (Numbers
7:11–12), and they led all the rest of the tribes in the conquest of the land
of Canaan (Judges 1:1–2), and in the battles against the tribe of Benjamin
(Judges 20:18). The first Judge of Israel was Othniel of the tribe of Judah
(Judges 3:9–11). 'Judah is My lawgiver' (Psalm 60:7; 108:8) said the Lord,
'and the Lord said Judah first' (Judges 20:18; 1:1–2) until He came to
Shiloh.

In saying that 'the scepter [SHEBET] shall not depart [SUR] from Judah
. . . ' (Genesis 49:10), Jacob prophesied that Judah's sovereignty or leader-
ship would not cease until certain things came to pass. The Hebrew word
SHEBET means 'rod' of authority (Exodus 21:20; Psalms 23:4; 74:2;
Jeremiah 10:16; 51:19; Micah 7:14) or correction (Proverbs 10:13; 13:24;
22:15; 23:14; 26:3; 29:15). Thus, when the Lord said in Zechariah 10:11
that 'the scepter [SHEBET] of Egypt shall depart [SUR],' He meant that
Egypt's sovereignty would cease.

Just when did Judah's scepter start to depart, and his initial leadership
begin to wane? Certainly not at Gilgal where the tribes set up camp just
after they had crossed the river Jordan. Because in Gilgal Judah was
again to the fore when Caleb claimed and received there (Joshua 14:6–15)

the first portion of the land of Canaan that was to be divided among the tribes. Also in the same place, the first lot of land fell in favor of the tribe of Judah (Joshua 15:1–63). But from the time that the twelve tribes came to Shiloh, Judah's primacy declined and Benjamin's ascended to gain the ruler's scepter.

Shiloh is located about nineteen miles north of Jerusalem to the east of the road that goes up from Jerusalem to Shechem via Bethel. Hence it is described as being situated 'on the north side of Bethel on the east of the highway that goes up from Bethel to Shechem' (Judges 21:19).

Following the subjugation of the land, the Ark of the Covenant which had been kept at Gilgal during the conflict, was transferred to Shiloh and kept there from the last days of Joshua to the time of Samuel the seer (1 Samuel 4:3). It was in Shiloh, when at last 'the land was subdued before them' (Joshua 18:1), that the final division of the land for the children of Israel took place. 'Joshua cast lots for them in Shiloh before the Lord' (Joshua 18:10) and the lot of Benjamin came up first (Joshua 18:11–28), then the tribes of Simeon, Zebulon, Issachar, Asher, Naphtali and Dan received their lots and the division of the land was completed. Also in Shiloh, the tribe of Levi obtained by lot the forty-two Levitical cities (Joshua 21:1–41) situated among the twelve tribes. These were to be the habitations of the priests and other members of the Levite clan whom the Lord scattered among His people so that every tribe would benefit from the religious guidance and teachings of His priestly tribe. From these cities the Levites went to serve in the Tabernacle a part of each year. The remainder of the time they occupied themselves in agricultural work in the fields which adjoined their homes among the tribes. According to Moses' instructions (Numbers 35:6–28), six cities of refuge (Joshua 20:1–9) were added to the forty-two Levitical cities given to the priestly tribe at the time of the final division of the land in Shiloh.

It was while the Tabernacle was in Shiloh that the Lord gave His people 'rest all around according to all that He had sworn to their fathers. And not a man of all their enemies stood against them; the Lord delivered all their enemies into their hand' (Joshua 21:44). This occured when He was in the place where He had to set His name: Shiloh (Deuteronomy 12:5,11,21; 14:23–24; 16:6,11; 26:2; Jeremiah 7:12). All the children of Israel assembled together at Shiloh and the land was subdued before them there (Joshua 18:1).

Shiloh was the place where the Lord was honored in His title: *'Lord of Hosts'* (1 Samuel 1:3,11; 4:4) who is 'the God of *Israel*' (1 Samuel 1:11,17;

1 Chronicles 17:24; Psalm 59:6; Isaiah 21:10; 37:16; Jeremiah 7:3,21; 9:15; 16:9; 19:3,15; 25:27; 27:4,21; 28:2,14; 29:4,8,21,25; 31:23; 32:14,15; 35:13,17,18–19; 38:17; 39:16; 42:15,18; 43:10; 44:2,7,11,25; 46:25; 48:4; 50:18; 51:33; Zephaniah 2:9) just as in turn, *'the Almighty'* is 'the God of *Jacob'* (see p. 33). Furthermore, it is in His designation as 'the Lord of Hosts' that God is called 'King' (Isaiah 6:5; 44:6; Jeremiah 46:18; 48:15; 51:57; Zechariah 14:16; Psalm 24:10) and that He reigns (Isaiah 24:23). It was in Shiloh, the sanctuary of the Lord of Hosts, that the Lord reigned as King over His people although they did not realize it and asked instead to be ruled by an earthly king (1 Samuel 8:5–22; 12:12–13).

In Shiloh 'the Lord of Hosts' dwelt enthroned between the two Cherubim of the Ark of the Covenant (1 Samuel 4:4; 2 Samuel 6:2; 2 Kings 19:15; Isaiah 37:16; Psalm 99:1; Exodus 25:22). And while in Shiloh the Lord 'plainly revealed' (1 Samuel 2:27 Literal Translation, see KJV and NASB) Himself to Eli; something He had not done to the members of the House of Levi while they were still in Egypt subject to Pharaoh. Then, for a time the Lord of Hosts hid Himself because of the wickedness of Eli's sons (1 Samuel 2:12–17,22) but 'the Lord appeared again in Shiloh, for the Lord revealed Himself to Samuel in Shiloh' (1 Samuel 3:21), when young Samuel had come to maturity. And while the Tabernacle was in Shiloh, the Lord of Hosts revealed to the people what they were to do, He instructed them through the use of the oracular stones found in the breastplate of the high priest: 'the Demonstration and Truth [i.e., the Urim and Thummim] *revealed* all things in *Shiloh'* (Ps. Philo, *Biblical Antiquities* XXII. 9). For Shiloh was the place of 'the Lord of Hosts, the God of Israel' who is the Revealer of all things (2 Samuel 7:27; Isaiah 21:10; 22:14; Amos 4:13) and who revealed Himself through His Word in Shiloh (1 Samuel 3:21).

Knowing that the God of Jacob is the Almighty and the God of Israel is the Lord of Hosts, and knowing that Jacob-Israel are but one and the same person, we can understand why both the Almighty and the Lord of Hosts are called the Redeemer for are they not designations of the One and same God?:

> 'I the Lord am your Saviour and your Redeemer, the Mighty One of Jacob' –Isaiah 49:26; 60:16.

> 'Thus says the Lord, the King of Israel and his Redeemer the Lord of Hosts' –Isaiah 44:6.

> 'Our Redeemer, the Lord of Hosts is His name' –Isaiah 47:4.

'Their Redeemer is Mighty, the Lord of Hosts' —Jeremiah 50:34.

His people knew that the Redeemer-Messiah was to spring forth from the patriarch Jacob-Israel, and that the most ancient proper name ascribed to the Messiah in Holy Scripture is Shiloh as found in Genesis 49:10. 'What is the Messiah's name? His name is Shiloh, for it is written [Genesis 49:10]: "Until Shiloh come"' (Sanhedrin 98b, Babylonian Talmud; Midrash Genesis Rabbah 98.8; Midrash Lamentations Rabbah I.16; Midrash Mishlei sect. 19 [re Proverbs 19:21]; Midrash Haggadol on Genesis 49:10; Lekah Tob and Sekel Tob on Genesis 49:10; Yalkut Shimoni fol. 160; Tanchumah Vayehi 10; Yelammedenu 35 [In Jellinek's *Beth haMidrash* VI. p. 84] and Targums Onkelos, Jerusalem and Pseudo-Jonathan *ad loc.*). Early Christian tradition also interpreted Genesis 49:10 Messianically (Justin Martyr, *Apol.* I. p. 41; *Hom. in Gen.* 17; Cyprian, *Contra Jud.* I. 20; Cyril, *Hieros. Cat.* XII; Eusebius, *H.E.* I. 6; Chrysostom, *Hom.* 67 *in Gen.;* Augustine, *De Civ. Dei* XIV. 41; Theodoret, *Quest. in Gen.* 110; Jerome, *Quest. in Gen. ad loc.*).

It was inferred that because the sovereignty of Judah would cease when Shiloh would come or when someone would come to Shiloh that therefore 'Shiloh' would have to be a person and none other than the Messiah Himself to whom all the peoples would give their allegiance. After all, the consecutive verses in Genesis 49 continue to say of him that 'binding his foal to the vine and his ass's colt to the choice vine, he washed his garments in wine and his vesture in the blood of grapes. His eyes are darker than wine and his teeth are whiter than milk' (Genesis 49:11–12). But first we should see if there was any relationship between the period of time that His people had the Tabernacle in Shiloh or the time when someone in particular came to Shiloh, and the subsequent decline of the sovereignty of Judah. It would do well to study Benjamin and his tribe if we would obtain insight into the matter.

Benjamin was the youngest and last son of Jacob and the only one born after he was named Israel. He is therefore Israel's only son and at the same time the only one of the family born in the land of Israel. Among all the sons of Jacob, only Benjamin could be rightfully named 'Israel, son of Israel.' Jacob's chief son was Judah, and Israel's chief and only son was Benjamin. Judah was to lead all the tribes but so was Benjamin when all the people of the Lord came to Shiloh, the Sanctuary of the God of Israel.

From his birth Benjamin was separate from his brothers, for we know that he was the only one born of Israel, and in the Holy Land. He did not bow before Esau and he was the only one named by his father. He had no part in the sale of his brother Joseph and remained home with his father while his brothers went to Egypt. Later on, it was in his sack that Joseph's cup of divination was hid, and he ate separate from his brothers at Joseph's table and received five times greater portions of food than they did; he alone did not bow before Joseph. Among the twelve he was the only one considered sinless (Baba Bathra 17a; Shabbath 55b, Babylonian Talmud; Zohar I. 57b), and said to be the beloved of the Lord (Deuteronomy 33:12), 'in whose possession the Sanctuary shall stand in this world as well as in the time of the Messiah, and in the future world' (Sifre to Deuteronomy 352; Midrash Tannaim 216–217; see also Megillah I. 72d, Jerusalem Talmud; Zebaim 118b; Yoma 12a, Babylonian Talmud; Mechilta Bachodesh 4.65b; Midrash Genesis Rabbah 99.1). In the time of the Judges, the children of Benjamin battled against all the rest of the tribes (Judges 20:14–48). And was it not said that the children of the 'son of the right hand' (i.e., Benjamin) were uniquely left-handed? (Judges 3:15–21; 20:16; 1 Chronicles 12:2).

Understanding the distinctness of Benjamin, we are able to discover hidden references to him in the prophetic utterances of Jacob and Moses:

> 'Blessings . . . shall be on the head of Joseph, and on the crown of the head of him who is separate from his brothers : Benjamin is a ravenous wolf, in the morning he devours the prey and in the evening he shall divide the spoil' –Genesis 49:26,27.

> 'Let the blessing come on the head of Joseph, and on the crown of the head of him [Benjamin, v. 12] who is separate from his brothers' –Deuteronomy 33:16.

Joseph and Benjamin or Joseph's children and Benjamin, are often paired throughout the Holy Scriptures (Genesis 35:24; 42:4; 45:12; 46:19–22; 49:22–27; Numbers 1:10–11,32–37; 2:18–23; 10:22–24; Deuteronomy 27:12; 33:12–13; Judges 1:21–22; 5:14; 10:9; 1 Chronicles 2:2; 9:3; 27:20–21; Psalm 80:2; Ezekiel 48:32; Hosea 5:8–9; Revelation 7:8). Thus, it is not surprising to find the reference to Benjamin hidden in the couplets of Genesis 49:26,27 and Deuteronomy 33:16. The relationship of the houses of Joseph and Benjamin was so close that Shimei described himself as being of 'the house of Joseph' (2 Samuel 19:20) although he was a Benjaminite (2 Samuel 19:16; Genesis 43:29).

Benjamin hides and things are hidden in Benjamin. It was in Benjamin's sack that Joseph's cup was hid (Genesis 42:2,12). The Benjaminites hid in the wilderness (Judges 20:45,47) and in the vineyards of Shiloh

(Judges 21:20). King Saul the Benjaminite 'could not be found' for he had 'hidden himself among the things' (1 Samuel 10:21,22) and later on 'disguised himself and put on other garments' (1 Samuel 29:8). And even today, no one knows where the one thousand missing men of the tribe of Benjamin (compare Judges 20:15,35,46) hid themselves (see Rabbi Isaac Abarbanel and Radak's commentaries on Judges 20:15 and Abraham Zacuto's *Sepher Yohasin Hashalem* p. 7 *ad loc.*). Joab did not number the men of Benjamin (1 Chronicles 21:6), perhaps because he knew how well they were able to hide themselves from him.

It was from the tribe of Benjamin that the Lord chose Saul, first King of Israel (1 Samuel 9:15–17; 10:1; 12:13). And just as He had chosen from 'the fewest of all people' (Deuteronomy 7:7) His people Israel 'to be a special people to himself above all the people on the face of the earth' (Deuteronomy 7:6), so did He specially choose their first King from the tribe of Benjamin, 'the smallest of the tribes of Israel' (1 Samuel 9:21). God does all things exceedingly well. Let us try to discover why it was from the tribe of Benjamin that the Lord gave His people their first King.

Long ago the Lord promised Abraham and Jacob that Kings would come forth from them (Genesis 17:6,16; 35:11). He also promised Abraham that he would be the father of many nations. This truly came to pass because Abraham had children from Sarah, Hagar and Keturah who were descendants of the three sons of Noah: Shem, Ham and Japheth (Yalkut Reubeni on Genesis 26.2,36c; Yalkut on Job [Chapter 8]; 1 Maccabees 12:10,21; 14:20; 2 Maccabees 5:9). We saw the wisdom of God in His choosing the tribe of Judah to be the one from which His Messiah would spring forth (see Chapter 13). We shall also see that through suitable marital unions the Lord would enable one of the tribes to have the right to provide for His people their first King: Saul, the Lord's anointed one from the tribe of Benjamin. For by a series of events the Lord made the tribe of Benjamin to be truly Israel. He did so when by His wonderful wisdom and marvelous justice He incorporated all the rest of the tribes into that one tribe. Was not Benjamin (the only son of Israel) born at the price of the death of his mother Rachel? Likewise, the new Benjamin-Israel tribe would be born, but at the terrible cost of the death of all the women of the tribe of Benjamin.

It all began with the death of 'a concubine from Bethlehem in Judah' (Judges 19:1–30) through the brutality of some men of Gibeah who were of the tribe of Benjamin. This incident led to the internecine warfare between the rest of the tribes and the tribe of Benjamin which resulted in the massacre of all the Benjaminites except for *six hundred* male survivors (Judges 20:1–48). It was then that the rest of the tribes realized that there was great danger that one of the tribes was going to be cut off forever from the congregation of Israel. For women were no longer available to the men of Benjamin either from their own tribe or from the daughters of the rest of the tribes because the assembly of the tribes had solemnly sworn not to give any of their daughters in marriage to the men of Benjamin (Judges 21:1,7).

While they were debating among themselves what to do, some of the leaders of the tribes noted that the inhabitants of Jabesh Gilead had not participated in the war against the tribe of Benjamin, and had not come into the assembly to take the vow. In reprisal, 'twelve thousand of the bravest men (Judges 21:10) from the rest of the tribes stormed the town of Jabesh Gilead and slew all the people in it except *four hundred* virgins' (v. 12) which they spared and brought to *Shiloh* and there gave them as wives to the men of Benjamin (Judges 21:9–14). But these were not sufficient to provide a mate for each man of the remnant of Benjamin. And as they were forbidden by oath to give them any of their daughters, the elders of the congregation devised a plan whereby wives could still be acquired by the men of Benjamin. The elders knew that every year, as prescribed by Moses, all the men of the tribes with their families had to convene at Shiloh, the place where the Lord was to set His name (Deuteronomy 12:5,10–12,21; Jeremiah 7:12). They also knew that it was customary at the yearly festival for the young daughters of all the tribes to take part in the maiden dances held in the fields by the vineyards of Shiloh.

When the time of the yearly festival in Shiloh came around, the elders of the congregation gathered the as yet unwedded men of Benjamin and commanded them to 'go, and lie in wait in the vineyards and watch; and when the daughters of Shiloh come out to dance in the dances, then come out of the vineyards and *seize* each man his wife from the daughters of Shiloh, and go to the land of Benjamin . . . and the men of Benjamin did so; they took themselves enough wives for their number from those who danced whom they caught. Then they went and returned to their inheritance and they rebuilt the cities and dwelt in them' (Judges 21:20–21,23). Thus, the tribe of Benjamin was not only preserved for posterity but through intermarriage with all the rest of the tribes it became *in itself* a true congregation of *Israel* in Shiloh. Is it any wonder that the rabbis said that the flag of Benjamin was a veritable rainbow containing all the colors of the rest of the tribes? (Midrash Genesis Rabbah 2.7).

It was when the tribe of Benjamin came to Shiloh that their primacy was made manifest because the first lot cast before the Lord went to them (Joshua 18:1,10–28). Again, years later, when Benjamin came to Shiloh it was there that the intermarriages occured that made them the true Israel. And it was also when 'a man from *Benjamin* ran from the battle lines and *came to Shiloh*' (1 Samuel 4:12) bearing the sad news that Israel had been defeated, and the Ark of God captured by the Philistines, that the people decided they needed a King to rally them and fight their battles. And to him they would give their obedience. The scepter and staff of Judah departed when Saul of Benjamin came to Shiloh and was made the first King of Israel.

That the tribe of Benjamin married into all the rest of the tribes is intimated in the Babylonian Talmud (Baba Bathra 116a; Taanith 30b). And there is an old tradition that the fifteenth day of Ab (the fifth month in the Jewish religious year or the eleventh month in the civil year), was a day of rejoicing because it was 'the day when the tribe of Benjamin was allowed to reenter the community of Israel' (Midrash Lamentations Rabbah, *Proem* XXXII). On that day the tribes were allowed to intermarry, and all the young single women of Jerusalem, both rich and poor alike, would dress in uniformly white garments and go by the vineyards to sing and dance before the young men who gathered there in search of a life partner (Gemara to Taanith IV 9,10, Jerusalem Talmud; Baba Bathra 121a, Babylonian Talmud).

Although Jerusalem was situated in the land allotted to Judah and Benjamin (Joshua 15:1,8; 18:11,16,28), it was considered to belong to all the tribes (Yoma 12a, Babylonian Talmud) for it was the national shrine, as Shiloh was in its day. The young men and women who particiated in the singing and dancing on the fifteenth day of Ab belonged to all the tribes who convened in Jerusalem for the holy days. If they were allowed to intermarry on that day, it was in commemoration of the intermarriage of the tribe of Benjamin in Shiloh with all the tribes of Israel. And 'the daughters of Jerusalem' also danced, as did 'the daughters of Shiloh' (Judges 21:21) long ago by the vineyards, where the men of Benjamin were hiding and watching.

Hundreds of years later, Saul of Benjamin was the issue of that union of the tribes which happened in Shiloh. Had the tribes not asked for a King? Here was a stalwart young man before them called Saul ('asked for' in Hebrew). A good offspring was he, 'a choice and handsome young man. There was not a more handsome person than he among the children of Israel. From his shoulders upwards he was taller than anyone else' (1 Samuel 9:2). No one had more the appearance of a leader than he who was presented to the tribes by Samuel in these terms: 'See him whom the Lord has chosen, there is no one like him among all the people' (1 Samuel 10:24). And none of the tribes had more right to provide a king than the tribe of Benjamin which had become in itself the new Israel. Deliverance from their enemies could be expected to come from their king of the tribe of Benjamin: the tribe of the 'son of the right hand' of salvation. Thus it was that 'little Benjamin their ruler' (Psalm 68:27) led them all including 'the princes of Judah and their adherents' (ibid.).

It was the dismemberment of an assaulted woman by her husband and the dispersion of parts of the body to the twelve tribes that resulted in the tribe of Benjamin being cut off from the rest of the tribes (Judges 19 and 20). And it was when women from the twelve tribes united with the men of Benjamin that their tribe was able to survive and become attached to the rest of the tribes, for we should not forget that there were no Benjaminite women left.

Bethlehem-Ephrathah, the city which provided the line of Kings (see p. 102), again enters into the picture. For the woman whose death initiated all the events leading to the formation of the new Benjamin-Israel tribe, was 'a concubine from Bethlehem-Judah' (Judges 19:1).

The phrase 'until Shiloh comes' or 'until he comes to Shiloh' (Genesis 49:10) has always been enigmatic, so much so, that *The Interpreters Bible* (Abingdon Press, Vol. I p. 821) calls it 'cryptic in the extreme.' The earliest interpretation is perhaps found in the book of the prophet Ezekiel: 'Until he comes whose right it is' (Ezekiel 21:27; see also St. Matthew 11:3). The ancient Greek (Septuagint) translation rendered it:

> 'Until the things in store for him shall come' –Septuagint and Theodotion version of Genesis 49:10.

> 'Until for whom it is in store shall come' –Aquila and Symmachus versions of Genesis 49:10.

The old Syriac version rendered it: 'Until he whose it is comes,' and the Latin Vulgate: 'Until he comes who is to be sent.' The Targums, in turn, paraphrased it:

> 'Until the *Messiah* comes, whose is the Kingdom' –Targum Onkelos.

> 'Until the time that *King Messiah* shall come, whose is the Kingdom' –Targum Jerusalem.

'Until the time *King Messiah* shall come whose is the Kingship'
—Targum Neofiti I.

'Until the *King Messiah* shall come, the youngest of his sons' —
Targum Pseudo-Jonathan or Targum Jerusalem I.

We can see from these texts that the word Shiloh was interpreted as meaning someone who has a right to the Kingdom or for whom things are kept as an inheritance awaiting the time when they shall be given to him. According to the Targums and early Jewish and Christian tradition, this person is the Messiah.

Whether Shiloh refers to the sanctuary or to the name of the Messiah who was to come, one thing is certain: that when Shiloh would come or when he would come to Shiloh, the sovereignty of Judah was to cease. We saw that Judah's sovereignty did depart for a time when Saul of Benjamin became King of Israel. We can also see that not long after the Messiah-Son of Man came, the Kingdom of Judah ceased to exist, and the Judean Davidic royal line became exhausted and can no longer be traced because of the Diaspora. Another thing was certain to occur at the coming of Shiloh or at his coming to Shiloh, which is that the obedience of the people would be to him. True, it was to King Saul that all the people of Israel gave their allegiance, and it is to the Messiah-Son of Man that all peoples shall give their obedience (Daniel 7:13–14).

What are the things that are kept as an inheritance for the one who is to be sent? They are the precious hidden things of God's wisdom and knowledge which shall be fully understood by him, the Messiah-Son of Man. For he is the great Teacher and Revealer of 'all the treasures of that which is hidden' (Enoch 46:3), and from 'his mouth shall pour forth all the secrets of wisdom and counsel' (Enoch 51:3). Because 'in him dwells the spirit of understanding and of might' (Enoch 49:3; Isaiah 11:1–2) giving knowledge of God and perfect peace (see pp.124–127).

We know the rabbinic traditions concerning the coming of the Messiah as a great teacher (pp. 141–142) to give understanding and knowledge of God, and thereby peace. For His people knew that knowledge and understanding help to turn many away from evil, and persuade them to be good so that they may enjoy 'the peace of righteousness' (Baruch 5:4). Great is the power of understanding to turn the many from unrighteousness:

'Give me understanding, and I shall keep Your Law, yes, I shall observe it with all my heart' —Psalm 119:34,32,104.

'O Lord, You have put understanding in the heart of Your servant that he may do what is good and right before You, and restrain himself against deeds of wickedness' —1QH 14:8–9, Dead Sea Scrolls.

'You have taught him understanding of Your mysteries that he may not sin against You' —1QH 17:21,22, Dead Sea Scrolls.

'Give to Your people a heart of wisdom and an understanding of prudence and . . . they shall not sin' —Ps. Philo's *Biblical Antiquities* XXI.2.

'He shall instruct them [to make them understand] in all that has been found . . . so that they may separate themselves from all those who have not departed from all perversity' —1QS 9:20, Dead Sea Scrolls.

'He [God] opens the understanding of men . . . to turn a man from unrighteousness' —Job 33:16,17 Greek Text.

'The temperate understanding is able to be superior to the passions and to transform some and destroy others' —4 Maccabees 2:18.

'The temperate understanding repels all these malignant passions' —4 Maccabees 2:16.

'The temperate understanding has power to conquer the pressure of the passions' —4 Maccabees 3:17; Megillah 3a, Babylonian Talmud.

'The understanding has skill to direct the irrational powers within us like a pilot or a charioteer' —Philo, *Det.* 54.

'The affections of our appetites are resisted by the temperate understanding and bent back again' —4 Maccabees 1:35.

'A wise heart that has understanding will abstain from sins and have success in the works of justice' —Sirach 3:32, Latin Vulgate.

'When I understand [BIN], I am afraid of Him' —Job 23:15.

'Will you not understand so as to fear Him who created the foundations of the earth?' —Targum to Isaiah 40:21.

'All men shall fear and shall declare the work of God for they shall understand [SAKAL] what He has done' —Psalm 64:9.

'If a man understands the design of God by which all things are ordained, he will despise all material things and his vices will be healed' —Corpus Hermeticum, *Asclepius* III. 22a.

'They who are understanding [SAKAL] . . . turn many to righteousness' —Daniel 12:3.

'By His knowledge shall My righteous Servant make the many [to understand and thereby] to be righteous' —Isaiah 53:11.

'I will teach transgressors Your ways and sinners shall be converted to You' —Psalm 51:13.

'They shall be converted by Your glorious mouth' —1QH 6:14
Dead Sea Scrolls.
Because 'out of His mouth comes knowledge and great understanding' —Proverbs 2:6.

'If men saw this, not with bodily eyes, but rather with the eyes of the understanding; they would certainly be converted to virtue' —Philo, *Q. Gen.* IV. 51.

'Teaching understanding to those whose spirit has gone astray and instructing in doctrine those who murmur' —1QS 10:26–11:1
Dead Sea Scrolls (Dupont-Sommer).

'The Lord give you understanding [SAKAL] and insight [BINAH] . . . that you may keep the Law of the Lord your God' —1 Chronicles 22:12.

'The Levites taught the multitude . . . they all wept when they heard [and understood] the Law' —1 Esdras 8:48,49,50.

'The Levites caused the people to understand the teaching . . . they read distinctly from the book from the Law of God and gave the explanation and caused them to understand [BIN] the reading and . . . they all wept when they heard [and understood] the words of the Law' —Nehemiah 8:7,8,9.

'He shall go before Him in the spirit and power of Elijah, to turn the hearts of the fathers to the children and the disobedient to the understanding [PHRONĒSEI] of the righteous' —St. Luke 1:17.

'The teaching of Truth was in his mouth . . . and he did turn many away from iniquity' —Malachi 2:6.

'The Lord has directed my mouth by His Word, and He has opened up my understanding by His light . . . and gave me the ability that I might speak the fruit of His peace to convert the souls of those who are willing to come to Him' —Odes of Solomon 10:1–3.

'Be transformed by the renewing of your understanding' — Romans 12:2; Ezekiel 11:19–20; 36:26–27.

'Be renewed in the spirit of your understanding, and put on the new man, created after the likeness of God in righteousness and true holiness' —Ephesians 4:23–24.

The Messiah came not only to redeem us as the Suffering Servant of the Lord but He also came as the Son of Man to give us understanding. For indeed 'the Dayspring from on high has visited us to give light to those who sit in the darkness and the shadow of death, to guide our feet into the way of peace' (St. Luke 1:78,79). 'He is our peace' (Ephesians 2:14) because as the Son of Man He is Understanding. There is no peace without understanding, and no understanding without Him who is our righteousness (2 Corinthians 5:12; Romans 3:21; 5:19,21; Philippians 3:9; 2 Peter 1:1). Yeshua the Son of Man shall be revealed the day we shall know that He is Understanding made flesh, who walked in our midst 'full of grace and truth.' 'For the Law was given through Moses, but grace and truth came through Yeshua, the Messiah' (St. John 1:14,17). He is the Giver of understanding to those who desire to know the hidden things (see pp. 82–83), for all the secret treasures of the Torah are entrusted to Him (pp. 141–143, 197), and 'from His mouth shall come out all the secrets of Wisdom' (Enoch 51:3; 46:3; 49:1–3).

Chapter 24

The Parables Of Yeshua The Son Of Man

'Let not the parable be lightly esteemed in your eyes because
by means of it a man arrives at the true meaning of the words
of the Torah.' —Midrash Song of Songs Rabbah I.1.8.

He came to fulfill the Law (St. Matthew 5:17–20) that was given for the
sake of righteouness (2 Baruch 67:6; Romans 10:5), and He taught by His
example that 'the righteouness which is in the Law' (Philippians 3:6) conduces towards the lovingkindness [ḤESED] of those who are truly godly
[ḤASSID]. For all true keeping leads to giving. 'Therefore love is the fulfil-
ment of the Law' (Romans 13:10), 'for the end of the commandment is love
out of a pure heart and a good conscience and sincere faith' (1 Timothy
1:5). That kind of love and lovingkindness are found in the children of
God, made His children by their faith in Yeshua the Messiah (St. John
1:12). For it is by Him that the Truth is made known, the Truth that sanc-
tifies and makes one a perfect child of God (St. John 17:17; 8:32,35–36).

The Messiah who is the Truth (St. John 14:6; Ephesians 4:21) reveals
the Truth and makes known 'the things which have been kept secret from
the foundation of the world' (St. Matthew 13:35,11,16–17; Psalm 78:2).
These things were brought to light in His parables, the parables of Yeshua
the Messiah who as the Son of Man is Understanding incarnate.

When Yeshua the Messiah spoke to the crowds 'He taught them many
things in parables' (St. Mark 4:2). 'He did not speak to them without a
parable' (St. Matthew 13:34; St. Mark 4:34). The Hebrew word for 'parable': MASHAL means 'to set side by side', 'to make resemble', i.e., 'to equate
one thing to another'; it also means 'to rule', 'to have dominion' or 'power
over'. Another Hebrew word: MOSHEL analogously means 'to be like' (Job
41:33) and also 'dominion' (Daniel 11:4; Zechariah 9:10). Yeshua the Son
of Man spoke in parables because in His excellent parables He was able
to both make known and conceal—as the unrevealed Messiah—His great
understanding and knowledge of all the hidden truths and wisdom of the
Torah. To the ears of the undiscerning the parables would sound like simple stories but to those in the crowd with knowledge, the speaker's great
understanding and mastery over all the secrets of the Torah was made

manifest. We can take the parable of The Sower as an example:

> He spoke to them many things in parables, saying: 'Behold, the sower went forth to sow. And as he sowed, some seed fell by the wayside; and the birds came and devoured them. Some fell upon rocky places, where they did not have much earth; and they immediately sprang up, because they had no depth of earth. But when the sun was up they were scorched, and because they had no root they withered away. And some fell among thorns, and the thorns sprang up and choked them. But others fell on good ground and yielded fruit, some a hundredfold, some sixtyfold, and some thirty-fold. He who has ears to hear, let him hear!' – St. Matthew 13:3–9; St. Mark 4:2–9; St. Luke 8:4–8.

The majority of the crowd hearing the Messiah would have wondered, without a doubt, why He called for particular attention at the end of the parable. For it seemed to be just an ordinary narrative about a sower sowing seed that fell upon different portions of the ground of a field. Nevertheless, the Messiah did consider it a very important parable for when His disciples asked Him about the meaning of that parable He said to them: 'Do you not know this parable? How then will you know all the parables?' –St. Mark 4:13,10.

Those in the crowd who had knowledge of the Holy Scriptures would realize that the Lord Messiah would know that they were truly the ground of the field which is the world (St. Matthew 13:38). And that God would relate with them as Sower to field and Seed to ground. How could the Seed flourish if the ground of their hearts was hardened as that of a foot trodden path cutting across the field or if it were shallow as the thin layer upon the rocks, and overburdened as that in the patch choked by the thorns and brambles of worldly cares and distractions? Only if they were like the good ground would the Seed thrive in their hearts and bear the fruit of understanding to His glory (St. Matthew 13:18–23). Furthermore, they would apprehend that when the Messiah would come down from heaven to teach them, He would come at first as a Sower to sow in them words that would make His ways known to them and bring them a greater knowledge of God. For if the Messiah was to teach them true righteousness, what better way would He have than to sow it into them? It was known that righteousness is sown:

> 'Sow to yourselves righteousness and reap lovingkindness [ḤESED]' –Hosea 10:12.

'To one who sows righteousness—a reward of Truth [EMETH]' —
Proverbs 11:18.

They knew that the Law which was given for the sake of righteousness,
was sown in their hearts: 'Behold, I sow My Law in you and it shall bring
forth fruit in you.' This was called 'the fruit of the Law' which is 'the fruit
of righteousness' (2 Esdras 9:31,32; 2 Baruch 32:1; Amos 6:12). For they
knew that the Word of God is to be kept in our hearts as a seed: 'Your Word
I have hid in my heart so that I may not sin against You' (Psalm 119:11).
That Word has within it the light of knowledge, and understanding which
are for those who hold fast to the Seed of His Word: 'the unfolding of Your
words gives light, giving understanding to the simple' i.e., to those who
'believe every word' (Psalm 119:130; Proverbs 14:15), and keep it. It was
already said that 'light is sown [ZARA] for the righteous' (Psalm 97:11,
Literal Translation), and that this light would arise from their hearts
when they have become upright (Psalm 112:4). Because 'the fruit of light
[PHOS] is found in all goodness and righteousness and truth' (Ephesians
5:9).

When He explained the parable of The Sower, in private to His disciples
(St. Matthew 13:10–23; St. Mark 4:10–20; St. Luke 8:9–15), the Messiah
told them that 'the Seed is the Word of God' and that 'the Sower sows the
Word' (St. Luke 8:11; St. Mark 4:14). He made it clear to them that we are
the ground upon which the Word is sown, the varied terrain being the
types of hearers of the Word. He told them that those who shall bring
forth fruit in abundance are they who hear the Word and understand it.
They are the ones who have accepted and kept the Word in the good
ground of their hearts 'with patience' (St. Luke 8:15; St. Matthew 13:23;
St. Mark 4:20).

There was already the intimation in the Holy Scriptures that 'God sows'
('Jezreel' as in Hosea 2:22 etc.) and that 'righteousness will remain in the
fertile field' (Isaiah 32:16) until 'the peaceable fruit of righteousness'
(Hebrews 12:11) is brought forth from the seed of righteousness that was
sown in the heart. The work of that seed is to transform us into peacemaking children of God (St. Matthew 5:9) for 'the work of righteousness shall
be peace' (Isaiah 32:17). That is why one of the Messiah's understanding
disciples wrote (St. James 3:18; St. Luke 24:45) that 'the fruit of righteousness is sown in peace by those who make peace': God's loving children. In
the parable of The Sower, the Messiah reveals His knowledge that God
sows His Word in us, and that the bearing of fruit from that Seed-Word
of God depends on the state of the ground of our hearts.

And because it takes time for all things that are sown to bear fruit, the parable of The Sower is followed by the parable of The Secretly Growing Seed:

> He said, 'The kingdom of God is as if a man should cast seed upon the ground, and should sleep by night and rise by day, and the seed sprouts up and grows, he himself does not know how. For the earth brings forth fruit by itself: first the blade, then the head, after that the full grain in the head. But when the grain is ripe, immediately he sends forth the sickle, because the harvest has come' —St. Mark 4:26–29.

In this parable the Messiah makes known that the Seed has a life of its own, and shall proceed to do its work which is to be brought to fruit by the heart of the ground. This work of righteousness goes on day by day without observation because it takes place within the heart where the Seed-Word of God reigns in those who hold it fast. For what was truly sown in them was 'the Word of the Kingdom' (St. Matthew 13:19), and that Word is the very Kingdom of God which was to be sown in their hearts by the Messiah. Long ago, the Lord had already promised through the prophet Jeremiah that He would put His Law in their hearts (Jeremiah 31:33, see Midrash on Psalm 119.10). And they were to obey the Law as faithful subjects do the commands of their king. The Messiah revealed that in His lovingkindness God desired to reign in their hearts first, before He would come later on in His justice to establish His Kingdom throughout the world.

Once, when the Messiah 'was asked by the Pharisees when the Kingdom of God would come, He answered them and said, "The Kingdom of God does not come with observation; nor will they say 'Lo, here it is!' or 'There it is!' for behold, the Kingdom of God is within you" ' (St. Luke 17:20,21, Literal Translation). The Pharisees did not expect to receive such an answer for it was commonly taught that when the Messiah came he would manifestly inaugurate the Reign of God by overcoming all the enemies of Israel in battle, thus establishing by his prowess a universal peace on this earth. Furthermore, in his time Satan and the wicked would be no more. And the Truth would be revealed and triumph over all lies. Then, the righteous would flourish forever (Psalms of Solomon 17:29(31), 32(35), 34(38); Testament of Levi 18:4; Testament of Judah 24:1, 6; Testament of Simeon 6:4; 2 Baruch 73:1; Sibylline Oracles III. 373–376, 653, 655 ff.; Jubilees 23:29; 25:20; 40:9; Assumption of Moses 10:1; Enoch 38:5; 52:14; 105:2). And they would banquet with the Messiah in the Kingdom of God

(Baba Bathra 74a–75a, Babylonian Talmud; 2 Baruch 29:4; Midrash Leviticus Rabbah 13.3; St. Luke 13:29). In that era, God Himself would appear before the righteous (Midrash Numbers Rabbah 13.2; Sifre Deuteronomy 343; Midrash Tannaim 211), as their visible King.

'The mystery of the Kingdom of God' (St. Mark 4:11; St. Luke 8:9) which the Messiah revealed in His parables, is that it would first come as a hidden reign in the heart of man before it became manifest in its final establishment on this earth. Did they not say that the Messiah was to be the one who would inaugurate this Kingdom? If the Messiah himself was to be hidden at first (see Chapter 17; St. John 7:27,41; 14:22), was it not to be expected that the Messiah would usher in the Kingdom of God also in a hidden way?

Basically, a kingdom consists of a king, his subjects and an area of land. Even if there was only one subject besides the king, that area would be considered a kingdom and the king would 'reign' if the subject obeyed the commands of the king. God reigns in the heart as King if His commands are obeyed. No one obeyed the commands of God better than Yeshua the Messiah (see pp. 48–49) who is Himself the *incarnate* Kingdom of God just as He is also the Wisdom of God:

> 'Even so you too, when you see all these things happening, recognize that *He* [Yeshua] is near' –St. Matthew 24:33; St. Mark 13:29.

> 'Even so you too, when you see these things happening, recognize that *the Kingdom of God* is near' –St. Luke 21:31, see also St. Matthew 12:28.

> 'Therefore *I* [Yeshua] send you prophets and wise men and scribes, some of whom you will kill and crucify, and some you will scourge in your synagogues and persecute from town to town' – St. Matthew 23:34.

> 'Therefore also *the Wisdom of God* said, I will send them prophets and apostles, some of whom they will kill and persecute' –St. Luke 11:49; see also 1 Corinthians 1:24,30.

We see that He is truly the Wisdom of God when we realize that what the Messiah sows in the hearts of those who believe in Him is in reality *His* seed: 'the Sower went out to sow his seed' (St. Luke 8:5). The Sower who is the living Word of God (St. John 1:1,14) has power to sow Himself in the hearts of those who accept Him. And what He sows in their hearts is the Seed of Himself to be brought forth by them as a mother brings forth a child from the seed in her womb.

A woman keeps the child being formed in her with loving care, knowing that it comes from the one she loves. She anticipates the time of motherhood when she will bring forth the baby and be able to cuddle it in her arms. In the meantime, she is aware that she carries within her a precious life, an unborn being whom she loves. The Word and Law of God with all His commandments, precepts and testimonies are meant to be kept and loved (Psalm 119:47,48,97,113,119,127,140,159,163,165,167) for they lead us to Him and bring about His perfect reign in our hearts.

Knowing how difficult it had been for His people to keep and love the Law of righteousness, God made it into flesh in the person of Yeshua the Messiah who is the perfect fulfillment of all that was meant to be kept and loved in the Law. He incarnated in His Messiah the perfect obedience which establishes the reign of God in the heart of Man, and He gave His Messiah the power to sow Himself in the hearts of those who accept Him. In so doing, God made it easier for us to be good because what is sown and what we are asked to keep in our hearts is not only the seed of the Law but that of a Being. The human heart was made to keep and love a person far more readily than a thing. It is the seed of Someone who loved us and gave up His life for us that we are asked to keep in our hearts. Thus, the Messiah is truly in the hearts of those who receive Him, as a child is in the womb of his mother waiting to be brought forth by her love. In the Messiah the Law became a Person. He said, 'I am the way, the truth, and the life' (St. John 14:6), in keeping *Him* we keep the way of true righteousness which is the Law, but we can now keep it with all eagerness and joy, because it enables us to keep and form Him whom we love in our hearts. Blessed are they who hunger and thirst to be good (St. Matthew 5:6), for they shall bring Him forth and be able to embrace Him whom they once carried in the womb of their hearts.

Truth is the manifestation of His hidden Word. And the Truth may be said to be the offspring of the reign of God in the heart of man, because perfect obedience to the will of God brings forth the lovingkindness, truthfulness, and peacefulness of the children of God. The Truth belongs to the faithful and true who have brought it forth from their hearts.

In the parable of The Good Seed and the Darnel (St. Matthew 13:24–

30,36–43) the Messiah reveals the presence of another sower in the field of the world: the devil. The Son of Man sows the good seed-words of Truth which He brought forth, the devil sows lies, his own offspring for he is the father of lies (St. John 8:44). And the enemy of the Son of Man sows his lies in the midst of all the good things the Son of Man sowed, because he wants to confound the ground. But as in the parable of the Dragnet (St. Matthew 13:47–50), the Messiah taught that there will be a day of final reckoning and separation of the just from the unjust, and of the truth from all the lies of the evil one.

Yeshua the Son of Man knew that just as those who are faithful and true bring forth the truth from their hearts, so do the wicked 'travail with iniquity, and conceive mischief and bring forth lies' (Psalm 7:14) as children of their evil hearts. For they are ever 'conceiving [HARAH = becoming pregnant] and uttering from their hearts words of falsehood' (Isaiah 59:13): their offspring. But the good bring forth the fruit of righteousness which contains the good seeds of truth. And since the fruit of righteousness is the product of their obedience to the rule of God in their hearts, the Messiah said that 'the good seed are the children of the Reign [or Kingdom of God]' –St. Matthew 13:38.

In His time, hearing the parable of The Good Seed and the Darnel, the instructed among the people would have perceived the Messiah's great wisdom. For they knew that there is 'evil seed' (2 Esdras 4:31), and that 'evil is sown' (2 Esdras 4:28,29), and that it is 'sown along with good' (2 Esdras 4:29) in the heart of man. Was not the Law of God to be sown in their hearts so that the 'Law might bring forth fruit in them'? (2 Esdras 3:21; 9:32). They knew that it was said of the wicked one that 'the root of evil' (2 Esdras 8:53) and 'the plant of wickedness has taken root in him' (Sirach 3:28), to make him produce 'the fruit of lies' (Hosea 10:13), and 'the bread of deceit' (Proverbs 20:17) for the evil sower, 'the father of lies'–'the devil' (St. John 8:44). They also knew that 'in His mysteries of understanding and in His glorious wisdom, God has set an end for the existence of deceit; and at the time of His Visitation, He will destroy it forever. Then the Truth of the earth [TEBEL = fruitful earth] shall arise for ever . . . and God will cleanse by His Truth all the works of every man, and will purify for Himself the bodily fabric of every man to banish all spirit of deceit from his members' (1QS 4:18,19, 20,21, Dead Sea Scrolls).

All deceit will vanish when the truth will be fully manifested (see pp. 74–75). Until the time of the harvest, the wheat and the darnel in its midst grow together in the field of the world. But when the grains are ripe, the field is harvested and the darnel is collected into bundles to be burned while the wheat is gathered into His barn (St. Matthew 13:26–30). Thus, Truth and deceit grow side by side until the humble Sower who is the Son of Man (St. Matthew 13:37) shall return as Lord of the harvest. 'As therefore the darnel is collected and burned in the fire, so will it be at the completion of the age. The Son of Man will send forth His angels and they shall collect out of His Kingdom all the stumbling blocks and those doing the lawlessness, and cast them into the furnace of fire. There shall be wailing and gnashing of the teeth. Then shall the righteous shine forth as the sun in the kingdom of their Father. He who has ears to hear let him hear!' (St. Matthew 13:40–43; see also St. Mark 4:29).

When all the tax collectors and the sinners drew near to Him to hear Him . . . , the Pharisees and scribes murmured saying, 'this man receives sinners and eats with them' (St. Luke 15:1–2). In response, the Messiah told them three apt parables which were directed to the three groups of people in question: the sinners, the tax collectors, and the Pharisees and scribes. For the sake of sinners in general (Isaiah 53:6), Yeshua told the Pharisees and scribes the parable of The Lost Sheep (St. Luke 15:4–7) making known to them that the Lord goes after a repentant sinner as a shepherd goes after a lost sheep until he has rescued it. In the meantime he leaves the rest of the flock in the wilderness. 'And when he has found it, he lays it on his shoulders rejoicing. And when he comes home he calls together his friends and neighbors, saying to them, "Rejoice with me, for I have found my sheep which was lost!" ' (St. Luke 15:5–6). Next, by telling them the parable of The Lost Coin (St. Luke 15:8–10), the Messiah took into consideration the tax collectors who were regarded as sinners by the scribes and Pharisees because of their avarice. He taught them that the Lord goes after repentant publicans as a woman goes after a lost silver coin, deligently searching her house for it. 'And when she has found it, she calls her friends and neighbors together, saying, "Rejoice with me, for I have found the silver piece which I lost!" ' (St. Luke 15:9).

The scribes and the Pharisees were the elders, they were the interpreters of the Law and the spiritual guides of the people. It was to them that the Messiah next addressed His beautiful parable about The Two Brothers, the beloved story better known as the parable of The Prodigal Son (St. Luke 15:11–32). It is about a father who had two sons, the younger son demanded from his father that portion of the property to which he was entitled, and which accordingly he received. It probably amounted to one third of the estate since according to the Jewish law (Baba Bathra VIII. 3–4, Bekoroth VIII. 1–2, Mishnah; Bekoroth 3a, Babylonian Talmud) the eldest brother was entitled to two thirds of the property. Having received his portion, the younger brother departed to a distant land and in a short time squandered his whole fortune in riotous living. A great famine then began to prevail in the land and he was there reduced to seeking the help of a citizen of that country who sent him to his farm to tend swine, the lowest and most contemptible of all occupations.

Yet even in this degrading work he could not earn enough to keep himself from starving. He would have gladly satisfied his hunger with the carob pods that the swine ate, but no one gave him anything. Want and misery now opened the younger son's eyes to his folly. He remembered his father's house where even the least among the servants and laborers were so well cared for. He contrasted his wretched condition with theirs and he said to himself: 'How many of my father's hired servants abound with bread and here I perish with hunger! I will arise and go to my father, and say to him, "Father, I have sinned against heaven and before you and I am no longer worthy to be called your son. Make me like one of your hired servants" ' (St. Luke 15:17–19).

He carried out his resolve at once, and arose and took the road homewards. While he was still afar off, his father saw him and had compassion, and ran and embraced him and kissed him. The son began his humble confession but the father did not seem to listen for he at once called his servants and told them to quickly bring out the best robe and put it on his son and put a ring on his hand and sandals on his feet. And he ordered them to bring out the fatted calf and kill it to prepare a banquet, 'because this my son was dead and is alive again; he was lost and is found.' And they began to be merry. Now his older son was in the field. And as he drew near to the house, he heard music and dancing. So he called one of the servants and asked him what these things meant. And he said to him, 'Your brother has come, and because he has received him safe and sound, your father has killed the fatted calf.' But he was angry and would not go in. Therefore his father came out and began entreating him. So he answered and said to his father, 'Lo, for so many years I have been serving you, and I have never transgressed your commandments at any time; and yet you never gave me a young goat, that I might make merry with my friends. But as soon as this son of yours came who has devoured your livelihood with harlots, you killed the fatted calf for him.' And he said to him, 'Son you are always with me, and all that I have is yours. But it was right that we should make merry and be glad, for your brother was dead and is alive again, and was lost and is found' (St. Luke 15:24–32).

It was to the Pharisees and the scribes that this parable was directed, therefore, the Messiah in His wisdom left it purposely unfinished. For they represented the elder brother in the story and Yeshua waited to see their response to His appeals. The parable invited them to rejoice and welcome back the repentant sinners and tax collectors with gladness, for they were, after all, their brothers. And were they not returning to the Father whom they loved?

The Messiah knew about the two stages of mankind. Thus, His parables about trees and fruit (St. Matthew 7:16–21; 12:33–35; St. Luke 6:43–46) precede the ones concerning the seeds, field, grain and bread (St. Matthew 13:1–9,18–23,24–33; St. Luke 8:11–15,18–20). In both these sets of parables, Yeshua the Messiah drew attention to the heart: 'By their fruits you shall know them. Do men gather grapes from thorns, or figs from thistles? Even so, every good tree brings forth good fruit, and the evil tree brings forth evil fruit. A good tree cannot bring forth evil fruit, neither can an evil tree bring forth good fruit. Every tree that does not bring forth good fruit shall be cut down and shall be cast in the fire' (St. Matthew 7:16–19; see also St. Matthew 3:10; St. Luke 3:9). 'Either make the tree good and its fruit good or make the tree evil and its fruit evil. For by the fruit, the tree is known. O generation of vipers, how can you speak good things when you are evil? For out of the abundance of the heart the mouth speaks' (St. Matthew 12:33–35).

Indeed, 'there is nothing that enters a man from outside which can defile him; but the things which come out of him, those are the things that defile a man . . . for from within, out of the heart of men, proceed evil thoughts, adulteries, fornications, murders, thefts, covetousness, wickedness, deceit, licentiousness, an evil eye, blasphemy, pride, foolishness. All these evil things come from within and defile a man' (St. Mark 7:15,21–23). The Messiah knew that 'the heart is deep beyond all things and that it is the man' (Jeremiah 17:9, Greek Text). And that 'as in water face reveals face, so a man's heart reveals the man' (Proverbs 27:19). Nothing was hid from the Messiah because He knew the thoughts of men's hearts (St. Luke 9:47; 5:22; 11:17; 24:38; St. Matthew 9:4; 12:25; St. Mark 2:8).

Yeshua the Messiah knew that we shall not have truly repented unless we have repented from our heart, and we shall not have really forgiven unless we have forgiven from our heart (St. Matthew 18:35). He taught that all outward righteousness is false that does not come from the heart: 'Woe to you, scribes and Pharisees! For you clean the outside of the cup and of the dish but inside they are full of robbery and unrighteousness . . . first clean the inside of the cup and of the dish, so that the outside may also become clean' (St. Matthew 23:25–26). We are what we are within our hearts, and those who bring forth the 'hundredfold' (St. Luke 8:8) are 'they who, hearing the Word hold it fast in an outwardly good [KALE = exterior beauty and goodness] and inwardly good [AGATHE = intrinsic goodness] heart, bearing fruit with patience' (St. Luke 8:15). Outward appearances can be deceptive: 'Woe to you, scribes and Pharisees, hypocrites! For you are like whitewashed tombs which indeed appear beautiful outwardly, but inside are full of dead men's bones and all uncleanness. Even so you also outwardly appear righteous to men, but inside you are full of hypocrisy and lawlessness' (St. Matthew 23:27–28).

Yeshua knew that when God wants man to remember, He writes on the tablets of the heart (Jeremiah 31:33; Hebrews 8:10), for He knows that if we 'lay up His words in 'our' hearts' (Job 22:22) we shall never forget them. 'His mother kept all these [His] sayings in her heart,' 'pondering them in her heart' (St. Luke 2:51,19) because she knew that 'to ponder upon wisdom is perfect understanding' (Wisdom 6:15), if the pondering is done in the heart, for we do 'understand with the heart' (Isaiah 6:10; see pp. 45–46). The Messiah warned us in His parable of the Sower that we are to strive to keep His sown Word in our heart even if we do not as yet understand it (see St. Luke 2:50,51b) because the devil is always ready to snatch it away (St. Matthew 13:19; St. Mark 4:15; St. Luke 8:12) so that we may not be able to ponder it and understand.

And what shall be understood by them who do the pondering is that the Messiah did not come to abolish the Law or the Prophets but to bring to completion all the teaching of the Torah:

> 'Do not think that I came to abolish the Law or the Prophets. I did not come to abolish but to fulfill.
> Truly, I say to you, till heaven and earth pass away, not one jot or one tittle will pass away from the Law till all is fulfilled. Whoever therefore breaks one of the least of these commandments, and teaches men so, he shall be called least in the Kingdom of heaven; but whoever does and teaches them, he shall be called great in the Kingdom of heaven' —St. Matthew 5:17–19.

The Old Covenant was effected by the *keeping* and doing of all the commandments, precepts, statutes, ordinances, testimonies and judgments of the Lord. The New Covenant is effected by the *giving* of the fruit of all that was kept in the Law. Yeshua the Messiah inaugurated the New Covenant because He is the One who brought forth the fruit of all keeping which is selfless love. And this was manifested in His dying to redeem us so that we might have new Life through Him.

The fruition of all righteousness is lovingkindness. One truly loves who has first kept and done His commandments (Deuteronomy 7:9; 11:1; 30:16; St. John 14:15,21,23; 15:10; 1 Timothy 1:5; 1 John 5:2,3; 2 John v.6; Sirach 2:15, Greek Sinaiticus Text; Testament of Joseph 11:1, Armenian Text). 'A good understanding have all those who do His commands' (Psalm 111:10). 'Yeshua began to do [first] and teach [after]' —Acts 1:1. From the very beginning He fulfilled all righteousness (St. Matthew 3:15) before He ministered and instructed. He taught well because He has 'the understanding of the righteous' (St. Luke 1:17).

Yeshua the Son of Man taught in parables and proverbs because as the Son of Man He is Understanding incarnate. There is a definite relationship between 'parables *and* understanding' (Ecclesiastes 1:17, Greek Text). Thus, they are called 'the parables of understanding' (Sirach 1:25). We may be sure that 'a parable shall be found in the lips of the understanding' (Sirach 21:16, Greek Sinaiticus Text). And we have to listen very carefully (St. Matthew 13:9,43; St. Mark 4:9,23; St. Luke 8:8; 14:35) when we know that these parables have come from the Son of Man Himself. 'Let not the parables of understanding [BINAH] escape you' (Sirach 6:35, Hebrew Text). And 'let not the parable be lightly esteemed in your eyes because by means of it a man arrives at the true meaning of the words of the Torah' (Midrash Song of Songs Rabbah I.1.8). We have to pay close attention to 'enigmatic parables' (Sirach 47:15) for they are full of understanding. The Messiah also spoke in proverbs (St. John 10:6; 16:25) because there is also a close relationship between proverbs and understanding. In the days of old, 'those who had understanding . . . poured forth fitting proverbs' (Sirach 18:29). Who has not heard about 'the proverbs of Solomon . . . to receive [from them] the instruction of understanding'? (Proverbs 1:1,3). For there was a time when 'Solomon . . . overflowed like a river with understanding' (Sirach 47:13,14). But 'to depart from evil is understanding' (Job 28:28). Solomon lost his understanding because later on he did not depart from evil (1 Kings 11:1–8). Thus, it is written: 'Solomon . . . how wise you were in your *youth,* you overflowed like a river with understanding' (Sirach 47:13,14) but not in your old age when 'you did stain your honor and pollute your seed' (Sirach 47:20). For 'there is [also] a wisdom that abounds in evil [see St. James 3:15–16] and there is no understanding' (Sirach 21:15, Latin Vulgate) because evil abounds.

If 'the finding out of parables is a painful labor of the mind' (Sirach 13:26) it is because we must really study 'to penetrate the subtleties of parables' (Sirach 39:2) so as to be able to 'seek out the hidden meaning of proverbs and be at home with the enigmas of parables' (Sirach 39:3) that we may rejoice, because from them we shall receive understanding:

> 'Hear me [my son] and *receive my proverbs*' —Sirach 16:24, Hebrew Text.

> 'Hear me, my son, and *learn understanding*' —Sirach 16:24, Greek Text.

We know that 'a parable shall be found in the lips of the understanding' (Sirach 21:16, Sinaiticus Text). Conversely 'like a lame man's legs, which hang limp, is a parable in the mouth of fools' (Proverbs 26:7), and 'like a thorn that goes up into the hand of a drunkard is a proverb in the mouth of fools' (Proverbs 26:9), 'they shall not be found where parables are spoken' (Sirach 38:33), because they are foolish. 'Weep for the fool, for he lacks understanding' (Sirach 22:11) and apt proverbs and parables shall not be heard from his lips.

Yeshua the Son of Man hid His great understanding in His parables and proverbs. It was said of a patient man of understanding that 'he will hide his words until his time [of exaltation] and the lips of many shall declare his understanding' (Sirach 1:24), when those words are revealed. For 'a man shall be exalted according to his understanding' (Proverbs 12:8) found hidden in his words. The Son of Man once said: 'My hour is not yet come' (St. John 2:4) and 'My time is not yet come' (St. John 7:6; St. Matthew 24:35–36; Acts 1:6–7). But the time is here for Him to be exalted among His own because His understanding is now revealed.

Chapter 25

The Parable Of The Steward
Of Unrighteousness

'Let not the parables of understanding
escape you' —Sirach 6:35, Hebrew Text.

We have seen that 'the finding out of parables is a painful labor of the
mind' (Sirach 13:26), even more so, should it attempt to find out [i.e., un-
derstand] the parable of The Steward of Unrighteousness which the Messiah told to the disciples and Pharisees (St. Luke 16:1–15). The majority
of biblical scholars agree that 'this is the most difficult of all parables'
(*Peake's Commentary on the Bible,* edited and revised by Matthew Black
and H. H. Rowley, p. 836, Nelson 1963) for it seems to present impedi-
ments to any satisfactory interpretation. 'The literature dealing with the
parable of the unjust steward is staggering, and after all the effort expend-
ed, its meaning still eludes us. Indeed, more than any other parable it can
be expected to keep its mystery for future generations of exegetes, for it
bristles with difficulties' (L.J. Topel S.J. in *CBQ* XXXVII:2, 1975, p. 216).

Just as the garden of Paradise is closed except to those who believe in
Him, so does this parable of understanding open only to those who have
faith and confidence in the Son of Man, who in His wisdom, understanding and knowledge told the parable:

And He also said to the disciples, 'There was a certain rich man
who had a steward who was accused [DIEBLĒTHĒ] of scattering
[DIASKORPIZŌN] his goods. And he called him and said to him,
'What is this I hear about you? Turn in the account of your
stewardship for you can no longer be a steward.' And the steward
said within himself, 'What shall I do? for my master is taking the
stewardship away from me. I am not strong to dig, and I am
ashamed to beg. I have known [EGNŌN] what I am to do, so that
when I am removed from the stewardship, they will receive me
into their homes.' So he called every one of his master's debtors
to him and said to the first, 'How much do you owe my master?'
And he said, 'A hundred baths (Hebrew liquid measure) of oil.' So
he said to him, 'Take your bill, and sitting down quickly write

fifty.' Then he said to another, 'And how much do you owe?' And he said 'A hundred kors (Hebrew dry measure) of wheat.' And he said to him, 'Take your bill, and write eighty.' And his master praised [EPĒNESEN] the steward [OIKONOMON] of [TES] unrighteousness [ADIKIAS] because he had acted with understanding [PHRONIMŌS]. For the sons of this age are more understanding [PHRONIMŌTEROI] in their generation than the sons of light. And I say to you, make friends for yourselves by means of the mammon of unrighteousness that when it fails they may receive you into eternal dwellings. He who is faithful in that which is least is faithful also in much; and he who is unrighteous in what is least is unrighteous also in much. If therefore you have not been faithful in the unrighteous mammon, who will entrust to you the true riches? And if you have not been faithful in what is another man's, who will give you what is your own? No servant can serve two masters; for either he will hate the one, and love the other, or else he will hold fast to the one and despise the other. You cannot serve God and mammon.' Now the Pharisees who were lovers of money, also heard all these things, and they turned up their noses [EXEMUKTĒRIZON] at Him. And He said to them, 'You are those who justify yourselves before men, but God knows your hearts. For what is exalted among men is an abomination in the sight of God.' —St. Luke 16:1–15.

This difficult parable told by the Son of Man has not yet been understood because from the very beginning all commentators have taken it for granted that the charges laid upon the unfortunate steward were true, and that he was indeed guilty of wasting his master's goods as 'accused of' [DIEBLĒTHĒ] —St. Luke 16:1. The Greek word DIEBLĒTHĒ which the Evangelist used, is the aorist passive tense of DIABALLO which means 'to slander,' 'to misrepresent,' 'to deceive,' 'to set someone in opposition by slandering,' and as such it is used not only in classical Greek texts (Herodotus III.1; V.35; VIII.22,110; Thucydides III.4,4; Sophocles, *Philoctetes* 578; Euripides, *Hecuba* 863; Plato, *Politicus* VIII. p. 566b; Aristotle, *Politica* V. II, etc.) but also in the Septuagint and New Testament Greek (2 Samuel 19:27; Psalm 31:13 [Symm.]; Proverbs 6:24; Daniel 3:8; 6:24; Sirach 19:15; 28:9; 38:17; 51:2,6; 1 Maccabees 1:36; 2 Maccabees 3:11; 14:27; 3 Maccabees 6:7; 4 Maccabees 4:1; 1 Timothy 3:11; 2 Timothy 3:3; Titus 2:3). The inspired Evangelist could have used the common Greek words for 'accused' [KATĒGOREO as in St. Luke 6:7; 23:2,10] or ENGKALEO [as in Acts 23:28,29; 26:27], but knowing the Messiah's intent, he used DIEBLĒTHĒ which literally means 'he [the steward] was slandered to him [the master].'

The Son of Man hoped that His listeners would recall the many times that the good were slandered before their masters (Genesis 39:14–20; 2 Samuel 16:1–4; 19:24–30; Daniel 3:8–13; 6:24; 2 Maccabees 14:23–28; Sirach 51:1–6; Testament of Joseph 10:3; Ahikar 3:1–4:6; etc.), and how they were justified in the end as the steward would be. 'If a ruler pays attention to [slanderous] lies, all his servants are wicked' (Proverbs 29:12). Thus, rulers and kings were warned not to give credence to common slander:

> The king asked how he could be free from error. And he replied, 'If you always act with deliberation and never give credence to slanders but prove to yourself the things that are said to you and decide by your own judgment' —Letter of Aristeas V. 252.

For they would have cause to regret the loss of innocent good administrators by their giving credence to slander:

> 'Alas for you Ahikar, scribe [of the king] and wise in the conversation of men, for I [King Senqerim] through [listening to] the tittle-tattle of men destroyed you. For you once did arrange well the affairs of our kingdom. Now if anyone gave you back to me, I would give him whatever he asked of me no matter how great a treasure of gold and silver' —Story of Ahikar 5:7, Armenian Text.

Before the Messiah told the parable of the Steward of Unrighteousness, He warned His listeners to 'take heed and beware of all covetousness, for a man's life does not consist in the abundance of the things which he possesses' (St. Luke 12:15). And He told them about the Rich Fool, the parable concerning a rich man whose barns were bursting at the seams, and he was in a quandary and thought within himself, saying. 'What shall I do, since I have no room to store my crops?' So he said, 'I will do this, I will pull down my barns and build greater ones, and there I will store all my crops and my goods. And I will say to my soul, Soul, you have many goods laid up for many years, take your ease, eat, drink, and be merry.' But God said to him, 'You fool! This night your soul is required of you; then whose will those things be which you have provided?' So is he [a fool] who lays up treasure for himself, and is not rich towards God' (St. Luke 12:17–21; see Sirach 5:1).

What is it to be rich towards God? It is to 'be rich in good works, ready to give, willing to share' (1 Timothy 6:18), for 'he who has pity on the poor lends to the Lord, and He will pay back what he has given' (Proverbs 19:17). A generous giver to the needy is described as a scatterer of goods:

'He (the 'good man' v. 5) has scattered [PAZAR-ESKORPIZEN] in giving to the poor, his righteousness endures forever, his horn shall be exalted' (Psalm 112:9, Hebrew and Greek Texts). It is called 'scattering' because when 'the righteous gives, he does not spare' (Proverbs 21:26). And he shall be rewarded in the end, 'for there is one who scatters and yet increases more, and there is one who withholds more than is right, but it leads to poverty' (Proverbs 11:24; Deuteronomy 15:7–10; Proverbs 11:25–31; Sirach 35:1–11; 29:12–13). Therefore 'stretch forth your hand to the poor, so that your blessing may be complete' (Sirach 7:32). 'Blessed is he who understands [SAKAL-SUNION] concerning the poor, the Lord shall deliver him in time of trouble' (Psalm 41:1, Hebrew and Greek Texts). The Lord is glorified by our generosity towards the poor. *'Give to the poor'* (Sirach 35:8, Syriac Text) and you *'glorify the Lord'* (Sirach 35:8, Greek Text).

It is the poor who are humble and meek and for that reason they are the recipients of the Lord's good judgment. The poor may be needy regarding the goods of this earth, but they are rich in the knowledge of God, and in good judgment. For it is written that 'the humble [ANAV] He will guide in judgment [MISHPAT], the humble He will teach His way' (Psalm 25:9). Thus 'God . . . gives judgment [MISHPAT] to the poor' (Job 36:5,6), consequently, 'the needy speaks with [good] judgment [MISHPAT]' —Isaiah 32:7. We are assured that 'the Lord will do the judgment [DIN] of the humble, and the judgment [MISHPAT] of the poor' (Psalm 140:12). In the end, we shall see that it is 'the meek of the earth who have done His judgment' (Zephaniah 2:3). The poor not only have knowledge and good judgment but they have also the gift of understanding, for 'has not God chosen the poor of this world to be rich in faith?' (St. James 2:5) and it is 'through faith that we understand' (Hebrews 11:3). Thus it is 'the poor man who has understanding' (Proverbs 28:11), and 'the poor man is honored for his understanding' (Sirach 10:29, Hebrew Text) and for his knowledge as well because it is 'the poor man who knows' (Ecclesiastes 6:8).

True righteousness is compassionate and generous towards the poor for 'righteous men pity and are kind' and 'the righteous one is generously merciful and compassionate' (Proverbs 13:9b; 21:26, Greek Texts). Thus, the Hebrew word TSEDAKAH not only means 'righteousness' but 'liberality' and 'almsgiving' as well. And when the compassionate give to the poor from what they possess, the Lord repays them (2 Corinthians 8:14) out of the abundance possessed by the poor: their understanding, knowledge and good judgment. 'The righteous always have light' (Proverbs 13:9a,

Greek Text) and 'unto the upright there arises light in the darkness because he [the upright] is gracious and full of compassion and righteous' (Psalm 112:4). 'Deal your bread to the hungry, bring the poor who are cast out, into your house . . . , cover the naked . . . , help those in need. Then shall your light break forth as the morning' (Isaiah 58:7,8). 'If you draw out your soul to the hungry, and satisfy the afflicted soul, then shall your light arise' (Isaiah 58:10). We can now understand why it is written that:

> 'The righteous knows (through the understanding and knowledge he has received in helping them) the judgment of the poor, but the wicked do not understand knowledge' —Proverbs 29:7.

Conversely, 'light is withheld from the wicked' (Job 38:15), because 'the heart of the wicked is without pity' (Proverbs 12:10, Greek Text); therefore, 'they are darkened in their understanding . . . due to their hardness of heart' (Ephesians 4:18,19). Thus, the Psalms tell us:

> 'Deliver the poor and needy, free them from the hand of the wicked. They [the wicked who oppress the poor] do not know, nor do they understand; they walk about in darkness' —Psalm 82:4–5.

And because 'ruthless men retain riches' (Proverbs 11:16) and are not generous towards the poor, it is said that 'a ruler who is a great oppressor lacks understanding' (Proverbs 28:16), and that 'a man of violence does not receive understanding' (Sirach 32:18, Hebrew Text MS. E). 'Great in folly and lacking in understanding was he' [merciless Rehoboam] —Sirach 47:23, Hebrew Text. It is because of their hardness of heart and lack of compassion towards the poor, that 'the wicked do not understand knowledge' (Proverbs 29:7), and that 'evil men do not understand judgment' (Proverbs 28:5, Literal Translation): the knowledge and good judgment possessed by the poor.

We are told in the Holy Scriptures that because 'a good man shows favor and lends, he will guide his affairs with [good] judgment' (Psalm 112:5), and because he has 'scattered abroad, he has given to the poor' (Ibid. v. 9a), he is able to act well with the understanding, knowledge and good judgment he has received in aiding them. Thus, 'he will not be afraid of evil tidings' (Ibid. vv. 7,8) and he shall be justified in the end (Ibid. vv. 9b–10) for he knows what to do.

Let us take up the case of the steward of unrighteousness. He 'was accused of scattering [DIASKORPIZŌN] his goods' (St. Luke 16:1), goods presumably belonging to the master. Was it the same type of scattering done by the younger son who squandered his patrimony in riotous living? For in the parable of The Prodigal Son it is specifically stated that 'the younger son gathered all together, journeyed to a far country, and there scattered [DIESKORPISEN] his substance in *debauched* [ASŌTŌS] living' (St. Luke 15:13). His 'scattering' was not the commendable kind we have seen done towards the poor (Psalm 112:9; Proverbs 11:24; see p. 217). In the parable of The Steward of Unrighteousness, the qualification is in the type of accusation made to the master regarding the steward. It was a *slanderous* one which made it appear that the steward was guilty of grossly wasting his master's goods. It led to his summary dismissal by the master who gave the steward no time (contrast St. Matthew 22:12–13) to verbally defend himself (St. Luke 16:2).

The sudden evil tidings of his removal from office greatly distressed the poor steward who now found himself in dire straits and said to himself, 'What shall I do? For my master is taking away the stewardship from me. I am not strong to dig, and I am ashamed to beg' (St. Luke 16:3). He found himself penniless and had no other option than to find employment as a steward in some other household. It is at this instant that we can have insight as to the type of 'scattering' the steward really did, for he immediately knew what to do in his predicament. The steward said, 'I have known [EGNŌN] what I am to do, so that when I am removed from the stewardship, they will receive me into their houses' (St. Luke 16:4). And what he knew had to be done was to exercise good judgment, for he had the knowledge and good judgment he acquired in being generous towards the poor.

He was an efficient steward, he kept good records, and was able to call *'every one'* of his master's debtors to him' (St. Luke 16:5), something that a dissipated man living riotously would not have been able to do. And when he asked the first debtor who came to him, 'How much do you owe my master?' he replied 'A hundred baths of oil' (Ibid. v. 6), a large amount of olive oil indeed! because one bath was equivalent to ten gallons. Thus, the man owed his master a thousand gallons of olive oil which has been calculated to be the total yield of 146 olive trees! and worth a thousand denarii in those days ($45,000 today). When the steward asked the second debtor how much he owed his master, he replied, 'A hundred kors of wheat' (Ibid. v. 7). Again, this was a large amount, comprising a thousand bushels of wheat because one kor was the equivalent of ten to eleven bushels of wheat. The man owed the master the calculated yield of a hundred acres of grain! A thousand bushels of wheat were worth two-thousand and five-hundred denarii in those days ($100,000 today). These were princely amounts of oil and grain which made one recall the 'one-hundred talents of silver, *one-hundred kors of wheat,* one-hundred baths of wine, *one-hundred baths of oil,* and salt without prescribed limit' (Ezra 7:22) generously given by King Artaxerxes [c. 465–424 B.C.] to Ezra and the seventeen-hundred and seventy-two persons (Ezra 8:1–19) that he took with him to the Temple in Jerusalem. For King Artaxerxes decreed that 'whatever is commanded by the God of heaven, let it be done with munificence [ADRAZDA] for the house of the God of heaven, lest there be wrath [of God] against the realm of the king and his sons' (Ezra 7:23; 1 Esdras 8:20).

We should not forget that the steward was slanderously accused of scattering his master's goods. Jealous co-workers, seeing the large amounts of oil and grain being carted away, and the provisions that may have been freely given to the needy by the steward, painted the liberality in an unfavorable light to the steward's detriment. Prejudged and discharged without being given the opportunity to defend himself, the steward now had to 'bring forth judgment [MISHPAT] for the sake of truth' (Isaiah 42:3, Literal Translation). He did so, for immediately after the first debtor was called, the steward said to him, 'Take your bill, and sitting down quickly write fifty' (St. Luke 16:6, Literal Translation), and in an instant the debt was cut in half.

If we search the Holy Scriptures we will see that the steward did judgment, for he told the first debtor to *sit down,* and to write *quickly,* and to thus *divide* the sum *in half.* First of all we 'sit in judgment' (Judges 5:10; Psalm 9:4; Proverbs 20:8; Isaiah 16:5; 28:6; Daniel 7:9–10,26; 1 Esdras 3:15; Wisdom 9:12; Sirach 4:9; 11:9; 38:33; History of Susannah vv. 50,60–61; Enoch 69:27–29; 3 Enoch 24:21; 26:12; 28:3,8; 31:1; 33:1; 2 Esdras 7:33; 2 Maccabees 13:26; St. Matthew 19:28; 27:19; St. Luke 22:30; St. John 19:13; Revelation 20:4) for we 'sit to judge' (Joel 3:12). And good judgment and retribution are *swift*:

> 'He [God] . . . sends swiftly the lightnings of His judgment' – Sirach 43:13.

> 'His judgment comes quickly' –Sirach 21:5.

> 'I have heard of the swiftness of the Judge who is to come' –2 Esdras 8:18.

> 'I will enter into judgment . . . I will recompense your deed upon your own head quickly and speedily' –Joel 3:2,4.

'He will come upon you terribly and swiftly because severe judgment falls on those in high places' —Wisdom 6:15.

'God who rules all things, quickly rendering vengeance to him according to his deserts' —Additions to Esther 16:18.

'Almighty God having quickly returned to him [Haman] a fitting recompense' —Esther 8:13, Greek Text.

'He [God] will avenge them quickly' —St. Luke 18:8.

'Quick [OXUS] shall I be found in judgment' —Wisdom 8:11.

In Hebrew, when the steward began 'to take stock' [DIN as in Baba Bathra 90b, Babylonian Talmud; Tosephta to Yebamoth 79a; Aboth of R. Nathan chap. 32], he began 'to judge' [DIN]. And in the same language, if he were 'to decree a judgment' [GAZAR DIN], he would be literally 'dividing [GAZAR] a judgment [DIN].' Another Hebrew word: CHATHAK, means 'to decree' [as in Daniel 9:24; Megillah 15a, Babylonian Talmud] or 'to decide' [Sanhedrin 7b; Berakoth 61a; Shebuoth 30b, Babylonian Talmud], and also 'to sever' [Megillah IV. 75a; Hullin IV. 6]. In King Solomon's famous judgment (1 Kings 3:16–28), his quick decision to divide in half by sword the contested child, immediately revealed the true mother of the child. Solomon's wisdom drew upon a disregarded decision of his father King David to divide a property in half (2 Samuel 19:29), and the subsequent response of poor slandered Mephibosheth to that judicial decision (2 Samuel 16:1–4; 19:24–30). King David's unjust treatment of Mephibosheth by giving credence to the slander of his servant Ziba, is commented upon by the Jerusalem Talmud: Yebamoth II. 4a, and by the Babylonian Talmud: Yoma 22b (see also Alphabet of Ben Sira [in J.P. Eisenstein's *Otzar Midrashim* N.Y. 1915] and Pseudo Jerome re 2 Samuel 19:29). Could this be a reason why, in judgment, King David's kingdom was in turn divided in half [Judah and Israel] by Ahijah, the prophet from Shiloh? [1 Kings 11:29–38]. Executed judgment often cuts in half:

'Your kingdom is divided [in half] and given to the Medes and Persians' —Daniel 5:28.

And Daniel [in judgment] said, 'Very well, you have lied against your own head, for even now the angel of God has received the sentence of God to cut you in two' . . . then Daniel said to him [the other wicked judge], 'Well, you have also lied against your own head, for the angel of God waits with the sword to cut you in two' —History of Susannah vv. 55,59.

'The lord of that servant [the unfaithful steward] will come on a day when he does not expect him and at an hour which he does not know, and shall cut him in two [DICHOTOMĒSEI] and appoint him his portion with the hypocrites' —St. Matthew 24:50–51; St. Luke 12:45–46.

We have seen that when 'judgment shall sit' (Daniel 7:26), it shall do judgment quickly; and when warranted, it shall divide to reveal the truth of a matter. 'Do judgment that you may be saved' (Sirach 3:1, Syriac Text). But to be able to do good and saving judgment one must be good because 'evil men do not understand judgment' (Proverbs 28:5, Literal Translation). The Lord delights in good judgment (Jeremiah 9:24; 22:15; Isaiah 42:1; Hosea 12:6; Micah 6:8) because He delights in the righteousness (Psalms 11:7; 33:5; 45:7; 146:8) that is able to accomplish it. 'Judgment and righteousness' go together (Genesis 18:19; Deuteronomy 16:18; 33:21; 2 Samuel 8:15; Psalms 33:5; 89:14; 97:2; 99:4; 103:6; Proverbs 2:9; 21:3; Ecclesiastes 5:8; Isaiah 1:21; 33:5; Jeremiah 4:2; 9:24; 22:3; 23:5; 33:15; Ezekiel 45:9; St. John 7:24; 16:8, etc.). Therefore, 'the Lord . . . loves righteousness and judgment' (Psalm 33:4,5). And if judgment is as running waters, then righteousness is the mighty torrent that directs those waters and pushes all obstacles aside (Amos 5:24).

In having the first debtor quickly cut in half the amount of oil that he owed, the steward sent a message to the master as to who was really responsible for the profligate scattering of goods. For the loan of a hundred baths of oil was indeed an extravagant extension of credit, and likewise the hundred kors of wheat advanced to the second debtor. These loans were contracted between the master and them: 'How much do *you* owe *my master?*' (St. Luke 16:5,7). Having been told the amounts they owed the master in the hundreds, the steward did not ask them to obliterate the original amount or alter it in such a way as to disguise it but simply told the first debtor to 'quickly write fifty' (v. 6), and the second one to 'take your bill and write eighty' (v. 7). In so doing the steward made sure that the master would become aware of the changes made when he received back the tallied accounts, because the record of the original amount would still remain there.

'A man's agent is like himself' (Baba Metzia 96a; Baba Kamma 113b; Kiddushin 41b–42a, 43a; Nazir 12b; Negaim 72b, Babylonian Talmud). By virtue of their office, stewards were empowered by their masters to sell their crops, to extend credit, and even to forgive debts. But it was the master who determined the overall policy, whether to keep or to give (St.

Luke 12:42; St. Matthew 24:45), whether to store or to sell, and to whom. He was also the one who set a limit on the amount of credit to be extended to borrowers. We have seen in the book of Ezra that the king himself determined the amount of silver, grain, wine and oil that were to be given to Ezra and his contingent for the Temple service (Ezra 7:21–22; 1 Esdras 8:19–20). These were the same princely amounts of grain and oil given not to a large group of people, but to two individual borrowers. The almost unlimited amounts of oil and grain that were given on credit established the first and second debtors as being rich men themselves who would deal *directly* with the master, and into whose houses the steward hoped to be received. The big loans were contracted between them and the master, and the steward had to ask them: 'How much do you owe my master?' (St. Luke 16:5,7). Their names may have been in the accounts receivable book, but they held their own pledges in hand: 'take your bill . . . and quickly write fifty . . . take your bill, and write eighty' (vv. 6,7).

Concerning the second debtor, there were no symbolic acts of judgment performed, such as the sitting down, and writing quickly, and cutting the amount owed in half which was done by the first. The man who owed the hundred kors of wheat was merely told by the steward to 'take your bill and write eighty' (St. Luke 16:7). It was time for the steward to exert *his* rights. He did so, when he took off, in principle, his commission from the amount in that particular pledge to the benefit of the debtor. For the steward-keepers got *twenty percent* (Song of Songs 8:12). There is an old tradition that the Ishmaelites, to whom Joseph had been sold, priced him for a hundred gold pieces in Egypt, and that the eunuch-steward from Potiphar's household who had been sent with that sum to buy him, paid the Ishmaelites only eighty gold pieces, and pocketed the twenty as his commission (Testament of Joseph 16:3–5, Greek B Text, Armenian and Slavonic Texts). Was it to be a sign that Joseph who was later on placed over Pharaoh's house (Genesis 41:40) as the greatest of stewards was himself originally sold to the Ishmaelites for twenty pieces of silver?

As in the case of the first debtor, the steward duly noted in his accounting to the master (St. Luke 16:2) the alteration in the second debtor's pledge. He thereby sent another written 'message' for his lord to see that if any scattering of goods had been observed as coming from the steward's own hands it should not have been subject to criticism. Because he had right to dispose as he saw fit any portion of goods that would have normally accrued from commissions he never took as steward, the first two pledges gave evidence of that. The steward had been as generous in scattering towards the poor as the master was in extending liberal credits to his rich debtors. Unlike dishonest stewards, our steward was in a state of penury when discharged for he never accumulated towards his own financial security. Nevertheless, his generosity towards the poor served him in good stead for he now possessed the understanding and knowledge needed to do judgment, and at the same time to ingratiate himself into the households of other rich masters who would not hesitate to receive him for they knew his worth. There was also an old tradition that the patriarch Joseph in Egypt did not enrich himself through his stewardship:

> 'For the young man's [Joseph's] honesty was exceedingly great, so much so that though the times and state of affairs gave him numerous opportunities for gaining wealth, and he might have soon become the richest of his contemporaries, his reverence for the truly genuine riches rather than the spurious, the seeing rather than the blind, led him to store up in the king's treasuries all the silver and gold which he collected from the sale of corn and refuse to appropriate for himself [as his commission] a single drachma' —Philo, *De Iosepho* 258.
> (On the charitableness of Joseph the steward, see Testament of Joseph 3:5; Midrash Tanchumah [Buber] I.31; Tanchumah Noah 3; Yelammedenu in Recanati, Wa-Yesheb; Zohar I. 208a.)

And was not Ahikar, the slandered steward of the King, saved by his almsgiving? (See Story of Ahikar 8:2, Syriac Text.) And in the end, was he not exalted by his understanding and knowledge?

When in the Gospel according to St. Luke [16:8a] the master praised [EPĒNESEN = 'to highly praise'] 'the steward [OIKONOMON] of unrighteousness [ADIKIAS],' he did not call him 'the unrighteous steward' or 'the unjust steward' or 'the dishonest steward' or 'the devious employee' as most English translations of the Gospels have done, but simply referred to him as 'the steward of unrighteousness' because he was 'of this world' (v. 8b) of unrighteousness. In those days, due to the prevalence of wickedness, the world was referred to as 'the realm of ungodliness' (1QH 2:8; 3:24, Dead Sea Scrolls). For they knew about 'the corruption that is in the world through lust' (2 Peter 1:4), the 'worldly [KOSMIKAS] lusts' (Titus 2:12) that debase. They said that 'the whole world lies under the sway of the wicked one' (1 John 5:19): who is 'that serpent of old, called the Devil and Satan who deceives the whole world' (Revelation 12:9). But although they were 'in this present evil world' (Galatians 1:4), some of the 'children of the world' (St. Luke 16:8) were praised as being 'more understanding [PHRONIMŌTEROI] than the children of light' (Ibid.) who 'are not of this world' (St. John 15:19). Such a one who was highly praised 'because he had acted understandingly [PHRONIMŌS]' (St. Luke 16:8) was 'the steward of unrighteousness' or 'the steward [of this world] of unrighteousness' (Ibid.).

One must be righteous and depart from evil in order to have 'the understanding [PHRONĒSEI] of the righteous' (St. Luke 1:17) for 'to depart from evil is understanding' (Job 28:28). If we are to be 'guileless [AKERAIOI] as doves' and 'prudently understanding [PHRONIMOI] as serpents' (St. Matthew 10:16), it is because unlike simple doves, serpents are very prudent in getting away from what is not good for them. The master praised his steward for his 'understanding' [PHRONĒSIS] because he saw that 'the understanding [PHRONĒSIS] of God was in him to do judgment' (1 Kings 3:28, Greek Text). We need the 'understanding' [PHRONĒSIS] that the steward had, in order to be able to judge well. Thus, St. Paul said: 'I speak as to *understanding* [PHRONIMOIS] men; *judge* [KRINATE] for yourselves what I say' (1 Corinthians 10:15). The master realized, regarding his servant, that 'a man who has understanding [PHRONĒSIN] is better than [one having] a large estate' (Proverbs 24:5, Greek Text), 'for if understanding [PHRONĒSIS] works, who is a greater worker than understanding?' (Wisdom 8:6). 'Happy is he who has found understanding' [PHRONESIN] in his servant (Sirach 25:9). For we know that good servants understand.

It is good to remember that it is the righteous who understand. 'Righteousness and understanding' (1QH Fragment 7:8, Dead Sea Scrolls) go together. 'A righteous man understands' (Proverbs 21:12, Hebrew and Greek Texts) because 'a good understanding have all those who do His commandments' (Psalm 111:10). If it is said that 'Wisdom rests in the heart of him who has understanding' (Proverbs 14:33, Hebrew Text) it is because 'Wisdom rests in the heart of the righteous' (Proverbs 14:33, Syriac Text). Therefore, 'the breastplate of understanding' (Testament of Levi 8:2) is 'the breastplate of righteousness' (Ephesians 6:14). 'Holy understanding' (Proverbs 2:11, Greek Text) and 'godly [EUSEBES] understanding' (4 Maccabees 11:21) is 'the understanding of the holy ones' (Proverbs 2:11, Syriac Text). 'We contribute towards understanding [PHRONĒSEOS] . . . by desire for virtue, by zeal for noble things, by continuous study therein, by persistent self training, by unwearied and unflagging labor' (Philo, *Ebr.* 20,21). The steward would not have been able to act with '*understanding* [PHRONĒSIS]' if he had not been first of all a righteous and compassionate man.

We saw how well the steward first proceeded to do judgment on his master's scattering of liberal credits, and then take off the commission he was entitled to, because 'an understanding [PHRONIMOS] man proceeds rightly on his way' (Proverbs 15:21, Greek Text). Had the steward in the parable been an 'unrighteous' or 'unjust' or 'dishonest' or 'devious' (usual renderings of St. Luke 16:8 in English translations of the Bible) steward, he may have been able to act 'shrewdly' [ARUM-PANOURGIA] or 'deceitfully' [MIRMAH-DOLOŌ] or even 'wisely' [HAKAM-SOPHOS] with the type of 'wisdom' [SOPHIA] that is 'not from above but earthly, sensual, demonic' (St. James 3:15) as is 'the wisdom of this world' which 'is foolishness with God' (1 Corinthians 3:19), and which the Messiah would never have commended in His parable.

If we are attentive and careful to render faithfully the words of His parables, we shall be able to discover the hidden wisdom and understanding found in them, and we shall not be scandalized in Him (St. Luke 7:23). In another parable (St. Luke 18:1–8) which should be referred to as the Parable of the 'Judge [KRITES] of [TES] Unrighteousness [ADIKIAS]' (St. Luke 18:6, Literal Translation), the Messiah told about a judge (whom He compared to God [vv. 1,6–8] who took his time to attend to the supplication of a widow who asked him to give her full justice against her adversary: 'Vindicate me against my adversary' (v. 3). But 'for a while he [the judge] refused' (v. 4) because then, as in today's courts, there may have been other cases scheduled to be heard before hers. And since Yeshua the Son of Man told them this parable 'to the effect that they ought always to pray and not lose heart' (v. 1), the widow in the parable obtained a quick judgment in her behalf, ahead of time, through her pertinacious pleading, inasmuch as the judge had said to himself, 'Even though I do not fear God nor respect man, yet because this widow troubles me I will vindicate her, lest by her continual coming she exhausts me' (vv. 4–5). The Messiah went on to say that just as the widow obtained a quick judgment on her behalf by her repeated supplications, 'Shall not God vindicate His chosen ones who cry to Him day and night? Will He delay long over them? I tell you, He will vindicate them speedily' (St. Luke 18:6–8). As in the Parable of the Steward of Unrighteousness, most English translations of the New Testament do not render faithfully the written term 'judge [KRITES] of [TES] unrighteousness [ADIKIAS]' but change it to 'unjust judge,' 'unrighteous judge' and even 'corrupt judge.' Would the Messiah compare His Father in heaven to a corrupt, unrighteous or unjust judge? Would He have commended in His parable a dishonest, unrighteous or unjust steward? In common with the 'judge who neither feared God nor regarded man' (v. 2), God does not fear God nor does He revere man for 'God is a righteous judge and He is no respecter of persons' (Psalms of Solomon 2:18; see also Deuteronomy 10:17; 2 Chronicles 19:7; Job 34:17–19; Wisdom 6:7; Enoch 63:8; Jubilees 5:15–17), 'for God shows no partiality' (Romans 2:11; Galatians 2:6; Ephesians 6:9; Colossians 3:25); and neither did the judge in the parable because as a righteous judge (Deuteronomy 1:17; 16:18–20; Leviticus 19:15; Proverbs 24:2) he also was no respecter of persons since it is written that he did not regard man (St. Luke 18:2,4). Furthermore he had no reason to fear God (in the Gospel, God is to be feared when we have done wrong [St. Matthew 10:28; St. Luke 12:5; 23:40]), because he was a just judge who only took his time just as God does until we storm heaven by our prayers as the widow did the judge's house. We can now see that the Messiah had good reason to say as He did: 'steward of unrighteousness' and 'judge of unrighteousness.' If He had meant to say 'unjust steward' or 'unjust judge,' He would have said just that. For He called an evil man an 'evil [PONĒROS] man [ANTHRŌPOS],' and a wicked slave a 'wicked [KAKOS] slave [DOULOS],' and an evil slave an 'evil [PONERE] slave [DOULE]' (St. Matthew 12:35; 24:48; 25:26; 18:32) instead of referring to them as 'a man of evil,' 'a slave of wickedness' or 'a slave of evil.'

In the parable of the Steward of Unrighteousness, the kind of understanding that the steward had was PHRONĒSIS (as rendered in the Greek of the Gospel according to St. Luke 16:8), and that type of 'understanding' comes from above: 'I prayed and understanding [PHRONĒSIS] was given to me' (Wisdom 7:7). For 'God . . . gives understanding [PHRONĒSIN] to those who have understanding [SUNESIN]' of what it is all about (Daniel 2:21, Greek Text). 'Happy . . . is the person who knows understanding [PHRONĒSIN]'! –Proverbs 3:13, Greek Text.

Yeshua the Messiah who understands all things expects His own to have good *'understanding* [PHRONĒSIS]':

> 'Every one then who hears these words of Mine and does them shall be likened to an *understanding* [PHRONIMŌ] man who built his house upon the rock; and the rain fell, and the floods came, and the winds blew and beat upon that house but it did not fall, because it had been founded on the rock' –St. Matthew 7:24–25.

> 'The Kingdom of Heaven shall be likened to ten virgins who took their lamps and went out to meet the bridegroom. Now five of them were foolish, and five were *understanding* [PHRONIMOI]. For when the foolish took their lamps, they took no oil with them, but the *understanding* [PHRONIMOI] ones took vessels of oil with their lamps' –St. Matthew 25:1–4.

> 'Who then is the faithful and *understanding* [PHRONIMOS]

steward whom his master will set over his household, to give them their portion of food in due season? Blessed is that servant, whom his master when he comes will find so doing. Truly I tell you, he will set him over all his possessions' —St. Luke 12:42–44; St. Matthew 24:45–46.

Notice that ideally the Lord Messiah expects each of His stewards to be 'faithful and understanding [PHRONIMOS].' Shall a steward have 'understanding [PHRONĒSIS]' without also being faithful? We may be sure that the steward in the parable who 'had acted with understanding [PHRONĒSIN]' was a good man.

Even Pharaoh in his court called attention to the understanding of Joseph, the formerly slandered steward: 'There is not a more understanding [PHRONIMŌTEROS] and intelligent [SUNETŌTEROS] man than you' (Genesis 41:39, Greek Text). For Joseph too was a charitable and patient man, and he also held his tongue, as our steward did, when he was falsely accused. Because 'a patient man is understanding [PHRONIMOS]' and 'an understanding [PHRONIMOS] man bears up under many things' (Proverbs 17:27; 14:17, Greek Texts). Do we not know that 'He who holds his peace is understanding [PHRONIMOS]'? —Proverbs 17:28, Greek Text; see also Sirach 19:31. Who was the Messiah referring to if not to our steward when He said: 'He who is faithful in a very little is faithful also in much'? (St. Luke 16:10). We should remember that he was able to call one by one all his master's debtors who were under his stewardship (St. Luke 16:5).

When we are told not to let 'the parables of understanding' (Sirach 6:35) escape us, it is because they are 'enigmatic parables' (Sirach 47:15, Literal Translation) full of deep 'words of understanding [PHRONĒSEŌS]' to which we have to 'give ear to know [the] understanding [PHRONĒSIN]' we shall find in them (Proverbs 1:2; Baruch 3:9, Greek Text). Did not the Son of Man who is full of understanding ask them to give ear when He spoke His parables? 'He who has ears to hear let him hear!' (St. Matthew 11:15; 13:9,43; St. Mark 4:9,23; 7:16; St. Luke 8:8; 14:35).

Other children of this world of unrighteousness, besides the steward, received praise from the Messiah. When Yeshua heard the reply of the Roman centurion, who belonged to the world of unrighteousness but was nevertheless a kind man (see St. Luke 7:2–5), He marveled at his faith and said to those who followed Him: 'Truly, I say to you, I have not found such great faith, not even in Israel' (St. Matthew 8:10; see also St. Matthew 15:21–28; St. Luke 10:30–37; 17:11–19; Acts 10:22). For it is possible to be 'of this world' (St. Luke 16:8; 20:34) yet 'not conformed to this world'

(Romans 12:2) of unrighteousness. The Messiah taught that we are 'not to love the world [of unrighteousness], neither the things that are in the world [of unrighteousness]. 'If anyone loves the world, the love of the Father is not in him. For all that is in the world,—the lust of the flesh, the lust of the eyes, and the pride of life—is not of the Father but is of the world' [of unrighteousness] —1 John 2:15–16.

When we are told to keep ourselves 'unspotted from the world' (St. James 1:27), it is really meant that we are to keep ourselves unstained from unrighteousness. In those days, to say 'the world' was to say 'unrighteousness' and vice versa. 'The steward of unrighteousness' could be also known as 'the steward of this world.' The steward in the parable dealt with the material things of this world of unrighteousness in a righteous way: through his generosity towards the poor. And just as there are stewards of unrighteousness or of this world, there are also stewards of righteousness or as it were stewards of 'the Kingdom of Heaven.' They are the ones who shall 'bring forth out of His treasury what is new and what is old' (St. Matthew 13:52) to His glory for it is they who are 'stewards of the mysteries of God' (1 Corinthians 4:1).

'It is required in stewards that one be found faithful' (1 Corinthians 4:2) especially in dealing with 'the mammon of unrighteousness' (St. Luke 16:9) or 'riches [MAMMON is derived from MAMŌNA, Aramaic for 'riches'] of the world.' The steward in the parable never accumulated any riches for himself but gave away what he had. Moreover, he was a faithful steward for he could account for all the riches that his master gave away in liberal credits. 'Blessed is the man who is found perfect [TAMIM] and has not gone after mammon' (Sirach 31:8, Hebrew Text), because along with covetousness and riches comes false dealing:

> 'From the least of them even to the greatest, of them, everyone
> is given to *covetousness*; and from prophet even to the priest,
> everyone *deals falsely*' —Jeremiah 6:13; 8:10.

'The mammon of unrighteousness' (St. Luke 16:9) and 'the mammon of falsehood' (Targums to 1 Samuel 8:3; 12:3; 2 Samuel 14:14; Proverbs 15:27) are one and the same for to trust in unrighteousness is to trust in a lie and conversely:

> 'He has made you to trust in *a lie*' —Jeremiah 29:31, Hebrew
> Text.

> 'He has made you to trust in *unrighteousness*' —Jeremiah
> 29[36]:31, Greek Text, Literal Translation.

'They prophesy to you *a lie* —Jeremiah 27:16, Hebrew Text.

'They prophesy to you *unrighteousness*' —Jeremiah 27[34]:16, Greek Text, Literal Translation.

The Messiah gave warning to 'beware and guard against all covetousness' (St. Luke 12:15) for 'the love of money [PHILARGURIA] is the root of all evil' (1 Timothy 6:10; Proverbs 1:19; Diogenes [Quoted in Diogenes Laertius' *Hist.* VI. 50]). The steward was certainly not covetous for he 'scattered' so much that he was impecunious when he was unjustly fired. Moreover the covetous do not know how to do the good judgment that the steward did:

> 'Your rulers are rebels and companions of thieves; they all love bribes and chase after gifts. They do not judge [SHAPHAT] the fatherless, nor does the cause of the widow come before them' — Isaiah 1:23.

> 'Wicked men . . . their houses are full of deceit therefore they have become great and grown rich. They have grown fat, they are sleek; yes, their wickedness has no limit. They do not judge [SHAPHAT] the cause, the cause of the fatherless' —Jeremiah 5:26,27,28.

Nor do they know or understand because they are greedy:

> 'They do not know [YADA], they are all dumb dogs . . . yes, they are greedy dogs which never have enough, and they are shepherds who cannot understand. They all look to their own way, everyone for his gain, to the last one' —Isaiah 56:10,11.

When the Messiah told the parable, there were some Pharisees listening to Him 'who were lovers of money [PHILARGUROI] and they turned up their noses [EXEMUKTĒRIZON] at Him' (St. Luke 16:14). How could they understand His deep parable of understanding since they were also greedy and covetous? (St. Matthew 23:14). 'A man without understanding turns up his nose [MUKTĒRIZEI]' at what he does not understand (Proverbs 11:12, Greek Text), forgetting that Wisdom said: 'All the words of my mouth are said in righteousness; there is nothing crooked or perverse in them. They are all clear to him who understands, and right to those who find knowledge' (Proverbs 8:8–9). For just 'as His ways are plain to the holy so are they stumbling blocks to the wicked' (Sirach 39:24) because 'the wicked do not understand' (Proverbs 29:7; 28:5; Daniel 12:10; Isaiah 56:11, Greek Text).

And what they did not understand, is that 'the mammon of unrighteousness' (St. Luke 16:9) or 'the riches of this world' if not utilized to the benefit of others and the glory of God, remains part and parcel of the world of unrighteousness, and as such, deserves to be called 'unrighteous mammon' (v. 11a). Nevertheless, those who dealt with the riches of this world for commercial profit were expected to be honest in their transactions, even though they were trafficking with 'the unrighteous mammon.' However, if 'the mammon of unrighteousness' were to be used to do good and fill the needs of the poor, it would then be doing the work of righteousness which is not of this world but of the heavens far above this world of unrighteousness. And it will be there that 'the unrighteous mammon' shall become 'the true riches' (Ibid. v. 11b), stored up for those who redeemed its unrighteousness by their lovingkindnesses on this earth.

Chapter 26

The Son Of Man
And
The Ladder Of Understanding

The Lord promised that in the end, 'He will magnify the Law and make it honorable' for 'in the end. . . . knowledge shall increase' (Isaiah 42:21; Daniel 12:4), and 'the Law shall be found perfect' for 'in those days . . . the children of the earth shall see . . . and shall understand' and 'the holy people shall be given the delights of Paradise . . . and there shall be given to them a heart that understands the good' (Sirach 34:8; Enoch 100:1,6; Apocalypse of Moses 13:3,4,5). Did not the Lord say through the prophet Jeremiah [23:20; 30:24] that 'in the latter days you shall understand [BIN] with understanding [BINAH]'? Because then 'the earth shall be full of the knowledge of the Lord as the waters cover the sea' (Isaiah 11:9; Habacuc 2:14). Knowledge shall be given that we may truly be able to glorify the Lord, then 'the earth shall be filled with the glory of the Lord' (Numbers 24:21), and 'foolishness shall be no more' (1Q Myst. I.7 [Book of Mysteries], Dead Sea Scrolls). 'When the Most High will visit the world which was made by Him . . . then you shall understand' (2 Esdras 9: 2,4). And 'to whom the Law has now been a hope, and understanding an expectation . . . shall wonders appear in their time for they shall behold the world [of understanding] which is now invisible to them' (2 Baruch 51: 7,8).

Long ago the Messiah promised that the time would come when the heavens would be opened and His people would see the angels of God ascending and descending upon the Son of Man (St. John 1: 47–51). Because He is the Ladder of Understanding, and as the Son of Man-Messiah, He is the giver of understanding and the revealer of all the secrets of wisdom and knowledge (Enoch 46:3; 49:1–3; 51:3, see also pp. 141–142). To those who believe in Him, Yeshua the Messiah makes known what is hidden in the Holy Scriptures so that at last they can understand and see what was veiled from their eyes (2 Corinthians 3:14–17).

Having known that as the Son of Man the Messiah is Understanding incarnate, we have understood the relationship between *Man* and *Son of Man; Knowledge* and *Understanding.* Along the same lines we can see the correlation between the Creator and the Former, the Most High and the Almighty. Image and Form, and Jacob and Israel [Chapters 1–7,9] so that we can note the appropriateness of writing:

> Who is the *Man* who can *know* the *command* of God? And who is there of all the *sons of Man* who can *hear* [and understand] the *words* of the Holy One?
> Who is the *Man* who can *see* [and know] all the *works of heaven* . . . ? Or who is there from among the *sons of Man* who is able to *understand* and measure the length and *breadth* of the whole *earth?*–4QEn IV^g [Pl.xxiv.10–14], Dead Sea Scrolls.

Was it not right that the *Seers* [and knowers, vide l Samuel 3:7] to whom the word of the Lord would *appear* [l Samuel 3:15, 21] would come first? And that the *Prophets* [and hearers] to whom the word of the Lord would *speak* would come after? Shall we:

> Cry out to the Seer, 'eat fruit and see for us!' [Adam and Eve saw after they ate the fruit].
> And say to the Prophet, 'eat bread and prophesy' (Amos 7:12) for us?

> Can Reuben ('*see!* a son') the eldest son, see this? And can Simeon ('a *hearing*'), the second son, hear it?–(Genesis 29:32–33).

We can now understand why the *Watchers* [IRIM who *see* and *know* (not NATSARIM)], and the *Holy Ones* [who *hear* and *understand,* see Proverbs 30:3] are respectively found among the angels (Daniel 4:13,17,23 [4:10,14,20. Hebrew Text]). And are there not some of them noted to be with 'the *appearance* [MAREH] of a *Man*' (Daniel 8:15; 10:18), and others with 'the *likeness* [DEMUTH] of the *sons of Man*' (Daniel 10:16)? If we hope to have their knowledge and understanding let us:

> 'Put on the new *Man* who is renewed in *knowledge* according to the *image* of Him who *created* him'–Colossians 3:10.

> And take on the new *son of Man* who is renewed in *understanding* [Romans 12:2; Ephesians 4:23] after the *likeness* of Him who *formed* him (2 Enoch 44:1 B Text, see pp. 43–44).

Man [ADAM] ate the forbidden *fruit* from the tree of *knowledge* but 'the *sons of Man* ate *bread* which came down from the dwelling of the angels': 'the *bread of understanding*' (Targum to Psalm 78:25; Sirach 15:3). Shall we eat *flowers* as Esdras did so that we may *see*? (2 Esdras 9:24–26,38; 10:32;12:51) and '*the fruit of knowledge*' (Sirach 37:22, Hebrew Text) that we may *know,* and '*the bread of understanding*' so that we may *understand* as the *good* sons of Man do? For we must be obedient and righteous before we shall be given knowledge and understanding because:

> 'A brutish *man* will not *know*
> And a fool [*a foolish son of Man*] will not *understand* this'–Psalm 92:6.
> '*Foolish sons* are they, yes, they have *no understanding*'–Jeremiah 4:22.

Have we seen 'the *vision* of *knowledge*'? (1QH 4:18, Dead Sea Scrolls), and has 'the *light* of *knowledge*' (Hosea 10:12, Greek Text; Sirach 4:27 Codex Alexandrinus and Greek MS 248 texts; Testament of Levi 4:3; 18:3; Testament of Benjamin 11:2 B Text, see also Wisdom 6:22; Sirach 24:37 Latin Vulgate and 1QS 11:3,4; 1Q Sb 4:27, Dead Sea Scrolls) shined upon us?

Have we heard the *voice* of *Understanding*? (Proverbs 8:4, see p. 145). Then, 'hear my voice and understand' (2 Esdras 8:19). 'If you now have understanding, hear this: hear the voice of my words' (Job 34:16):

> 'Hear O you mountains . . .
> And let the hills hear Your voice'–Micah 6:2,1
>
> 'Unto you O men, I call
> And my voice is to the sons of Man' –Proverbs 8:4.

Because it is they and the 'hills' who have understanding.

Knowing the relationship between *Man* and *Knowledge,* and *Son of Man* and *Understanding,* we can trace Man and Son of Man parallelisms hidden throughout the Holy Scriptures. Let us take as an example Isaiah 56:1:

> Thus says the Lord, 'Keep judgment [MISHPAT] and do righteousness [TZEDAKAH]'

This verse may be rendered:

> Thus says the Lord to Man, 'Keep judgment', and to the Son of Man, 'do righteousness'

Because had Man [Adam] kept the commandment of God, he would have also kept the knowledge of God and of good and evil, and consequently the good judgment found within the seed of God's command (see pp. 5–7). Thus, in keeping that seed, Man would have kept potential good judgment. Concomitantly, because righteousness is of the sons of Man (see pp. 15–17, 22), it is theirs to have the ability to 'do righteousness'. We can see why the second verse in Isaiah 56 would say:

> 'Blessed is the *man* who does this [i.e. keeps judgment], and the *son of Man* who holds it [i.e., righteousness] fast'–Isaiah 56:2.

For he who holds fast his righteousness and integrity as Job did (Job 27:6; 2:3,9) shall go on from righteousness to godliness and he shall 'do righteousness'[TZEDAKAH] which is the term used for the generous lovingkindnesses done by the children of God. Concordantly, the Man who has kept the commandment of God has also kept the inherent good judgment found in it and becomes himself a worthy 'judge' [ELOHIM. See St. Matthew 19:28; St. Luke 22:28–30; 1 Corinthians 6:2,3; Revelation 20:4; Daniel 7:22). If we do not forget the close association of the term 'Man' and 'judgment' we shall have insight concerning the grievance of the Lord found in Isaiah 59:15,16:

> The Lord *saw* it and it displeased Him that there was no *judgment*. And he *saw* that there was no *Man* [to do judgment with his knowledge of good and evil]. And He was astonished [*'understood it well'* in the Greek Text] that there was no [*son of Man*] *intercessor*.

We have no doubt that the 'intercessor' referred to in Isaiah 59:16 is a son of Man, because we know from the book of Job that it is they who do the interceding:

> 'O that one might supplicate for a man with God,
> As a son of Man [intercedes] for his neighbor'–Job 16:21.

Again, just as the art of good judgment would have been allocated to the ideal Man who would have obtained knowledge through obedience, so is the gift of good counsel acquired by the righteous sons of Man for it is they who understand. We must have understanding before we can give good counsel:

> 'A man of understanding will obtain powerful counsel [TACHBU-LOTH]'–Proverbs 1:5

> Powerful counsel is rooted in understanding–Sirach 37:17
> Hebrew Text
>
> Counselors by their understanding–Sirach 44:3 Hebrew Text.
>
> 'The counsel of understanding' –Sirach 6:24 Latin Vulgate
>
> Seek counsel always from the understanding–Tobit 4:18 Greek
> Vaticanus B Text.
>
> As the water jar contains water, understanding contains . . .
> counsel–Philo, Q. Gen. IV. 98

Knowledge and *judgment* pertain to *Man,* and *understanding* and *counsel,* to the *sons of Man.* Thus, if knowledge and counsel were to be purposely hidden, then: '*Knowledge* is hidden from *Man,* and the *counsel* of prudence from the *sons of Man*' (1QS 11:6, Dead Sea Scrolls). And the time of *judges* would take place at the very earliest: the time of *Man,* and the time of *counselors* would be that of those who follow after: the *sons of Man.* Thus it is written:

> 'I will restore your *judges* as at the *very first* [RISHON],
> And your *counselors* as at the beginning'–Isaiah 1:26

We can now also understand why the Lord said through His prophet Micah:

> They do not *know* [as *Man*] the *thoughts* of the Lord ['In Your
> *thought* is all *knowledge*–1Q H 11:8, Dead Sea Scrolls]. Neither
> do they *understand* [as *sons of Man*] His *counsel* –Micah 4:12

Furthermore, the Lord said through the prophet Isaiah:

> 'I *saw* and there was no *man* among them [to *see* and *know* Me]
> And there was no *counselor* [i.e., an understanding *son of Man*]
> who when I inquired of them could *answer* a word'–Isaiah 41:28.

Because just as it takes understanding to be able to give good counsel, so does one need to have understanding before one can give a good answer. For 'how shall I be able to answer unless You make me understand?' (1QH 10:7, Dead Sea Scrolls). 'The Lord gave me enough understanding to answer' (Pesikta Rabbati, Piska 33.3). 'As long as I have understanding I will answer' (2Esdras 8:25). 'If you have understanding answer your neighbor'

(Sirach 5:12), and give him good counsel like a true son of Man. Were not the teachers in the Temple 'astonished at His understanding and answers' when they first heard the young Messiah—Son of Man? (St. Luke 2:47). Now we know why the Lord asked:

'Why, when I came there was no *man* [to *see* and *know* Me]? And when I called there was no one [i.e. a *son of Man*] to *answer*?' — Isaiah 50:2

Moreover, it takes knowledge to be able to 'declare' [NAGAD], and by 'declaring' [NAGAD] we can show things so clearly that others will thereby know:

'Declare [NAGAD] if you know'—Job 38:4

'Declare [NAGAD] if you know it all'—Job 38:14

'Who has declared [NAGAD] from the *very first* [RISHON] that we may *know*?'—Isaiah 41:26

'I have *declared* [NAGAD] the *very first* [RISHON] things from the beginning . . . because I have *knowledge* [DAATH]'—Isaiah 48:3,4

If we want a 'declaration' [NAGAD] that will make us 'know' [YADA] let us ask it of *Man* for he is the one supposed to have *knowledge*:

'Gird up your loins now like a *Man,* for I will demand of you that you make Me *know* [YADA]'—Job 38:3

'Gird up your loins now like a *Man,* I will demand of you that you *declare* [NAGAD] to Me'—Job 40:7

And if we want a *good answer* that will make us understand let us ask it of the *Son of Man,* 'Oh that I knew where I might find Him, that I might come to His seat! . . . I would know the words which He would cry out to me, and *understand* what He would *answer* me' (Job 23:3,5). He would make us understand why the Lord said through the prophet Isaiah:

'Have you not [seen and] *known* [as Man]?
Have you not *heard* [and understood as a *son of Man*]
Has it not been *declared* [NAGAD] to you from the *very first* [RISHON]?
Have you not *understood* from the foundation of the earth?' — Isaiah 40:21

He would also make us understand that because it takes *understanding* to be able to *speak* (My soul recovered the spirit of understanding and I began to speak—2 Esdras 5:22), an angel who had 'the *likeness* of the *sons of Man*' (Daniel 10:16) was the one sent to Daniel to enable him to speak when he 'became dumb' (Daniel 10:15). For it is the *sons of Man* who are supposed to *understand,* and be able to speak well with their understanding.

And knowing that it takes *knowledge* to be able to '*declare*' [NAGAD], and that it is of '*Man*' to have that *knowledge,* it was only fitting that an angel with 'the *appearance* of a *Man*' (Daniel 10:18) be the one who was sent to Daniel. It was that manly angel who said to Daniel:

> 'Do you *know* why I have come to you? . . . I will *declare* [NAGAD] to you what is written in the Scripture of Truth'—Daniel 10:20,21

For he had knowledge to make Daniel know the Truth.

There may be some who will say that if we have 'understanding' [BINAH] we can also 'declare':

> 'Declare [NAGAD] if you have understanding' [BINAH]—Job 38:4

But we must not forget what the book of Proverbs says about that kind of understanding:

> The *knowledge* of the holy ones is *insight* [BINAH]—Proverbs 9:10

Just as the wisdom of the same angelic holy ones is knowledge of all things on this earth:

> The wisdom of an angel of God to know [YADA] all things that are in the earth—2 Samuel 14:20

The Essenes were wise when they said that in the end:

> 'The righteous [sons of Man] will understand the knowledge of the Most High, and the perfect of way [i.e. children of God] will have insight [BINAH] of the wisdom of the angels' [literally 'sons of Heaven']—1QS 4:22 Dead Sea Scrolls

Which means that as perfect children of God they will have perfect knowledge of all things.

We must have knowledge before we can know between good and evil, but have we heard about the relationship between taste and understanding? For it is written that:

'As the palate tries the taste of a thing so an understanding [BIN] heart the taste of a lie'–Sirach 36:24, Hebrew Text.

And 'as the palate tastes different kinds of venison so does an understanding heart [taste and reject] false speeches'–Sirach 36:29 Greek Text

Thus, Job rhetorically asked: 'Is there iniquity in my tongue? cannot my taste understand [BIN] falsehood?'–Job 6:30

Applying the *Man/Son of Man* line of thought to this added knowledge, we can understand why wise old Barzillai the Gileadite said to King David:

'Can I *know* [as a Man] between *good* and *evil*? Can your servant *taste* [and *understand* as a son of Man] what I eat and drink?'–2 Samuel 19:35

The Messiah phrased it well when He said:

Your Father in heaven makes His *sun* to rise on the *evil* and on the the *good* [Motifs of *light, good* and *evil* pertaining to *Man*] And sends *rain* on the *righteous* and on the *unrighteous* [Motifs of *water* and *righteousness* pertaining to the *sons of Man*]–St. Matthew 5:45

Remembering the associations between the term 'Man' and 'Creator', 'image', 'light', 'seeing', 'knowledge' and the 'Most High'; and the associations between the term 'son of Man' and 'Former', 'likeness', 'water', 'hearing', 'understanding' and the 'Almighty', we shall have insight into other *Man/Son of Man* parallelisms in the Holy Scriptures:

'If they through delighting in their *beauty* [image perceived by the eyes] supposed these things to be *gods* [it would be rendered ELOHIM in Hebrew] let them *know* [GNŌTŌSAN] how much better the Master of them is, for the *Originator* of beauty *created* them [all themes of image, seeing, gods, knowing, creating, and Originator pertaining to the *Most High* and *Man*].
But if they were astonished at their *power* and working, let them

understand [NOĒSATŌSAN] from them how much *mightier* is He [the Almighty] who *fashioned* them' [themes of power, understanding, mightiness and fashioning relevant to the *Almighty* and *sons of Man*]—Wisdom 13:3–4.

We can have added insight into the ancient text of Isaiah 53:11 that is found both in the Greek Septuagint and in the Hebrew text of the Isaiah [1QIs^a] Dead Sea Scroll:

'The Lord is also pleased to take away the travail of his [the Suffering Servant's] soul and to show him light, And to form him with understanding'

This may be rendered:

The Lord is also pleased to take away the travail of his soul and to show him, as Man, light of knowledge.
And to form him, as son of Man, with understanding [See Isaiah 52:14 for similar comparison of the Suffering Servant to Man and son of Man].

Because, just as a newborn babe sees the light after the arduous travail of his passage from the womb, so is Man given the light of knowledge as the reward of his labors in the field of the Lord. Moreover, knowing the relationship between 'son of Man' and 'form' and between 'forming' and 'understanding', and not forgetting that whoever does any forming 'painfully forms' (Wisdom 15:7), we can understand that the suffering son of Man would receive as his reward: the gift of understanding. 'Why is light given to him who is in misery' (Job 3:20) if not so that he may be comforted by the light of knowledge? All you sons of man who are bitter in soul and have been formed by suffering, comfort your souls and strengthen your hearts with 'the bread of life and understanding'!—Sirach 15:3, Latin Vulgate.

Bread comes from seeds [i.e., grain], and the sons of Man also come from seeds sown in the womb, but when the Lord God created and formed Man He made him complete and fully grown as the original trees which were created mature with fruits in their branches:

'You [God] will destroy their *fruit* from the *earth* [as *Man* who came from the *earth* perished],
And [You will destroy] their *seed* from the *sons of Man* [who shall also die]'—Psalm 21:10, Literal Translation.

It is because the term 'Man' is associated with 'trees', 'fruit' and 'knowledge' that the blind man healed by the Messiah was given the insight to say:

'I see [BLĒPO] *men* that I behold [ORŌ = intellectual vision] as *trees* walking'–St. Mark 8:24

And it is because the term 'son of Man' is associated with 'bread', 'grapevines' (see pp. 10–11), and 'understanding' that we can see why the Messiah-Son of Man referred to Himself as the 'True Vine' (St. John 15:1) and 'True Bread' (St. John 6:32). For is He not as the Son of Man truly 'the bread of understanding' (Sirach 15:3), and the finest wine to gladden and comfort the heart (Psalm 104:15, Proverbs 31:6b,7; Ecclesiastes 10:19; Zechariah 10:7) just as understanding does? 'There is no joy above the joy of the heart' (Sirach 30:16), but because 'God made . . . the heart for understanding' (Testament of Naphtali 2:8), the heart rejoices when it understands since He also formed 'the understanding for joy' (2 Enoch 30:9).

The Psalms tell us that 'wine gladdens the heart of man' (Psalm 104:15), and because ancient man knew that it is in the heart that we understand, they used to say 'wine makes glad the understanding' (Homer, *Iliad* 3.246, 247).
To be wise in heart was to be wise in understanding:

'Wise in heart'–Exodus 28:3, Job 9:4 Hebrew Text
'Wise in understanding'–Ibid. Greek Text

'Every wise hearted man'–Exodus 36:1, 31:6 Hebrew Text
'Everyone wise in understanding'–Ibid. Greek Text

'Speak to all who are wise hearted'–Exodus 28:3 Hebrew Text
'Speak to all who are wise in understanding' –Ibid. Greek Text

'A fool shall be servant to the wise in heart'–Proverbs 11:29
Hebrew Text
'A fool shall be servant to the man of understanding'–Ibid. Greek
Text

Because 'the wise in heart is a man of understanding'–Proverbs
16:21, Syriac Text
Truly, 'a wise heart understands' –Sirach 3:27, Hebrew Text.

Wine and understanding bring joy to the heart of man. And to be wise in heart is to have the joy of understanding:

'May He grant you *wisdom of heart*—Sirach 50:23 Hebrew Text
'May He grant you *joyfulness of heart*' —Ibid. Greek Text

When a father says to his son: 'My son if your heart is wise, my heart will rejoice' (Proverbs 23:15), he is really saying to him: 'My son if you are understanding, you will make my heart glad.' Because what is expected by the fathers of the sons of Man is that they have the understanding needed to appreciate the parental wisdom and knowledge. It is because He is par excellence a *Son,* that the Son of Man is Himself Understanding incarnate. And being Understanding, He gave Himself to us as the bread and wine of understanding which were made flesh and blood to give us life, strength and joy. Yes, there is life in understanding:

'Are they living and understanding?'—Philo, *Som.* I.22

'Give me understanding and I shall live' —Psalm 119:144

'Set in motion, formed and given life by the understanding'—Philo., *Op.* 9

'Understanding is a wellspring of life to him who has it'—Proverbs 16:22

'May He enlighten your heart with life-giving understanding'—1QS 2:3, Dead Sea Scrolls

'Through Your precepts I get *understanding*'—Psalm 119:104
'I will never forget Your precepts because through them You have given me *life*'—Psalm 119:93

'The breath of the Almighty gives them *understanding*'—Job 32:8
'The breath of the Almighty has given me *life*' —Job 33:4

'O Lord . . . give us the seed of a new heart and cultivation to our *understanding* [as a vine] so that there may come fruit from it whereby everyone shall *live*'—2 Esdras 8:6

'The understanding of the Spirit is life and peace'—Romans 8:6

'Learn where insight [PHRONĒSIS] is . . . and where understanding [SUNESIS] is, so that you may be able to know where there is length of days and life'—Baruch 3:14

Learn where understanding is 'and with all your getting get understanding' (Proverbs 4:7) so that you may be lifted up some day (see pp. 64–65, 90–92).

And then shall we understand why it is written:

> 'O Lord what is *Man* that You *know* [YADA] him? And the *Son of Man* that You *understand* him?'–Psalm 144:3, see pp. 13–14

> 'What is *Man* that you should *magnify* him? Or [the *Son of Man*] that You set Your *understanding* [LEB-NOUN, see. pp. 45–46] upon Him?'–Job 7:17 Hebrew and Greek Texts.

For You have indeed set Your understanding upon Him so that the Son of Man may be exalted before the eyes of His own in His good time.

Epilogue

He fulfilled all that the prophets had foretold concerning Him. And He brought to completion the ancient Law that was given to His people Israel to teach them to keep what is good and reject evil. Then, in the fullness of time He came to give them the new Law which would show them how to give.

The Messiah did not come to abolish the Old Law but to bring it to fruit because perfect giving can only spring forth from faithful keeping. For to love is to keep, and to give out of love the fruit of what was kept which is the seed of His commandments:

> 'Do not think that I came to abolish the law or the Prophets. I did not come to abolish but to fulfill. For truly, I say to you, until heaven and earth pass away, not one jot or one tittle shall pass away from the Law, until all is accomplished. Whoever then breaks one of the least of these commandments, and so teaches others, shall be called least in the kingdom of heaven; but whoever keeps and teaches them shall be called great in the kingdom of Heaven' —St. Matthew 5:17–19.

It is well known that in His time the Scribes and Pharisees were righteous men who strove to fulfill 'the Law of righteousness' (Romans 9:31). The Messiah Himself acknowledged their righteousness yet He said to those who believed in Him: 'I say to you that unless your righteousness surpasses that of the Scribes and Pharisees, you shall by no means enter the Kingdom of Heaven' (St. Matthew 5:20). It is to those who believed in Him and received Him into their hearts that Yeshua the Messiah 'gave power to become sons of God' (St. John 1:12). Those who accepted Him were no longer allowed to rest in the righteousness of the servants of God, they had now to strive for the perfection of the children of God. It is in the striving for perfection that the followers of the Messiah shall see the fruition of all righteousness into lovingkindness and truthfulness. For the Messiah came to bring peace and those who make peace are the true and loving children of God. Thus, 'the fruit of righteousness (which is lovingkindness and truth [Hosea 10:12; Proverbs 11:18]), is sown in peace by those who make peace' (James 3:18) through their lovingkindness and truthfulness. This 'peaceable (EIRĒNIKON) *fruit* of righteousness'

(Hebrews 12:11) is the one brought forth by the children of God who kept the original *seed* of righteousness sown in their hearts. Within the fruits of righteousness are the children seeds of righteousness true as the seed of righteousness that was sown. These children seeds within the fruits of righteousness are in turn sown into the hearts of others 'by those who make peace': the children of God. Rightly then did the Messiah say: 'Blessed are the peacemakers for they shall be called children of God' (St. Matthew 5:9).

Man is body and soul, and he lives not only by food for the body but also by that for the soul. Because 'Man does not live by bread alone, but by every word that proceeds out of the mouth of God' (St. Matthew 4:4 Deuteronomy 8:3). To be 'poor in spirit' is to be humble and know that our thoughts are not His thoughts nor our ways His ways, for as the heavens are higher than the earth so are God's ways higher than our ways and His thoughts than our thoughts (Isaiah 55:8,9). Yeshua, the Messiah, said: 'Blessed are the poor in spirit for theirs is the Kingdom of Heaven' (St. Matthew 5:3). The reward of those who are poor in spirit are the treasures of the Kingdom of Heaven: the gift of spiritually understanding the wisdom and knowledge of God. Thus, the high things of the heavens above belong to the lowly and humble of spirit. 'A man of understanding is poor in spirit' –Targum to Proverbs 17:27, Literal Translation.

And the Son of Man went on to say: 'Blessed are the meek for they shall inherit the earth' (St. Matthew 5:4 Vaticanus, Sinaiticus, and Ephraemi Greek Texts, Vetus Latina, Latin Vulgate, Syriac and Coptic Texts). To be meek is to be pliable towards God and let Him do what He wants with us. It is to accept His will and His dealings with us as good, and therefore offer no resistance nor dispute with Him. In loving submission, meekness makes us trust in Him and allow His hand in our lives to purify and transform us. Meekness willingly bears the yoke and drags the burden of the plow because it has confidence in the Plower behind it all. Happy are the meek for they shall inherit the new earth that shall have also been transformed by Him.

It is not easy to be humble and meek in the face of opposition, insult and injury. For as the Messiah was persecuted in His time so are His followers to suffer in turn (St. John 15:20) but not without solace, because He said to them: 'Blessed are they who mourn, for they shall be comforted' (St. Matthew 5:5) by the One who is called 'the Comforter: the Holy Spirit' (St. John 14:26). He shall give them understanding concerning the will of God which is that they become perfect, loving, and truthful children of God. Because 'the things of God no one knows except the Spirit of God'

(1 Corinthians 2:11) and 'the Holy Spirit teaches' (1 Corinthians 2:13) 'that all may learn, and all may be comforted' (1 Corinthians 14:31) by His teaching in their tribulation. 'Blessed is the man whom You shall instruct O Lord, and shall teach him out of Your Law, so that You may give him relief from the days of tribultation' (Psalm 94:12,13). Truly, 'if Your teaching had not been my delight, I would have perished in my affliction' (Psalm 119:22).

Having understood, in the midst of their suffering: God's mysterious designs, the humble and meek remember what the Psalmist said:

> 'Give me understanding, and I shall keep Your Law, yes, I shall observe it with all my heart' —Psalm 119:34

> 'I will run the way of Your commandments when You shall enlarge my understanding' —Psalm 119:32.

And they are filled with a great desire to be good, for they now understand His will. Thus, in His wonderful wisdom Yeshua the Messiah went on to say: 'Blessed are those who hunger and thirst for righteousness, for they shall be filled' (St. Matthew 5:6). They who have mourned and been comforted by the Holy Spirit know that they must really hunger and thirst to be just, and to do His will (St. John 4:34) if they hope to be good and accomplish it.

And because true fidelity is always in the company of loving compassion, He next said to them: 'Blessed are the merciful, for they shall obtain mercy' (St. Matthew 5:7). Righteousness and mercy go hand in hand, for the merciful should also be faithful, and the righteous, kind.

It is the humble and meek, righteous and merciful who can advance towards that 'holiness without which no one shall see the Lord' (Hebrews 12:14). All who are righteous and compassionate long for the sight of the Lord. But they know that they must first be holy, because it is holiness which brings one close to God. For 'whom the Lord chooses shall be holy' (Numbers 16:7), and 'that one whom He chooses He will cause to come near to Him' (Numbers 16:5). Yeshua the Messiah taught that no one is holy who is not holy from within (St. Matthew 12:35; 15:8, 17–20; 23:25–28; St. Mark 7:6–23; St. Luke 11:39; 6:45; 16:15) because the Lord looks at the heart (1 Samuel 16:7; 1 Chronicles 28:9; 29:17; 2 Chronicles 6:30; Psalm 7:9; Proverbs 17:3; Jeremiah 17:10; 11:20; 20:12; St. John 2:24–25). We can see the beautiful order found in the Beatitudes of the Son of Man when we note that the Messiah went on to say: 'Blessed are the pure in heart for they shall see God' (St. Matthew 5:8). The truly holy are the pure in heart, and it is they who shall see God in all His works and in all His ways.

Step by step the Messiah taught us that by being humble, meek, righteous, compassionate, and holy we shall be able to see and know God, and 'attain to...the knowledge of the Son of God, unto a perfect man' (Ephesians 4:13), 'renewed in knowledge after the Image of Him who created him' (Colossians 3:10). We are all meant to walk towards the perfection of a child of God for all 'holiness leads to godliness' (Shekalim 9, Babylonian Talmud). The 'pure in heart' or truly holy ones go on towards the godliness and perfection of the children of God. We must not forget that none but His children have true knowledge of God. Thus, He said to them: 'No one fully knows (EPIGINŌSKEI) the Father, but the Son, and anyone whom the Son wills to reveal Him' (St. Matthew 11:27; St. Luke 10:22; St. John 10:15; 7:29; 8:55; 17:25).

The Messiah came 'to guide our feet into the way of peace' (St. Luke 1:79) by His teaching. For 'through His (the Messiah's) teaching shall peace be greatly increased upon us' (Targum to Isaiah 53:5). Did not the prophet Isaiah say that when 'all your children shall be taught by the Lord, great shall be the peace of your children'? (Isaiah 54:13). Because to be taught by the Lord is to receive His knowledge, and it is the knowledge of God which shall bring peace on this earth (see pp. 124–127). We know that it is the children of God who possess this peacemaking knowledge. We can see the Messiah's great knowledge of God, and become aware of His infinite understanding when we observe that right after He praised true holiness (St. Matthew 5:8), Yeshua said to them: 'Blessed are the peacemakers, for they shall be called children of God' (St. Matthew 5:9). And as such they shall be able to make peace through His holy knowledge: 'to turn the hearts of the fathers to their children, and the hearts of the children to their fathers' (Malachi 4:6 [3:24 Hebrew Text]).

All crooked things will go right, and the word will come into the riddle, and the key into the puzzle, and we shall be so delighted to know that it was right all along and that we trusted Him when things were darkest and most incomprehensible. —Mother Stuart, RSCJ.

Postscript

The Holy Scriptures tell us about the angels but they give us the names of only three of them: the archangels Michael ('Who is like unto God?' see Daniel 10:13, 21; 12:1; Jude 9; Revelation 12:7), Gabriel ('Strength of God' Daniel 8:16; 9:21; St. Luke 1:19, 26), and Raphael ('Healing of God,' Tobit 3:17; 5:4; 8:2; 9:1, 5; 12:15). From *The Revelation of the Son of Man* we know that Gabriel is the angel who gives us the gift of understanding from the Lord (see p. 94). Gabriel appeared to Zacharias 'standing on the right side of the altar of incense' (St. Luke 1:11) because there is a definite relationship between understanding and the right hand or side (see pp. 149–153).

Furthermore, having understood the connection between 'seeing' and 'knowing' (see pp. 19–21) we may surmise, in turn, that Raphael is the angel who gives us the gift of knowledge from God. For was he not sent to give *sight* to blind Tobit? And to Sarah the grace to finally be able to *know* man? (she was the unfortunate damsel who had seven bridegrooms consecutively snatched from her before she was able to consummate her marriages [Tobit chapters 2–3, 6, 8, 11]). And just as the right hand is the hand of understanding so is the left hand symbolically the hand of knowing (YAD = 'left hand' and YADA = 'to know,' see St. Matthew 6:3). Needless to say, Raphael would stand on the left side of the altar, and he would be concerned with the left hand of knowledge.

In Jewish tradition (see p. 94) the angel Gabriel was the one assigned to protect the tribes encamped in the eastern section. And rightly so, because there is also a connection between the dawn and the understanding (see pp. 87–88). Furthermore, it was to be expected that the rabbis who said that 'Gabriel's place is in the east' (Pesikta Rabbati, Piska 46.3) would also say that 'Raphael's place is to the west' (Ibid.). For if the dawn brings forth understanding, then the evening comes with knowledge. Thus, the sun may understand his rising in the east, but 'the sun *knows* his setting' (Psalm 104:19) in the west. We can now understand why it is written that 'day unto day [upon arising] brings forth answer [AMAR, see pp. 236–237 for relationship between "answering" and "understanding"], and night unto night shows knowledge' (Psalm 19:2, see also p.88).

In the cover painting of the book there are two spectral hands that are pulling aside the prayer shawl that covered the face of the Messiah. These represent the right hand of Gabriel and the left hand of Raphael, symbolic of the understanding and knowledge needed to reveal the Son of Man in all His kingly glory, wearing the royal garments and crown of a prince. For 'the Son of Man is revealed' [APOKALUPTETAI = 'unveiled' in St. Luke 17:30] on the day that we shall see that He is truly the promised Messiah, Son of David. The traditional color of the tribe of Judah [see Midrash Numbers Rabbah II.7] is displayed in the blue band across the prayer shawl.

The pen name Levi Khamor means in Hebrew: 'joined [LEVI] donkey [KHAMOR]' signifying a joint effort by a donkey and an ox, or by a son of man and a man, which means to say a work done by understanding and knowledge. For just as we can see that the term 'Man' connotes 'knowledge,' and 'son of Man': 'understanding' (see pp. 13–17, 19–23 etc.), so do the Hebrew words for ox (or bull), and donkey signify knowledge and understanding. The bull knows, and the donkey understands (see p. 135). Thus, it is written that:

> 'The ox [SHOR = 'ox' or 'bull'] *knows* his owner,
> And the ass [*understands*] his master's manger;
> But Israel does not *know*,
> My people do not *understand*' —Isaiah 1:3.

The Revelation of the Son of Man was written by a hermit who is a Scriptural and Rabbinic scholar. He was aided throughout the writing by the dedicated prayers of a carpenter who also daily offered up the burden of his labors for the sake of the work. They both agreed before the Lord to undertake the task together with all their heart and soul. The author is right-handed, and the one who prayed is left-handed; the former was born in the east and the latter in the west. It may be said that this work was done by a man, and a son of man who desired to bear witness to Him, for it takes two to bear witness to the Truth.

'To Him be all the glory both now and forever. Amen, Amen.'

D.J.M.   **A.M.O.**

Bibliography

1) General References

2) Bible and Bible Texts and Commentaries

3) The Old Testament Pseudepigrapha

4) Apocrypha of the New Testament

5) Dead Sea Scrolls

6) Targumim

7) Mishnah

8) Tosefta

9) Post-Biblical Pre-Talmudic Jewish Works

10) Talmud

11) Midrash

12) Zohar

13) Early Christian and Patristic Writings

14) Early and Medieval, and Talmudic Literature

15) Collectanea Operum Judaicarum

16) Judeo-Christian Theme Texts

17) Texts on the Messiah and Messianic Speculations

18) Karaism

19) Hermetica and Gnostic Texts

20) Relevant Non-Israelite Ancient Texts

21) Classical Greek and Latin Authors

22) Holy Land Literature

23) Contemporary Rabbinic Works

24) The Parables

25) Son of Man Literature

GENERAL REFERENCES

[Concordances, Dictionaries, Encyclopedias, Grammars, Indices, Lexicons and Standard Texts]

Aland, K. and Aland, B. *The Text of the New Testament.* An introduction to the Critical Editions and to the Theory and Practice of Modern Textual Criticism. Leiden, 1987.

Arndt, W. F., and Gingrich, F. W. *A Greek-English Lexicon of the New Testament and Other Early Christian Literature.* Chicago, 1957.

Aistleitner, J., ed. *Worterbuch der Ugaritischen Sprache.* 4th Edition. Berlin, 1974.

Assyrian Dictionary (The) of the Oriental Institute of the University of Chicago. Vols. I–IX, XVI, XXI, [A–M, S and Z]. Chicago, 1956 ff.

Barthelemy, D., and Rickenbacher, O. *Konkordanz zum Hebraisher Sirach mit Syrische-Hebraischen Index.* Gottingen, 1973.

Bezold, C. *Babylonische-Assyrisches Glossar.* Heidelberg, 1926.

Ben Yehuda, E. *Thesaurus Totius Hebraitatis.* 8 vols. London and New York, 1960.

Berlin, M., and Zevin, S. Y., eds. *Encyclopedia Talmudit.* 10 vols. Jerusalem, 1946 et seq.

Blass, F., and Debrunner, A. *A Greek Grammar of the New Testament and Other Early Christian Literature.* Translated and revised by R. W. Funk. Chicago, 1961.

Blass, F., and Debrunner, A. *Hebraische Grammatik.* Aufl, 1909.

Boeckh, A., ed. *Corpus Inscriptionum Semiticarum.* Paris, 1881.

Borger, R. *Babylonische-Assyrische Lesestucke I–III.* Rome, 1963.

Brederek, E. *Konkordanz zum Targum Onkelos.* Berlin, 1906.

Brockelmann, K. *Lexicon Syriacum.* Olms, 1928.

Brockelmann, K. *Syrische Grammatik.* Berlin, 1899, [repr. Leipzig, 1965].

Brown, F.; Driver, S. R.; and Briggs, C. A. *An English and Hebrew Lexicon of the Old Testament.* Oxford, 1959.

Budge, E. A. W. *An English Hieroglyphic Dictionary.* 2 vols. N.Y., 1978, [repr. of 1920 edit.].

Buxtorff, J. *Lexicon Chaldaicum, Talmudicum et Rabbinicum.* 2 vols. Leipzig, 1869–75.

Deimel, A. *Sumerisches Lexicon und Akkadisch-Sumerisches Glossar.* 9 vols. Rome, 1928–50.

Dekkers, E., and Gaar, A. *Clavis Patrum Latinorum.* Rome, 1961.

Denis, A. M., ed. *Concordance de l'Apocalypse grecque du Baruch.* Louvain, 1967.

Eisenstein, J. D., ed. *Ozar Yisrael: An Encyclopedia of All Matters Concerning Jews and Judaism* [Hebrew]. London, 1935.

Encyclopaedia Judaica [German]. 10 vols. Berlin, 1928–34.

Encyclopaedia Judaica. 16 vols. Jerusalem-New York, 1972.

Erman, A., and Grapow, H., eds. *Worterbuch der Aegyptischen Sprache.* 6 vols. Leipzig, 1926–31.

Gesenius, W., and Kautzsch, E. *Hebraische Grammatik.* Aufl, 1909.

Gesenius, W., and Buhl, E. *Hebraisches und Aramaisches Handwortenbuch das Alte Testament.* Leipzig, 1921.

Gianotti, C. R. *The New Testament and the Mishnah*, [a Cross Reference Index]. Grand Rapids, 1983.

Ginsburg, C. D. *Introduction to the Masoretico-Critical Edition of the Hebrew Bible.* London, 1897, [Repr. New York, 1966, with an introduction by H. M. Orlinsky].

Goldschmidt, L. *Oznayim LaTorah. Konkordantsiyah leTalmud Babli.* ed. R. Edelman, Copenhagen, 1959.

Gordon, C. H. *Ugaritic Handbook.* [Analecta Orientalia XXV]. Rome, 1947.

Gordon, C. H. *Ugaritic Manual.* [Analecta Orientalia XXXV]. Rome, 1955.

Gordon, C. H. *Ugaritic Textbook.* [Analecta Orientalia]. Rome, 1965.

Graffin, R., ed. *Patrologia Orientalis.* 25 vols. Paris, 1903–07.

Graffin, R., ed. *Patrologia Syriaca.* 3 vols. Paris, 1894–1926.

Gross, M. B. *Otzar Ha-agadot.* 3 vols. Jerusalem, 1954.

Haiman, M., ed. *Sefer Torah, Ha-Ketubah, ve-Ha-Masorah 'al Torah, Nebi-'im ve-Ketubim,* [Index by Biblical passage, of comments on that biblical passage in Rabbinic literature]. 3 vols. Tel Aviv, 1965.

Hatch, E., and Redpath, H. A. *A Concordance to the Septuagint and the Other Greek Versions of the Old Testament and Apocryphal Books.* 2 vols. Supplement. Oxford, 1897–1906.

Jastrow, M. A. *A Dictionary of the Targumim, the Talmud Babli and Yerushalmi and the Midrashic Literature*. 2 vols. New York, 1950.

Kahle, P. *Prolegomena to Kittel's Biblia Hebraica*. Leipzig, 1937.

Kasher, M. M., ed. *Torah Shelemah*. 28 vols. Jerusalem, 1927–75 ff.

Kasovsky, H. J. *Concordance to the Targum Onqelos*. 5 vols. in 2. Jerusalem, 1939–40.

Kasovsky, C. J., and B. *Thesaurus Talmudus*. Jerusalem, 1954, ff.

Kasovsky, C. J. *Thesaurus Mishnae*. 4 vols. Jerusalem, 1960.

Kasovsky, C. J., *Thesaurus Tosephthae*. 6 vols. Jersualem, 1952–61.

Kittel, G., and Friedrich, G., eds. *Theological Dictionary of the New Testament, with Index* by R. E. Pitkin. 10 vols. Grand Rapids, 1964–76.

Kohut, A., ed. *Aruch Completum*. 8 vols. Vienna, 1926.

Kohut, A., Krauss, S., et al., eds. *Complete Talmudic Targumic and Midrashic Lexicon*. New York, n.d.

Kosovsky, B., ed. *Thesauris Sifra*. 4 vols. Jerusalem, 1967–69.

Kosovsky, B., ed. *Thesaurus Sifrei*. 5 vols. Jerusalem, 1971–74.

Krauss, S., et al. *Sypplement Volume to Kohut, Aruch Completum*. New York, 1965.

Kuhn, K. G., Denis, A. M., et al. *Konkordanz zu den Quamran-texten*. Gottingen, 1960.

Kuhn, K. G., et al. *Nachtrage zur Konkordance zu den Quamran-texten*. RDQ IV, Heft 14. 1963.

Lampe, G. W. H. *Patristic Greek Lexicon*. Oxford, 1968.

Leisegang, I. *Philoneus Alexandrini Opera Supersunt, Indices*, [Concordance to Philo]. Berlin, 1926.

Levy, J. *Worterbuch uber die Talmudim und Midrashim*. 4 vols. Darmstadt, 1963, [repr. of Leipzig, 1875–89 edit.].

Levy, J. *Chaldaische Worterbuch uber die Targumim*. 2 vols. Koln, 1959.

Lisowsky, G., and Rost. L. *Konkordanz zum Hebr. Alten Testament*. 1958.

Mandelkern, S. *Veteris Testamenti Concordantiae Hebraicae atque Chaldaice*. Graz, 1955.

Margolioth, M. *Encyclopedia of Talmudic and Geonic Literature*. 2 vols. Tel Aviv, 1946, repr. 1962.

Mayer, G. *Index Philoneus*. Berlin, 1974.

Metzger, B. M. *New Testament Studies* [Philological, versional and patristic]. Grand Rapids, 1980.

Metzger, B. M., ed. *New Testament Tools and Studies.* Grand Rapids, 1972.

Migne, J. P., ed. *Patrologia cursus completus: Series Latina.* 221 vols. Paris, 1844–66.

Migne, J. P., ed. *Patrologia cursus completus: Series Graeca.* 161 vols. Paris, 1857–66.

Montefiore, C. G. and Loewe, H. *A Rabbinic Anthology.* London, 1938.

Moore, G. F. *Judaism in the First Centuries of the Christian Era: the Age of the Tannaim.* Cambridge, Mass. 1927–30.

Morrish, G. *A Handy Concordance of the Septuagint, Giving Various Readings from Codices Vaticanus, Alexandrinus, Sinaiticus, and Ephraemi.* London, repr. 1970.

Noy, Dov. [Neumann, D.] *Motif-Index of the Talmudic Midrashic Literature.* Ann Arbor, 1954.

Payne Smith, R. *Compendious Syriac Dictionary.* Oxford, 1957.

Payne Smith, R. *Thesaurus Syriacus.* 2 vols. Oxford, 1879–1901.

Pritchard, J. B., ed. *Ancient Near Eastern Texts relating to the Old Testament.* Princeton, 1969.

Roberts, A.; Donaldson, J.; and Menzies, A., eds. *The Ante-Nicene Fathers.* 9 vols. Grand Rapids, 1974–75.

Schaff, P., ed. *Nicene and Post-Nicene Fathers. First Series.* 9 vols. Grand Rapids, 1975.

Schaff, P. and Wace, H., eds. *Nicene and Post Nicene Fathers. Second Series.* 14 vols. Grand Rapids, 1974–76.

Schurer, E., ed. *A History of the Jewish People in the Time of Jesus Christ.* 5 vols. Edinburgh, 1885–91. Revised and edited by G. Vermes and F. Millor. Vol I, 1973.

Shunami, S. *Bibliography of Jewish Bibliographies.* Jerusalem, 1965.

Singer, I., ed. *The Jewish Encyclopedia.* 12 vols. New York, 1907.

Smend, R. *Griechisch-Syrisch-Hebraischer Index zur Weisheit des Jesus Sirach.* Berlin, 1907.

Soden (von), W. *Akkadische Handworterbuch.* Wiesbaden, 1959.

Stephanus, H. *Thesaurus Linguae Graecae.* Paris, 1831–65.

Strack, H. L., and Billerbeck, P. *Kommentar zum Neuen Testament aus Talmud und Midrasch.* 4 vols. Munich, 1922–28.

Van Zijl, J. B. *A Concordance to the Targum of Isaiah.* Missoula, 1979.

Wachsman, A. *Hanothen Bajam Derech,* [Talmudic Lexicon]. Budapest, 1938.

Winter, M. M. *A Concordance to the Peshitto Version of Ben Sira.* [Monograph of the Peshitto Institute 2]. Leiden, 1976.

Zevin, S. J., ed. *Encyclopedia Talmudica.* English Translation by I. Epstein and H. Freedman. Jerusalem, 1969.

Zorell, F. *Lexicon Hebraicum et Aramaicum Veteris Testamenti.* Rome, 1968.

BIBLE AND BIBLE TEXTS AND COMMENTARIES

Aland, K.; Black, M.; Metzger, B. M.; and Wikgren, A., eds. *The Greek New Testament.* Philadelphia, 1966.

La Bible. Edited by Rabbi S. Cahen. 18 vols. Paris, 1838–55.

Bible Rabbinique de Bomberg. Amsterdam, 1700–1705.

Bible Rabbinique de Buxtorf. Biblia Sacra Hebraicae et Chaldaica. Basle, 1619.

Ceriani, A. M. *Translation Syra Pescitto Veteris Testamenti ex Codice Ambrosiano.* Milan, 1876.

Deane, W. J., ed. *The Book of Wisdom.* Oxford, 1881.

Delitzsch, F. *Das Salomonisch Spruchbuch.* Leipzig. 1873.

Di Lella, A. A. *The Hebrew Text of Sirach.* The Hague, 1966.

Edersheim, A. ed. *Ecclesiasticus.* London, 1888.

Emerton, J. A., ed. *The Peshitta of the Wisdom of Solomon.* Leiden, 1959.

Enslin, M. S. *The Book of Judith.* New York, 1973.

Fang Che-Yong, M. *De discrepantis inter textum Graecum et Hebraicum libri Ecclesiastici seu Ben Sira* (Diss. man. scrip.). Rome, 1963.

Gerleman, G. *Studies in the Septuaginta. III: Proverbs.* Lund, 1956.

Geyer J. C. L., ed. *The Wisdom of Solomon.* London, 1963.

Goodrick, A. T. S. *The Book of Wisdom.* New York, 1913.

Hanhart, R., ed. *Judith* [Septuaginta Vetus Testamentuum Graecum VIII, 4]. Gottingen, 1976.

Hart, J. H. A., ed. *Ecclesiasticus,* The Greek Text of Codex 248. Cambridge, 1909.

Herkenne, H. *De Veteris Latinae Ecclesiastici Capitibus I–XLIII.* Leipzig, 1899.

Hertzenauer, P. M., ed. *Biblia Sacra Vulgata*. Rome, 1914.

The Holy Scriptures: According to the Masoretic Text. Philadelphia, (Jewish Publication Society), 1917.

Kittel, R. *Biblia Hebraica*. 3rd ed. Leipzig, 1937.

Knabenbauer, J., ed. *Ecclesiasticum cum Appendix Ecclesiastici Hebraeus*. Paris, 1902.

Lagarde, P. A. (de), ed. *Codex Amiatinus* [Contains Latin Text of Sirach]. Mitteilungen I, 1884.

Lagarde, P. A. (de), ed. *Libri Veteris Testamenti Apocryphi Syriace* [contains Syriac Text of Sirach]. London, 1861.

Lee, S. *Vetus Testamentum Syriace*. London, 1823.

Levi, I., ed. *The Hebrew Text of Ecclesiasticus*. [Semitic Study Series No. III.] Leiden, 1969.

Mikraot Gedolot (Hebrew Text of the Bible with Targum and Commentaries of Rashi, Ibn Ezra, Ramban, and Sforno). New York, Pardes Publishing Co., 1951.

Myers, J. M., ed. *I and II Chronicles*. [Anchor Bible Series, vols. 12 and 13.] Garden City, N.Y., 1965.

Myers, J. M., ed. *Ezra-Nehemiah*. [Anchor Bible Series, vol. 14.] Garden City, N.Y., 1965.

Myers, J. M., ed. *I and II Esdras*. [Anchor Bible Series, vol. 42.] Garden City, N.Y., 1974.

Rahlfs, A., ed. *Septuaginta*. 2 vols. Stuttgart, 1937.

Rudolph, W., ed. *Vom Buch Kohelet*. Munster, 1959.

Sperber, A. *The Bible in Aramaic* [Targums]. 4 vols. London, 1959.

Sperber, A., ed. *The Hebrew Bible* [With pre-Masoretic Tiberian vocalization. The Prophets, according to the *Codex Reuchlinianus* (in a critical analysis)]. Leiden, 1969.

Swete, H. B. *The Old Testament in Greek,* 2 vols. 3rd edit. Cambridge, 1907

Toy, C. H. *The Book of Proverbs*. Edinburgh, 1899.

Tov, E., ed. *The Book of Baruch also called 1 Baruch*. [Pseudo-epigrapha Series 6]. Missoula, 1975.

Tur-Sinai, N. H. *Mishle Selomoh* [Proverbs]. Tel Aviv, 1950.

Tur-Sinai, N. H. *The Book of Job: A New Commentary*. Jerusalem, 1967.

Vattioni, F., ed. *Ecclesiastico [Sirach]: testo ebraico con apparato critico e versione greca, latina e siriaca*. Naples, 1968.

Walton, B. *Biblia Sacra Polyglotta*, [edit. Hebrew, Greek, Latin, Aramaic, Syriac, Arabic and Geez]. 6 vols. London, 1964–65, repr. of 1657 edition.

Zeitlin and Enslin M. S., eds. and transls. *The Books of Judith*. Philadelphia, 1972.

Ziegler, J., ed. *Sapientia Iesu Filii Sirach*. [Septuaginta Vol. XII, 2.] Gottingen, 1965.

Ziegler, J., ed. *Sapientia Salomonis*. [Septuaginta Vol. XII, 1.] Gottingen, 1962.

Zimmerman, F. *The Book of Tobit*. New York, 1958.

Yadin, Y., ed. *The Ben Sira Scroll from Masada*. Jerusalem, 1965.

THE OLD TESTAMENT PSEUDEPIGRAPHA

Baars, W., ed. *The Psalms of Solomon* [Syriac, Peshitta]. Leiden, 1972.

Bernard, J. H., ed. *The Odes of Solomon*. Cambridge, 1912.

Bidawid, R. J., ed. *The Old Testament in Syriac According to the Peshitto Version* [Contains 2 Esdras in Syriac]. Leiden, 1966.

Black, M., ed. *The Book of Enoch or 1 Enoch* [A New English edition with commentary and textual notes]. Leiden, 1985.

Box, G. H., ed. *The Ezra Apocalypse*. London, 1912.

Box, G. H., and Landsman, J. L., eds. *The Apocalypse of Abraham*. London, 1918.

Box, G. H., ed. *The Testament of Abraham*. London, 1927.

Campbell, B. J., ed. *The Last Chapters of Enoch in Greek*. London, 1937.

Ceriani, A. J., ed. *Monumenta sacra et profana*. Vol. V, fasc. I. [Syriac Version of 2 Esdras in Codex Ambrosianus]. Milan, 1868.

Charles, R. H., ed. *The Apocrypha and Pseudepigrapha of the Old Testament*. 2 vols. Oxford, 1913.

Charles, R. H., ed. *The Apocalypse of Baruch*. Oxford, 1896.

Charles, R. H., ed. *The Ascension of Isaiah*. London, 1909.

Charles, R. H., ed. *The Assumption of Moses*. Oxford, 1897.

Charles, R. H., ed. *The Book of Enoch*. 2nd ed. Oxford, 1912.

Charles, R. H., ed. *The Book of the Secrets of Enoch*. Oxford, 1896.

Charles, R. H., ed. *Jubilees*. 2nd ed. Oxford, 1908.

Charles, R. H., ed. *The Testaments of the Twelve Patriarchs with Greek, Armenian and Slavonic Variants.* Oxford, 1908.

Charlesworth, James H., ed. *The Odes of Solomon.* Oxford, 1973.

Charlesworth, James H., ed. *The Old Testament Pseudepigrapha.* 2 vols. Garden City, New York: Doubleday, 1983–85.

Conybeare, F. C.; Harris, J. R.; and Lewis, A. S. eds. *The Story of Ahiqar from the Aramaic, Syriac, Arabic, Armenian, Ethiopic, Old Turkish, Greek and Slavonic Versions.* Cambridge, 1913.

Gebhardt (von), O. *Psalmoi Solomontos* [Codex Casanatentis]. Leipzig, 1895.

Gry, L., ed. *Les dires prophetiques d'Esdras* [2 Esdras]. 2 vols. Paris, 1938.

Hadas, M., ed. *The Third and Fourth Books of Maccabees.* New York, 1953.

Harris, J. R., and Mingana, A. eds. *The Odes and Psalms of Solomon.* 2 vols. Manchester, 1916–1920.

Holm-Nielsen, S., ed. *Die Psalmen Salomos.* Guttersloh, 1977.

Jonge (de), M., ed. *The Testaments of the Twelve Patriarchs.* Assen, 1962.

Jonge (de), M., ed. *Testamenta XII Patriarchum* [Greek Text]. Leiden, 1964.

Klyn, A. F. J., ed. *Die Syrische Baruch-Apokalypse.* Tubingen, 1976.

Knibb, M. A. and Ullendorff, E., eds. *Ethiopic Book of Enoch: New edition in the light of the Aramaic Dead Sea Fragments.* 2 vols. Oxford, 1978.

Kraft, R. A. and Purintum, A. E., eds. and trans. *Paraleipomena Jeremiou.* Missoula, 1972.

Lagarde (de), P. *Libri Testamenti Apocryphi Syriace.* Leipzig-London, 1861.

Leemhuis, F., Klijn, A. F. J. and Van Gelder, G. J. H. eds. *The Arabic Text of the Apocalypse of Baruch [Parallel English and Syriac Translations of the Arabic Text]. Leiden, 1986.*

Malan, S. C., ed. The Book of Adam and Eve. Edinburgh, 1882.

Metzger, B. M. *An Introduction to the Apocrypha.* London, 1957.

Milik, J. T. and Black, M., eds. *The Book of Enoch* [Aramaic Fragments of Qumran Cave 4]. Oxford, 1976.

Morfill, W. R., trans. and Charles, R. H., ed. *The Book of the Secrets of Enoch* [2 Enoch], Oxford, 1896.

Myers, J. M., ed. and trans. *I and II Esdras*. [Anchor Bible Series 42.] Garden City, 1974.

Odeberg, H., ed. *Third Enoch or the Hebrew Book of Enoch* [3 Enoch]. Cambridge, 1928.

Oesterly, W. O. E., ed. *II Esdras*. London, 1933.

Rabin, C., ed. and trans. *The Zadokite Documents*. Oxford, 1954.

Rzach, A. *Oracula Sibyllina*. Leipzig, 1891.

Schechter, S., ed. *Fragments of a Zadokite Work*. Cambridge, 1910.

Schodde, G. H., ed. *The Book of Jubilees*. Oberlin, Ohio, 1888.

Stone, M. E., ed. *Testament of Levi* [English Translation of the Armenian Text]. Jerusalem, 1969.

Stone, M. E., ed. and trans. *The Armenian Version of IV Ezra* [2 Esdras]. Missoula, 1979.

Stone, M. E., ed. *Jewish Writings of the Second Temple Period*. Philadelphia, 1984.

Swete, H. B., ed. *The Psalms of Solomon [Greek Text] with the Greek Fragments of the Book of Enoch*. Cambridge, 1899.

Thackeray, H. J., ed. *The Letter of Aristeas* [Greek Text]. Found in the Appendix to H. B. Swete's: *The Introduction to the Old Testament in Greek*. Cambridge, 1902.

APOCRYPHA OF THE NEW TESTAMENT

Guillamont, A.; Puech, H. C.; Quispel, G.; Till, W.; and Yassach, A. A. M., eds. *The Gospel According to Thomas*. Leiden–New York, 1959.

Hennecke, E., ed. *Neutestamentliche Apokryphen*. Tubingen, 1924 [2nd edition].

Hennecke, E., ed. *New Testament Apocrypha*. 2 vols. N. Y., 1963–65.

James, M. R., ed. *The Apocryphal New Testament*. Oxford, 1924.

DEAD SEA SCROLLS

Brownlee, W. H., ed. *The Dead Sea Scrolls Manual of Discipline* [1QS]. New Haven, 1951.

Burrows, M., and Trever, J. C., eds. *The Dead Sea Scrolls of St. Mark's Monastery*. 2 vols. New Haven, 1950–51.

Carmignac, J., ed. *La Regle de la Guerre des fils de lumiere contre les fils de tenebres* [1QM]. Paris, 1958.

Carmignac, J., ed. *Les Textes de Qumran, II*. Paris, 1963.

Delcor, M., ed. *Les Hymnes de Qumran (Hodayot) Texte Hebreau* [Hebrew Text of 1QH and Fragments]. Paris, 1960.

Dupont-Sommer, A., ed. *The Essene Writings from Qumran* [English Translation from the French by G. Vermes]. Oxford, 1961.

Holm-Nielsen, S., ed. *Hodayot: Psalms from Qumran* [1QH and Fragments]. Aarhus, 1960.

Licht, J., ed. *The Thanksgiving Scroll* [1QH–Hebrew]. Jerusalem, 1957.

Mansoor, M., ed. *The Thanksgiving Hymns* [1QH]. Leiden, 1961.

Rabinowitz, I. *'The Qumran hebrew Original of Ben Sira's Concluding Acrostic on Wisdom'* [Hebrew Union College Annual, Vol. XLII (1971), pp. 173–194]. Cincinnati.

Sanders, J. A., ed. *The Psalms Scroll of Qumran Cave 11* [11Q Ps[a]]. Oxford, 1965.

Sukenik, E. L., ed. *Otzar Hammegiloth haggezanoth* [Hebrew Text of 1QH and Fragments]. Jerusalem 1954–57.

Wernberg-Moller, P., ed. *The Manual of Discipline* [1QS], Leiden, 1957.

Yadin, Y., ed. *The Scroll of the War of the Sons of Light against the Sons of Darkness* [1QM]. Oxford, 1962.

TARGUMIM

Barnstein, H. *Targum Onkelos to Genesis*, London, 1896.

Berliner, A., ed. *Targum Onkelos*. Berlin, 1884.

Churgin, P. *Targum Jonathan to the Prophets*. New Haven, 1927.

Churgin, P. *Targum Ketuvim* [Hagiographa]. New York, 1945.

Diez Macho, A. *Targum Palestinense Neofiti*, Madrid, 1968.

Etheridge, J. W.. trans. *The Targums of Onkelos and Jonathan ben Uzziel on the Pentateuch with the Fragment of the Jerusalem Targum from the Chaldee*. New York, 1968, repr. of 1862 edition.

Ginsburger, M., ed. *Das Fragmententhargum* [Targum Jerusalem on the Pentateuch Fragments]. Berlin, 1899.

Ginsburger, M., ed. *Pseudo-Jonathan* [Targum Jonathan ben Uzziel on the Pentateuch]. Berlin, 1903.

Gollancz, H., trans. *Targum to the Song of Songs.* London, 1908.

Greenup, A. W. *The Targum on the Book of Lamentations.* Sheffield, 1893.

Grossfeld, B., ed. *The Targum to the Five Megilloth.* New York, 1973.

Levine, E., ed. *The Aramaic Version of Lamentations.* New York, 1976.

Levine, E., ed. *The Aramaic Version of Qohelet.* New York, 1978.

Melamed, R. H., *The Targum to Canticles.* Philadelphia, 1921.

Munk, L., ed. *Targum Sheni* [On Esther]. Berlin, 1876. [Also found in Churgin's Targum Ketuvim, pp. 214–235.]

Sperber, A., ed. *The Bible in Aramaic* [The Targums]. 4 vols. London, 1959.

Stenning, J. F. *The Targum of Isaiah.* Oxford, 1949.

MISHNAH

Albeck, Chanoch, ed. *Shisha Sidre Mishnah.* 6 vols. Jerusalem, 1954–59.

Albeck, H. *Mavo laMishnah* [Introduction to the Mishnah]. Jerusalem, 1959.

Danby, H. *The Mishnah.* Oxford. 1933.

Epstein, Y. N. *Introduction to the text of the Mishnah* [Hebrew]. Jerusalem, 1964.

Mishnah [Hebrew]. Pardes Publishing House, N.Y., 1963.

Shisha Sidre Mishnah. 12 vols. Jerusalem, 1954–1958.

TOSEFTA

'Additions' to the Mishnah

Horowitz, C. M., ed. *Tosefta Atiqta.* Frankfurt, 1890.

Lieberman, S., ed. *The Tosefta and Tosefta Kifshutah* [a comprehensive commentary on the Tosefta]. 9 vols. New York, 1955–73.

Lieberman, S., ed. *Tosefeth Rishonim,* 4 vols. Jerusalem, 1938–39.

Zuckermandel, M. S., ed. *Tosefta, Mischna und Baraitha.* 2 vols. and Suppl. Frankfurt, 1908–10.

POST-BIBLICAL PRE-TALMUDIC JEWISH WORKS

Aucher, J. B., ed. *De Providentia [Philo]: I and II* [Latin Translation of the Armenian Text]. Paris, 1822.

Charles, R. H., ed. *Apocrypha and Pseudepigrapha of the Old Testament.* 2 vols. Oxford, 1913.

Charlesworth, James, H., ed. *The Old Testament Pseudepigrapha.* 2 vols. Garden City, New York: Doubleday, 1983–85.

Daniel, S., ed. *Philo–de Specialibus: I and II.* Paris, 1975.

Dietzfelbinger, C., ed. *Pseudo-Philon Liber Antiquitatum Biblicarum.* Tubingen, 1975.

James, M. R., ed. *The Biblical Antiquities of Philo.* London, 1917.

Kisch, G. *Pseudo-Philo's Liber Antiquitatum Biblicarum.* Notre Dame, Indiana, 1949.

Philo. Translated by F. H. Colson and G. H. Whitaker. 12 vols. Loeb Classical Library Series, Cambridge, Mass., 1932–1962.

Thackeray, H. St. J.; Marcus, R.; and Feldman, H., eds. *Josephus.* 9 vols. Loeb Classical Library, Cambridge, 1926–65.

Whiston, W., trans. *The Works of Flavius Josephus.* New York, 1853.

TALMUD

Jerusalem Talmud

Schwab, M. *Le Talmud de Jerusalem.* 6 vols. Paris, 1960.

Palestinian Talmud. *Codex Vaticanus 133.* Jerusalem, 1971.

Talmud Yerushalmi. 7 vols. New York, 1959 [Reprint of the Vilna 1922 edition with additional commentaries].

Babylonian Talmud

Babylonian Talmud [Hebrew]. 20 vols. New York: Otzar Hasefarim, 1965 [Reprint of the Vilna 1895 edition with additional commentaries].

Babylonian Talmud Codex Munich 95. 3 vols. Jerusalem, 1971.

Cohen, A. *The Minor Tractates of the Talmud.* London, 1911.

Epstein, I., ed. *The Talmud Babli with Minor Tractates*. 35 vols. London: Soncino, 1935–52.

Higger, M. *The Seven Minor Tractates*. New York, 1930.

Higger, M. *The Additional Tractates*. New York, 1931.

MIDRASH RABBAH, MIDRASHIM AND AGGADOTH

Midrash Rabbah

Albeck, C., and Theodor, J., eds. *Bereshith [Genesis] Rabbah*. 3 vols. Jerusalem, 1965.

Freedman, H., and Simon, M., eds. and English transls. *Midrash* [Rabbah]. 10 vols. London, 1961.

Halevi, E. E., ed. *Midrash Rabbah*. 8 vols. Tel Aviv, 1956–63.

Lieberman, S., ed. *Midrash Debarim [Deuteronomy] Rabbah*. 2nd ed. Jerusalem, 1964.

Margulies, M., ed. *Midrash Wayyikra [Leviticus] Rabbah*. 5 vols. Jerusalem, 1953–60.

Midrash Bereshith Rabbah. Codex Vatican 60. Jerusalem, 1972.

Midrash Rabbah. Vilna: Romm, 1921.

Mekhilta

Midrash on certain chapters of Exodus

Epstein, J. N., ed. *Mekilta de Rabbi Simeon ben Jochai*. Jerusalem, 1955.

Horovitz, H. S., and Rabin, I. A., eds. *Mechilta D'Rabbi Ismael*. 2nd ed. Jerusalem, 1955.

Lauterbach, J. Z., ed and English trans. *Mekilta de-Rabbi Ishmael*. 3 vols. Philadelphia, 1976.

Pesikta

Midrashic homilies on the Jewish
festivals and Special Sabbaths

Braude, W. G., ed. and English trans. *Pesikta Rabbati*. 2 vols. [Yale Judaica Series]. New Haven, 1968.

Braude, W. G., and Kapstein, I. J., eds. and transls. *Pesikta De-Rab Kahana.* Philadelphia, 1975.

Friedmann, M., ed. *Pesikta Rabbati.* Vienna, 1880.

Friedmann, M., ed. *Pesikta Hadta* [a Midrash]. Vienna, 1880.

Mandelbaum, B., ed. *Pesiqta deRab Kahana* [Hebrew]. 2 vols. New York, 1962.

Margollioth, E., ed. *Pesikta Rabbati de Rab Kahana.* Warsaw, 1893.

Sifra

Tannaitic midrashic commentary on *Leviticus.*
Also known as *Sepher debe Rab*

Finkelstein, L., ed. *Sifra: or Torat Kohanim According to Codex Asemani.* New York, 1956.

Friedmann, M., ed. *Sifra, der alteste Midrasch zu Leviticus.* Breslau, 1915.

Weiss, I. H., ed. *Sifra on Leviticus.* Vienna, 1862.

Sifre

Tannaitic midrashic commentaries
on Numbers and Deuteronomy

Berlin, N. Z. J., ed. *Sifre.* Jerusalem, 1959.

Epstein, J. N., ed. *Mebooth leSifruth haTannaim.* Jerusalem, 1957.

Friedmann, M., ed. *Sifre on Deuteronomy.* Vienna, 1864.

Finkelstein, L., ed. *Siphra ad Deuteronium.* New York, 1969.

Kuhn, K. G., ed. *Der Tannatische Midrasch Sifre zu Numberi.* Stuttgart, 1959.

Levertoff, P. P., trans. *Midrash Sifre on Numbers.* London, 1926.

Sifre Zuta

'Little' Sifre on Numbers:
another Tannaitic midrash on Numbers

Horovitz, H. S. *Siphre Zuta.* Lodz, 1929.

Liberman, S., ed. *Spry Zwt*. New York, 1968.

Pirkei

Pirke Aboth

'Chapters' or sayings of the Fathers. Found
in the Seder Nezikin section of the Mishnah

Hertz, J. H. *Sayings of the Fathers or Pirke Aboth* [Hebrew Text and English trans.]. New York, 1945

Taylor, C., ed. *Sayings of the Jewish Fathers*. Prolegomenon by Judah Goldin. Ktav, New York: 1969 [repr. of 1897 Cambridge edition].

Aboth de Rabbi Nathan

Aggadic elaborations and
additions to the Pirke Aboth

Goldin, J., ed. *The Fathers according to Rabbi Nathan*. [Yale Judaica Series. Vol. X.] New Haven, 1955.

Saldarini, A. J., ed. *The Fathers according to Rabbi Nathan* [Version B]. Leiden, 1975.

Schecter, S., ed. *Aboth de Rabbi Nathan*. New York, 1945 [repr. of 1897 Vienna edit.]

Pirke de Rabbi Eliezer

Aggadic discussions on all the most important
events described in the Pentateuch

Friedlander, G., ed. *Pirqe Rabbi Eliezer*. London, 1916.

Higger, M., ed. *Pirqe Rabbi Eliezer*. Horeb, VIII, 1944, 1948.

Midrashim and Aggadoth

Albeck, H., ed. *Midrash Bereshith Rabbati* [a midrash on Genesis by Rabbi Moshe haDarshan no longer extant]. Jerusalem, 1940.

Astruc, En Saloma. *Midrashe ha-Torah*. Edited by Simeon Eppenstein. Berlin, 1899.

Bietenhard, H., ed. *Midrash Tanchumah B*. Bern, 1980.

Braude, W. G., ed and English trans. *The Midrash on Psalms*. 2 vols. [Yale Judaica Series XIII]. New Haven, 1959.

Buber, S., ed. *Yalkut Makiri*. 2 vols. Berdyczew, 1899.

Buber, S., ed. *Midrash Lekah Tobh* [Pesikta Zutarta]. 2 vols. Wilna, 1880.

Buber, S., ed. *Midrash Tehillim* [Shocher Tobh]. Wilna, 1891.

Buber, S., ed. *Midrash Shir haShirim*, Wilna, 1887.

Buber, S., ed. *Midrash Mishle* [On Proverbs]. Wilna, 18

Buber, S., ed. *Midrash Tanchumah* [Yelammedenu] 3 vols. Wilna, 1885 [repr. Jerusalem, 1964].

Buber, S., ed. *Midrash Samuel*. Cracow, 1893.

Buber, S., ed. *Midrash Ruth Zuta*.

Buber, S., ed. *Midrash Aggadah*. Vienna, 1894.

Buber, S., ed. *Midrash Zuta on Megilloth*. Berlin, 1894.

Buber, S., ed. *Midrash Sechel-Tobh* [On Genesis 11–Exodus 15]. Berlin, 1900–01.

Buber, S., ed. *Aggadath Bereshith*. Cracow, 1902.

Buber, S., ed. *Aggadath Esther*. Cracow, 1897.

Eben-Schmuel, J. [J. Kauffman], ed. *Midrash Geulah* [Midrashic texts relative to the Redemption of Israel], Jerusalem, 1954.

Epstein, A., ed. *Midrash Tadshe* [On Genesis 1:11]. Vienna, 1887 [Also found in Jellinek's *BHM* 3. pp. 164–193].

Epstein-Lewin, ed. *Midrash Tanchumah*. Jerusalem, 1967.

Fisch, S., ed. *Midrash Haggadol* [to Sefer *Devarim*]. Jerusalem, 1972.

Hoffman, D., ed. *Midrash Tannaim zum Deuteronium*. Berlin, 1908–09.

Margalioth, M., ed. *Midrash haGadol*. Bereshith, Jerusalem, 1975.

Midrash Agur [Midrash Sheloshim u-Shetayim Middot] found in H. G. Enelow, ed. Midrash Mishnat Rabbi Eliezer (1933), p. 10 f. and L. Ginzberg's *Tarbiz* 4 (1933), pp. 297–342.

Rabinowitz, Z. M., ed. *Midrash haGadol to Leviticus*. Jerusalem, 1967.

Schechter, S., ed. *Midrash haGadol* [on Genesis, contains quotations from the Targums, Midrashim and Talmudim]. Cambridge, 1902.

Schecter, S., ed. *Aggdath Shir haShirim*. Cambridge, 1896.

Yalkut
'Collection'

[When the word *Yalkut* is used by itself it refers to the Yalkut Shimoni collection by Rabbi HaDarshan of the 13th Century.]

Buber, S., ed. *Yalkut haMakiri* [Collection of Midrashim culled by R. Makir ben Abba Mari mostly on the Prophetical books and hagiographa]. 2 vols. Berdyczew, 1899.

Epstein-Lewin, ed. *Yalkut Reubeni* [collection of kabbalistic comments on the Pentateuch culled by Rabbi Reuben ben Hoshke Cohen]. Warsaw, 1899.

King, E. G. *The Yalkut on Zechariah*. Cambridge, 1882.

Shimeon Hadarshan. ed. *Yalkut Shimoni* [Homiletic Midrashim on the whole Pentateuch]. 2 vols. New York, 1944 [repr. of Salonica 1501, 1506–07 editions].

Spira, J. Z. K., ed. *Yalkut Makiri* [to Isaiah]. Berlin, 1894 [repr. Jerusalem, 1964].

Tanna debe Eliyyahu Rabba and Zuta

The Lore of the School of Elijah,
an ethical Midrashic work composed of two parts:
the 'Great' (Rabbah) and the 'Small' (Zuta)

Braude, W. G., and Kapstein, I. J., eds. and transls. *Tanna Debe Eliyyahu*. Philadelphia, 1981 [English translation includes Zuta Seder].

Friedmann, M., ed. *Seder Eliahu Rabba und Seder Eliyyahu Zuta*. Vienna 1902–04 [repr. Jerusalem, 1960].

Sefer ha Yashar

Midrash on Genesis, Exodus, Numbers
and Joshua written in heroic terms

Hilman, S. I., ed. *Sefer Or HaYashar al Yerushalmi*. Jerusalem, 1947.

Noah, M. M., trans. *Sefer ha Yashar*. [*The Book of Yashar*—English translation.] New York, 1840.

Sepher Hassidim

Ethical Midrash written by
Judah ben Samuel heHasid; died 1217

Margoliot, R., ed. *Sepher Hassidim* [Bologna Version]. Jerusalem, 1957.

Wistinelzsky, J. H., ed. *Sepher Hassidim* [Parma Version]. Berlin, 1891–94.

ZOHAR AND COMMENTARIES

The book of 'Splendour' originally written
in Aramaic and attributed to Rabbi Simeon ben Yohai;
A commentary on the Bible (Pentateuch)

Zohar

Mapsik, C., ed. *Le Zohar* 2 vols. La Grosse, 1984.

Margolis, R., ed. *Zohar.* 3 vols. [Hebrew]. Jerusalem, 1940–46. [Repr. Jerusalem, 1964. 4th ed.]

Pauly (de), J., ed. *Sepher haZohar* [Le Livre de la Splendeur]. 6 vols. Paris, 1906–11 [this is a revised edition].

Sperling, H.; Simon, M.; and Abelson, J., eds. and transls. *Zohar* [English translation; not the complete text]. 5 vols. London, 1950.

Commentaries on the Zohar

Ashlag, R., ed. *Commentary to the Zohar.* 2 vols. Jerusalem, 1961.

Lachower, F., and Tishby, I., *Mishnat ha-Zohar.* 2 vols. Jerusalem, 1971.

Margolioth, M., ed. *Zohar: With Commentaries.* 3 vols. [Hebrew]. Jerusalem, 1964.

Margolis, R. *Sha'arei Zohar* [Commentary]. Jerusalem, 1956.

Mendel, M. *Yalkut haZohar* [Commentaries]. Piotrikov, 1912.

Zohar Chadash and other Portions of the Zohar

Kipnis, S. *Midrashei haZohar Leket Shemu'el.* 3 vols. Jerusalem, 1957–60.

Margolis, R., ed. *Zohar Chadash* ['New' Zohar; a commentary on Canticles]. Jerusalem, 1978.

Margolis, R., ed. *Tikkunei Zohar.* Jerusalem, 1978.

EARLY CHRISTIAN AND PATRISTIC WRITINGS

Bardy, G., ed. *Eusebe de Cesaree: Histoire Ecclesiastique.* 3 vols. [Sources Chretiens, 31, 41, 55]. Paris, 1952–58.

Bigg, C., ed. *The Clementine Homilies.* Oxford, 1890.

Blunt, A. W. F., *The Apologies of Justin Martyr.* Cambridge, 1891.

Butterworth, G. W., ed. *Clement of Alexandria with an English Translation.* Loeb Classical Library, London, 1919.

Coxe, A. C., ed. *The Dialogues of Justin, Philosopher and Martyr with Trypho a Jew.* [Ante-Nicene Fathers, Vol. I.]

Grant, R. M., ed. Theophilus of Antioch; *Ad Autolycum.* Oxford, 1970.

Grant, R. M., and Graham, H. H., eds. *The Apostolic Fathers.* Vol. II–First and Second Clement. New York, 1965.

Gwynn, J., ed. *Demonstrations of Aphrahat* [Aphraates], *the Persian Sage.* Grand rapids, 1955.

Hart, F. J. A., and Mayor, J. B., eds. *Clement of Alexandria, Miscellanies* [Stromata] Book VII. London–New York, 1902.

Joly, R., ed. *Hermes: Le Pasteur.* Paris, 1968.

Lake, K., ed. *The Apostolic Fathers.* 2 vols. Cambridge, 1946.

Lightfoot, J. B., and Harmer, J., eds. *The Apostolic Fathers.* 2 vols. New York, 1891.

Marrou, H. I., and Harl, M., eds. *Clement d'Alexandrie.* Paris, 1960.

Owen, W. B., ed. *Athenagoras with Explanatory Notes.* New York, 1904.

Salvioni, J. M., ed. *Ephraem, Syrus, Opera omnia quae extant graecae, syriacae, latinae . . .* Vatican, 1732–46.

Saltman, A., ed. *Pseudo Jerome. Questiones* [on the Book of Samuel]. Leiden, 1975.

Snyder, G. F., ed. *Shepherd of Hermas.* [The Apostolic Fathers. Vol. 6.] New York, 1968.

Stahlin, O., ed. *Clement of Alexandria* [Stromata I–IV] found in [Die griescheischen Christlichen Schriftsteller, vols. 15–17]. Leipzig, 1897.

Strawley, J. H., ed. *The Epistles of St. Ignatius of Antioch*. London, 1935.

EARLY AND MEDIEVAL RABBINICAL, AND TALMUDIC LITERATURE

Abarbanel, Don, I. *Commentary on the Former Prophets*. Jerusalem, 1955.

Abarbanel, Don, I. *Commentary on the Pentateuch*. Jerusalem, 1956.

Angelino, J. [David ben Yehudah he-Hasid]. *Livnath ha-Sappir*. Jerusalem, 1970.

Berliner, A., ed. *Rashi al haTorah* [New edition of Rashi's Commentaries on the Bible with an appendix of variants in the readings of Rashi]. Jerusalem, 1964–70.

Cohen, A., trans. *Ibn Gabirol: The Choice of Pearls* [Mibchar haPeninim]. New York, 1925.

Cordovero, Moses. *Pardes Rimmonim* [Hebrew]. Cracow, 1951.

Elfenbein, I., ed. *Responsa Rashi*. New York, 1943.

Filipowski, S., ed. *Sepher Yuchasin* [Of Abraham Zacuto]. London, 1857 [repr. Jerusalem, 1963].

Gollancz, H., trans. [R. Joseph Kimchi's] *Shekel Hakodesh*. Oxford, 1919.

Greenup, A. W., ed. *Sheqel ha-Qodesh* [Rabbi Joseph Kimchi's]. London, 1911.

Hirsch, S. R., ed. *Horeb*. 2 vols. London, 1962.

Ibn Ezra, A. *Commentary on the Pentateuch*. Edited by Y. L. Krinsky. 5 vols. Tel Aviv. [Reprint of the 1928 Vilna ed.]

Landover, S., ed. *Saadia Gaon's: The Book of Beliefs and opinions*. Translated by S. Rosenblatt. New York, 1948.

Maimonides. *The Guide to the Perplexed* [Trans. S. Pines.]. Chicago, 1962.

Maimonides. *Hilkhoth haYerushalmi of Rabbi Moses Ben Maimon*. Edited by S. Lieberman. New York, 1947.

Maimonides. *Mishnah Im Perush Rabenu Moshe Ben Maimon*. Edited by Qapiach. 7 vols. Jerusalem, 1963–69.

Maimonides. *Mishnah Torah: With additional commentaries*. New York, 1963.

Maimonides. *Moreh NeBukhim* [trans. I. Tibbon]. Jerusalem, 1959.

Maimonides. *Sefer Ha-Misvot.* Edited by C. Heller. Jerusalem, 1946.

Nachmanides. *Commentary on the Torah.* Edited by H. D. Chavel. 2 vols. Jerusalem, 1962–63.

Recanati, Menahem. *Peruch al haTorah al Derekh haEmeth.* Venice, 1523.

Saadia Gaon, R. *Siddur.* Edited by I. Davidson, S. Hassaf, and B. I. Joel. Jerusalem, 1941, Emunot vedeot. Leiden, 1881.

Vidas (De), Elijah. *Reshit Hokhmah, Shaar ha-Ahorah.* Tel Aviv, n.d.

Vital, Hayyim. *Sepher 'Es Hayyim* [Hebrew]. Koretz, 1784.

Wise, S. S., trans. *Gabirol's* [Ibn] *Improvement of the Moral Qualities.* New York, 1902.

Zucker, M., ed. *Rav Saadya Gaon's Translation of the Torah.* New York, 1959.

COLLECTANEA OPERUM JUDAICARUM

Bacher, W., ed. *Die Agada der babylonischen Amoraer.* Strassburg, 1878.

Bacher, W., ed. *Die Agada der palastinischen Amoraer.* Strassburg, 1892.

Bacher, W., ed. *Die Agada der Tannaiten.* Strassburg, 1890.

Eisenstein, J. D., ed. *Bibliotheca Midraschica: a Library of 200 Minor Midrashim.* New York, 1915.

Eisenstein, J. D., ed. *Ozar Midrashim.* 2 vols. New York, 1915.

Ginzberg, L., ed. *Legends of the Jews.* 7 vols. Philadelphia, 1909–46

Grunhut, L., ed. *Sefer ha-Likkutim: Sammlung alterer Midraschim und wissenschaftlicher Abhandlangen.* 6 vols. Jerusalem, 1898–1903.

Jellinek, A., ed. *Beth ha Midrash.* 6 vols. Leipzig, 1853–77.

Levin, B. M., ed. *Otzar haGaonim.* 13 vols. Haifa and Jerusalem, 1928–43.

Rabbinovicz, R., ed. *Diqduqe Sofrim. Variae Lectiones in Mischnam et in talmud Babylonicum.* 12 vols. New York, 1960.

Wertheimer, S. A., ed. *Batte Midrashot.* 4 vols. Jerusalem, 1893–97.

Wertheimer, S. A., ed. *Otzar Midrashim.* 2 vols. Jerusalem, 1913–14 [revised and edited by his grandson A. J. Wertheimer].

Wertheimer, S. A., ed. *Leket Midrashim.* Jerusalem, 1904.

JUDEO-CHRISTIAN THEME TEXTS

Abrahams, I. *Studies in Pharisaism and the Gospels.* New York, 1967.

Bonsirven, J. *Les idees Juives au temps de Notre Seigneur.* Paris, 1933.

Bonsirven, J. *Le Judaisme palestinien au temps de Jesus-Christ.* 2 vols. Paris, 1934.

Bonsirven, J. *Palestinian Judaism in the time of Jesus Christ.* New York, 1964.

Bonsirven, J. *Textes Rabbiniques des deux premiers siecles Chretiens.* Rome, 1955.

Bowker, J. *Jesus and the Pharisees.* Cambridge, 1969.

Dalman, G. *Jesus Christ in the Talmud, Midrash, Zohar and the Liturgy of the Synagogue.* Translated and edited by A. W. Streave. New York, 1893.

Dalman, G. *Jesus-Jeschua.* Leipzig, 1922.

Dalman, G. *Die Worte Jesu.* Leipzig, 1930.

Daube, D. *The New Testament and Rabbinic Judaism.* New York, 1956.

Davies, W. D. *Torah in the Messianic Age and/or The Age to Come.* Philadelphia [SBL], 1952.

Davies, W. D. and D. Daube, eds. *The Background of the New Testament and its Eschatology.* Cambridge, 1956.

Davies, W. D. *Christian Origins and Judaism.* Philadelphia, 1962.

Davies, W. D. *Paul and Rabbinic Judaism* 4th edition. Philadelphia, 1980.

Derrett, J. D. M. *Midrash, in Action as a Literary Device* [Studies in the New Testament Vol. II]. Leiden, 1978.

Derrett, J. D. M. *Midrash, Haggadah and the Character of the Community* [Studies in the New Testament Vol. III]. Leiden, 1982.

Derrett, J. D. M. *Midrash, the Composition of the Gospels and Discipline* [Studies in the New Testament Vol. IV]. Leiden, 1986.

Finkel, A. *The Pharisees and the Teacher of Nazareth.* Leiden, 1964.

Flusser, D. *Jesus.* New York, 1969.

Herford, R. T. *Christianity in Talmud and Midrash.* London, 1903.

Lagrange, M. J. *Le Judaisme avant Jesus-Christ.* Paris, 1931.

Montefiore, C. J. G. *Rabbinic Literature and Gospel Teachings.* London, 1930.

Neusner, J. *The Rabbinic Traditions about the Pharisees before 70.* 3 vols. Leiden, 1971.

Odeberg, H. *Pharisaism and Christianity.* Saint Louis, 1964.

Smith, M. *Tannaitic Parallels to the Gospels.* Philadelphia, 1968.

TEXTS ON THE MESSIAH AND MESSIANIC SPECULATIONS

Beutzen, A. *King and Messiah.* Edited by G. W. Anderson, 2nd edition. Oxford, 1970.

Brierre-Narbonne, J. J. *Exegese des prophecies messianiques.* Paris, 1934.

Brierre-Narbonne, J. J. *Exegese Talmudique des prophecies messianiques.* Paris, 1934.

Brierre-Narbonne, J. J. *Exegese Midrashique des prophecies messianiques.* Paris, 1935.

Brierre-Narbonne, J. J. *Exegese Targumique des prophecies messianiques.* Paris, 1936.

Brierre-Narbonne, J. J. *Exegese Apocryphe des prophecies messianiques.* Paris, 1937.

Brierre-Narbonne, J. J. *Exegese Zoharique des prophecies messianiques.* Paris, 1938.

Briggs, C. A. *Messianic Prophecy.* Edinburgh, 1886.

Browne, L. E. *The Messianic Hope in its Historical Setting.* London, 1951.

Coppens, J. *L'Esperance Messianique: ses origines et son developement.* Bruges, 1963.

Delitzsch, F. *Messianic Prophecies in Historical Succession.* English transl. by S. I. Curtiss. Edinburgh, 1891.

Greenstone, S. *The Messiah Idea in Jewish History.* Philadelphia, 1906.

Gross, G. *Le Messianisme Juif.* Paris, 1969.

Klausner, J. *The Messianic Idea in Israel.* Transl. from the third Hebrew Edition by W. F. Stinespring. New York, 1955.

Lagrange, M. J. *Le Messianisme chez les Juifs.* Paris, 1909.

Landman, L. *Messianism in the Talmudic Era.* New York, 1979.

Levey, S. H. *The Messiah in Aramaic Interpretation: The Messianic Exegesis of the Targum.* Cincinatti, 1974.

Laperrousaz, E. M. *L'Attente du Messie en Palestine a la Veille et au Debut de l'Ere Chretienne.* Paris, 1982.

Mowinckel, S. *The Messiah in the Old Testament.* London, 1956.

Neusner, J. *Messiah in Context.* Philadelphia, 1984.

Oesterley, W. O. E. *The Evolution of the Messianic Idea.* New York, 1909.

Patai, R. *The Messiah Texts.* New York, 1979.

Ringgren, H. *The Messiah in the Old Testament.* London, 1956.

Sarachek, J. *The Doctrine of the Messiah in Medieval Jewish Literature.* New York, 1932.

Scholem, G. *The Messianic Idea in Judaism.* New york, 1972.

Silver, A. H. *A History of Messianic Speculation in Israel from the First to the Seventeenth Centuries.* New York, 1927.

Teeple, H. M. *The Mosaic Eschatological Prophet* [Deut. 18:15]. Philadelphia, 1957.

Wunsche, A. *Die Leiden des Messias.* Leipzig, 1870.

KARAISM

Furst, J., ed. *Geschichte des Karaerthums: eine Kurze Darstellung seiner Entwickelung, Lehre und Literatur mit den dazugehorigen Quellen nachweisen.* 3 vols. Leipzig, 1862–69.

Nemoy, L., ed. *Karaite Anthology: excerpts from the early literature translated from Arabic, Aramaic and Hebrew sources with notes.* New Haven, 1952.

Szyszman, S. *Le Karaisme. Ses doctrines et son histoire.* Lausanne, 1980.

Vajda, G. *Deux Commentaires Karaites sur l'Ecclesiaste.* Leiden, 1971.

HERMETICA AND GNOSTIC TEXTS

Festugiere, R. P., ed. *La Revelation d'Hermes Trimegiste.* 4 vols. Paris, 1949– 60.

Nock, A. D., and Festugiere, M., eds. *Corpus Hermeticum.* 4 vols. Paris, 1945– 54.

Reitzenstein, R. *Poimandres.* Leipzig, 1964.

Robinson, J. M. (Dir.) et al. *The Nag Hammadi Library in English* [Nag Hamadi Library Gnostic Texts]. New York, 1984.

Scott, W., ed. *Hermetica: The Ancient Greek and Latin Writings which contain religious and philosophical teachings ascribed to Hermes Trimegistus.* 3 vols. Oxford, 1924–26.

RELEVANT NON-ISRAELITE ANCIENT TEXTS

Egyptian Texts

Budge, E. A. W., ed. and trans. *The Book of the Dead*. London, 1899.

Budge, E. A. W., ed. and trans. *The Book of the Dead. Facsimiles of the Papyrus of Ani in the British Museum*. London, 1890.

Budge, E. A. W., ed. and trans. *The Gods of the Egyptians*. 2 vols. London, 1904.

Devaud, E., *Les maximes de Ptahhotep* [Papyrus Prisse]. Fribourg, 1918.

Faulkner, R. O., ed. and trans. *The Ancient Egyptian Pyramid Texts*. Oxford, 1962.

Gardiner, A. H., ed. *The Admonitions of an Egyptian Sage from a Hieratic Papyrus in Leiden*. Leipzig, 1909.

Gardiner, A. H., ed. *Hymns to Amon from a Leiden Papyrus*. [Zeitschrift fur Agyptische Spruche und Altertumskunde 42, (1905), pp. 12–42].

Gunn, B. G. *The Instruction of Ptah-Hotep*. London, 1906.

Jequier, G., *Le Papyrus Prisse*. Paris, 1911.

Lepsius, C. R., ed. *Denkmaler aus Aegypten und Aethiopien*. 6 vols. Leipzig, 1897–1913.

Sethe, K., ed. *Die altagyptischen Pyramid-texte*. 4 vols. Leipzig, 1908–22.

Navile, E., ed. *Das Agyptische Todtenbuch der XVIII bis XX Dynastie*. Berlin, 1886.

Mesopotamian and Ugaritic Texts

Dietrich, M., and Loretz, O., eds. *Konkordanz der Ugaritischen textzahlungen*. [Alter Orient und Altes Testament. 19:144, 1972.]

Driver, G. R., ed. *Canaanite Myths and Legends*. [Old Testament Studies 3.] Edinburgh, 1956.

Fischer, L. R., ed. *Ras Shamra Parallels: Texts from Ugarit and the Hebrew Bible*. 2 vols. [Analecta Orientalia 49 and 50]. Rome, 1972–75.

Gray, J. *The Keret Text in the Literature of Ras Shamra*. 2nd edition. Leiden, 1964.

Heidel, A. *The Babylonian Genesis*. Chicago, 1963.

Heidel, A. *The Gilgamesh Epic*. Chicago, 1954.

Heidel, A. *The Gilgamesh Epic and old Testament Parallels.* Chicago, 1946.

Kapelrud, A. S. *Baal in the ras Shamra Texts.* Copenhagen, 1952.

King, L. W., ed. *Legends of Babylon and Egypt in relation to Hebrew tradition.* London, 1918.

King, L. W., ed. *The Seven Tablets of Creation.* [Luzac's Semitic Text and Translation. Series Nos. 12 and 13.] London, 1902.

Langhe (de), R., ed. *Les Textes de Ras Shamra Ugarit et leurs rapports avec le milieu de l'Ancien Testament.* 2 vols. Paris, 1945.

Longdon, S. *Babylonian Wisdom.* [Babyloniaca VII (1923), pp. 129–229.] Paris.

Meek, T. J. *Cuneiform Bilingual Hymns, Prayers, and Penitential Psalms.* [Beitrage zur Assyrologie und semitischen Sprachwissenschaft. 6:1 (1913), pp. 1–127.] Strassburg.

Montgomery, James A. *Aramaic Incantation Texts from Nippur.* Philadelphia, 1913.

Rogers, R. W. *Cuneiform Parallels to the Old Testament.* New York, 1926.

Tallqvist, K. L., ed. *Cuneiform Texts from Babylonian Tablets in the British Museum.* 41 vols. London, 1896–1931.

Virolleaud, C., trans. *Baal Text 1.* [Syria Vol. XV. (1934), pp. 305–336], Paris.

Whitehouse, O. C. *The Cuneiform Inscriptions and the Old Testament.* 2 vols. London, 1888.

Wilcke, C. *Das Lugalbanda-Epos.* Berlin, 1969.

Other Ancient Texts

Mercer, S. A. B., ed. *The Tell-El-Amarna Tablets.* 2 vols. Toronto, 1939.

Torczyner, H. *The Lachish Letters* [Tell-el-Amarna]. Jerusalem, 1938.

CLASSICAL GREEK AUTHORS AND WRITINGS

Aeschylus

Weir Smyth, H., ed. and trans. *Aeschylus.* 2 vols. Loeb Classical Library, London.

Callimachus Fragment

Bowra, C., ed. *Pindari Carmina*. Oxford, 1947. (Callimachus Fragment 133 found here.)

Mair, A. W., and G. R., eds. *Callimachus, Lycophron, Aratus*. Loeb Classical Library. (Text of Hymn 2 to Apollo will be found here.)

Diogenes Laertius

Estienne, H., ed. *Diogenes Laertius: Vies, doctrines, et pensees de philosophes illustres*. 4 vols. Leipzig, 1828–31.

Herodotus

Herodotus. Edited and translated by A. D. Godley. 4 vols. Loeb Classical library, London, 1920–25.

Herodotus. Translated by H. Cary. London, 1894.

Homer

Buckley, T. A. *The Iliad of Homer* [Literally translated]. London, 1879.

Murray, A. T., ed. and trans. *Iliad*. 2 vols. Loeb Classical Library, London, 1924–25.

Plotinus

Armstrong, A. H., ed. and trans. *Plotinus*. 6 vols. Loeb Classical Library, London, 1966.

Creuzer, F. *Plotinus*. 3 vols. Oxford, 1835.

Sophocles

Campbell, L. *Sophocles*. London, 1879.

Storr, F., ed. and trans. *Sophocles*. 2 vols. Loeb Classical Library, London, 1928–39.

CLASSICAL LATIN AUTHORS

Suetonius

Suetonius, Tranquilos, Gaius. *The Lives of the Caesars.* Translated by J. C. Rolfe. Loeb Classical Library, London, 1920.

Tacitus

Annals of Tacitus. Translated and annotated by A. J. Church and W. J. Brodrib. New York, 1906.

The Histories of Tacitus. Translated by C. H. Moore. 2 vols. Loeb Classical Library, London, 1962.

HOLY LAND LITERATURE

Davies, W. D. *The Gospel and the Land.* Berkeley, 1974.

Feliks, Y. *Agriculture in Palestine in the Period of the Mishnah and Talmud.* Jerusalem, 1963.

Freyne, S. *Galilee from Alexander the Great to Hadrian 323 B. C. E. to 135 C. E.: A Study of Second Temple Judaism.* Notre Dame, 1980.

Kallai, Z. *Historical Geography of the Bible*, The Tribal Territories of Israel. Leiden, 1986.

Meistermann, B. *New Guide to the Holy Land.* London, 1923.

Neubaer, A. *Geographie du Talmud.* Paris, 1868.

Rapporport, A. S. *Myths and Legends of ancient Israel.* Revised Edition with an Introduction by R. Patai. New York, 1961.

Vaux, R. de. *Ancient Israel, its Life and Institutions.* New York, 1961.

Vilnay, Z., ed. *Legends of Galilee, Jordan and Sinai.* Phildelphia, 1978.

Vilnay, Z., ed. *Legends of Jerusalem.* Philadelphia, 1973.

Vilnay, Z., ed. *Legends of Judea and Samaria.* Philadelphia, 1975.

CONTEMPORARY RABBINIC WORKS

Abelson, J. *The Immanence of God in Rabbinical Literature.* London, 1912.

Arama, R. Isaac. *Akedat Yitshak.* Jerusalem, 1962.

Birnbaum, P., ed. *Daily Prayer Book [Ha-Siddur Ha-Shalem].* New York, 1949.

Buchler, A. *Studies in Sin and Atonement in the Rabbinic Literature of the First Century.* New York, 1967.

Kadushin, M. *The Rabbinic Mind.* New York, 1952.

Mamorstein, A. *The Doctrine of Merits in Old Rabbinic Literature and the Old Rabbinic Doctrine of God.* New York, 1968.

Lauterbach, J. Z. *Rabbinic Essays.* Cincinnati, 1951.

Patai, R. *Adam weAdamah* ('Man and Earth' in Hebrew Custom, Belief and Legend). 2 vols. [Hebrew]. Jerusalem, 1942–43.

Schechter, S. *Some Aspects of Rabbinic Theology.* London, 1909.

Scholem, C. *Major Trends in Jewish Mysticism.* New York, 1961.

Singer, S. *The Authorized Daily Prayerbook.* Revised ed. London, 1962.

Spiegel, S. *The Last Trial. On the Legends and Lore of the Command to Abraham to offer Isaac as a Sacrifice. The Akedah.* [Translated by J. Goldin.] New York, 1979.

Urbach, E. E. *The Sages: Their Concepts and Beliefs.* Translated by I. Abrahams. Jerusalem, 1975.

THE PARABLES

Armstrong, E. A. *The Gospel Parables.* London, 1967.

Barbour, I. G. *Myths, Models and Paradigms.* New York, 1974.

Breech, J. *The Silence of Jesus.* Philadelphia, 1985.

Cadoux, A. T. *The Parables of Jesus: Their Art and Use.* New York, 1931.

Callan, C. J. *The Parables of Christ.* London, 1940.

Carlston, C. E. *The Parables of the Triple Tradition.* Philadelphia, 1975.

Cerfaux, L. *The Treasure of the Parables.* De Pere, Wis., 1968.

Crossan, J. D. *In the Parables.* New York, 1973.

Crossan, J. D. *Cliffs of Fall: Paradox and Polyvalence in the Parables of Jesus.* New York, 1980.

Derrett, J. D. M. *Law in the New Testament.* London, 1970.

Derrett, J. D. M. *New Resolutions of Old Conundrums.* Shipston-on-Stour, 1987.

Dupont, J. *Pourquoi des Parables? La Methode parabolique de Jesus.* Paris, 1977.

Eichholz, G. *Einfuhrung in die Gleichnisse.* Neukirchen, 1963.

Eichholz, G. *Gleichnisse der Evangelien.* Neukirchen, 1971.

Feldman, A. *The Parables and Similes of the Rabbis.* Cambridge, 1924.

Fiebig, P. *Die Gleichnisreden Jesu im Lichte der rabbinischen Gleichniss des neutestamentlichen Zeitalters.* Tubingen, 1912.

Finlay, L. A. *Jesus and His Parables.* London, 1950.

Fonck, L. *The Parables of the Gospels.* New York, 1915.

Harrington, W. J. *A Key to the Parables.* Glen Rock, 1964.

Harrington, W. J. *He Spoke in Parables.* Dublin, 1964.

Hermaniuk, M. *La Parabole Evangelique. Enquete exegetique et critique.* Bruges–Paris, 1947.

Jeremias, J. *The Parables of Jesus,* Rev. Ed. New York, 1955.

Jones, G. V. *The Art and Truth of the Parables.* London, 1964.

Julicher, A. *Die Gleichnisreden Jesus.* Darmstadt, 1963.

Kohlefeld, H. *Parables and Instructions in the Gospels.* Montreal, 1966.

Kingsbury, J. D. *The Parables of Jesus in Matthew 13.* Richmond, 1969.

Lambrecht, J. *Once More Astonished. The Parables of Jesus.* New York, 1981.

Linnemann, E. *Jesus of the Parables.* New York, 1966 [1961].

Maillot, A. *Les paraboles de Jesus aujourd'hui.* Geneva, 1973.

Meinertz, M. *Die Gleichnisse Jesu,* 4th Ed. Munster, 1948.

Michaelis, W. *Die Gleichnisse Jesu.* Hamburg, 1956.

Oesterley, W. O. E. *The Gospel Parables in the Light of their Jewish Background.* New York, 1963.

Perkins, P. *Hearing the Parables of Jesus.* New York, 1981.

Sheppard, J. B. *A Study of the Parables Common to the Synoptic Gospels and the Coptic Gospel of Thomas.* Ann Arbor [University of Michigan– Micro-film], 1965.

Smith, B. T. D. *The Parables of the Synoptic Gospels.* Cambridge, 1937.

Smith, C. W. F. *The Jesus of the Parables.* Philadelpia, 1975.

Swete, H. B. *The Parables of the Kingdom.* London, 1920.

TeSelle, S. *Speaking in the Parables.* Philadelphia, 1975.

Via, D. O. *The Parables: Their Literary and Existential Dimension.* Philadelphia, 1967.

Voste, I. M. *Parabolae Selectae Domini Nostri Jesu Christi*, 2 Vols. Rome, 1933.

SON OF MAN LITERATURE

The list of books and articles consulted on the Son of Man theme is too extensive to be included in the Bibliography. Discussion of the term is to be found among the works of the following authors:

Abbott, E. A.
Aland, K.
Barr, J.
Barrett, C. K.
Beardslee, W. A.
Bentzen, A.
Birdsall, J. M.
Black, M.
Borsch, F. H.
Bowker, J.
Bowman, J.
Boussett, W.
Breckelmans, C. H. W.
Brown, J. P.
Brown, R. E.
Bruce, F. F.
Campbell, J. Y.
Casey, M.
Catchpole, D. R.
Collins, J. J.
Conzelmann, H.
Coppens, J.
Cortes, J. B.
Creed, J. M.
Cullmann, O.
Dalman, G.
Daube, D.
Davies, W. D.

Delcor, M.
Denis, A. M.
Dion, H. M.
Ellis, E. E.
Emerton, J. A.
Flusser, D.
Ford, J. M.
Formesyn, R. E.
Freed, E. D.
Freedman, D. N.
Gaster, M.
Gertner, M.
Giles, P.
Ginsberge, H. L.
Glasson, T. F.
Grelot, P.
Gressmann, H.
Hahn, F.
Harvey, A. E.
Higgins, A. J. B.
Hooker, M. D.
Horton, F. L.
Jeremias, J.
Jonge, M.
Jungel, E.
Kaiser, O.
Kelly, R. G. H.
Kim, S.

LeDeaut, R.
Lehmann, K.
Leinestad, R.
Lietzmann, H.
Lindars, B.
Lindeskog, G.
Loader, W. R.
Maddox, R.
Manson, T. W.
Marshall, I. H.
Meeks, W. A.
Michaelis, W.
Michel, O.
Milik, J. T.
Moe, O.
Moule, C. F. D.
Moulton, J. H.
Mowinckel, S.
Muller, K.
Muller, U. B.
Neugebauer, F.
Noack, B.
Odeberg, H.
Otto, R.
Parker, R.
Pesch, R.
Perrin, N.
Ploger, O.
Pollard, T. F.
Preoss, T.
Quell, C.
Quispel, G.
Robinson, J. A. T.
Rogerson, J. W.
Rollins, W. G.
Rost, L.
Rowland, C. C.

Schippers, R.
Schnackenburg, R.
Schneider, G.
Scholem, G. G.
Schultz, S.
Schweizer, E.
Scott, R. B. Y.
Seitz, O. J. F.
Sharman, H. B.
Silver, A. H.
Sjoberge, E.
Smith, M.
Smolley, S. S.
Stahlin, G.
Stauffer, E.
Stone, W.
Stott, W.
Taylor, V.
Teeple, H. M.
Todt, H. E.
Ullendorf, E.
Vermes, G.
Vielhauer, P.
Vogtle, A.
Volter, D.
Voltz, P.
Voss, G.
Walker, W. O.
Wegner, M.
Widengren, G.
Wifall, W.
Wilson, R.
Woude, A. S.
Wrede, W.
Young, E. J.
Zahn, T.
Zimmerli, W.

Reference Index

OLD TESTAMENT

Genesis

1:11	4
1:11,29	8
1:26	3
1:26–27	42
1:27	42,15
1:27,31	15
1:28	7,15
1:29–30	15
2:5	4
2:6–7	3,4
2:7	35,42,114
2:8–9	4,8
2:8–15	4
2:15	4,60
2:16–17	4
2:17	15,134
2:19	15
2:22	114
3:5	25
3:16–17	179
3:17–19	8
3:19	3,8,112–13
3:22	6
3:23	4,8,106
4:12	8
4:17	116
6:9	15
6:14–16	111
6:17	134
6:22	15
7:1	15
7:5	15
8:21	15
9:1–2	15
9:2	15
9:3	15
9:6	15
9:21	113
11:5	111,116
12:5 to 13:1–12	106
13:10	60,106
14:18–20,22	29
14:19	32
16:1–4	115
17:1	29
17:4	32
17:6,16	103,193
18:19	222
22:1–13	165,166
22:6	179
22:11	134
22:17	135
24:49	76
25:27	186
26:24	65
29:32–34	96,233
29:35	96(2x)
30:1,3,6	115
30:1–24	96
30:9–13	115
30:20	117
32:28	43,96
34:1–31	188
35:10	43
35:11	193
35:16–18	187
35:16–19	102(2x)
35:18	96
35:18,21	96
35:21–22	103
35:22	188
35:24	192
36:9–11	97
37:5–8	9
37:26–27	188
38:1–5,12	96
39:1–2,20	67
39:14–20	216
40–41	122
41:15	144
41:32	134
41:40	223
41:52	187
42–47	106
42:2,12	192
42:4	192
43:3–4,8–9	188
43:29	192
44:9–34	96
44:16,18–34	188
44:23	144
45:12	192
46:10	100
46:12	100
46:19–22	192
46:28	188
47:29	76
48:3	33
48:7	102
48:13–19	149
49:3	187
49:3–4	188
49:5–7	188
49:10	188(2x),191,196
49:11	177
49:11–12	191
49:22	161
49:22–27	192
49:24	33
49:26,27	192

Deuteronomy, Greek [Septuagint]

Joshua

Joshua,Greek [Septuagint]

Judges

41:20	37,133
41:25	119
41:26	237
41:28	236
42:1	222
42:3	220
42:8	49
42:16,17	126
42:21	232
43:1	40,43
43:5	93
43:6	120
43:7	40
43:10	19,44,136
43:10–11	129
44:1–2	62
44:2	39(2x)
44:4	143
44:6	190(2x)
44:9	19
44:18	19,21
44:19	19
44:20	161
44:21	63
44:23	63
44:28	106
45:4	62
45:8	158,159
45:9	3,39
45:15	39,121,129
45:17	170
45:18	40
45:19	74
46:13	158
47:4	190
48:3,4	237
48:10	178
48:11	49
48:13	149,150
48:18	127
48:20	62
48:22	127
49:1–7	122
49:2	122
49:3	63
49:6	122
49:7	122
49:9	122
49:9–10	106
49:26	33,190
50:2	237
50:6	67
51:2	32
51:5	158
51:8	158
51:9	150,154,156

51:9	171
51:10	171
51:12	33
51:13	39
51:23	8
52:1	74
52:10	160,161,170
52:13	64,65,71,92
52:13,15	90,122,164
52:14	33,38,43,67,92,240
53	172
53:1	155,170
53:1–10	92,122,185
53:1–11	67
53:1–12	168–169,171
53:1–12	174
53:3	71
53:3–5	173
53:3,5–12	173
53:3–7,10–11	53
53:4	173,174
53:4,12	172
53:4–5,10	172
53:4–6	173
53:5	172(2x),173(4x)
53:6	179,208
53:7	172
53:7–8	123
53:8	130
53:11	92,126,185,199
53:11–12,	122
53:12	172
54:13	128,248
55:1,3	141
55:8,9	246
55:10,11	4,141
56:1	234
56:2	33,235
56:10,11	19,116,230
56:10–12	128
56:11–12	180
57:1,2	127
57:15	164
57:21	127
58:7,8	218
58:10	218
59:8	127
59:13	59,207
59:15,16	235
59:16	156,171
59:16–17	158
60:10	116
60:16	33,190
60:17	127
61:3	7
61:8	73(2x)

9:10	124,201
10:1	143
10:11	188
12:1	36
13:7	106
14:16	190

Zechariah, Greek [Septuagint]

3:8	92
6:12	92
9:9	135,163
10:7	241

Malachi

1:6	49,60,61
1:6–14	167
2:3	7
2:6	200
2:7	57
3:24	248
4:6	248

1 Maccabees

1:36	215
2:52	178
7:18	74
12:10,21	193
14:20	193

2 Maccabees

1:2	65
3:11	215
5:9	193
6:30	52
7:37,38	167
9:7,9,11	54
13:26	220
14:23–28	216
14:27	215

NEW TESTAMENT

Matthew

1:1–16	96
1:1–25	105
1:21	156,160,169
2:1–2	94
2:1–6	101
2:1–22	106
2:15	106
3:8	159
3:9	32
3:10	210

3:10,12	9,123
3:13–17	178
3:15	68,159,212
3:16–17	138
3:17	178
4:1–11	178
4:4	246
4:13–17	118
5:3	246
5:4	246
5:5	246
5:6	206,247
5:7	246
5:8	15,62,64,248(2x)
5:9	203
5:17–19	211,245
5:17–20	201
5:20	51,245
5:44–45	75,239
5:44–48	73
5:48	51,72
6:24	184
7:16–19	210
7:16–21	210
7:24	66,113
7:24–25	227
8:10	228
8:18	108
8:20	184
8:24–7	138
9:4	210
9:13	159
9:30	108
9:36	128
10:16	225
10:26	130
10:28	227
11:3	196
11:14–15	136
11:15	228
11:27	56
11:29	68,107,178,183
12:1–8,22–30	114
12:16	108
12:25	210
12:28	205
12:33–35	210(2x)
12:35	227
12:42	119,120
13:3–9	202
13:9,43	212,228
13:1–9,18–23, 24–33	210
13:10–23	203
13:15	177,178
13:18–23	202
13:19	204,211

Letter of Aristeas

v. 252	216
v. 276	80

3 Maccabees

6:2	34
6:7	215

4 Maccabees

1:10–11	167
1:35	198
2:(15)16	70
2:16	198
2:18	70,198
2:21,22	90
3:17	198
4:1	215
6:28–30	167
11:21	225
17:20–22	167

Odes of Solomon [Syriac and Coptic]

1:5	159(2x)
3:11	109
6:6,10–12	29
8:6	171
8:9	30
8:18	35
10:1–3	200
12:3,4	29
17:7	31
18:13	19
23:16	31
23:18	31(2x)
25:1,2	171
25:9	171
38:1	59
38:4	58
41:13–14	31
25:2	171
23:4	30

Paraleipomena Jeremiou

7:8	15

Psalms of Solomon

2:18	226
2:35	54
2:37	50
2:37	91
3:14	17
7:17	106
9:8	17
13:10	178(2x)

14:3–4	4
15:5	58
17:23,31,35	157
17:23–27	156
17:29,32,34	204

Pseudo-Philo, Biblical Antiquities

XV.6	153
XVI.5	36
XX.2,3	28
XX.3	80
XX.21	96
XXI.2	198
XXII.9	190
LIX.4	103

Sibylline Oracles

I.4	30
I.67–69	111
III.286	164
III.373–376	204
III.562	109
III.580,584	34
III.584–585	30
III.652	93
III.653,655 ff.	204
III.670	180
V.108,256–259, 414–428	177

Story of Ahikar

v. 26	70 Slavonic
v. 28	70 Greek
v. 112	70 Slavonic
2:8	98 Armenian
2:92	183 Armenian
3:1 to 4:6	216 Multiple
5:7	216 Armenian
6:16	144 Syriac
7:19	29 Arabic
8:2	244 Slavonic

Testament of Job

32.12 [vii.36]	149

Testaments of the Twelve Patriarchs

Testament of Simeon

4:8	69
6:4	204

Testament of Levi

4:3	54,144,234
8:2	225

18.6	143
22.3	124
22.5	157
22.5a	143,117
23.9	167
26.11 end	167

Pesikta Rabbati

5.6	140
15.10	156,178
15.10.14	121
15.14–15	101
31.2	179
33.3	236
33.6	164,177
34.2	120,174,177(2x)
36.1	94,118,142,173, 174,175,177(2x)
34.1–2	124
36.2	101
37.1,2	174,175
40.5	167
37.1	164,173,177
46.3	93,94(2x),95,117

Aboth de Rabbi Nathan

27.3	183
32	221
34	148
35.3–4	117
37,110	134
43.121	117

Pirke R. Eliezer

pp. 94,96,101,118,124,143,164,177

Midrash Haggadol on Genesis

1:1	143,177
32:6	124
33:11	143
41:1	124,130
49:1	124
49:10	173,191

Midrash Haggadol

I.325–326	167
I.581	11
I.682	100
I.735–739	101

Midrash Rabbati on Genesis [Moses haDarshan]

1:3	173
24:67	173

37:22	173

Midrash Aggadat Bereshith [Genesis]

82	100
159–160	100

Midrash Haggadah on Genesis [Buber]

15:12	101
19:15	101
38:15	100

Lekah Tob

pp. 119,143(2x),174,175,191

Sekel Tob

pp. 101,117,124,191

Midrash Tanchumah

pp. 10(2x),97(2x),100,124,130,137,143(2x), 166,167,177,179,191,224

Yelammedenu

pp. 101,224

Tanna Debe Eliyyahu Rabba and Zuta

pp. 63,68,112,118,140,174,175,182,183(3x)

Yalkut Genesis

99	167
158	100
479	167
645	167
782	167

Yalkut Joshua

12	167

Yalkut Job

8	193

Yalkut Proverbs

962	10

Yalkut Isaiah

508	167

Yalkut Daniel

1066	114

Yalkut Jonah

550	175

Yalkut Micah

555   167

Yalkut HaMakiri

Psalm 110   148

Yalkut Reubeni

pp. 143,193

Yalkut Shimoni

pp. 101,121,124,130,143(3x),148,156(4x),
157,164(5x),170,173(2x),177(3x),191

ZOHAR

I.4b	148,177
I.25b,82b	101
I.38a,b	174
I.38b	175,177
I.39a	148
I.47b	148
I.53b	148
I.57b	192
I.81b	120
I.119a	119
I.120b	186
I.123b	15
I.169b	148
I.174b	148
I.188b	101
I.208a	224
I.231b	177
I.238a	101,124
I.243a	183
I.247b	117
I.267b	174
II.7b,8a	121
II.8a	174,175
II.8b	104
II.85	173
II.115b	173
II.172b	164,121
II.203b	101
II.211a,b	174
II.212a	173(2x),175(2x)
II.236a	100
II.278b	101
III.7b	119
III.7b,9e	93
III.8b	119
III.35a	183
III.130b	164
III.164a,b,	177
III.166a	174

III.167a	177
III.203b	164,175
III.220a	119
III.238a	124
III.275b	124
III.276b	173
III.278	124
III.278b	175
III.289	164

APOCRYPHA OF THE NEW TESTAMENT

Apocryphon of John

14:15   3

Gospel of Thomas

Logion 78   181

EARLY CHRISTIAN AND PATRISTIC WRITINGS

Ambrose

De Officis

I.11.37   72

Aphraates

Demonstration

XVII.7   43

Athenagoras

Embassy

XXV   82

Augustine

De Civ. Dei

XIV.41   191

Homily on Psalm

119:104   66

Chrysostom

Hom. in Gen.

67   191

1 Clement

33:3	151
36:2	82

Clement of Alexandria

Exhortation to the Pagans [Protreptikos]

I.2.3	149
I.10.2	82
X.105,1	19
XI.120.4	171
LXVIII.18,98	42

The Instructor [Paedagogus]

I. 98	42
I.IX.76.1	185
X. 94.2	185

Stromata [Miscellanies]

I. 1	74
II. 2	179
II. 4	144
IV. 6	187
IV. 17	82
V. 6	186
V. 11	83
V. 87 f.	42
VI. 80 f.	42
VII. 4.1–2	49

Cyprian

Contra Jud.

I. 20	191

Treatises

XII. ii. iv.	171

Cyril

Hieros. Cat.

XII	191

Cyril of Scythopolis

Euthym.

86,133	104

Didache

2:21	27
9:3	83

Epistle of Barnabas

6:9	8
6:10	83
9:1,4	83
10:12	83
19:2	42

Epistle to Diognetus

7:4–5	58
8:17	36
9:6	35
12:1–2	4

Eusebius

Hist. Eccl.

I.6	191

Gregory

Morals on Job

XXV.30	68

Hyppolytus

Re Genesis

49:5	100

Ignatius

Philipp.

VII.1	31

Jerome

Comm. on Isaiah

66:14	171

Onomastikon

43,62,68	104

Quest. in. Gen.

Gen. 49:10	191

Justin Martyr

Apol.

I.41	191
I.44.29	57,74

Dial.

8,10	122
33,83	148

Hom. in Gen.

17	191

Melito Bishop of Sardis

p. 171

Pseudo Jerome

2 Sam. 19:29	221

Shepherd of Hermas

Mandates

V. 1. 33:1	69
V. 2. 34:4	70
V. 2. 34:7	70
VI.5. 65:3	181
X. 1. 40:6	82

Similitudes

II. 51:8	19
V. 4. 57:4	82
VI. 5. 65:3	181
IX. 2. 79:6	82
IX. 14. 91:4	152
IX. 19. 96:2	57
IX. 30. 107:4	181

Visions

I. 3. 3:4	151
II. 2. 6:1	182

Tertullian

Adv. Jud.

10	100

Adv. Marc.

3.18	100
5.9	148

Ap. C.

V.III. xvi	171

Praxeas

XIII	171

Theodoret

Quest. in Gen.

110	191

RABBIS AND OTHER WRITERS

Abarbanel pp. 164,166,171,193

Abraham Zacuto p. 193

David de Pomis p. 166

David Kimchi pp. 10,143,174

Eleazar ben Pedat p. 148

Eliezer Hakkalir p. 172

ElijahVidas p. 172

Huna ben Hanina p. 148

Ibn Ezra pp. 143,148,164

Ibn Gabirol pp. 52,185

Isaac ben Moses Arama p. 148,166

Joseph Kimchi pp. 46,68(3x)

Kalafta ben Dosa p. 174

Levi Yitzchak p. 142

Maimonides pp. 10,101(2x),119,174

Moshe ha Darshan p. 172

Moshe Kohen Crispin p. 172

Moshe Sheikh of Safed p. 171

Nachmanides p. 166

Naphtali ben Asher Altschuler p. 174

Obadiah ben Joseph Sforno p. 148

Radak p. 193

Saadia Ibn Danan p. 174

Rashi pp. 100,101,124,131,174

Saadia Gaon pp. 119,131

Simeon bar Yohai p. 174

COLLECTANEA OPERUM JUDAICARUM

Beth HaMidrash [Jellinek]

I. 55–57	174
II. 23–29	174,175
II. 29	177
II. 48–51	174,177
II. 54–57	174
II. 55	119
II. 58–63	174
III. 12–64	142
III. 78–81	174
III. 80	121
III. 83–108	167
III. 132,195	177
III. 141–143	174
IV. 122	119
V. 167–8,187–8	101
V. 168	130–131
V. 189–190	121,158
VI. 22,25–6,84	101
VI. 36–70	142
VI. 47	173
VI. 79–90	174
VI. 84	191
VI. 112–116	174
VI. 150ff.	131

Lachish Letters
II.4   97

Ludlul bel Nemeqi
ll.36–37   23

Nippur Fragment
III.3–8   134

Sippar Text
55   134

Sumerian Hymn
No. 23, l. 10   115

Ancient Central American Texts
Popol Vuh
p. 41–42

GREEK PAGAN WRITERS

Aeschylus
Ag.
176f.,   52
249f.,   52

Aristotle
Politica
V.11   215

Callimachus Fragment
133   149

Diogenes Laertius
Hist.
VI. 50   230

Euripides
Hecuba
863   215

Herodotus
I. 207   52
III. 1   215
V. 35   215
VIII. 22,110   215

Homer
Iliad
3.246,247   241

Odyssey
10.515   113

Hymn to Apollo
No. 2,l. 29   149

Plato
Politicus
VIII. 566b   215

Sophocles
Philoctetes
578   215

Oed. Col.
lll.1–7   52

Thucydides
III.4,4   215

PAGAN LATIN WRITERS

Suetonius
Vespasian
4   93

Tacitus
Histories
V.13   93

Acknowledgments

Special thanks to Rev. Donald J. Arsenault for his prayers and intercessions and to Hiroko Endo, Laura Poyatos, Adèle Bolduc, Rev. Cyril Karam, OSB, Norman and Rena Arsenault, Florence Maron, Thomas B. Constantino, Greg Glazov, Rev. Daniel Twomey, Bill and Marilyn Jones, Mary Lee Skinner, Berna Kensinger, Murray Littlejohn, Robert Fricke, and many others for their kind help and prayers.

So shall it be on the day
the Son of Man is revealed...
one will be taken
and one will be left
—cf. Luke 17:22, 34

More Titles from St. Bede's

Cosmos, The World and the Glory of God
Louis Bouyer

Addresses all possible questions relating to the world: its constitution and origin; the history of its treatment from cosmogonic myth to philosophical cosmologies; from biblical cosmogenesis to the "big bang" theory. The nature of spirit and matter, the history of ideas and movements of thought in the attempt to fathom the mystery of the universe, are only two of the themes addressed in this searching and masterful inquiry into the cosmos. Fr. Bouyer shows his genius in penetrating this mystery, showing it to be a reflection of that other cosmos which it merely reflects: the inner being of God.

Paperback, 274 pages   ISBN 0-932506-66-6   **$17.95**

STUDIES IN HISTORICAL THEOLOGY

Does God Change?
Thomas Weinandy, OFM, Cap.

Did God undergo change as a result of the Incarnation? Can the impassible God be born, suffer, die, and love as man? Fr. Weinandy explores these questions, synthesizing patristic, medieval, and contemporary Christology and offers a unique solution that is in keeping with the teachings of the Church.

Paperback, 212 pages   ISBN 0-932506-42-9   **$15.95**

The Christian Trinity in History
Bertrand de Margerie, SJ
Foreword by Jaroslav Pelikan

In this remarkable book, you will encounter a complete and up-to-date theological study on the mystery of the Trinity from a historical perspective. A must for every library and seminary, or for anyone giving a course on the Trinity. *"The most important book on this doctrine to appear in this century! It deserves to be read widely."* **From the Foreword**

Paperback, 387 pages   ISBN 0-932506-14-3   **$17.95**

Process Theology and the Christian Tradition
Illtyd Trethowan

The author claims that process philosophers/theologians misconstrue the Christian tradition about God's relations with His world, but allows that they have some excuse for doing so. He argues that the eternity/immutability of God is part of the tradition and that it does not lead to contradictions in our thinking, although it has not always been properly defended. An excellent introduction to and refutation of modern process thought.

Paperback, 124 pages   ISBN 0-932506-44-5   **$9.95**

MAGI BOOKS
AVAILABLE EXCLUSIVELY FROM ST. BEDE'S

Aquinas Scripture Series

These Commentaries are the first of their kind to appear in English. They not only contain the personal theology of Aquinas himself, but also his ample use of the rich thought of the Fathers and Doctors of the Church, such as Jerome, Augustine, Ambrose, and Gregory. Taken together, these sources provide a deeper understanding of the text.

Vol. 1: Commentary on St. Paul's Epistle to the Galatians
Hardback, 222 pages   ISBN 0-87343-021-2 $10.00

Vol. 2: Commentary on St. Paul's Epistle to the Ephesians
Hardback, 314 pages   ISBN 0-87343-022-0 $10.00

**Vol. 3: Commentary on St. Paul's First Letter to the Thessalonians
    and the Letter to the Philippians**
Hardback, 122 pages   ISBN 0-87343-047-6 $10.00
Paperback,   ISBN 0-87343-028-X $6.00

Vol. 4: Commentary on the Gospel of St. John, Part 1
Hardback, 506 pages   ISBN 0-87343-031-X $35.00
(Part 2, the final part, in preparation)

Why God Became Man   *Anselm of Canterbury*
Included in this edition is *The Virgin Conception and Original Sin* with its own detailed outline and full notes, historical and theological.

   These two major works of a giant of theology and a Doctor of the Church are used not only in philosophical and theological programs, but also in general presentations of the history of Western Civilization. A landmark in the history of thought.
Paperback, 245 pages   ISBN 0-87343-025-5   **$6.95**

The Great Dialogue of Nature and Space   *Yves R. Simon*
Especially written to interest a general audience, particularly those concerned with the modern sciences, in the basic ideas that both philosophers and scientists discuss. Simon simply and clearly explains with precision ideas such as space, time, chance, determinism, and the role of facts and seeming conflicts among scientists and philosophers. Some chapters have been newly translated from the French.
Paperback, 224 pages   ISBN 0-87343-035-2   **$6.00**

STUDIES IN SCRIPTURE

Old Testament Priests and the New Priest,
According to the New Testament   *Albert Vanhoye, SJ*

How are the priesthood of the faithful and the ministerial priesthood interrelated? Fr. Vanhoye takes you through the Old Testament into the New, focusing especially on Hebrews, 1 Peter, and Revelation, and explains that the common priesthood is personal *offering*, while the pastoral ministry is a tangible manifestation of the priestly *mediation* of Christ. Thus are the two aspects of priesthood made visible in different ways by the laity and the clergy. This complementarity reflects the basic unity of the priesthood in Jesus Christ. Excellent for seminarians, priests, religious, and all concerned with an understanding of the vocation of service at the heart of Orders.

Paperback, 333 pages   ISBN 0-932506-38-0   **$17.95**

The Truth of Christmas Beyond the Myths   *Rene Laurentin*

Are the Infancy Narratives fact or theological creations? What kind of historicity underlies these narratives? In this masterful study of the Gospel stories of the Birth of Christ according to Matthew and Luke, Fr. Laurentin looks beyond the myths to the internal evidence presented in the Gospels themselves.

Paperback, 569 pages   ISBN 0-932506-34-8   **$21.95**

Jesus and His Mother   *Andre Feuillet*

A fascinating look at Mary's role in Salvation History presented by a renowned biblical scholar. The book examines the Christological and Marian scenes of Luke 1 & 2, compares them with the Johannine tradition, and concludes with a discussion on the role of women in the Church and world of today.

Paperback, 290 pages   ISBN 0-932506-27-5   **$15.95**